ERRATA

On p. 143, read "Mohsen" for "Moshen" Mirabi

On p. 299, read "Bertram" for "Bertrams" S. Brown

The Chronically Mentally Ill
Research and Services

The Chronically Mentally Ill
Research and Services

Edited by
Mohsen Mirabi, M.D.
Chief, Adult Psychiatry Services
Texas Research Institute of Mental Sciences
Houston, Texas

Lore Feldman
Technical Editor

CALIFORNIA SCHOOL OF PROFESSIONAL PSYCHOLOGY
LOS ANGELES

MEDICAL & SCIENTIFIC BOOKS
A DIVISION OF SPECTRUM PUBLICATIONS, INC.
NEW YORK

SPECTRUM PUBLICATIONS, INC.
175-20 Wexford Terrace
Jamaica, NY 11432

Library of Congress Cataloging in Publication Data
Main entry under title:

The Chronically mentally ill.

    Bibliography: p.
    Includes index.
    1. Mentally ill—Care and treatment. 1. Chronically ill—Care and treatment. I. Mirabi, Mohsen. [DNLM: 1. Mental disorders—Congresses. 2. Chronic disease—Congresses. WM 100 C557 1982]
RC480.53.C49   1984   362.2   84-6799
ISBN 0-89335-202-0

Printed in the United States of America

Contributors

William A. Anthony, Ph.D. • Director, Center for Rehabilitation Research and Training in Mental Health, Boston, Massachusetts

Bertram S. Brown, M.D. • President and Chief Executive Officer, Hahnemann University, Philadelphia, Pennsylvania

Karen S. Danley, Ph.D. • Center for Rehabilitation Research and Training in Mental Health, Boston University, Boston, Massachusetts

J.R. Elpers, M.D. • Director, Los Angeles County Department of Mental Health, Los Angeles, California

Ian R.H. Falloon, M.D. • Department of Psychiatry, University of Southern California School of Medicine, Los Angeles, California

David W. Foy, Ph.D. • Director of Training and Rehabilitation Research, Brentwood Veterans Administration Medical Center, Los Angeles, California

Charles M. Gaitz, M.D. • Assistant Director and Head, Gerontology Center, Texas Research Institute of Mental Sciences, Houston, Texas

Howard H. Goldman, M.D., M.P.H., Ph.D. • Department of Psychiatry, Langley Porter Institute, University of California, San Francisco, California

Jack R. Gordon, M.D. • Head, Clinical Research Division, Texas Research Institute of Mental Sciences, Houston, Texas

Herbert J. Grossman, M.D. • Director, Institute for the Study of Mental Retardation and Related Disabilities; Professor, Department of Pediatrics, Neurology, and Psychiatry, University of Michigan, Ann Arbor, Michigan

Joanne Howell, M.S. • Massachusetts Rehabilitation Commission, Quincy, Massachusetts

Dale L. Johnson, Ph.D. • Department of Psychology, University of Houston, Houston, Texas

Samuel J. Keith, M.D. • Chief, Center for Studies of Schizophrenia, National Institute of Mental Health, Rockville, Maryland

Robert Paul Liberman, M.D. • Department of Psychiatry, University of California at Los Angeles School of Medicine; Chief, Rehabilitation Medicine Service, Brentwood Veterans Administration Medical Center, Los Angeles, California

Mark H. Licht, Ph.D. • Department of Psychology, Florida State University, Tallahassee, Florida

Marco J. Mariotto, Ph.D. • Department of Psychology, University of Houston, Houston, Texas

Susan Matthews, B.A. • Center for Studies of Schizophrenia, Clinical Research Branch, National Institute of Mental Health, Rockville, Maryland

Gary E. Miller, M.D. • Commissioner, Texas Department of Mental Health and Mental Retardation, Austin, Texas

Mohsen Mirabi, M.D. • Chief, Adult Psychiatry Services, and Acting Director, Psychiatry Residency Program, Texas Research Institute of Mental Sciences, Houston, Texas

Vona Morton, R.N. • Texas Research Institute of Mental Sciences, Houston, Texas

Gordon L. Paul, Ph.D. • Cullen Distinguished Professor of Psychology, University of Houston, Houston, Texas; Director, Clinical Research Unit, Adolph Meyer Mental Health Center, Decatur, Illinois

Christopher T. Power, Ph.D. • Associate Director, Clinical Research Unit, Adolf Meyer Mental Health Center, Decatur, Illinois

Robert F. Prien, Ph.D. • Chief, Affective Disorders Section, Pharmacologic and Somatic Treatments Research Branch, National Institute of Mental Health, Rockville, Maryland

Cyrus Sajadi, M.D. • Chief, Psychiatric Evaluation Section, Texas Research Institute of Mental Sciences, Houston, Texas

Nina R. Schooler, Ph.D. • Chief, Schizophrenic Disorders Section, Pharmacologic and Somatic Treatments Research Branch, National Institute of Mental Health, Rockville, Maryland

Joanne B. Severe, M.S. • Schizophrenic Disorders Section, Pharmacologic and Somatic Treatments Research Branch, National Institute of Mental Health, Rockville, Maryland

Alla Shvartsburd, M.S. • Texas Research Institute of Mental Sciences, Houston, Texas

Robert C. Smith, M.D., Ph.D. • Chief, Biological Psychiatry Section, Texas Research Institute of Mental Sciences, Houston, Texas

John S. Strauss, M.D. • Department of Psychiatry, Yale University School of Medicine, New Haven, Connecticut

John A. Talbott, M.D. • Department of Psychiatry, Cornell University Medical College; Associate Medical Director, The Payne Whitney Psychiatric Clinic, The New York Hospital, New York, New York; President, American Psychiatric Association

Charles J. Wallace, Ph.D. • University of California at Los Angeles School of Medicine, Los Angeles, California

Preface

The topic of chronic mental illness has been much discussed, but there is still no widely accepted strategy of intervention for patients suffering from disorders of this kind. These patients have received little attention until recently, because they are difficult to treat effectively. Although methods of patient care are changing rapidly, the application of new techniques has been slow. Services for chronically disabled patients have been poorly funded. Government support has decreased while deinstitutionalization has increased the demand for community services.

This volume focuses on emerging trends and developments in the field and offers comprehensive coverage of state-of-the-art methods of diagnosis, evaluation, and treatment of the chronically mentally ill population. Many leading clinicians, scientists, and mental health advocates discuss new suggestions and solutions to longstanding problems, presenting biological and psychosocial perspectives. We introduce readers to current movements in the diagnosis and treatment of schizophrenia, depression, chronic alcoholism, mental retardation, and the mental illnesses related to aging. Recent trends in psychopharmacology, psychotherapy, and social management that may enable patients to live more satisfying and productive lives are particularly highlighted.

This book is based on a symposium on the chronically mentally ill which was sponsored by the Texas Research Institute of Mental Sciences, the training and research arm of the Texas Department of Mental Health and Mental Retardation. To our colleagues who shared their experience and knowledge with us we express our deep appreciation. Many thanks to Myriam Albertini, Dr. Maxine Weinman, and Dr. Sandra Magnetti, whose administrative and organizational expertise helped to make the symposium a reality.

Mohsen Mirabi, M.D.

Contents

I
An Overview of the Chronically Mentally Ill

1
The Chronic Mental Patient:
A National Perspective

JOHN A. TALBOTT

The census in state hospitals nationwide reached its peak of 560,000 in 1955 and has gone down steadily since then to its current low of under 140,000 (Meyer, 1974-1975) (Figure 1). This represents a 70-percent reduction nationwide, a rate mirrored in most states. Some have exceeded it; for instance, Massachusetts has gone from 24,000 to under 3,000. New York State (Figure 2) had a slow slope for some time and then, in the late 60s, it accelerated a great deal. Now the trend has again slowed. The reasons for this phenomenon are many.

REASONS FOR DEINSTITUTIONALIZATION

The first force behind deinstitutionalization was the community mental health movement itself. The movement began in part in response to the scandalous conditions in state hospitals—overcrowding, poor care, patient abuse, inhumanity—and the idea that one should treat people close to their families, homes and jobs, in an attempt to avoid institutionalization (Joint Commission on Mental Illness and Health, 1961).

The second influence derived from the technological advances within psychiatry, both sociological and pharmacological. The open-door system, milieu treatment, and the introduction of chlorpromazine and the other phenothiazines were major factors (Brill and Patton, 1959).

The third was the civil liberties movement, which advocated treatment in less restrictive environments, an end to involuntary commitment, and the right to refuse treatment (Stone, 1975).

Finally, and probably least understood early in the deinstitutionalization process and certainly by now discredited and denied by most states, the economic issue. The fact that, in the last 29 years, with the provision of Medicaid, Medicare, and Supplemental Security Income (SSI), states were able in large part

3

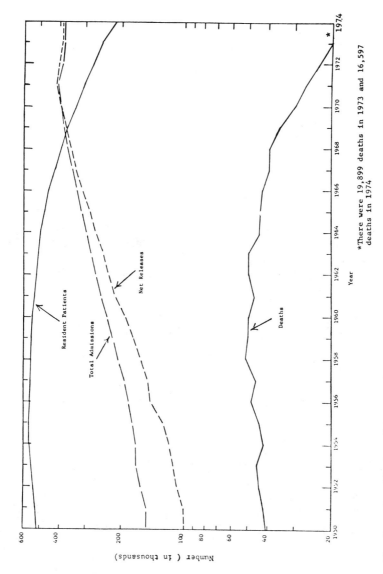

Figure 1 Number of resident patients, total admissions, net releases, and deaths, state and county mental hospitals, United States 1950-1974. Source: National Institute of Mental Health.

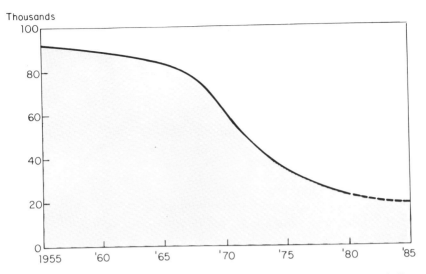

Thousands

Figure 2 New York State total resident population. Source: New York State Office of Mental Health.

to shift the funding from 100 percent state funding to largely federal funding with some local share (Scull, 1977).

These factors resulted in what is now known as "deinstitutionalization," which is really comprised of two parts: the shift of people from institutional to community settings; and the blockage of new admissions into institutions with the intention of not having anyone else become institutionalized, that is, become chronic, in institutions.

The 50s and 60s were replete with the hopeful notions that we really did not need hospitals, that no one would become chronically ill if we didn't have hospitals, and that people do not become chronic or relapse in the community. Such thinking has been generally abandoned by now. There are now very few people who advocate closing all hospitals, and the evidence is convincing that the relapse rate for schizophrenia will persist despite deinstitutionalization.

PROBLEMS OF DEINSTITUTIONALIZATION

In 1975, the American Psychiatric Association's Committee on the Chronic Mental Patient conducted a study of psychiatrists' opinions about the problems of deinstitutionalization. We asked simply, "What are the problems encountered and posed by the chronic mentally ill?" The answers, listed in rank order, were (Table 1, Talbott, 1978):

1. Deinstitutionalization itself.
2. Funding that has not followed patients from hospitals to community

Table 1   Summary of Most Important Issues Identified by Psychiatrists

Deinstitutionalization
Funding for chronic mental patients
Need for a continuum of community care facilities
Need for a model service system
Adequate housing, job opportunities, and rehabilitation services
Low status accorded chronic patients by psychiatrists
Definition of the role of psychiatrists in caring for chronic mental patients
Suitable training for psychiatrists in caring for the chronic mental patient
Involvement of families in caring for chronic mental patients
Description of effective programs for the chronic patient
Achievement of continuity of care
Adequate provision of community care facilities
Role of long-term medication
Determination of what patients should be treated where
Establishment of responsibility for coordination of care
Utilization of a case manager or continuity agent

Source: Talbott, 1978.

settings; discrimination against chronic and for acute illness, against long-term and for short-term care, and against private and for public funding of services for the chronic mentally ill.

3. The need for a continuum of community care facilities. Most respondents noted that their states or counties had a state hospital, a nursing home, and an aftercare clinic. There was no continuum of care settings that would enable patients to move from the most restrictive to the least restrictive settings in a step-wise, graded way.

4. The need for a model service system. Our respondents asked "Where can we look at a model system, to see what they have, and to adapt that system back home?"

5. Adequate housing, job opportunities, and rehabilitation services.

6. Low status accorded chronic patients by mental health professionals.

7. Definition of the role of psychiatrists in caring for chronic mental patients. Psychiatrists have been leaving the public sector, especially its leadership positions, in droves, in the last 20 years. This is often attributed to their relegation to isolated roles, for example, as prescription writers and paper pushers, rather than being involved with all aspects of treatment planning and implementation.

8. Suitable training for psychiatrists in caring for the chronic mental patient. Most clinicians were trained either in a psychoanalytic approach or a biological approach, for example, using medication and other somatic treatments. Today

using either approach alone is not considered optimally helpful to chronically mentally ill people because it ignores their interactive effect and the necessity of social and vocational rehabilitation.

9. Involvement of families in caring for chronic mental patients. Psychiatrists for the last hundred years have tended to blame families for the illnesses of their relatives, rather than try to work with them on devising optimal treatment plans.

10. Description of effective programs for the chronic patient. Again our respondents asked "What programs can we look at that deliver good services for the chronic patient?"

11. Achievement of continuity of care. It is a rare instance when we provide continuity of care so that someone is able to be followed by the same group of people or person through a variety of services.

12. Adequate provision of community care facilities. The third item referred to a continuum; this one refers to sheer numbers. There are only 9,000 halfway house slots in the country for some 900,000 schizophrenic patients living in the community. Therefore, every schizophrenic person has a one-in-a-hundred chance of being in a halfway house; clearly not enough.

13. The role of long-term medication. All medications have side effects, and many psychiatric medications have long-term side effects. The cost-benefits of those medications, social as well as economic, are a serious ethical and professional problem.

14. Determination of what patients should be treated where. We know, after the fact, that many people are in hospitals who should not be there, and many people are in the community who should be in hospitals. But the prospective determination of where those people should be treated and cared for, and how many of each service and setting are needed, has yet to be worked out.

15. Establishment of responsibility for coordination of care. In most parts of the country, we have moved from a system in which states, with their state hospitals, were responsible for the severely and chronically ill, to a wide spectrum of different services which, for the most part, are ill-coordinated and ill-defined, and constitute a scattered effort rather than an umbrella of services. As a result, the chronic mentally ill have fallen into the cracks.

16. Utilization of a case manager or continuity agent. Our respondents asked "Would designation of a single, responsible person help ensure provision of services?"

From this laundry list of problems emerged seven questions, whose answers may bring us closer to a public policy:

1. Who are the chronic mental patients and where are they? What are their needs?
2. What programs work and what programs don't work to meet the needs of chronic mental patients?

3. What are the obstacles to implementing effective programs and what are the solutions to surmount these obstacles?
4. What are the economic issues involved in providing effective care for the chronic mental patient (cost-benefit analyses)?
5. What are the pros and cons of case-client-patient assessment and resource management?
6. Who has and should have responsibility for coordinating, implementing, and monitoring services for chronic mental patients?
7. What are the rights of patients, ex-patients, and providers of services?

DEFINING THE POPULATION

Thus far, I have been using such terms as chronic mental patient and chronically mentally ill without defining them. They are incorrect terms, in that they imply homogeneity; for example, that these people are all the same, which implies that if we provide the same treatment, everyone will respond the same way. That is clearly not the case. The chronically mentally ill are all very different people, with different needs; their treatment plans, therefore, need to be different.

Leona Bachrach, a leading sociologist in the field, has defined this group as people who, but for the deinstitutionalization movement, might be in public hospitals, like state hospitals, today; and I will use her definition (Bachrach, 1976). It is an important definition because it does not insist on a person's ever having been hospitalized and discharged. We are now finding, in most places in the country, a new cohort of young chronic patients created by demographic factors that is all too familiar to you. This group is a consequence of the large, post-World War II baby boom, and it is now moving up the age charts. Figure 3 shows that in 1970 this big bulge was in the 15- to 24-year age period, when people develop signs and symptoms of schizophrenia that require intervention. In the succeeding decades, they will develop primary affective disorders, that is, manic-depressive disorders. In addition, the group 65 and older will double in size by the year 2030, and their risk for developing mental illness is quite high as well (Figure 4).

The reason we cannot talk about only those people who were previously hospitalized in state hospitals is because currently 30 to 40 percent of people coming into programs serving chronic patients have never before been in either state hospitals or, often, in any mental health facility. This population of "new chronic patients," who show all the symptoms of chronicity we see in those hospitalized for 20 years, present a grave problem, because many community support program criteria specifically rule out these never-hospitalized people. States usually assume responsibility only for patients who were previously hospitalized in state facilities. Yet, we are facing this huge bulge in our population. The incidence of schizophrenia and manic-depressive illness is not changing. What is changing is the nation's demography. We will experience an explosive growth in

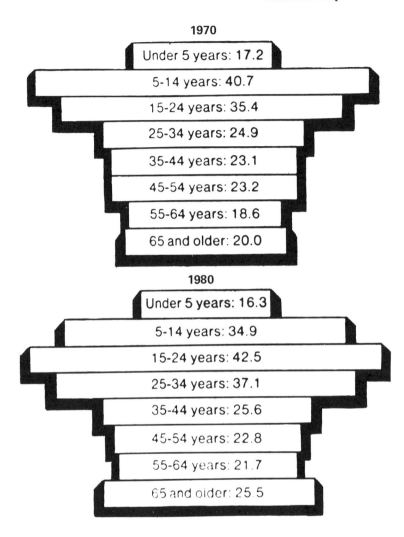

Figure 3 Profile of the population by age groups (figures rounded off, in millions). Source: Bureau of the Census.

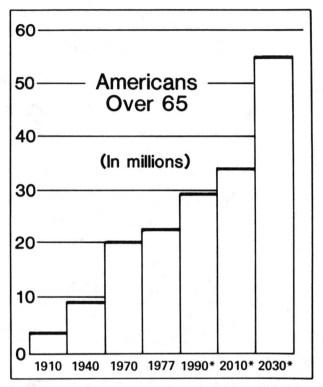

60 ——————————————————————————

50 ———— **Americans** ————
Over 65

40 ——————————————————

(In millions)

30 ——————————

20 ——————

10 ————

0

1910 1940 1970 1977 1990* 2010* 2030*

*Assuming (1) a fertility level of 2.1 children born per woman and (2) that mortality rates decrease at a rate whereby life expectancy at birth increases by about .05 year per year.

Figure 4   Source: U.S. Bureau of the Census

the number of people who will become vulnerable to chronic mental illness at the same time that the number of state hospitals and state hospital beds is shrinking.

In referring to the chronically mentally ill we are dealing with disability as well as disease. Many people recover from acute and recurrent episodes of illness and go back to live normal lives. Many, though, have some emotional scarring. That scarring tends to occur in areas of everyday living we take very much for granted—the ability to shop, to prepare food, to live, to bank, to travel. These deficits impair the ability to compete in the market place, and they can be seen in much the same way as a physical disability: even after the active disease process is over, a disability often is still present.

Finally, we tend to forget children when it comes to chronic mental illness. Children comprise four percent of this population, a significant number. In addition, of all the children who are mentally ill as children, 40 to 60 percent carry that illness with them into adulthood.

MAPPING THE CHRONICALLY ILL

If we try to draw a map of the chronically mentally ill (Minkoff, 1978), what does that map look like?

	Number of the Chronically Mentally Ill
Schizophrenics	900,000 in the community
	200,000 in institutions
	1.1 million total
Elderly	1 million in institutions
	1 million psychotic in the community
	2 million total
SSI-Eligible	1.7 million in institutions
	1.5 million with mental disorders in the community
	3.2 million total

One problem with counting is that the chronic patient groups overlap. How many people are in all three categories—schizophrenic, elderly, and SSI-eligible? At a minimum, 1.1 million, and at the most 5 to 7 million (Figure 5).

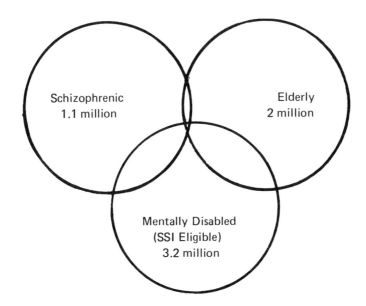

Figure 5 Number of the chronically mentally ill. Source: Minkoff, 1978.

The National Institute of Mental Health's conservative estimate is 1.7 to 3 million. In either case, we are talking about a minimum of three-quarters percent, and a maximum up to 3 or 4 percent, of the population of the United States—a large number of people who use up a lot of psychiatric services. A study of Medicaid utilization in New York State found that schizophrenic patients utilized the second largest single amount of money in the Medicaid system, alcohol/drug abuse patients were about fifth, and another mixed mental illness group was seventh. Thus, we had three large groups spending tremendous amounts of Medicaid money, which the report "attributed to the deinstitutionalization movement."

Where are these people? In the early days of deinstitutionalization, we placed patients who were easiest to place. Sixty-five percent of people originally went home to their families—half to their spouse, half to other relatives. That has changed completely. Now, only 25 percent go to live at home. The rest of them will live alone in some community setting or other. If you take a slice of the chronically mentally ill in the community, as Lamb did in California, fully half live in homes—board and care homes, nursing homes, and the like.

Of those institutionalized, 750,000 are in nursing homes and 150,000 in hospitals. There are two groups of persons in mental hospitals—150,000 who are

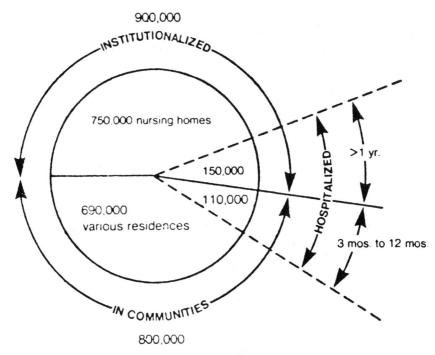

Figure 6 Location of the chronically mentally ill, United States, 1977. Source: *National Plan for the Chronically Mentally Ill* (Goldman et al., 1981).

there over a year, and 110,000 who are in and out rather rapidly. The larger population of 150,000 tends to be older and residual, whereas the smaller group tends to be younger and transient (Figure 6).

Figure 7 presents the percentage of Americans in institutions in 1950 and 1970, and it demonstrates the phenomenon of transinstitutionalization. We have deinstitutionalized one institution, the tuberculosis sanitarium, represented by the second bar from the top. We accomplished that for only one reason, effective medications for tuberculosis. We have not deinstitutionalized anybody else. The same percentage of Americans are in institutions in 1970 that were there in 1950. All we have changed is the proportion of Americans in the various institutions. The bottom-most group represents those in state hospitals, now a third of what it was. The next one up is the group in nursing homes; this has tripled. we have seen an exchange—a *transinstitutionalization*.

So if that's all we have done, why are all those people out on the streets? Why does New York City have 10,000 to 40,000 homeless people? Because of the second part of deinstitutionalization, which is blockage of new admissions to facilities.

Figure 8 shows who is left in the New York state institutions. The young people cluster at the 30-year age range; the older people at age 70. Services also changed dramatically between 1955 and 1973 (Figure 9). State hospitals and county hospitals, which formerly delivered 50 percent of mental health services, shrank to providing 12 percent. This was probably about the same actual number because the 1973 total numbers were much larger. Outpatient services, a quarter in 1955, were a half in 1973. Community mental health centers, which did not exist in 1955, constituted 23 percent 12 years later.

Figure 10 shows the forensic populations, classified in New York in two different categories. Some are already convicted and are in correctional facilities, the others are not. Both populations are increasing dramatically. I believe the two time bombs waiting to go off among the mentally ill are in, one, the nursing homes, and two, the prisons.

MEASURES OF FUNCTIONING

Let us look at how well the chronically mentally ill function. One can measure functioning in several ways: by readmission rates, symptomatology, work history, socialization, and aftercare.

Readmissions

Thirty years ago, 25 percent of patients admitted to hospitals were readmissions. Now, more than 60 percent of admissions to mental hospitals nationally are readmissions. There are two ways to remember this. Each person discharged from a hospital will have a 60 percent chance of being readmitted within two

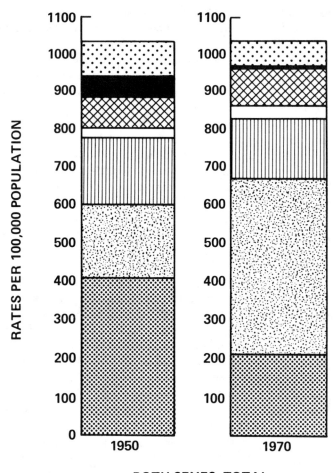

BOTH SEXES, TOTAL

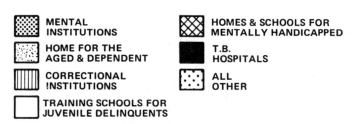

Figure 7 Distribution of persons in institutions per 100,000 population by type of institution, both sexes, United States 1950 and 1970. Source: U.S. Bureau of the Census, Persons in Institutions, 1950 and 1970.

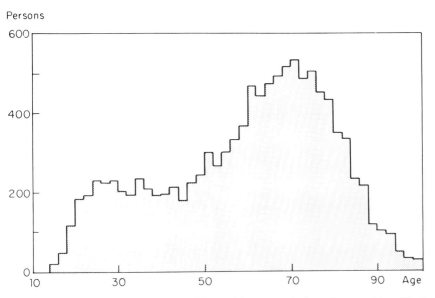

Figure 8 New York State age profile—resident population. Source: New York State Office of Mental Health.

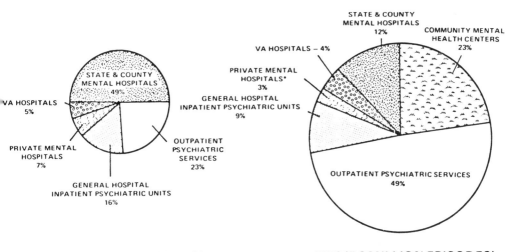

1955 (1.7 MILLION EPISODES)   1973 (5.2 MILLION EPISODES)

NCLUDES RESIDENTIAL TREATMENT CENTERS FOR EMOTIONALLY DISTURBED CHILDREN

Figure 9 Percent distributions of inpatient and outpatient care episodes in mental health facilities, by type of facility: United States, 1955 and 1973. Source: Division of Biometry, National Institute of Mental Health.

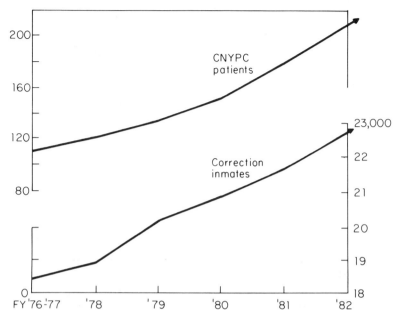

Figure 10 New York State forensic population: Central New York Psychiatric Center (CNYPC) and corrections. Source: New York State Department of Mental Health.

years, and 60 percent of persons admitted to any hospital constitute readmissions (Figure 11).

Symptomatology

Of all the chronically mentally ill people in the community, only one-third are asymptomatic, the rest have some symptoms. These include hallucinations, delusions, and others, in addition to social and vocational disabilities.

Work

Work remains one of the most critical outcome variables in psychiatry. Seventy percent of the patients who are admitted to hospitals and subsequently discharged go back to a less skilled job. Only 30 to 50 percent of those employed previously even return to work. In terms of its effect on the marketplace, mental illness has a tremendous impact.

Socialization

Only 25 percent of the chronically mentally ill have the sorts of social systems, whether family or other networks, that we consider adequate. A book by Susan Sheehan (1982), *Is There No Place on Earth For Me?*, expresses better

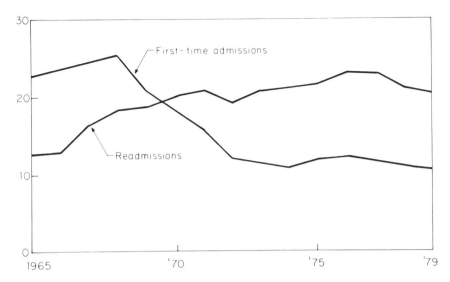

Figure 11 New York State admissions versus readmissions. Source: New York State Office of Mental Health.

than I can the problems the chronically ill have with socialization. Sheehan recounts in a poignant manner the continual, repetitive problems the chronic mentally ill encounter. In one incident, a group of patients visit a staff member's home on Christmas Eve. They sit around as if they were on a ward, and some sing carols. Most sit passively, doing almost nothing. The next day a staff member asks if they had a good time. A marvelous time, is the reply. To us it seems horrible.

Aftercare

All the outcome research available shows that only two things seem to prevent both relapse and readmission: medication and continuing contact, whether it's psychotherapy or counseling or mere person-to-person contact. It is disappointing, therefore, that among the chronically mentally ill in the community, fewer than 50 percent continue to take their medication, and fewer than 25 percent stay in some sort of aftercare program during the next year. This demonstrates the needs for continuity of care provided by some means or other.

NEEDS OF THE CHRONICALLY MENTALLY ILL

How about the needs of the chronically ill? (Turner, 1978; Peterson, 1978). Figure 12 graphically illustrates many of the problems we face. In the hospital, all the needs of a chronically ill patient are met under a single umbrella. Moving someone to his or her own apartment to live alone in no way satisfies all these

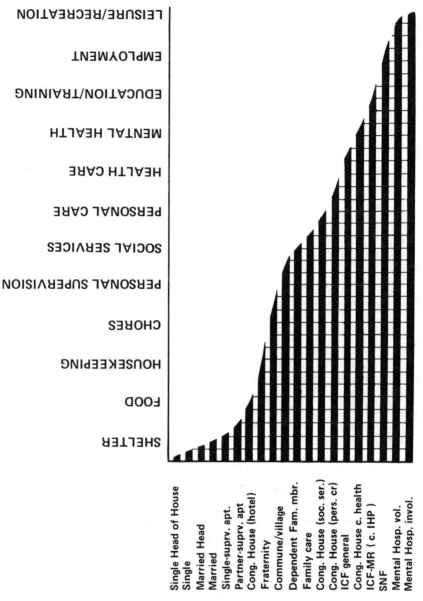

Figure 12   Needs and settings of the chronically ill. Source: E. Boggs, personal communication.

needs, and indeed removes the umbrella. We went, in 1955, from providing an umbrella of services to providing essentially nothing at all. What we need is quite another thing (Figure 13).

Housing

This is a critical need for this patient population. Right now, nursing homes are overcrowded with the chronically mentally ill, and we have too few alternatives because we do not have adequate funding for them.

Income

Income is a critical issue, whether it's continuing income and support or part-time employment. We have learned that the chronically ill can frequently work for a few half-days a week or even some full days, but not full-time.

Medical Care

This population has three times the morbidity and the mortality of the rest of us. Chronic mental illness is accompanied by chronic medical illness. Half of the psychiatric care in this country is delivered by nonpsychiatric health care providers, who often know too little about these patients' psychiatric and social needs. In addition, we need a different sort of mental health system. We need good quality hospitals, rather than the sorts of hospitals we have had. We need crisis stabilization. Study after study shows that the acutely ill person who is experiencing his or her first psychiatric break deserves the longest, most careful, most thorough hospitalization, much longer than any of the usual lengths of stay in most states, and longer than most insurance policies provide. In contrast, people who are experiencing their tenth, eleventh, or twelfth admission deserve a very rapid workup, assessment, re-equilibration on medication, and return to community care if this exists to return to. One obviously cannot allow patients to return to the street. But if there is a community support system in place, the patient stands a chance of improving. I want to emphasize that one cannot take people who have been living in a prison or a hospital for 25 years and turn them loose in either an urban or rural environment and expect them to survive without specific training in the skills of everyday living and an adequate community support system.

One problem identified in reports of the General Accounting Office, the American Psychiatric Association, and the President's Commission on Mental Health is that the needs of this population are met by funding from different federal agencies, and often this separation is perpetuated by different state agencies. In 1978 I attended an NIMH conference at which all directors of the various federal entitlement programs were on the podium together to tell us what was happening. They started by introducing themselves to each other. They didn't know each other! Here were the people from all the federal agencies re-

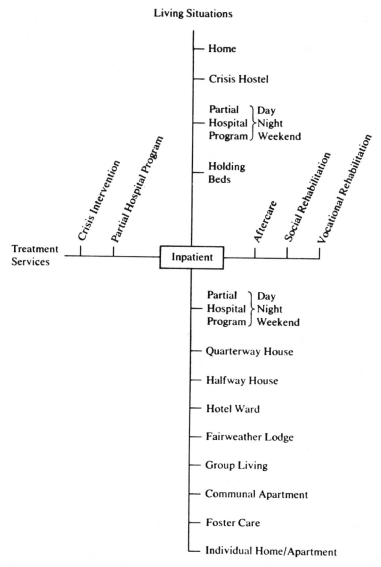

Figure 13 The spectrum of optimal treatment services and living situations.

sponsible for the chronic mentally ill, and they were madly taking notes on what the others' programs were like.

EFFECTIVE PROGRAMS

We now have adequate evidence (Glasscote, 1978; Barter, 1978) concerning the effectiveness of programs for the chronically mentally ill. I choose to divide these programs into two categories: preparatory programs that prepare people to move from institutions to community settings, and community support programs that maintain and sustain people in the community.

The best described and researched of the preparatory programs was conducted a few years ago in Illinois by Gordon Paul and Robert Lentz (1978). Patients who received their behavioral modification-oriented treatment were compared with a group in "milieu therapy." A third group received what was called "traditional" state hospital treatment—mainly medication and some group therapy. In the behavioral modification program, which taught survival skills, the researchers found that very few people were rehospitalized. During the first follow-up period, fewer than 10 percent of patients were rehospitalized, whereas 30 percent of the milieu-treated patients were readmitted, and 50 percent of the traditional state hospital-treated patients returned to the hospital.

The best described program of supportive services in the community is that of Leonard Stein and his group in Wisconsin (Stein and Test, 1980; Test and Stein, 1980; Weisbrod et al., 1980). The Stein and Test data are impressive. They had a higher staff-to-patient ratio than did most programs and offered a wider variety of services. They too attempted to teach patients the skills of everyday living. They provided medication and tried to treat people entirely in the community. They compared their program's patients with a hospitalized group and followed them up in the usual way our system does. The patients treated in their experimental program spent more time in sheltered employment, had fewer symptoms, spent much less time in hospital; the quality of their lives was no different, and the burden to their families and communities was the same. Stein and Test also found no difference in their patients' social contacts except that they had more contact with trusted friends. When the program stopped, however, the results were dramatic. Hospitalization and unemployment rates increased, and the patients' contacts with trusted friends and their ability to enjoy life and leisure time diminished.

The granddaddy of psychosocial rehabilitation programs, Fountain House in New York, has been replicated by almost 100 Fountain House-type programs throughout the country. These programs all provide what I call the psychosocial triad of housing, social rehabilitation, and vocational rehabilitation. Fountain House itself, and some of the others, actually offer medical care right on site, for people who can't or won't travel, but it also encourages the use of other services. Fountain House is able to cut in half the readmission rate of discharged state hospital patients at six months: 17 percent readmitted versus 37 percent of controls readmitted.

If one looks at all the elements of good programs, several common denominators emerge:

1. Continuing medication and personal contact.

2. Teaching people the skills of everyday living.

3. Provision of the psychosocial triad—housing, social rehabilitation, and vocational rehabilitation.

4. Program leaders who are dedicated to the work, understand chronicity, don't get discouraged, don't burn out, and who can walk that thin line between expecting enough and not expecting too much from their patients.

5. Aggressive outreach and monitoring systems. Our study a few years ago of readmissions to a New York state hospital was done so that I could demonstrate that I needed more money than other superintendents, and that the money was needed to buy buildings and hire new personnel. Much to my dismay I found that I had not shown that I needed buildings and new people. I needed to change some attitudes, so that patients who did not come in for appointments were followed up aggressively, and people transferred from one area to the other or whose housing changed were shown where to go for outpatient care. On discharging a patient, rather than merely saying, "Show up in the aftercare clinic three weeks from now," one had the professional from the aftercare program visit the patient in the hospital. The effectiveness of these sorts of measures was subsequently demonstrated in several studies.

6. Good patient advocacy systems. Until now patient advocacy has tended to mean "freedom at all costs." Legal advocates have made few attempts to ensure the provision of good services. Lawyers have argued for freedom for one patient on a ward, but not for the other 30 patients; for the right to treatment in the hospital but not for providing adequate services and the right to treatment in the community. This situation is beginning to change; good programs serving the chronically ill provide patient advocacy in terms of ensuring good services.

7. Good interagency referrals. In many state programs, staff members spend most of their time trying not to accept chronically ill patients. The federal community mental health center program that emanated from the first Commission on Mental Health Report, *Action for Mental Health*, did not take care of the chronically mentally ill. The centers competed with the private systems for the same patients. An amendment was needed in 1975 to ensure that the centers would begin to take care of these patients.

8. Good horizontal and vertical administrative structures, to facilitate communication among agencies and up the bureaucratic ladder.

9. Appreciation of small progress.

10. Stable resource bases. Successful programs have linkages with community leaders and decision makers that ensure continued support for their programs.

11. Good accountability and responsibility for the population.

How do you put all of this together? The funding streams must be made to come down together and finally be available to the patient (Figure 14). We must recreate in the community the sort of umbrella available in the state hospital.

One way of doing this is through a case management or resource management system (Lourie, 1978; Ozarin, 1978) (Figure 15). Why do we need case managers? If the patients have families who can advocate for them, the families clearly constitute the best case management system, but it is exhausing work. Someone must pull together the available resources. The National Plan on the Chronic Mentally Ill uses the term resource manager, which is more accurate than case manager. Marshalling resources for people rather than "managing" cases seems an infinitely more desirable concept to me.

OBSTACLES TO GOOD PROGRAMS

What are the obstacles? (Paul, 1978; Meyerson, 1978). And why, if we know what I have spelled out above, don't we do it? Why do we have only one Pyramid House in Houston or one Fountain House in New York? There are a host of reasons.

The first is attitudinal. It is hard to imagine a group that has less status and less lobbying clout than the chronically mentally ill. Chronic mental patients cannot compete with the parents of the mentally retarded, with alcoholics, with prisoners, with welfare mothers, and with all the other have-not groups, because their everyday functioning is so impaired.

Some of the reasons for their low status among professionals and all other citizens are neurotic and some are real. Among the crazy reasons is the fact that people are still afraid of working with the chronically mentally ill because they fear they'll get sick themselves. Then there are some very real reasons. We are no more successful in curing chronic schizophrenia than we are in curing chronic heart disease. We can care for it; we can manage it. The primary thing that discourages young physicians, whether they are pediatricians or internists or psychiatrists, is that chronically ill persons are frustrating to treat. Neither mental hospitals nor community programs have cured chronic mental illness.

Second are the legal and ethical barriers. Recent legislative and judicial judgments have tended to hamper good programs. The more regulation is built in, the more the quality of care will drop to the lowest common denominator, although some rank abuse will be eliminated. That is the trade-off. In New York State, there are 164 agencies that may audit and inspect our hospitals and ask us to fill out forms. With the exception of two, 162 agencies all do this at different times.

Every mental health facility has a cadre of people who do nothing but prepare for all these visits and fill out forms. Everyone else spends an inordinate amount of time with required papers. Twenty-five percent of our time, whether we are psychiatrists, directors of hospitals, ward clerks, or nurses, is spent com-

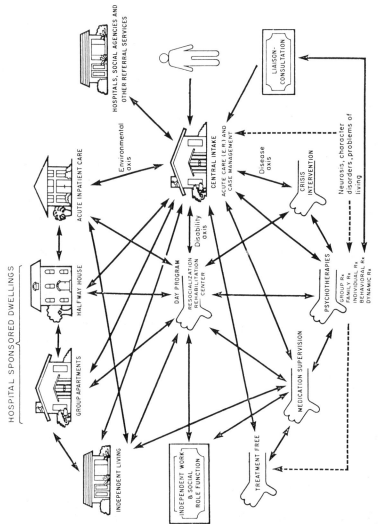

Figure 14   An integrated service delivery system. Source: J. Barter, personal communication.

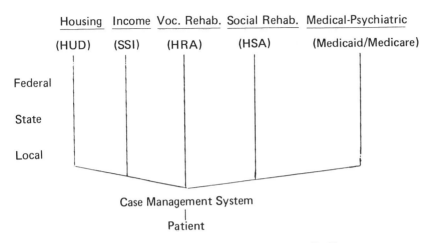

Figure 15   Needs of the chronically mentally ill.

plying with these regulations, and 25 percent of our salaries can be attributed to meeting regulatory requirements, above and beyond good clinical care.

Third are structural/administrative barriers. We have diffuse administrative structures, with different agencies having different standards and different criteria for eligibility. The red tape is incredible. The politics between cities and states, or counties and states are often very destructive to the mentally ill.

Fourth, funding problems are monumental, as mentioned in the section on problems of deinstitutionalization.

Fifth, we lack an integrated community care and support program. We have not recreated the umbrella we had in the state hospital out in the community. We have a multiplicity of systems and subsystems, and multiple levels of accountability.

Lastly, we have personnel insufficiently trained in modern treatment methods who will work with this population.

ECONOMICS OF MENTAL CARE

Let me give you some economic details (Sharfstein et al., 1978; Menninger, 1978) (Figure 16). Health today accounts for 10 percent of the gross national product, and 15 cents of every health dollar goes to mental health.

The largest single consumers of dollars for the mentally ill are nursing homes (Figure 17), followed by state, county, and other public mental hospitals. Thus over 50 percent of provider dollars (i.e., direct costs) goes to these institutions, whereas general hospitals, which are actually the largest providers of psychiatric services in the country, get only 11 percent of the money.

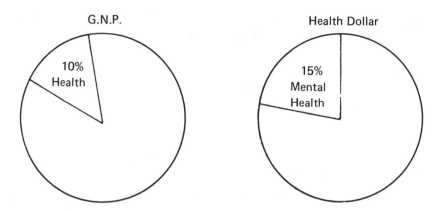

Figure 16   Economics. Source: Sharfstein et al., 1978.

Table 2   Estimated Costs of Mental Illness

	1963	1968	1971	1974[1]
Direct Costs	2,401,700	4,030,974	11,058,290	16,973,058
Indirect Costs	4,634,000	16,906,000[2]	14,179,382	19,812,768
Total Costs	7,035,700	20,936,974	25,237,681	36,785,827

[1]Total does not include comparability adjustments on management expenses.
[2]The 1968 estimate is greater than the 1971 estimate because of the vagaries of the methodology employed by the authors of the estimate. However, while their estimating procedure may be questioned, it is noted that allowances are made for a number of costs of mental illness which are not normally counted.
Source: Sharfstein et al., 1978.

In 1974, 36 billion dollars were estimated to be spent on mental health, split roughly evenly between direct and indirect costs (Table 2). Eighty-seven percent of that could be traced to the chronically mentally ill, and most of it went to maintaining inadequate programs.

We should be arguing not simply for more money, but for the existing money to be allocated in a different way.

COST-BENEFIT ANALYSES

What about cost-benefit analyses? For years we have been told about the immense savings of deinstitutionalizing people. The good news is that there *are* immense savings in housing the mentally ill in community settings. The bad news is

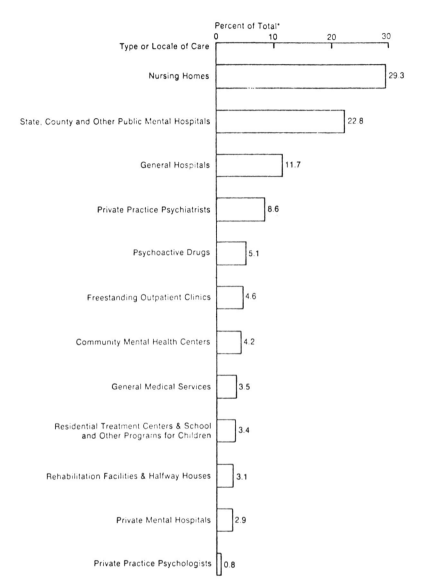

*Estimated total expenditures for direct care were $14.5 billion

Figure 17 Percentage distribution of expenditures for direct care of the mentally ill by type or locale of care, United States 1974. Source: *Statistical Note 125*, Division of Biometry and Epidemiology, National Institute of Mental Health.

that it costs much more to provide services, because of the combined problems of decentralization, need for coordination, and the necessity of providing a community umbrella. We now have about eight studies of the costs of institutional versus community care. They all conclude that there is some small saving in the long run. Sharfstein and Nafziger (1976) studied a single patient for 15 years and found that, for the first three years, the cost was about the same. Then there was a slight advantage to community care.

Leonard Stein and Burton Weisbrod in Wisconsin (Weisbrod et al., 1976) showed that some 11 percent more money was needed for caring for patients in the community than for those in control groups. You had to "prime the pump," because community services are more expensive, but you got 15 percent more back in taxes and other benefits. Thus there was a net gain. It is cheaper in the long run for the total economy, but legislators at all levels do not always see that. It is difficult to get them to prime the pump because it costs *more* to prime that pump even though the eventual result saves monies.

There is also the question of funding two systems, institutional and community. As a nation, we have come about halfway in moving from institutional to community care. Now we are stuck with both systems, each chewing up money. It is logical for some people to say that we must "go back to hospitals and get rid of the whole expensive community system," because it is more expensive in terms of services.

Figure 18 presents the economic picture in New York State. State monies constitute almost two-thirds of the total and local monies a third. People, how-

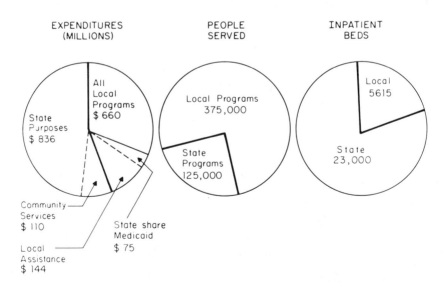

Figure 18 New York State state/local program shares. Source: New York State Office of Mental Health.

ever, are being served in the local programs. The reason for this maldistribution is that the inpatient beds are in the state hospitals.

Staffing ratios are demonstrated in Figure 19. State hospitals once had four patients to one staff member; the ratio now is more than one to one, a dramatic change. It makes possible somewhat better care, but at a tremendous cost.

GOVERNMENTAL RESPONSIBILITY

Built-in conflicts of interest exist at each level of government (Glenn, 1978; Muszinsky, 1978). Every level funds services and administers them directly, and also contracts with the next level down. When accreditation of state hospitals was threatened in California, the money flowed back from the community programs. To save the state hospitals, Medicare money had to be safeguarded. We now have a mental health system in transition, with two overlapping subsystems. Every time there is a threat, governmental monies will be withheld from the newer (community) systems. Some people have proposed that government withdraw from direct provision of services and contract for them instead.

Most persons agree that psychiatric services are best administered at the local level. Monies for such services need to come down from the federal level as categorical funding because, unless they do, the mentally ill will not successfully

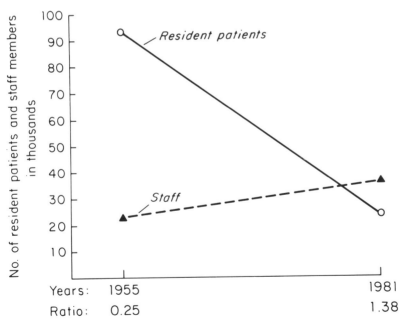

Figure 19 Ratio of resident patients to staff of New York State psychiatric centers. Source: New York State Office of Mental Health.

compete with other groups. These patients were lost in the community mental health center movement, and they will continue to be lost in whatever system we devise in the future, unless those services are funded by the state and federal governments and administered at the local level.

A way also has to be found to coordinate social services money with mental health funding. One can no longer discuss financing mental health without dealing with all the money allocated through Medicaid, Medicare, and Supplemental Security Income, federal housing, social and vocational rehabilitation programs.

AMERICAN PSYCHIATRIC ASSOCIATION RECOMMENDATIONS

Recommendations from the American Psychiatric Association (*A Call to Action* 1978) to move toward meeting the goal of providing adequate care for the chronically mentally ill include:

1. A reform of funding mechanisms.
2. The need for advocacy for services.
3. Research.
4. Expansion of training.
5. Continuity of services.
6. Technical assistance—requiring the federal government to educate community agencies on existing resources applicable to each community.
7. Finding a way for money to follow patients; a radical example of this is a voucher-type system. Clearly, if patients held vouchers, one voucher for services and another for housing, 50 percent of the money would not go to nursing homes and state and county hospitals, and our current system and delivery of care would be radically revised.

Many of the solutions to be worked out in the next few years are incorporated in the National Plan on the Chronic Mentally Ill, although many have to come from local initiatives in individual states. The problem we now have, first and foremost, is not new knowledge (except for the etiology of schizophrenia), but of applying what we already know. We must devise funding formulas so as not to leave this population in a worse position than they were in state hospitals two decades ago, or in the almshouses and workhouses two centuries ago.

REFERENCES

A Call to Action 1978. In J. A. Talbott (ed.), *The Chronic Mental Patient*, pp. 209-210. Washington, DC: American Psychiatric Association.

Bachrach, L. L. 1976. *Deinstitutionalization: An Analytical Review and Sociological Perspective*. Rockville, MD: U.S. Department of Health and Human Services.

Barter, J. T. 1978. Successful community programming for the chronic mental patient: Principles and practices. In J. A. Talbott (ed.), *The Chronic Mental Patient*, pp. 87-95. Washington, DC: American Psychiatric Association.

Brill, H., and Patton, R. E. 1959. Analysis of population reduction in New York state mental hospitals during the first four years of large-scale therapy with psychotropic drugs. *Am. J. Psychiatry* 116:495-509.

Glasscote, R. 1978. What programs work and what programs don't work to meet the needs of chronic mental patients? In J. A. Talbott (ed.), *The Chronic Mental Patient*, pp. 75-85. Washington, DC: American Psychiatric Association.

Glenn, T. D. 1978. Exploring responsibility for chronic mental patients in the community. In J. A. Talbott (ed.), *The Chronic Mental Patient*, pp. 173-193. Washington, DC: American Psychiatric Association.

Goldman, H., Gattozzi, A. A., and Taube, C. A. 1981. Defining and counting the chronic mentally ill. *Hosp. Community Psychiatry* 32-21-27.

Joint Commission on Mental Illness and Health 1961. *Action for Mental Health*. New York: Basic Books.

Lourie, N. V. 1978. Case management. In J. A. Talbott (ed.), *The Chronic Mental Patient*, pp. 159-164. Washington, DC: American Psychiatric Association.

Menninger, W. W. 1978. Economic issues in providing effective care for the chronic mental patient. In J. A. Talbott (ed.), *The Chronic Mental Patient*, pp. 151-156. Washington, DC: American Psychiatric Association.

Meyer, N. G. 1976. Provisional patient movement and administrative data, state and county psychiatric inpatient services, July 1, 1974-June 30, 1975. *Mental Health Statistical Note* 132. Rockville, MD: National Institute of Mental Health.

Meyerson, A. T. 1978. What are the barriers or obstacles to treatment and care of the chronically disabled mentally ill. In J. A. Talbott (ed.), *The Chronic Mental Patient*, pp. 129-134. Washington, DC: American Psychiatric Association.

Minkoff, K. 1978. A map of chronic mental patients. In J. A. Talbott (ed.), *The Chronic Mental Patient*, pp. 11-37. Washington, DC: American Psychiatric Association.

Muszynski, S. 1978. Who is responsible for overseeing services to chronic mental patients? In J. A. Talbott (ed.), *The Chronic Mental Patient*, pp. 195-206. Washington, DC: American Psychiatric Association.

Ozarin, L. D. 1978. The pros and cons of case management. In J. A. Talbott (ed.), *The Chronic Mental Patient*, pp. 165-170. Washington, DC: American Psychiatric Association.

Paul, G. L. 1978. The implementation of effective treatment programs for chronic mental patients: Obstacles and recommendations. In J. A. Talbott (ed.), *The Chronic Mental Patient*, pp. 99-127. Washington, DC: American Psychiatric Association.

Paul, G. L., and Lentz, R. 1978. *Psychosocial Treatment of Chronic Mental Patients: Milieu versus Social-Learning Programs*. Cambridge, MA: Harvard University Press.

Peterson, R. 1978. What are the needs of chronic mental patients? In J. A. Talbott (ed.), *The Chronic Mental Patient*, pp. 39-49. Washington, DC: American Psychiatric Association.

Scull, A. T. 1977. *Community Treatment and the Deviant: A Radical View*. Englewood Cliffs, NJ: Prentice-Hall.

Sharfstein, S., and Nafziger, J. 1976. Community care: Costs and benefits for a chronic patient. *Hosp. Community Psychiatry* 27:170-173.

Sharfstein, S. S., Turner, J. E. C., and Clark, H. W. 1978. Financing issues in the delivery of services to the chronically mentally ill and disabled. In J. A.

Talbott (ed.), *The Chronic Mental Patient*, pp. 137-150. Washington, DC: American Psychiatric Association.

Sheehan, S. 1982. *Is There No Place on Earth for Me?* Boston: Houghton Mifflin.

Stein, L. I., and Test, M. A. 1980. Alternative to mental hospital treatment. I. Conceptual model, treatment program, and clinical evaluation. *Arch. Gen. Psychiatry* 37:392-397.

Stone, A. A. 1975. *Mental Health and Law: A System in Transition*. Rockville, MD: National Institute of Mental Health.

Talbott, J. A. 1978. What are the problems facing and posed by the chronic mental patient: A survey of psychiatrists' concerns. In J. A. Talbott (ed.), *The Chronic Mental Patient*, p. 17. Washington, DC: American Psychiatric Association.

Test, M. A., and Stein, L. I. 1980. Alternative to mental hospital treatment. III. Social cost. *Arch. Gen. Psychiatry* 37:409-412.

Turner, J. E. C. 1978. Philosophical issues in meeting the needs of people disabled by mental health problems: The psychosocial rehabilitation approach. In J. A. Talbott (ed.), *The Chronic Mental Patient*, pp. 65-72. Washington, DC: American Psychiatric Association.

Weisbrod, B. A., Test, M. A., and Stein, L. I. 1980. Alternative to mental hospital treatment. II. Economic benefit-cost analysis. *Arch. Gen. Psychiatry* 37:400-405.

2
The Chronically Mentally Ill:
Who Are They? Where Are They?

HOWARD H. GOLDMAN

Once locked away out of sight, the majority of the chronically mentally ill now live among us. Some live with their families; others reside in nursing homes, board and care facilities, or residential apartments. Unfortunately, still others are homeless, barely surviving in urban America. The plight of the deinstitutionalized, chronically mentally ill has come to public attention through personal experience, government reports, the lay press, and the professional literature. The stories of "bag ladies" and "vent people" have become painfully familiar. So familiar, in fact, that we are beginning to know the chronically mentally ill by name: We know Sylvia Frumkin from the *New Yorker* (Sheehan, 1981); Al, Luther, and Angelita introduced the *National Plan for the Chronically Mentally Ill* (1980). In a recent series in the *Philadelphia Inquirer*, Donald Drake (1982) sensitively recounted the poignant tales of "The Forsaken," Janet Moore and Larry Levine, the Duck Lady, and Johnny No Name. The stories are reminiscent of the Depression portraits by James Agee and Walker Evans, Dorothea Lange and Ben Shahn. The chronically mentally ill remind us of the limitations of our treatment techniques and the shortcomings of our social policies. They are individuals with names and personal histories. Each is a unique member of a diverse group we call "chronically mentally ill." As clinicians, we are aware of their individuality; as planners and policy-makers, we must view them as a heterogeneous population. Who are they? Where are they? Let us turn from the personal perspective to a public health and epidemiological response to these questions.

Before the era of deinstitutionalization, the chronically mentally ill were easier to identify and count; they were the long-term residents of psychiatric

A major portion of this paper appeared as "Defining and counting the chronically mentally ill" by Goldman, H. H., Gattozzi, A. A., and Taube, C. A., in *Hospital and Community Psychiatry* 32(1):21-27, 1981 and is reprinted with permission of the editor.

hospitals. Today these institutions are no longer home to the majority of persons disabled by chronic mental illness. One consequence of the shifts in the pattern and locus of mental health care arising from deinstitutionalization is a lack of definitive information on the scope of the problem of chronic mental illness. Sources of data, like the affected individuals and their services, have been dispersed and decentralized. The difficulty is compounded by the absence of consensus on a definition that would delimit the target population.

Broadly speaking, a chronic condition is characterized by a long duration of illness, which may include periods of seeming wellness interrupted by flare-ups of acute symptoms, and secondary disabilities. This simple characterization is applicable to chronic mental illness, but the task of identifying persons who are chronically mentally ill is not at all straightforward. Although it is true that most such persons "are, have been, or might have been, but for the deinstitutionalization movement, on the rolls of long-term mental institutions, especially state hospitals" (Bachrach, 1976), any attempt to specify the attributes of state hospital patients must take into account the dynamic nature of clinical judgments about these patients.

Perceptions about the appropriateness of placement of patients in state hospitals and other psychiatric facilities have been changing rapidly in recent years (Faden and Goldman, 1979), and there is every reason to think they will continue to change in the future. As knowledge about the heterogeneity of patients' needs increases, the formulation of appropriateness should evolve. As the number and variety of community-based services expands, however, clinical judgments about appropriateness change. This variability in the assessment of needs is to be expected and encouraged in a dynamic service system.

DELIMITING THE TARGET POPULATION

One recent attempt to define the target population distinguished persons who are severely *mentally ill* (defined by diagnosis), those who are *mentally disabled* (defined by level of disability), and those who are *chronic mental patients* (defined by duration of hospitalization) (Minkoff, 1979).

These three dimensions—diagnosis, disability, duration—are sufficiently precise to serve as criteria for delimiting the target population (Figure 1). We can begin with the following general description: the chronically mentally ill population encompasses persons who suffer severe persistent mental or emotional disorders that interfere with their functional capacities in relation to such primary aspects of daily life as self-care, interpersonal relationships, and work or schooling, and that often necessitate prolonged hospital care.

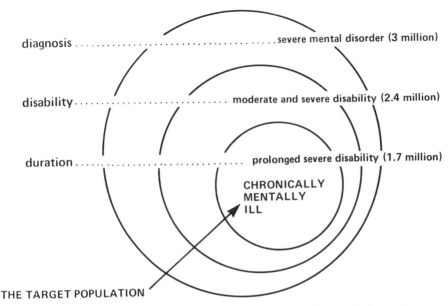

diagnosis .... severe mental disorder (3 million)

disability .... moderate and severe disability (2.4 million)

duration .... prolonged severe disability (1.7 million)

CHRONICALLY
MENTALLY
ILL

THE TARGET POPULATION

Figure 1   The dimensions of chronic mental illness, with population estimates.
Source: *National Plan for the Chronically Mentally Ill*, 1980.

Diagnosis

There is general agreement that the psychotic disorders predominate among this population, that is organic mental disorders, schizophrenia, depression and bipolar affective disorder, paranoid and other psychoses (American Psychiatric Association, 1980).

Other disorders may also lead to chronic mental disability—some of the personality disorders, for example, especially those designated as "borderline personality disorders." Furthermore, alcohol- and drug-abuse disorders and mental retardation may complicate the course of psychotic disorders (occasionally becoming designated as the primary diagnosis) or may become chronically disabling conditions themselves. Among children, schizophrenia, childhood autism, and some behavior disorders may lead to chronic disability; the same may be said of nonpsychotic organic brain syndrome, or "senility without psychosis," among the elderly.

Disability

Most definitions of disability center on the concept of functional incapacity, for example, "partial or total impairment of instrumental (usually vocational or homemaking) role performance" (Minkoff, 1979). One statutory definition refers to a condition that "results in substantial functional limitations in three or more of the following areas of major life activity: (1) self-care, (2) receptive and expressive language, (3) learning, (4) mobility, (5) self-direction, (6) capacity for independent living, and (7) economic self-sufficiency" (Public Law 95-602, 1978). However, objective measures of these "functional limitations" are not in widespread use.

In contrast, chronicity of disability may be operationally defined. Insofar as receipt of Supplemental Security Income payments (SSI) implies that the beneficiary has been unable to "engage in any substantial gainful activity" because of a disorder "which has lasted or can be expected to last for a continuous period of not less than 12 months," there is general agreement that approval of SSI eligibility is a measure of chronic disability for noninstitutionalized persons. Similar vocational criteria are common to other definitions of disability, such as those used in the Survey of Disabled Adults (Social Security Administration) and the Survey of Income and Education (Bureau of the Census). Chronicity also may be inferred from the need for extended hospitalization or other forms of supervised residence or sheltered work.

Duration

To infer disability from the need for extended hospitalization or supervised residential care requires specifying some duration of residence. Most would agree that one year of continuous institutionalization in a state mental hospital or of residence in a nursing home would qualify as a measure of chronic mental disability. Yet at least half of the population of chronically mentally ill are not continuously institutionalized (see Talbott, this volume, Figure 6). Although these individuals reside in the community, many of them were hospitalized in the past or are hospitalized during the course of the year. Some formula is necessary for determining what duration of hospitalization to use as a criterion for chronicity for the chronically mentally ill living in the community.

Treated prevalence estimates may be obtained by reference to the National Reporting Program of the National Institute of Mental Health Division of Biometry and Epidemiology, which uses a three-month period of follow-up for providing data on extended hospitalization. Eighty percent of all patients admitted to state and county mental hospitals, and virtually all patients admitted to private psychiatric hospitals and general hospital psychiatric units, are discharged within 90 days (unpublished data of the Survey and Reports Branch, Division of Biometry and Epidemiology, National Institute of Mental Health, 1975). Likelihood of release diminishes after this point; hence, we may consider that these unreleased patients represent a chronic intermediate-stay (3 to 12 months) population of the chronically mentally ill.

It should be noted that some persons with characteristics fitting the diagnosis and disability criteria have received short-term (less than 90 days) inpatient care, solely outpatient care from a medical or mental health professional, or no care at all save what their families or other natural support groups have provided. Although we are unable definitely to locate or enumerate such individuals, we include them in the target population. Prolonged functional disability caused or aggravated by severe mental disorders, not former hospitalization, is the chief distinguishing characteristic of chronic mental illness.

Having specified the dimensions we selected to delimit the target population, we now offer the following detailed definition:

The chronically mentally ill population encompasses persons who suffer certain mental or emotional disorders (organic mental disorders, schizophrenia, recurrent depressive and bipolar affective disorders, paranoid and other psychoses, plus other disorders that may become chronic) that erode or prevent the development of their functional capacities in relation to (three or more of) such primary aspects of daily life as personal hygiene and self-care, self-direction, interpersonal relationships, social transactions, learning, and recreation, and that erode or prevent the development of their economic self-sufficiency. Most such individuals have required institutional care of extended duration, including intermediate-term hospitalization (90 days to one year in a single year), long-term hospitalization (one year or longer in the preceding five years), nursing home placement because of a diagnosed mental condition or a diagnosis of senility without psychosis. Some such individuals have required short-term hospitalization (less than 90 days), others have received treatment from a medical or mental health professional solely on an outpatient basis, or—despite their needs—have received no treatment in the professional-care service system. Thus, included in the target population are persons who are or were formerly "residents" of institutions (public and private psychiatric hospitals and nursing homes), and persons who are at high risk of institutionalization because of persistent mental disability.

LOCATION OF THE POPULATION

Bearing in mind the caveat concerning the dynamic nature of any definition of this population, we propose to outline a series of separate segments of the population of the chronically mentally ill. The numbers of chronically mentally ill persons in each of these segments may be determined by a number of methods. The size of the population in each segment or location is subject to change because of the movement of people from one location to another.

Institutional Residents

For purposes of this report, the institutionalized chronically mentally ill are those individuals with any psychiatric diagnosis in mental hospitals for more than one year and those individuals in nursing homes (as defined by the National Center for Health Statistics, 1977) with a diagnosed mental condition or a diagnosis of senility without psychosis. The latter are included because simple senility, either alone or in combination with other chronic medical conditions, was a reason for admission to a state mental hospital before adoption of policies that encouraged deinstitutionalization and the transfer or diversion of the elderly into nursing homes.

Community Residents

Within communities, the chronically mentally ill are those individuals in a variety of residential settings (with families, in boarding homes, in single-occupancy hotel rooms) who are considered to be disabled by any one of several criteria, including SSI eligibility, episodic or prolonged hospitalization, or inability to work. The community-dwelling segment may be subdivided into several groups on the basis of their location, their use of mental health facilities, and the level and type of their disability.

COUNTING THE CHRONIC POPULATION

Having defined the target population in terms of disability and location, we now turn to determining their number. As Table 1 indicates, estimates of the number of the chronically mentally ill range from 1.7 million to 2.4 million, including 900,000 in institutions. Table 2 presents estimates of the types of disabilities suffered by persons with chronic illness and their utilization of mental health facilities. These estimates of the total number of chronically mentally ill are derived from a number of sources, including true prevalence estimates of chronic mental disorders, community estimates of chronic mental disability, and treated prevalence data on chronic mental patients.

Chronic Mental Disorders—True Prevalence Estimates

Based on the Report of the President's Commission on Mental Health (1978), about two million people in the United States could be given a diagnosis of schizophrenia. About 600,000 of them are in active treatment during a given year, accounting for more than 500,000 admissions in the specialty mental health sector. Any individual diagnosed as schizophrenic is at risk of becoming chronically mentally ill. However, because of the existence of other acute syndromes that mimic the overt symptoms of schizophrenia but do not invariably become progressive or chronic (e.g., schizophreniform psychosis, acute psychotic episode), not all of the two million individuals are to be counted among the chronically mentally ill. Estimates of the number of chronically mentally ill individuals with a diagnosis of schizophrenia would range from 500,000 to 900,000.

Serious depression has a prevalence rate ranging from 0.3 percent to 1.2 percent. Assuming that the lower end of the range represents the population at highest risk of chronicity, there are perhaps 600,000 to 800,000 chronically and severely depressed individuals in the United States. Furthermore, psychosis in the elderly (primarily organic brain syndrome, predominantly chronic) is estimated to account for between 600,000 to 1,250,000 individuals.

Table 1   Estimates of the Number of the Chronically
Mentally Ill, United States, 1975-1977

Institutionalized Population		
Location (unduplicated count)		
Mental health facilities[1]	150,000	
Nursing homes[2]		
Residents with mental disorder[3]	350,000	
Residents with senility without psychosis[4]	400,000	
Subtotal	900,000	
Community Population		
Level of disability (unduplicated count)		
Severe[5]	800,000	
Moderate[6] and severe		1,500,000
Subtotal (as range)		800,000-1,500,000
Total[7]		1,700,000-2,400,000

[1]Includes residents for one year or more in state and county hospitals, Veterans Administration inpatient facilities, private psychiatric hospitals, residential treatment centers, community mental health centers (Source: Division of Biometry and Epidemiology, NIMH, 1975)
[2]Based on 1.3 million residents of skilled nursing and intermediate care facilities sampled by National Center for Health Statistics, National Nursing Home Survey, 1977.
[3]Primary or nonprimary diagnoses based on section 5, *International Classification of Diseases*, 9th Ed. (Source: National Nursing Home Survey, 1977)
[4]Primary or nonprimary conditions coded 797, *International Classification of Diseases*, 9th Ed. (Source: National Nursing Home Survey, 1977)
[5]Includes persons with a mental disorder who were unable to work at all for one year and those who could work only occasionally. (Source: Urban Institute, Comprehensive Needs Survey, 1973; Social Security Administration, Survey of Disabled Adults, 1966)
[6]Includes so-called "partially disabled" individuals whose work, including housework, was limited by a mental disorder. (Source: Urban Institute, Comprehensive Needs Survey, 1973)
[7]The lower figure (1.7 million), representing the severely disabled chronic mentally ill, was used as the size of the target population for the *National Plan for the Chronically Mentally Ill.*

Other more prevalent disorders, such as personality disorders (7.0 percent prevalence), alcoholism and alcohol abuse (5 to 10 percent), and drug abuse and misuse (1 to 10 percent, depending on the type of drug), may become chronic or may be complicated by chronic mental disorder. Only a small minority of these individuals are, however, part of the target population (*National Plan for the Chronically Mentally Ill*, 1980).

Chronic Mental Disability—Community Estimates

Currently there are four major sources of national data on chronic mental disability in the community: the Bureau of the Census (Bureau of the Census Survey of Income and Education, 1979), the Social Security Administration

Table 2   Estimates of the Number of Chronically Mentally Ill by Type
of Disability and Utilization of Mental Health Facilities
(Duplicated Counts), United States, 1975-1977

Type of Disability	
Receiving SSI/SSDI[1]	550,000
Complete work disability[2]	350,000
Activity limitation[3]	700,000
Utilization of Mental Health Facilities[4]	
Admissions (stay 90 days or more)	150,000
Readmissions[5]	650,000

[1]Source: Anderson (1982) citing *Social Security Bulletin* (March 1981) 44:2-48.
[2]Prevalence of disability in 18 to 64 age group. (Source: *Digest of Data on Persons with Disabilities*, Bureau of the Census, 1979)
[3]Prevalence of disability in population three years old or older. (Source: Bureau of the Census, 1979)
[4]Includes state and county mental hospitals, private psychiatric hospitals, psychiatric units in general hospitals, and residential treatment centers. (Source: NIMH Division of Biometry and Epidemiology, 1975)
[5]Readmission counts overestimate chronic patients because some patients with less severe disorders may be readmitted briefly many times. (Source: NIMH Division of Biometry and Epidemiology, 1975)

(Bureau of the Census Survey of Disabled Adults, 1979), a 1975 Comprehensive Needs Assessment Study conducted by the Urban Institute for the Department of Health and Human Services, and a 1978 Social Security Administration Household Survey of Disabled Adults. These studies indicate that there are between 350,000 and 800,000 individuals severely disabled by emotional disorders in the community and perhaps an additional 700,000 people who have moderate disabilities.

According to data published by the Bureau of the Census, based on 1976 estimates of disability in the community, about 700,000 persons three years of age or older (2.5 percent of a total of 28 million) have an "activity limitation" caused by severe mental disturbance. A total of 350,000 individuals between the ages of 18 to 64 have some work disability (including total disability) secondary to severe emotional disturbance (Department of Health Education, and Welfare, 1979).

The data extrapolated from the Urban Institute study (1975)—that about 800,000 individuals in the community have a severe mental disability, and 700,000 more are moderately or partially disabled—are corroborated by the most recent Social Security Administration survey (1978), which estimated that about 1.07 million adults living in households were disabled by emotional disorder, (unpublished data provided by John Ashbaugh, Human Services Research Institute, Boston). Further estimates from the Social Security Administration suggest that 550,000 of the severely disabled are receiving Supplemental Security Income or Social Security Disability Income (Anderson, 1982).

Chronic Mental Patients—Treated Prevalence Data

Estimates of the number of chronic mental patients may also be derived from two sources of treated prevalence data. The first source is national data from the reporting program of the NIMH Division of Biometry and Epidemiology (DBE), the Veterans Administration, and the Long-Term Care Statistics Branch of the National Center for Health Statistics. The second source is the Monroe County (N.Y.) case register. Both data sources suggest that chronic mental patients number about 1.7 million.

The Monroe County figure is derived (by Carl Taube of DBE) by extrapolation from the 10-year follow-up experience of a cohort of patients from Rochester State Hospital in 1962. Although generalization from these data is problematic, the estimate is a useful verification of estimates derived from the national data.

The national data provide the following estimates: the institutional population totals 900,000 and includes two major subdivisions of chronic mental patients based on place of residence—specialty mental health facilities and nursing homes. About 150,000 chronic mental patients are served by the specialty mental health sector. Data from 1977 suggest 100,000 chronic mental patients are institutionalized for one year or longer in state and county mental hospitals. An additional 50,000—a crude estimate—are long-term (longer than one year) residents of other specialty facilities. About 20,000 persons are in Veterans Administration hospitals (Minkoff, 1979), about 10,000 in residential treatment centers, and about 20,000 in other facilities, including private psychiatric hospitals and community mental health center inpatient units.

Of a total nursing home population of 1.3 million, an estimated 750,000 are chronic mental patients. This figure, perhaps a slight overestimate, encompasses three groups: individuals with a primary mental disorder (about 250,000), those with a diagnosed mental condition that is not the primary cause of institutionalization (about 100,000), and those with senility without psychosis (about 400,000). The two former categories clearly are part of the target population; the latter group probably represents a population of elderly individuals who would have been admitted to state mental hospitals in the pre-deinstitutionalization era. For this reason, all three subpopulations of nursing homes are considered chronic mental patients.

The *community population* of severely disabled chronic mental patients numbers about 800,000. An additional 700,000 individuals are partially disabled by a mental condition. Their patterns of service utilization are more difficult to estimate because the community groups are dynamic, possibly using several facilities during the course of a year. They are also more mobile, living in a wide variety of residential treatment settings—with their families or in congregate care, for example, in single-room-occupancy residences, or in board and care homes. Using treated prevalence data alone will produce an undercount of the community population, some of whom receive no treatment or receive care exclusively in such other sectors as the general health care, social welfare, or criminal justice systems.

The severely disabled community population makes considerable use of hospital and ambulatory services during the course of one year. About 110,000 were inpatients for more than three months. At least 200,000 readmitted to state and county mental hospitals had inpatient stays of 90 days or less. An additional 450,000 were readmitted to other inpatient psychiatric facilities. These patients also use ambulatory services in community mental health centers, outpatient clinics, private practice settings, and hospital emergency rooms. Utilization data are scarce and tend to underestimate the scope of service needs of chronic patients in the community.

These chronic mental patients live in a variety of community residences. A service delivery assessment in Department of Health and Human Services Region 3 estimated that between 300,000 to 400,000 of these chronic mental patients reside in board and care facilities (Mellody, 1979). These domiciliary care residences and single-room-occupancy hotels often are criticized as substandard, isolating, and a form of "transinstitutionalization" and continued neglect (Schmidt et al., 1977; Mellody, 1979; Talbott, 1979).

Not all chronic patients are transinstitutionalized, however; some return to their families. Although about 65 percent of discharged mental patients return home (Goldman, 1980, 1982), not all of these are chronic patients. Several studies report that about one in four chronic patients is discharged to his or her family (Minkoff, 1979). Ashbaugh's unpublished analysis of data from the Social Security Administration Survey of Disabled Adults (1978) indicated that 59 percent of the 1.07 million mentally disabled Americans living in households were married and residing with a spouse.

THE CHALLENGE FOR THE FUTURE

The technical criteria for defining the chronically mentally ill described here establish the objective boundaries of the target population, which are vital to the activities of planners and policy-makers. But they do no more than hint at the clinical, socioeconomic, ethnic, and cultural heterogeneity of this population. Data from several national surveys are currently being analyzed and a few reports on the characteristics of chronic patients in national programs have been published (Tessler et al., 1982; Tessler and Goldman, 1982; Tessler and Manderscheid, 1982). But data cannot convey any sense of the individual people referred to, their frailties and strengths, their suffering and that of their families, their hope and striving, however falteringly, for normalcy.

The chronically mentally ill population includes persons whose clinical conditions and functional disabilities vary widely at any time and, moreover, change over time. Kramer's 1981 projections for the year 2005 indicate that chronic mental disability will increase dramatically. Variability makes an accurate determination of the size and nature of the population extremely difficult. At best we can provide an estimate to guide national policy-makers in a more scientific assessment of needs. Suffice it to note here that, although our definition encompasses persons with prolonged moderate-to-severe disability, a significant proportion possess the capacity to live in relative independence if adequate community-based services, social supports, and life opportunities are provided.

REFERENCES

American Psychiatric Association 1980. *Diagnostic and Statistical Manual of Mental Disorders, Third Ed.* Washington, DC.

Anderson, R. J. 1982. Social Security and SSI benefits for the mentally disabled. *Hosp. Community Psychiatry* 33:295-298.

Bachrach, L. L. 1976. *Deinstitutionalization: An Analytic Review and Sociological Perspective.* Rockville, MD: National Institute of Mental Health.

Bureau of the Census Survey of Income and Education 1979. *Digest of Data on Persons with Disabilities.* Washington, DC: U.S. Department of Health, Education, and Welfare.

Drake, D. 1982. The forsaken. Reprinted from *The Philadelphia Inquirer*, July 18-24.

Faden, V. B., and Goldman, H. H. 1979. *Appropriateness of Placement of Patients in State and County Mental Hospitals. Statistical Note 152.* Rockville, MD: National Institute of Mental Health.

Goldman, H. H. 1980. The post-hospital mental patient and family therapy: Prospects and populations. *Journal of Marital and Family Therapy* 6:447-452.

Goldman, H. H. 1982. Mental illness and family burden: A public health perspective. *Hosp. Community Psychiatry* 33:557-560.

Kramer, M. 1981. The increasing prevalence of mental disorder. Presented at Langley Porter Psychiatric Institute, San Francisco, August 6.

Mellody, J. 1979. *Service Delivery Assessment of Boarding Homes.* Technical report, Region 3. Philadelphia: U.S. Department of Health and Human Services.

Minkoff, K. 1979. A map of chronic mental patients. In J. A. Talbott (ed.), *The Chronic Mental Patient*, pp. 11-37. Washington, DC: American Psychiatric Association.

National Center for Social Statistics 1972. *Findings of the 1970 APTD Study.* Washington, DC: Social and Rehabilitation Service.

National Plan for the Chronically Mentally Ill 1980. Final draft report to the Secretary of the Department of Health and Human Services, Washington, DC.

Public Law 95-602, 1978. Rehabilitation, Comprehensive Services, and Developmental Disabilities Amendments of 1978.

Report to the President from the President's Commission on Mental Health 1978, vol. 1. Washington, DC: U.S. Government Printing Office.

Schmidt, W., Reinhardt, A. M., Kane, R. L., and Olsen, D. M. 1977. The mentally ill in nursing homes: New back wards in the community. *Arch. Gen. Psychiatry* 34:678-689.

Sheehan, S. 1981. The patient. I. Creedmoor Psychiatric Center. *The New Yorker*, May 25, pp. 49-111.

Talbott, J. A. 1979. Deinstitutionalization: Avoiding the disasters of the past. *Hosp. Community Psychiatry* 30:621-624.

Tessler, R. C., and Goldman, H. H. 1982. The *Chronically Mentally Ill: Assessing Community Support Programs*. Cambridge, MA: Ballinger.

Tessler, R. C., and Manderscheid, R. W. 1982. Factors affecting adjustment to community living. *Hosp. Community Psychiatry* 33:203-207.

Tessler, R. C., Rosen, B., Bernstein, A., and Goldman, H. H. 1982. The chronically mentally ill in community support systems. *Hosp. Community Psychiatry* 33:208-211.

Urban Institute 1975. *Report of the Comprehensive Service Needs Study*. Washington, DC: U.S. Department of Health, Education, and Welfare.

3
The Needs of the Chronically Mentally Ill: As Seen by the Consumer

DALE L. JOHNSON

My role in this volume on the chronically mentally ill is to say once again that the consumer's view of the treatment process is very important (Appleton, 1974; Hatfield, 1979; Lamb and Oliphant, 1978). I join the many others who have argued that the family of the patient must be involved in the treatment/rehabilitation process. Although someone should speak for the patients themselves, I cannot; I believe that I am better qualified to speak for families. Relatives of the mentally ill are consumers, they pay many of the bills for psychiatric care, and they have an important role in initiating and maintaining care. Furthermore, even though it may not often be acknowledged as such, it is the family system that is involved.

In writing this paper I have drawn on conversations with more than 100 relatives of the mentally ill, and with many patients and former patients. These contacts have been through our mutual involvement in Citizens for Human Development, a mental health advocacy group mainly concerned with continuity of care issues and with the Mental Health Association-sponsored parent support group, FAIR. I have also drawn on the literature contributed by patients and others about their experiences in living with mental illness.

Before describing these needs, I must say something about how I came to have an interest in the matter. I am a clinical and developmental psychologist and have had experience in working professionally with schizophrenic patients, but most of that was in the early years of my career as a psychologist. When I moved from a Veterans Administration hospital to a university in 1964, my interest in schizophrenia became quite literally academic. But in 1972, when my oldest child, then 19, became psychotic and was soon diagnosed as schizophrenic, my understanding of the disorder changed profoundly. I was rudely initiated into the fellowship of parents of the mentally ill, one I had never expected to join.

As my son had been a remarkably able child, his psychosis was a shock; that he had been involved with psychedelic drugs made it plausible.

THE IMPACT ON FAMILIES

I will not go into our personal family experiences, although to do so would be one way to bring in virtually all of the items on the list of needs. What we have found is that our son's psychosis and its impact on family, course of treatment and the like is commonplace. We have heard the same events and problems told over and over by members of Citizens for Human Development and in FAIR groups. When people come to these groups for the first time, they tell of their problems with sadness, frustration, and shame. As they hear others describe closely comparable events, they rush to say more, but the emotion now is anger. Let me assure you, my interest now is not academic, that is, impartial and disinterested, and the people I will refer to when I use the pronoun "we," the other family members associated with the advocacy groups, are not dispassionate either. We believe strongly that something must be done to improve services for the long-term mentally ill. We will keep on trying and we refuse to abandon our loved ones, although most of us have been told by professionals that we must do so. We have seen that services are too often designed and managed badly, to the extreme detriment of patients. The advice that we have received is so ambiguous and conflicting, determined more by politics and power plays than by concern for patient care, that we have often been in despair. Many of us have concluded that, "Psychiatry is not science nor art but confusion." The words are Harry Stack Sullivan's (1953) and we join him in his judgement with the addition that we would say that it is the mental health system that is confused and confusing. We also believe that this need not be the ordinary state of affairs.

Now I will turn to some of the problems. It has been our experience that mental health professionals do not seem to understand the impact of psychosis on families. This impact is unique. As psychotic conditions are relatively rare, and tend to be hidden, few families have had experience in coping. Dealing with a profoundly disordered person calls for a high level of understanding and skill, but the relatives of the mentally ill have not been prepared to have these skills. How does one select a therapist? How can the disturbed individual be brought to treatments? Is this just a passing phase? How serious is the disorder? This great uncertainty about a course of action often characterizes the professional, too, and this is a cause of further dismay.

This sense of helplessness is pervasive. The psychotic person's suffering is obvious, and so is the turmoil, yet one can do so little. Perhaps this seems to hit parents especially hard because they have been able to take care of their children's problems in the past, to "make it well." But not now; now we are confronted by pure tragedy. Nevertheless, the problem demands action: How can we find reliable help immediately? What is the right thing to do?

Perhaps the next emotion to enter is guilt. What did we do wrong? Did I cause this? Often this guilt is underlined by the disturbed one's angry lashing out with, "You're rotten parents." It is also emphasized by the comments of professionals who are quite clear in their belief that the parents have caused the disorder. I will say more on that later.

I cannot neglect another emotion that most of us have felt: fear. The person we know so well is now a stranger, acting in alien ways, transformed from a member of the family into an unpredictable antagonist. The fear is increased by threats such as, "If you try to put me into a hospital, I swear I'll kill you. I'll. . . . . . ." and this goes on to detail with bizarre threats as to how this will happen. This fear may continue for months or years. As you may know, psychotics and recovering schizophrenics tend to be night people, to sleep during the day and to move about at night. This means son or daughter roams the house at 3 a.m., slamming doors and cupboards and entering parents' room to demand money to buy cigarettes or to say that the family dog is possessed of evil spirits, or whatever. These nocturnal demands are often backed by threats and arguments. As sleep is impossible, parents become exhausted. There is also fear or apprehension of another kind. It is that others may be harmed by the patient, or that he or she will be harmed. We can relate many examples of this type. Another common feature is that our daughters and sons have run away—often for months with no word. The anxiety accompanying this uncertainty does not go away; it gnaws, day after day. We know, too, that some who have disappeared will not return, that they are dead, victims of suicide or murder. Life with schizophrenia is life at the raw edge of existence.

Having said so much about the harsher emotions, I will now add one of a different kind. As one sees these young people, at one time sociably involved, now cut off from friends, one feels compassion for their loneliness. That schizophrenic persons want companionship and intimacy seems to surprise many people —certainly one of the main features of the disorder is social withdrawal. It is an item in the *DSM-III*. Have they not withdrawn from society? Perhaps, but one senses that the leaving was not by choice and that they very much would like to return. We have all seen how each of our young people has, after a period of treatment and some recovery, tried to reestablish contact with old friends. While the friends are often marvelously accepting, the friendships are rarely renewed. The lives of the friends are too different. They are busy establishing careers, courting, getting on with life. The psychotic is not on that track at all: he or she is struggling to regain sanity, but in the process is bitterly lonely.

STAGES IN FAMILY ADJUSTMENT TO LONG-TERM MENTAL ILLNESS

We have come to see stages in the process of adjusting to mental disorder in the family. For many, the beginning is one of shock, confusion, and bewilderment, which may be followed by a period of denial. "This is not as serious as it seems."

"Yes, there is crazy behavior, but perhaps it is only a bad drug trip" (notice that, at this point, a drug freak-out seems minor by comparison). Or, "perhaps she is just finding herself and will emerge," as Laing has suggested, "stronger and wiser."

The reality of serious, chronic, perhaps life-long maladjustment does not hit home immediately. In the Piagetian sense, the information is not assimilated because there are no relevant existing cognitive schemas. The consequences are that family members may then make decisions based on this denial, such decisions as allowing the patient to discontinue medication, readily accepting discharge from a hospital though it is too soon, or urging return to college or work before the person is ready. As the patient is also wrapped up in denial, and professionals are often eager for quick cures, an unfortunate collusion develops.

A long period of sadness and anger, depression and rage, comes next as one finds that no progress has been made, or that, if any has been apparent, it is followed by relapse. By now, health insurance has run out, if it ever was available (47 percent of Houston families do not have psychiatric coverage), and it is necessary to move to other treatment facilities. The anger is often directed at individual mental health professionals. But often, as experience grows, the anger is with the system: something is grossly lacking.

What is this anger about? Let me offer some examples from interviews with family members.

"Grace was found by Travelers Aid in a dazed condition at the Greyhound Bus Station. She was nine months pregnant. She had been discharged from the state hospital so she was not their responsibility."

"Calvin was discharged from the army and from the VA hospital after 89 days of active service during which he suffered a psychotic breakdown. With 90 days of service he would have been eligible for continuing care at the VA hospital."

"Donald, a Rice University honors graduate, refused the prolixin shot because it made him feel worse. He also refused to spend his time making billfolds. He was sent away because he couldn't benefit from the program."

"Linda was discharged just before Christmas with a long list of daily medications. She said she felt worse after hospitalization because no one tried to help her, they just kept giving her more meds. They found her in the morning dead, apparently choked on her vomitus; zonked out on the meds, I suppose."

"A community clinic staff member said, 'James is not doing well. He may not come back, may not be involved in the day hospital or in the outpatient clinic. The doctor recommended the prolixin shot. This is a voluntary clinic, we can't treat people who won't be treated. He's not cooperating with the medications (he didn't want the shot). The doctor recommends that he not use this clinic. I doubt that he can get along any place. He has deteriorated.' "

The anger comes from the sense that what is happening is not right and that what is not right goes beyond the disorder itself to the way the disorder is treated.

The next stage after anger is one of action. Family members have seen that treatment and rehabilitation are not as effective as they might be and they want something better. They persist in this, perhaps because they are not as well-informed as professionals, perhaps because their responsibilities run deeper; maybe it is that they know that rehabilitation does not stop at five o'clock and is not shut down for the weekend. They also persist because they have a hope that something better is possible.

EFFECTS OF STRESS ON FAMILIES

Now I am drawing closer to the main point of this paper, which is that patients have families and these families provide most of the continuity of care that is so essential to the effective treatment of these disorders.

Psychosis has a dreadful impact on families and long-term mental illness can be fatally corrosive. We have seen the following effects on families. Conflict between parents, between siblings, between all members of families increases with psychosis. Conflict arises in the context of heightened emotionality, the uncertainty of what to do and the fact that the decisions to be made are hard decisions, such as to hospitalize, to seek commitment, to ask for an indefinite commitment, to permit extraordinary treatments such as electroshock. Family members are often sharply divided on such issues, and they receive little effective help in making the decisions.

Marital splits are common. As stress mounts, some spouses leave, sometimes to carry on independently in trying to help the disturbed child, but often just leaving.

There are other ways of leaving this kind of stress, and alcoholism and drug abuse are, I believe, more common than is generally recognized. Suicide of parents also occurs.

I have emphasized the impact on parents. They tend to be the ones who attend FAIR groups and advocacy meetings such as Citizens, but other family members are involved. Siblings are especially distressed by psychosis in the family. Many of the children have known the patient as elder sister or brother who was wise in the ways of the world, a leader to be followed, a guide through childhood and adolescence who is now strange, confused, threatened, asking for help, and a source of gross embarrassment. I might also mention that as these siblings look to their own futures with a mentally ill sibling in the family they wonder if it will some day fall on them to take care of this person. They also wonder if the disorder is genetic and whether their children will become schizophrenic. Answers to these questions are rarely forthcoming from professionals.

RECOMMENDATIONS FOR IMPROVED PROGRAMS

In attempting to specify some of the major needs of the long-term mentally ill, I have drawn upon a study done by the Citizens for Human Development. The topics were contributed by members of that group.

As we have looked back on our experience with mental illness we have agreed that our major concern is with continuity of care. This means that from the onset of symptoms through treatment and eventual disposition there must be continuity in the treatment and rehabilitative process. We have too often seen progress in our loved ones reversed when they are discharged from a hospital with no aftercare plans or are kicked out of a community care facility for a minor rule infraction. I was told by the staff of one hospital that my son was very psychotic, extremely resistant to medication, was probably incurable, and he was discharged to our care the next day. This is discontinuity of care. Too often, perhaps more often than not, patients are allowed to "drop through the cracks," as we have heard professionals put it. We believe that this discontinuity is unnecessary, as is attested to by the many programs that have been developed to ensure continuity. These exist now in communities in many states—Minnesota, Wisconsin, Kentucky, and Florida are a few. There will be more on this in later chapters.

Another important issue for us is that of providing emergency services. Psychotic episodes are often of a life-or-death nature, and immediate attention is necessary. We believe that 24-hour information and referral services should be maintained. They are in some communities, but not in Houston. We have found them unavailable when needed, and when told they are available we have tested them. My wife called the designated number at a quarter to five one afternoon and received no answer. When she tried again at night, after much ringing, a voice answered in Spanish saying that he was the janitor and that she should call again after nine o'clock in the morning. Communities should provide 24-hour information and referral services staffed by informed and helpful people.

Police need to be trained to work with acute cases. Galveston has a sheriff's department with an excellent record for handling psychiatric cases with humanity and without harm to the patient or to themselves. Houston does not and the case of Eddie Lee Johnson, who was obviously psychotic and was gunned down by 30 police officers in front of the police station, is fresh in our minds.

We need commitment procedures that protect the patient not only from false incarceration, but also the ravages of untreated mental illness.

We need emergency care that provides diagnosis and treatment immediately, not after many days. This is possible. The program developed at Northern State Hospital in Washington was designed to ensure that every patient who arrived at the admitting office would be seen by a physician within fifteen minutes, when a preliminary diagnosis would be made and treatment according to the hospital's comprehensive plan would be begun immediately (Deiter et al., 1965). This approach works. Why is it not adopted by other hospitals?

We agree that hospitalization is necessary in many instances, and we want hospital services that are effective and efficient, services that relieve the psychosis while avoiding the effects of institutionalization. For the very disturbed and long-term patients we advocate psychosocial programs like the one developed by Gordon Paul and his associates (Paul and Lentz, 1977).

Preparation for discharge from the hospital seems to us to be a critical time, yet it is so often handled badly. In our experience, when hospital staff members are impressed with the progress the patient has made in the hospital they seem to believe that post-hospital planning can be made with staff and patient only, excluding the family and post-hospital rehabilitation staff. A major problem with this is that patients typically do not have much insight into their condition and do not appreciate the need for continuing medications and rehabilitation efforts. Professionals seem to underestimate this lack of insight, even though it is a salient feature of psychosis. Instead, emphasis is placed on independence, springing from a kind of "sink or swim" philosophy. We can understand this desire to restore the patient to independent living and to minimize the effects of institutionalization, but we believe that the process of becoming independent when recovering from psychosis is slow and gradual, requiring much support and strong encouragement.

After hospitalization, or perhaps as an alternative, are community programs. We advocate the development of a wide variety of community rehabilitation arrangements. We advocate structured programs such as Fairweather Lodges; community centers like Fountain House, or here in Houston, Pyramid House; foster home care, supervised apartment training programs, halfway houses, boarding homes, co-op apartments, and home care. We have learned that the community needs of our family members are varied and that the only reasonable response is to plan for variety.

Most of us have found that home care is not satisfactory. It is too difficult for families to provide the best balance of stimulation and structure. Anderson et al. (1980) have warned against the hazards of overstimulating environments in provoking psychotic relapse. There is also the danger that, without planned remotivation efforts, the patient will sink into a nonfunctioning state. Recovering schizophrenics seem to do best when they are not allowed to vegetate but still are not the focus of highly emotional nagging.

We believe that the most effective programs are those that return patients to productive work at some functionally honest level as soon as possible. In our society, at least, to be work-shy is to be forever beyond the fringe of acceptability.

A major problem encountered in community programs is the use of time limits. Families have been told, "John can stay at our halfway house for 30 days, but then he must leave." This may be realistic for some individuals, but it is absurdly unrealistic for others. Twenty or so years ago Fairweather recognized the long-term nature of these disorders and he created a successful program without time limits. We urge community program staffers to take a more realistic view.

We are also greatly distressed by the use of termination from community programs as a disciplinary device. It is a classic Catch-22 situation: "You are here because your behavior is socially deviant, but if you act in socially deviant ways while you are here you must leave." Out of the program means onto the streets, not into another program. Of course limits are necessary, but methods must be used that do not interfere with the rehabilitative process.

THEORY AND FAMILY INVOLVEMENT

My emphasis throughout this paper has been on the role of the family in the treatment of the long-term mentally ill. I have tried to indicate that family involvement is virtually inevitable and certainly essential. Nevertheless, family members regularly report that they are not included in treatment, diagnosis, and the planning of follow-up programs. On the face of it, including the family in planning is nothing but common sense. Why then is it not done? Something more powerful than common sense must be at work, and I believe that the reason lies in the prevailing theoretical view of the role of the family in the etiology of mental disorder. The view that families cause the disorders tends to create distance between professionals and family members and to break continuity of care.

The view that parents, especially mothers, cause mental disorder is pervasive in our society. I have heard it from 10-year-old children and it is part of the conventional wisdom. But it seems that no one believes it quite as strongly as mental health professionals, and it is their beliefs and attitudes that have a powerful influence on the course of treatment.

We are all familiar with its origins in psychoanalytic thought. In Anna Freud's writings we find examples of how thought about the role of the family in the development of mental illness and its implications for professional practice developed. She was faced with the dilemma that confronts therapists working with children: should she work through the parents or with the child alone? In a 1926 paper she wrote as follows:

> But who bears this responsibility in a child's analysis? To remain consistent, we would have to say: the responsibility would rest with the persons concerned with the child's upbringing, with whom the child's superego is in any case still inseparably bound, that is with his parents. . . .But here we have some serious reservations. We cannot forget that it was these same parents or guardians whose excessive demands drove the child into an excess of repression and neurosis. The parents who are now called upon to help in the child's recovery are still the same people who let the child get ill in the first place. Their outlook has in most cases not been changed (Freud, 1974, pp. 58-59).

For answers she looked to theory, and following theory she reasoned that since the parents were the cause of the child's disorder, it would be better to work with the child apart from the parents. In this, she departed from her father's unique experiment, in the case of Little Hans, of treating a child through the parents. Nevertheless, her decision was the logical one to make based on the theory of the time. Her decision was a fateful one because it was instrumental in directing thousands of other professionals in the same direction. They, too, would not work with the family because it caused the disorder. There is an important difference between Anna Freud and these others. Whereas that great woman was a pioneer, moving into territory not yet explored, those who followed were not pioneers. Theory has changed, new theories are available, and new evidence is plentiful. But many continue to hold to that early theory despite the evidence. If the unexamined life is not worth living, the unexamined theory is not worth following.

The family etiology of schizophrenia was brought into focus by another historic idea, Bateson's theory of the double bind. Who today does not know the story?

> A young man who had fairly well recovered from an acute schizophrenic episode was visited in the hospital by his mother. He was glad to see her and impulsively put his arm around her shoulders, whereupon she stiffened. He withdrew his arm and she asked, "Don't you love me anymore?" He then blushed and she said, "Dear, you must not be so easily embarrassed and afraid of your feelings." The patient was able to stay with her only a few minutes more and following her departure he assaulted an aide. . . (Bateson et al., 1956, pp. 258-259).

As I read this again I hear it as pure drama, almost operatic in content, and I can see its great intuitive appeal. I know it appealed to me at one time. Despite the fact that study after study has failed to confirm the presence of double-bind behaviors in the families of schizophrenic patients, the idea persists. Much research on families and schizophrenia did appear after Bateson's. This outpouring of publications has been reviewed by a number of scholars, including Goldstein and Rodnick (1975), Hirsch and Leff (1975), Jacob (1975), Liem (1980), and Parker (1982). They have agreed that research evidence for a familial cause of schizophrenia is inconclusive. Typically, the studies are methodologically flawed, and even the best are correlational (Reiss, 1976). These studies have indicated that family communication style and conflict are related to schizophrenia, but cannot indicate direction of effects. The necessary longitudinal data are lacking. Liem (1974, 1976) has demonstrated that, in experimental studies of family interaction, it is the schizophrenic family member who structures the behaviors of those with whom he interacts, whether they be his own parents or nonrelated individuals. The results of many of the family studies can be reanalyzed in this light: it is difficult to communicate with a psychotic, one experiences considerable emotional arousal; in short, it is not a normal situation.

Perhaps I have gone too far in rejecting these family studies. Perhaps families are part of the development of schizophrenia. I have already argued that they are certainly involved in the course of rehabilitation. Vaughn and Leff (1976) and others have demonstrated that relapse can be predicted by the level of expressed emotionality by parents of schizophrenics. Highly emotional expressions of criticism and rejection are related to high rates of relapse and rehospitalization.

The important factor is to see where these family studies lead. They need not lead professionals to view relatives as antagonists. We believe they can lead to an awareness that families can effectively and cooperatively work with professionals toward common goals. Anderson et al. (1982), Gordon and Gordon (1981), Leff et al. (1982) are among those who have devised ways of including parents, by providing them with information and training. We need much more of this.

CONCLUSION

It has been my intention to describe something of what it is like to live with a schizophrenic family member. There are many other such accounts; those by Vine (1982) and Bernheim et al. (1982) are especially sensitive and should be on the reading lists of all professionals working with the long-term mentally ill.

I have also tried to say something about the problems family members have in trying to cope with mental illness, and have gone on to suggest a few of the things we think are necessary for rehabilitation. My list of recommendations has not been complete or detailed. What do consumers of mental health services really need? When this question was asked in a recent survey of former patients now living in the community, they replied that they wanted housing, jobs, and the sense of belonging to somebody. If I understand the families of these individuals correctly, I believe they are saying that they want the things that will make this simple request possible.

REFERENCES

Anderson, C. M., Hogarty, G. E., and Reiss, D. J. 1980. Family treatment of schizophrenia patients: A psycho-educational approach. *Schizophr. Bull.* 6: 490-505.

Appleton, W. S. 1974. Mistreatment of patients' families by psychiatrists. *Am. J. Psychiatry* 131:655-657.

Bateson, G., Jackson, D., Haley, J., and Weakland, J. 1956. Toward a theory of schizophrenia. *Behav. Sci.* 1:241-264.

Bernheim, K. F., Lewine, R. R. J., and Beale, C. T. 1982. *The Caring Family: Living with Chronic Mental Illness.* New York: Random House.

Deiter, J. B., Hanford, D. B., Hummel, R. T., and Lubach, J. E. 1965. Brief in-patient treatment—A pilot study. *Mental Hospitals* 16:95-98.

Fairweather, G. W. 1964. *Social Psychology in Treating Mental Illness: An Experimental Approach.* New York: John Wiley & Sons.

Freud, A. 1974. *Introduction to Psychoanalysis: Lectures for Child Analysts and Teachers, Vol. 1, 1922-1935*. New York: International Universities Press.

Goldstein, M., and Rodnick, E. 1975. The family contribution to the etiology of schizophrenia: Current status. *Schizophr. Bull.* 14:48-63.

Gordon, R. E., and Gordon, K. K. 1981. *Systems of Treatment for the Mentally Ill: Filling the Gaps*. New York: Grune & Stratton.

Hatfield, A. B. 1979. The family as partner in the treatment of mental illness. *Hosp. Comm. Psychiatry* 30:338-340.

Hirsch, S. R., and Leff, J. P. 1975. *Abnormalities in Parents of Schizophrenics*. New York: Oxford University Press.

Jacob, T. 1975. Family interaction in disturbed and normal families: A methodological and substantive review. *Psychol. Bull.* 18:35-65.

Lamb, H. R., and Oliphant, E. 1978. Schizophrenia through the eyes of families. *Hosp. Comm. Psychiatry* 29:805-806.

Leff, J., Kuipers, L., Berkowitz, R., Eberlein-Vries, R., and Sturgeon, D. 1982. A controlled study of social intervention in the families of schizophrenic patients. *Br. J. Psychiatry* 141:121-134.

Liem, J. H. 1974. Effects of verbal communications of parents and children: A comparison of normal and schizophrenic families. *J. Consult. Clin. Psychol.* 42:438-450.

Liem, J. H. 1976. Intrafamily communication and schizophrenic thought disorder: An etiologic or responsive relationship? *Clinical Psychologist* 29:28-30.

Liem, J. H. 1980. Family studies of schizophrenia: An update and commentary. *Schizophr. Bull.* 6:429-455.

Parker, G. 1982. Re-searching the schizophrenogenic mother. *J. Nerv. Ment. Dis.* 170:452-462.

Paul, G. L., and Lentz, R. J. 1977. *Psychosocial Treatment of Chronic Mental Patients: Milieu Versus Social Learning Programs*. Cambridge, MA: Harvard University Press.

Reiss, D. 1976. The family and schizophrenia. *Am. J. Psychiatry* 133:181-185.

Sullivan, H. S. 1953. *The Interpersonal Theory of Psychiatry*. New York: Norton.

Vaughn, C. E., and Leff, J. P. 1976. The influence of family and social factors in the course of psychiatric illness. *Br. J. Psychiatry* 129:125-137.

Vine, P. 1982. *Families In Pain*. New York: Pantheon.

4
The Needs of the Chronically Mentally Ill: The Perspective of a Director of a Large Urban Mental Health Program

J.R. ELPERS

The chronically mentally ill have been with us since the beginning of recorded history. Their care has continuously shifted from institutional to community settings and back again. Over time we have seen many innovative humane and even successful methods of providing care and rehabilitation; but the provision of services to the chronically ill is, by definition, a continuous responsibility that is frequently expensive and always frustrating. Had we discovered a cure for chronic mental illnesses, we would not need to write these papers and I and my staff would be engaged in pursuits other than that of public mental health. I make this point because the care of the chronically mentally ill has been and continues to be primarily the responsibility of government, principally state governments, and, in some states, local government.

During the last 25 years in California, we have seen a shift of responsibility for the treatment of the mentally ill from the state to the counties. During this time, we have seen a decline in the state hospital population from about 37,000 to fewer than 5,000. The state hospital population reduction has been the result of three factors: the advent of Aid to the Totally Disabled (ATD) and Social Security Insurance (SSI) support payments to allow the chronically ill to remain in community settings; the community mental health movement, which has persuaded the government and the public that the mentally ill should be treated in noninstitutional settings; and finally, and perhaps more importantly, new laws which made it impossible to keep people for long periods on open-ended commitments. This has limited the stays of most acutely ill, involuntary patients in any type of hospital to 17 days or less. The advent and continued improvement of psychotropic medications have undoubtedly eased this shift of patient care from institutional to community settings. These medications have not, however, obviated the need for treatment and rehabilitation of the mentally ill nor have they shown themselves to prevent chronicity.

Unfortunately, we have seen less than half of the resources that would have been spent in state institutions transferred to the communities. We are, therefore, faced with the challenge in the community of treating large numbers of severely and chronically ill individuals with limited resources. I shall discuss the administrative prerequisites, as well as the programmatic needs, for providing adequate services to this population.

To treat the chronically mentally ill effectively, a public mental health system must have a comprehensive range of services that is tailored to meet their needs. This tailoring must address issues of cultural relevance, ethnic identity, and age appropriateness. Services must be accessible, not overly restrictive of the patient's freedom, and appropriate to the clinical needs of the patient. In today's economic climate, an important prerequisite is that any service offered be cost-effective (not cheap).

In the past few years in California, I have had the opportunity to participate in an effort to devise an ideal system of care tailored to meet the needs of the chronically ill. The opportunity came about from a state legislative committee's request in the 1979-80 session to a constituent group to develop a model mental health system for California. The legislature wished to know exactly what we believed was needed and what the cost would be. Thus, the Legislative Work Group came into being. It consisted of representatives of all interested parties: professional organizations, provider groups, parent groups, and others who had a vested interest in improving the California mental health system. The meetings were chaired by the executive director of the state Mental Health Association, but staff work was done by a wide array of people, including staff members of the State Department of Mental Health.

The Legislative Work Group quickly decided that whatever planning was done had to be population-based and capable of being translated from a general principle to a specific catchment area. We decided to define all services for an "average" population of 100,000 people—assumed to be average in socioeconomic conditions, racial proportions, age groups, and other demographic characteristics. This method would allow an appropriate multiplication or division of the requirements of the prototype population to determine the average needs for any size service area. It assumed adjustments would be made according to local population characteristics. The group also decided that the model would address the needs of the public mental health system only and it would be done within the constraints of current law and regulation in California. The programs placed heavy emphasis on the chronically and severely ill populations because their needs were seen as the primary responsibility of the public mental health system.

The work group determined at an early stage that the model would have to take a general systems approach to the delivery of mental health services, that is, no single program or modality of services could stand alone. We assumed that the availability of any one component would influence the demands for and use of all components, and we further expected that patients could use multiple programs both sequentially and simultaneously. With these principles in mind, I would like to discuss the California Model as defined after two and a half years of work.

Table 1 displays the 24-hour residential services totaling 160 residential beds per 100,000 people. Only 15 of these are in the acute intensive care category, while in the least restrictive and least expensive setting, out-of-home placement, there are 75 beds. There was great debate in the Work Group and among other interested parties about how many of the acute intensive care beds should be in a hospital setting. We decided that the model should not place specific restrictions on this, although there seems to be a general consensus that about one-third of the patients would need the medical backup that only a hospital can provide. This point is important because the medical needs of acutely ill patients cannot be neglected, although an equally rich staffing pattern can be provided in a non-hospital setting at far less cost. This is because of the licensing structures, overhead costs, and logistical problems associated with locating mental health facilities in acute general hospitals. The other acute residential service is for short-term crisis treatment. Although these services are designed for persons in acute distress, they are not expected to serve people as ill as those in acute intensive care programs, that is, they should need much less medical support.

Twenty-four-hour transitional care is designed for persons who are still so disabled after their acute episodes that they need a longer period for support and rehabilitation before they can return to their homes, to less supportive settings or independent living in the community. We expect about half of the beds in these programs to be occupied by adolescents, a population that frequently requires a long-term, controlled environment to handle major adjustment problems. Generally this treatment does not need to be given in a hospital setting. Transitional care is different from long-term rehabilitative care in that the latter has an expectation of an even longer stay to accommodate the most severely chronically ill population. Persons in these programs represent those who formerly lived a long time in institutional settings, often without hope of improving. In our model we recognize that their rehabilitation is a long-term consideration, but we do hope for their eventual return to a more productive life.

Finally, out-of-home placement is that broad and diffuse category, generally known as board and care, group homes, etc. Community experience has also shown the need for semi-independent living arrangements that provide a step between more sheltered settings and complete residential independence. The patients are diverse, and so are the length-of-stay possibilities. Board and care will serve many people who are in transition to a full and productive life, while it also will be the ultimate residential setting for persons who are chronically ill and without any remaining family or community support systems. It cannot be overemphasized that 24-hour placement services must be linked with other

Table 1   24-Hour Care Services Summary

Level	Who is Served	Service Characteristics	Duration of Service	Where Provided	Minimum No. of Beds 100,000 Pop.
(1) 24-Hr. Acute Intensive Care	Patients who are severely and acutely mentally disordered, both voluntary and involuntary—marked by extreme impairments: intensive treatment required.	Immediate, intensive, round-the-clock, medically supervised treatment. Intended to restore a previous level of functioning.	• Up to 30 days • Often less than 10 days	• General hosp. • Psychiatric health facility • Augmented skilled nursing facility • Freestanding psychiatric hospital	15 in general or psych. hosp. and nonhospital. Local needs determine balance between hosp. and nonhospital, based on 85% occupancy
(2) Short-Term Residential Care	Clients undergoing acute situational crisis or severe stress reaction	Active social rehabilitation model intended to promote rapid restoration to previous level of functioning. Medication may not be required; facility typically not locked. Usually also use day treatment program off site.	10 days-two weeks	• Crisis house or community residential treatment system • Specialized family care setting (e.g., Southwest Denver)	10 beds
(3) 24-Hr. Transitional Care	Clients with impaired ability to cope because of severe emotional disturbances or mental disorder. Most appropriate 24-hr. setting for	Programs intended to assist clients to move to less protective care or more independent functioning after an episode of acute care. Examples: Adolescent group homes, adult halfway houses. Treatment services generally provided off-site.	3-12 months, 6 months average	• Transitional residential care of community residential treatment system • Psychiatric health facilities	10 adult transitional, 10 child and adolescent based on 90% occupancy

	Clients	Duration	Setting	Beds
(4) Long-Term Rehabilitative Care	Clients who are severely and persistently disabled and may be difficult to manage, because of serious mental disorders	Closely supervised and structured in-facility rehabilitation prog. intended to improve basic functioning. Emphasis on occup./rehabilitation therapy. In-house programming 12-16 hr/day, 7 days/wk	18-36 mos. average 1 year +	•Skilled nursing facilities with special treatment program •Long-term res. treatment prog. of community residential treatment system •Augmented intermediate care facility	40 beds based on 95% occupancy
(5) Out-of-Home Placement	Clients who are chronically disabled because of mental disorder	Provides for clients' basic needs and gen. supervision. Includes respite care beds. Rehab. and treatment provided through outpatient and community services.	6 mos. +	In "normal" residential surroundings, bd/care homes, group homes; SSI/SSA	60 supervised out-of-home 15 semi-independent living

Table 2 Nonresidential Services Summary

Level	Who is Served	Service Characteristics	Program Facilities Required	No. of Persons Served Annually
(6) Emergency Service and Evaluation	a) *Eval., Treatment, and Holding* Patients exhibiting acute symptoms; potentially violent/ suicidal; includes drug-induced psychosis.	Primary intake services for acutely ill persons, voluntary or involuntary 7 day/week, 24 hours/day; diagnosis and medication; 24-hour holding capability.	1 emergency unit	1,000 persons/ yr 1,000 units of service
	b) *Crisis Intervention* Any emergency or crisis in living	5 day/week, walk-in 24-hour, 7 day/week call-in information and referral	2 full-time staff	1,820 persons/ yr 1,820 units service
(7) Acute Day Treatment	• Severely disordered • Unable to function in normal roles—residence may be in 24-hr. care program or own home	Substitute for hospitalization; intensive and multidisciplinary Title 9 regulatory staffing: half-time physician required—3 to 6 months of treatment	1 acute day program 9 full-time staff (including clerical)	160 persons/yr (30-40 at any given time)
(8) Outpatient Services	• Crisis or sustained therapeutic intervention: Moderate to severe disturbance—should be accessible to all persons in target community.	Assessment and testing; full spectrum of typical outpatient care including medication; skills should be tailored to meet needs of population being served, including children, minorities.	1 clinic 20 full-time staff (average)	2,000 persons 16,250 units of service

(9) Case Management	Patients diagnosed as having chronic continuous mental disorder 5 years, with 2 or more hospital admissions in preceding year	Achieving continuity of care —identification, planning, monitoring; assurance of all necessary services, distinct and identifiable function.	8.6 case mgrs. + 2.6 support staff + tracking system	400 persons/yr 4,800 units of service av. caseload 50
(10) Community Support Services	•Chronically ill •Repeated hospitalizations; having few living/vocational skills; little familial support; socially isolated, withdrawn	a) *Day rehabilitation:* counseling/social rehabilitation—functional, vocational, and prevocational skill emphasis.	9 full-time staff 13 full-time staff and cler.	600 persons/yr
		b) *Socialization services:* assistance in daily living socialization activities.	2 full-time staff	
		c) *Semi-independent living program:* Assistance in daily living. Volunteers encouraged. Respite Care.	1 full-time staff 1 full-time staff	

treatment components of the system. Staffing and costs for the other components, such as day treatment and community support services, are built to incorporate services to persons in the various 24-hour programs.

Table 2 defines some of these other treatment components. They vary again from emergency services and evaluation at the front end of the system to case management for the long-term, chronically ill patients. We believe that proper linkage of acute day treatment services with various elements of the residential care system offers an effective alternative to acute hospitalization. We particularly like this model because it more closely approximates a normal living situation and thus avoids institutionalization. Outpatient services also encompass a broad array of modalities. They are usually the glue that holds the overall system together. They must be available to all patients in the community, whether they are living in residential placement, with their families, or independently. All mental health systems generally have outpatient services. In this model, we ask that these services be carefully tailored to meet the needs of the patients instead of fitting the selection of patients into the design of the outpatient program. Consequently, there is more emphasis on rehabilitation and a concomitant de-emphasis of long-term psychotherapy.

We think of case management as a special service tailored to the needs of those with a continuous mental disorder. This function is essential if we are to maintain continuity of care, appropriate program planning, and monitoring of residential services for the chronically ill. Perhaps more important, it is the case manager who must see that the chronically ill receive the therapies and adjunctive services essential to their functioning in the community.

Services we group under the title of community support services are particularly essential to the chronically ill patient. Day rehabilitation emphasizes vocational skills. Socialization centers teach individual and group socialization skills. Semi-independent living programs provide long-term assistance in the activities of daily living for those persons who wish to live alone but are not able to be totally independent. Community support services are perhaps the most essential resources to maintain chronically ill persons in the community in a manner comfortable for both the patient and his or her neighbors. Unfortunately, it is also the service component least likely to be available in the traditional mental health system.

Yet no mental health system is complete without a set of community and preventive services. As Table 3 shows, these include consultation, education, information, and community organization to develop services for outreach and referral systems. The Work Group was quite aware of the importance of these functions. We were particularly concerned that these efforts be directed to the underserved populations and to children and young people.

Mental health advocacy is important to keep the system human, to preserve the dignity and participation of the people we serve. Whether we like it or not,

Table 3   System Support and Unique Service Summary

Level	Who Is Served	Service Characteristics	Program/ Facilities Required
(11) Community Services: Consultation, Education/ Information, Community Organization and Outreach	General public and high-risk groups, particularly: •children/youth •cultural/linguistic and other minorities	Cultural and linguistic appropriateness is essential. *Consultation*: technical assistance to increase capabilities of caregivers and related agencies. *Education*: to communities about mental health, mental illness, and for mental health. *Information* about mental health and services to general and target communities. Efforts to reduce stigma of mental illness necessary to accomplish model's goals. *Community organization* to secure public participation and support for mental health action. *Outreach for prevention* aimed at alleviating problems of high-risk group by taking services to the community.	6 full-time staff members (including paraprofessionals), appropriate cultural/ language expertise 6,000 "contact" hrs/yr
(12) Mental Health Advocacy	Mentally disordered persons/clients	Assure client/staff understanding of rights, investigate complaints, intervene for individual clients or groups of clients, collect data on rights violations. Provide summary reports to local and state bodies.	Standard of 0.5 full-time staff member/100,000
(13) Services to the Justice System	Adults and juveniles under jurisdiction of justice system	Full range of services, parallel to those outlined above, tailored to local justice system.	See report on model for full details

advocates must be on the scene to sensitize and resensitize the professional staff.

Finally, we have a subset of services to the justice system which must be tailored to work closely with each community's law enforcement agencies as well as adult and juvenile corrections departments. We do not attempt to define these services in the same detail as other services because they generally are unique in each community.

Figure 1, showing the spectrum of treatment services, attempts to delineate in graphic form how the elements of the system interrelate and assist patients as they progress toward recovery or stabilization. Arrows pointing in both directions suggest that the clients can be served in both modalities concurrently.

Figure 2, the summary of standards per 100,000 population, includes costs of each component (in 1979 dollars) and shows the expected distribution of model service funds by age group in the standard population. The model anticipates that children will need a proportionately small share of emergency hospital, long-term rehabilitation, and community support services. They will, however, need higher percentages of 24-hour transitional, community, and justice-system services. The last item illustrates the Work Group's concern that adequate mental health care be provided to high-risk youngsters in the juvenile justice system.

Full implementation of the California model would require about twice the budget currently available; we have found it to be an invaluable asset, however, in evaluating our current services, adjusting their relative availability, and perhaps most importantly, defining for the legislature and the public what is needed to give us a truly competent public mental health program.

Beyond the availability of the components that I have described for the California model, I believe there are other prerequisites to providing adequate services to the chronically mentally ill. First you must have an administrative system that clearly fixes the responsibility for each patient's care on a given individual or clinical treatment team. This team must be responsible for providing the continuity of care, case management and follow-through, regardless of the treatment component the patient might be using at the moment. To accomplish this, the service spectrum must be administratively integrated, and interagency relationships must be both well defined and carefully nurtured. Above all, there must be clear administrative sanctions against the "dumping" of difficult, chronically ill patients on other components of the system or outside of the system.

In Los Angeles County, we have found that we cannot function as a public mental health system without the close working relationship and support of our constituent groups. We strongly support patient self-help groups and we believe that it is critical to extend ourselves to help these groups understand and cope with their illnesses. We are also nurturing close relationships with the myriad of family groups who, in previous years, were alienated from the mental health system and frequently considered to be at fault by mental health professionals.

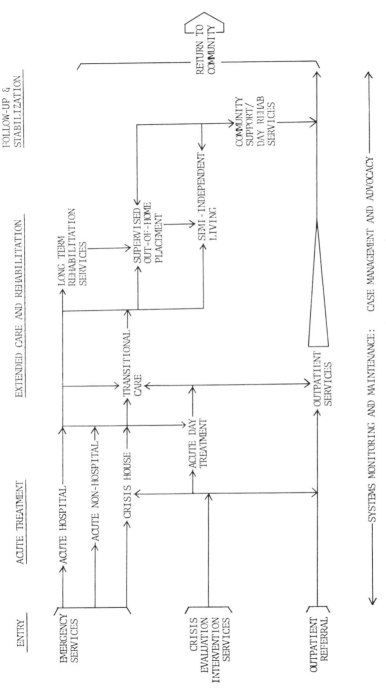

Figure 1   The spectrum of treatment services.

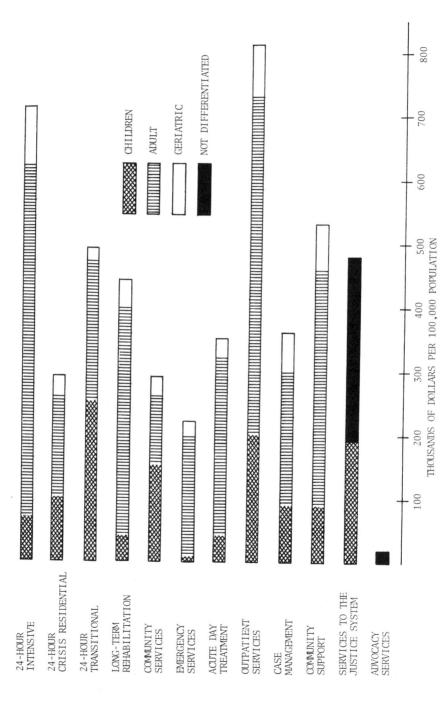

Figure 2 Summary of California model: standards of service for children, youth, adults, and aged persons.

We have found the families eager to work with us, knowledgeable about program needs, and an invaluable support group when it comes to arguing for budget increases. Finally, we believe that a strong and healthy relationship with our Mental Health Association members is a must. We respect their advocacy role and keep them fully informed of programmatic needs and directions and enlist their support wherever possible.

It is also critical that a large mental health system be willing to reach out to special groups who do not avail themselves of the more traditional services. One such group is the predominantly young, predominantly schizophrenic people we are now finding in our skid-row areas. In Los Angeles, after some violent episodes at a welfare office in a slum area, we were asked to intervene. From that has grown the Civic Center Project (Farr, 1982) in which a small but highly skilled staff is reaching out to provide services to a very difficult population on skid row. This population, of whom 10 percent are women, numbers from 8,000 in the summertime to 15,000 in the winter when the "snow birds" arrive from the northeast. A highly mobile population, it includes severely ill, predominantly schizophrenic, frequently paranoid people who are terrified of hospitalization or incarceration. The only way we have been able to reach this population is by a combination of working on the streets, working with existing organizations like the missions and voluntary agencies, and we have found that a great deal of our efforts go into such seemingly menial tasks as obtaining Social Security Insurance benefits and passes for the Rapid Transit District (RTD). But it is these efforts that develop trust by the clientele and their willingness to try out our medications and supportive services.

In Los Angeles County, a vast number of patients live in board and care facilities. Most of these patients receive prescriptions from private physicians working under Medi-Cal (Medicaid) but little, if any, other support or rehabilitative services. Through a pilot project, we are planning to integrate all Medi-Cal mental health services in Los Angeles County into the public mental health program. We expect to provide a much higher level of care for this population. We hope to bring activity centers, socialization centers, day treatment centers, and sheltered workshops into, or make them accessible to, these board and care facilities. By doing so, we believe that we can begin to provide a spectrum of services to these people who have been discharged from state hospitals and readmitted to perhaps less benign settings in the community. If successful, our efforts will result in a truly integrated single system of care for the chronically mentally ill. If adequately funded, it will represent a model of hope for the chronically ill.

REFERENCE

Farr, R. K. 1982. Skid row mental health project. Paper delivered to National Association of Counties conference as part of 1982 award to Los Angeles Department of Mental Health for new and innovative mental health projects, Washington, DC, July 12. Copies available from R. K. Farr, 2415 West 6th Street, Los Angeles, CA 90057.

II
Assessment and Information Needs
for Research and Services

5
The Utility of Assessment
for Different Purposes

MARCO J. MARIOTTO AND GORDON L. PAUL

Although formal assessment is a hallmark of scientific research, it is equally important to rational decision-making in management and clinical activities. The operation of mental health services systems for the chronically mentally ill requires a multitude of decisions at administrative and clinical levels, and each decision involves a choice among alternative courses of action. A facility director deciding, for example, on the level of funding for a treatment program chooses among at least three alternatives: increase funding, decrease funding, or maintain the status quo. Likewise, an individual clinician's decision to administer a neuroleptic drug to a particular patient involves a choice among drugs, dosage levels, and methods of administration. Even the tacit decision to continue activities "as usual" involves a choice *not* to change to alternative courses of action. All rational decision-making requires that choices among courses of action be based upon the probable gains and losses each alternative offers. The operation of mental health services for the chronically mentally ill involves choices that assume some level of assessment because they imply comparisons and predictions. Thus, formal assessment is as important to good services as it is to good research.

Formal assessment can be defined as "the gathering and evaluation of information about people, their environment, and their behavior within that environment" (Paul et al., in press). The major purpose of gathering such information is to enable people to make decisions. It is especially important to emphasize the decision-making goal of the assessment enterprise, as assessment undertaken without regard for the purpose of the information obtained may be a waste of time and resources.

Assessment is, thus, a continuous process in mental health systems at all levels (clinical, administrative, and research), whether it is done formally or not. It may range from subjective judgments of a supervisor that a staff member is "goofing off" to the precise determination of 72-hour blood serum levels of neuroleptic metabolites. Our goals in this chapter are to explain the major functions and purposes of assessment for the multifaceted decision processes involved in mental health systems for the chronically mentally ill, to delineate the domains and classes of variables that represent necessary targets for assessment, and to summarize a schema for evaluating the utility of information obtained from the assessment process. More detailed development and discussion of these subjects, especially as they apply to assessment in residential treatment environments, may be found in Paul et al. (in press).

MAJOR PURPOSES OF ASSESSMENT

At a global level, the major purposes of assessment for the chronically mentally ill are to provide information to aid decision-makers. As summarized by Weinstein (1975), information is needed to: (1) aid the clinician in serving individual clients; (2) aid the facility or service director in managing operations; (3) aid the state, county, or private mental health authorities in developing and monitoring overall programs in a service system; and (4) aid researchers in the field. At a more specific level, the multitude of decision problems facing personnel working with the chronically mentally ill can be categorized in a manner that accounts for most such decisions. Table 1 summarizes six categories of decision problems that regularly occur with regard to clients and staff in mental health service systems for the chronically mentally ill.

Placement and disposition decisions regarding clients occur whenever an individual is admitted into the system, placed into specific programs, or considered for discharge or transfer. Similarly, decisions on staff hiring, assignment to treatment programs, and discharges or transfers to other programs are continuous activities in service delivery systems.

Problem identification and description are fundamental to the effective operation of mental health services and research for the chronically mentally ill. The goals of the decision-maker are the identification of client assets, excesses and deficits, the establishment of treatment goals, and the formulation of a treatment plan to accomplish those goals. This decision category is so essential to the operations of service delivery systems and to research that *all* other decision categories require some level of information about client problems.

Staff development and utilization decisions are required in a parallel manner. Here the decision-maker strives to maximize cost-effective treatment by identification, specification, training and maintenance of staff performance. Included in this decision category are specifications or changes in treatment techniques, distribution of staff time and responsibilities, and personnel actions involving salaries, promotions, and performance evaluations.

Concurrent monitoring of operations comprises the majority of decisions after problem identification and treatment programming have taken place. Here

Table 1 Varieties of Decisions for Mental Health Service Delivery Systems
for the Chronically Mentally Ill

Regarding Clients	Regarding Staff
1. *Placement and Disposition* Admit into system Assign to treatment programs Retain, discharge, transfer	1. *Placement and Disposition* Hire Assign to treatment programs Retain, discharge, transfer
2. *Problem Identification and Description* Identify assets, excesses, deficits Establish treatment goals Establish initial treatment plan	2. *Development and Utilization* Specification or change in treatment Specification or change in staff time or responsibilities Personnel actions

3. *Concurrent Monitoring of Operations*

Desired change occurring? ⌐→ if not → └— modify and reevaluate —┘	Prescribed treatment being carried out? ⌐→ if not → └— modify and reevaluate —┘

4. *Absolute and Comparative Program Evaluation*

Intended population served? Desired change attained (as well as other effects)? └→ if not → └— modify and reevaluate —┘	Intended treatment programs employed? Nature of treatment implementations (as efficient, cost-effective as others?) └→ if not → └— modify and reevaluate —┘

5. *Legal and Ethical Regulation and Documentation*

Documentation of all above Compliance with external standards	Documentation of all above Compliance with external standards

6. *Specific Research Questions*

Measurement/control of 1,2,3 above Questions of specific focus	Measurement/control of 1,2,3 above Questions of specific focus

Adapted from Paul (in press).

rational decision-makers maximize treatment effectiveness by continuously assessing client changes and treatment implementation, and they modify treatment and reevaluate client functioning when desired changes do not occur. The information for this decision category is parallel to that needed for initial problem identification and staff development and utilization, but on a continuous basis.

Absolute and comparative program evaluations are required regularly at all levels of mental health services for the chronically mentally ill. The overall goal of the decision-maker, here, is to maximize cost-effective treatment by the allocation of resources and the provision of guidance and information to treatment personnel. A multitude of different decisions are required in this category depending on the particular goal being evaluated. For example, knowing whether the intended population is being served and/or whether a program is following a specified therapeutic procedure requires information at an absolute level. More commonly, comparative information on program evaluation is needed to make decisions because they involve comparisons of effectiveness between alternative treatment programs.

Legal and ethical regulation and documentation require decision-makers to insure that the right of clients and staff are protected by determining and documenting that appropriate and humane treatment conditions and procedures are provided. These decisions are usually based on after-the-fact determination that the results of all of the previously mentioned decision categories are in compliance with external standards or guidelines, and, if not, that appropriate changes are being made.

Specific research questions constitute the most variable set of decision problems within mental health systems for the chronically mentally ill. Both the design of and assessment procedures employed in scientific research must be determined by the nature of the question addressed. The goal of the decision-maker is to gain new knowledge regarding the nature, etiology, and treatment of chronic mental disorders. Questions of specific focus, in addition to assessment of particular variables germane to the research question, also need measurement of many of the above decision categories to increase the utility of research outcomes.

DOMAINS AND CLASSES OF VARIABLES

Given these categories of decision problems, what kinds of information are minimally necessary to address current clinical and research questions concerning the chronically mentally ill? Three domains of focus, with specific classes of variables within each domain, have been delineated as necessary targets of assessment for any clinical problem (Paul, 1969). These domains and classes of variables are particularly relevant as targets of information needed for rational decision-making involving the chronically mentally ill (Paul and Lentz, 1977). The domains are client, staff, and time.

Client domain. In this domain three classes of variables are necessary targets for assessment: problem behaviors, relatively stable personal-social characteristics, and the physical-social life environment. The *problem behaviors* class includes those aspects of client functioning that are distressing to either the client or significant others, which result in the decision to enter the mental health system. It includes distressing or maladaptive motoric, physiological, and cognitive activities that become the focus of treatment. Both excesses (e.g., delusions, hallucinations, and bizarre motor behavior) and deficits (e.g., in language, communication, interpersonal and cognitive functioning) are necessary targets of treatment intervention for chronically mentally ill clients (see Paul, this volume).

Relatively stable personal-social characteristics are variables on which clients may differ, other than problem behaviors. The variables are important because they may interact positively or negatively with treatment procedures and are often significant in defining appropriate client role behavior. Included in this class of variables are clients' demographic characteristics (e.g., age, sex, marital status), educational and vocational history, and physical status.

The *physical-social life environment* of clients may provide settings and experiences that interact positively or negatively with changes in problem behavior and set the time and/or place for the identification of such problems. The burgeoning data on the role of family variables in the relapse of chronically mentally ill clients (see Liberman et al., this volume) emphasizes the importance of assessment of these variables.

Staff domain. In the broad staff or therapist domain, three specific classes of variables are necessary targets for assessment: therapeutic techniques, relatively stable personal-social characteristics of staff, and the physical-social treatment environment. The *therapeutic techniques* class consists of aspects of interventions or staff functioning through which improvements in client behaviors are attempted. Included in this class are both discrete somatic treatments and complex actions and strategies of interpersonal interaction.

Relatively stable personal-social staff characteristics include the full range of variables on which staff members differ, other than therapeutic techniques. This class of variables is important since they may interact, positively or negatively, with the effectiveness of therapeutic procedures for given clients, settings, and problem behaviors. Potentially important variables for staff include age, sex, education and experience, theoretical orientation, and attitudes and opinions.

The physical-social treatment environment is the immediate setting in which treatment occurs. Variables in this class may interact with variables in other classes and affect treatment effectiveness. These variables include intramural characteristics like ward size and staff-patient ratios and extramural characteristics like home vs. clinic, public vs. private, and others.

Time domain. The third major domain of focus, time, is often neglected in assessment (Fiske, 1978). Variations in time specify the set of circumstances for assessing all other classes of variables and determine the focus and nature of such assessments. The importance of "real time" specifications of changes in variables in the client and staff domains is demonstrated in other chapters in this volume by Strauss, Licht, Power, and Paul. At a minimum, the "real time" of a client's or staff member's entry into and exit from particular treatment programs and the "real time" of major changes in any class of client or staff variables must be specified if assessment information is to be useful. The latter specification should include not only the time at which information was obtained but also the period covered by the assessment procedures. Recording of all time information in "real time" units allows comparisons and specifications of changes in other variables.

ASSESSMENT NEEDS FOR DIFFERENT DECISION CATEGORIES

If we cross the varieties of decision problems with the target domains and classes of variables, the resulting matrix demonstrates the wide range of assessment needs for rational decision-making at all levels of mental health services for the chronically mentally ill. Such a matrix is summarized in Table 2. The table highlights the nature and sheer volume of information needed for rational decision-making.

Of course, practical and technological constraints preclude precise assessment of all classes of variables to allow every decision at all levels to be completely data-based. Two points need to be emphasized, however. First, assessment of client problem behaviors and staff therapeutic techniques are minimally necessary for *all* decisions regarding the chronically mentally ill. Second, the quality and generalizability of the decision in each category shown in Table 2 are directly related to the quality of the information obtained for that class of variables. Precise, high-quality assessment information is, of course, not sufficient for rational decision-making; we are all aware of bad decisions based on good data. We do maintain, however, that good assessment information is a necessary condition for systematic, rational decision-making. Sometimes we're lucky and make good decisions on the basis of bad data, but luck is, unfortunately, a random rather than systematic factor.

POTENTIAL UTILITY OF ASSESSMENT PROCEDURES

Since the sheer volume of information needed for rational decision-making could easily overwhelm both staff and clients, the potential utility of assessment procedures must be determined to allow reasonable choices among different information-gathering approaches. Determining this potential value is not a simple task. Without straying into the intricacies and controversies of test and measurement theory, we can summarize the essential principles of assessment with a simple and sobering point. Anything less than *perfect, error-free* assessment of all components relevant to a particular decision—a clearly impossible task in most instances—represents generalizations and inferences from obtained informa-

Table 2 Information Needs for Different Categories of Decisions

| | Domains and Classes of Variables | | | | | |
| | Client Domain | | | Staff Domain | | |
Decision Category	Problem Behaviors	Stable Personal-Social Characteristics	Physical-Social Life Environment	Therapeutic Techniques	Stable Personal-Social Characteristics	Physical-Social Treatment Environment
Placement and Disposition:						
client admission/assignment	X	X	X	X	X	X
client discharge/placement	X	X	X	X	X	X
staff hiring/assignment	X	X	X	X	X	X
staff discharge/placement	X			X	X	X
Problem identification/description (initial treatment plan)	X	X	X	X		X
Staff development/utilization	X			X	X	X
Concurrent monitoring	X	X	X	X	X	X
Program evaluation	X	X	X	X	X	X
Legal and ethical regulation	X	X	X	X	X	X
Specific research questions	X	X	X	X	X	X

Adapted from Paul et al. (in press).

tion (Cronbach et al., 1972). In most cases, we infer and forecast from fallible data. Evaluation of assessment approaches involves estimating the fallibility of the information obtained to choose assessment procedures that maximally decrease the fallibility and increase the utility for valid decisions. An important point is that the principles of evaluation of assessment information apply to *any* information-gathering procedure used as a basis for decision-making, be it the subjective clinical analysis of a client's mental status or the determination of funding allocations (Wiggins, 1973; Curran and Mariotto, 1980).

Administrators, clinicians, and researchers working with the chronically mentally ill must evaluate the potential utility of particular assessments for particular purposes. Employing the logic of mathematical decision theory (Wald, 1950; Cronbach and Gleser, 1965), guidelines for choosing assessment procedures can be delineated. We have called these the "four R's" of assessment procedure utility: representativeness, replicability, relevance, and relative cost (Paul et al. in press).

Representativeness refers to the adequacy of an assessment procedure in covering information desired for any particular decision. This adequacy is traditionally referred to as concurrent, content, and/or predictive validity. No measure has general "validity," however. Rather, it has validity for a particular purpose (Cronbach and Gleser, 1965). Validity can best be indexed as the *degree* to which the information obtained from the assessment could be generalized to represent the information on which the particular decision in question would be based, if we had perfect, error-free assessment of all relevant information. Thus, the validity of obtained information will depend on how well important conditions or domains of measurement for this particular decision problem have been sampled. Conditions or domains of measurement that must be taken into account, depending on the particular decision, include people (i.e., clients or staff), content (i.e., problem behaviors, therapeutic techniques), and occasions (specific situations and times). In general, the greater the adequacy of sampling appropriate domains, the greater is the representativeness of the information for particular decisions, and the greater is the assessment procedure's potential value.

Replicability refers to the trustworthiness or dependability of the information obtained from the assessment procedures, specifically the degree to which the same information is replicable over independent assessors. Traditionally, dependability has been referred to as the reliability of the assessment information, and various reliability indexes have been developed over the years. For decision-making concerning chronically mentally ill patients, the most important reliability index for determining the potential utility of an assessment procedure is interobserver agreement. This index reflects the degree to which the same information is obtained by different observers or assessors, the intersubjectivity of the obtained information (Fiske, 1978). Observer intersubjectivity should remain constant over differing situations and times of observation; assessors should agree that the same events occurred no matter where or when the observation is made. Thus, whether the assessors are clients or staff members, professional assessors, or external nonparticipating observers, the recorded information must be replicable. Further, the greater the replicability, the greater is the trustworthiness of the obtained information and the greater is the potential value of the assessment procedure.

Relevance is the appropriateness of the information obtained for a variety of decision problems. The overall potential utility of an assessment procedure is proportional to the number of separate decisions for which the information can be used. An assessment procedure that provides useful information for both problem description *and* program evaluation will have greater potential value than a procedure that can only provide information for one or the other. Licht (this volume) and Power (this volume) discuss several assessment procedures that have a wide range of applicability for decision problems concerning the chronically mentally ill. In general, the greater the number of decisions to which obtained information can contribute, the greater is the relevance to overall decision-making, and the greater is the potential value of the assessment procedure.

Relative cost refers to the expense of an assessment procedure *in comparison to* alternative procedures that provide the same information. Costs include not only the direct costs of assessment staff and materials, but also the indirect costs of the amount of professional and administrative time involved in using the information for decisions. Also, costs of assessment procedures may differ between "start-up" and "maintenance" expenses. Relative cost must also take into account the value placed on the outcome of decisions that result from the assessment information. In some instances of decision-making for the chronically mentally ill, relatively straightforward estimates of the value of various decision outcomes can be made. For example, if one assessment procedure is more relevant to a greater number of treatment decisions than another, it might lead to greater treatment efficacy as indexed by shorter hospitalization and/or lower recidivism rates. This can be translated directly into dollar values. Other outcomes, like increased staff morale or the prevention of a suicide, are not so easily translated into dollars. Indeed, the difficulty of transforming such outcomes into numerical values is the "Achilles heel" of the use of mathematical decision theory to index the utility of assessment procedures (Cronbach and Gleser, 1965). Nevertheless, the logic of decision theory requires decision-makers to specify some relative value to gains and losses of various decision outcomes, including the decision as to which assessment procedure should be used for a particular decision problem. These outcome values must then be entered along with direct and indirect costs to determine the relative costs of an assessment procedure. "Net" relative cost, then, includes the direct and indirect costs of the assessment procedures, less the dollar costs potentially saved by the information obtained, less the value of potential gains in treatment effectiveness, less the value of potential assurance of legal, ethical, and humane operations. The lower the costs and/or the greater the representativeness, replicability, and relevance of the information obtained, the lower is the net relative cost, and the greater is the potential value of an assessment procedure.

CONCLUSION

We have outlined the varieties of decisions, the domains and classes of variables relevant to those decisions, and a schema for evaluating the utility of information-gathering procedures of importance in working with the chronically mentally ill. Formal assessment operations are crucial, not only for gaining useful knowledge about the basis of problems and the effectiveness of interventions, but for the humane and cost-effective operation of services. Other writers in this volume discuss specific variables that have already demonstrated important relationships to understanding and treating the chronically mentally ill. The more precisely we can measure such variables, the more closely can we approach the elevation of mental health service delivery to the status of an applied, rational science.

REFERENCES

Cronbach, L. J., and Gleser, G. C. 1965. *Psychological Tests and Personnel Decisions*. Urbana: University of Illinois Press.

Cronbach, L. J., Gleser, G. C., Nanda, H., and Rajaratnam, N. 1972. *The Dependability of Behavioral Measurements*. New York: Wiley.

Curran, J. P., and Mariotto, M. J. 1980. A conceptual structure for the assessment of social skills. In M. Hersen, D. Eisler, and P. Miller (eds.), *Progress in Behavior Modification*, pp. 1-37. New York: Academic Press.

Fiske, D. W. 1978. *Strategies for Personality Research*. San Francisco: Jossey-Bass.

Paul, G. L. 1969. Behavior modification research: Design and tactics. In C. M. Franks (ed.), *Behavior Therapy: Appraisal and Status*, pp. 29-62. New York: McGraw-Hill.

Paul, G. L. in press. The impact of public policy and decision-making on the dissemination of science-based practices in mental institutions: Playing poker with everything wild. In R. A. Kasschau, L. Rehm, and L. P. Ullmann (eds.), *Psychological Research, Public Policy and Practice: Towards a Productive Partnership*. New York: Praeger.

Paul, G. L., and Lentz, R. J. 1977. *Psychosocial Treatment of Chronic Mental Patients*. Cambridge, MA: Harvard University Press.

Paul, G. L., Mariotto, M. J., and Redfield, J. P. in press. Assessment purposes, domains, and utility for decision-making. In G. L. Paul (ed.), *Observational Assessment Instrumentation for Institutional Research and Treatment*. Cambridge, MA: Harvard University Press.

Wald, A. 1950. *Statistical Decision Functions*. New York: Wiley.

Weinstein, A. S. 1975. Evaluation through medical records and related information systems. In E. L. Struening and M. Guttentag (eds.), *Handbook of Evaluation Research, vol. 1*, pp. 397-481. Beverly Hills: Sage Publications.

Wiggins, J. S. 1973. *Personality and Prediction*. Reading, MA: Addison-Wesley.

6
Assessment of Treatment in Outpatient Settings

JOHN S. STRAUSS

A truism that is often forgotten in theory and practice is that treatment assessment must relate to real patients in real treatment conditions. The thesis of this report is that, to live up to this dictum, we must make major modifications in how we evaluate the treatment of psychiatric disorders.

The planning and assessment of treatment requires three kinds of information: appropriate concepts and measures of outcome, accurate prognostic baselines that suggest what is the most likely course of a particular disorder for a particular kind of patient, and accurate descriptions of treatment. Our field has had long-standing problems with all of these requirements, but in the last few years much progress has been made to resolve these difficulties. The change has important implications for planning and assessing treatment in outpatient and inpatient settings.

Strangely, the advances in understanding outcome, prognosis, and treatment were accomplished without major technologic breakthroughs. Rather, they depended on the application of basic descriptive principles which were elaborated and refined by the use of standardized interviews and rating schedules, operational diagnostic criteria, careful sampling, and some relatively basic statistical procedures.

Use of these techniques has generated four findings that are the basis for the revolutionary changes that have occurred. First is the finding in several long-term studies that the outcome of chronic mental illness is not always permanent dysfunction. Persons with such illness may improve markedly, even recover, after many years of suffering continuous and severe disorders (Bleuler, 1978; Ciompi, 1980; Harding and Brooks, 1980). The results of the long-term studies have freed up a range of conceptual and treatment possibilities. If the chronically mentally ill do not always remain severely incapacitated for the rest of their lives, then what might contribute to improvement, and how can these forces be harnessed in the treatment process?

The second major cause of progress in outcome studies has been the finding that carefully made, symptom-based diagnoses do not have definitive prognostic value. Even for schizophrenia, a disorder originally defined by its supposedly deteriorating course, there is no diagnostic system using symptoms alone that has more than a modest ability to predict patient outcome (Strauss and Carpenter, 1974a; Brockington et al., 1978). This finding complements the results of long-term follow-up studies to show that neither chronicity nor symptom-based diagnosis is definitive in establishing a conclusive, pessimistic statement about the course of the individual's disorder and life. Such findings contradict frequently heard statements that chronic patients or people with schizophrenia always deteriorate and never recover.

The third dramatically important finding is that so-called "outcome" is not a single phenomenon, but seems to be constituted of many relatively independent areas of function (Ciompi, 1980; Schwartz et al., 1975; Strauss and Carpenter, 1972). Thus, knowing a patient's level of symptom severity at a given follow-up point provides only a modest prediction of his or her social relations or work function, or whether he or she is likely to be hospitalized. The same is true for all of the other variables. Hospitalization, once considered to be an adequate estimate of outcome and often used as the sole basis for assessing treatment effectiveness, has actually been found to be the variable least correlated with the other major areas of outcome functioning. Frequently, patients who are rehospitalized stay only for brief periods and then return to the community and to effective functioning. Conversely, many persons discharged from the hospital and not rehospitalized may remain in the community at the most marginal levels of functioning, perhaps living in some back room, but never requiring return to the hospital.

The finding that several prognostic variables are helpful in predicting individual outcome characteristics is the fourth important advance in knowledge. Social-relations functioning (Phillips, 1953), work functioning, previous duration of hospitalization (Strauss and Carpenter, 1974b) all have significant predictive value. Strikingly, the predictive power of these variables is usually greatest for the corresponding variable at follow-up, previous social relations being the best predictor of later social-relations functioning, previous work functioning being the best predictor of later work functioning.

These findings related to the various aspects of outcome and prediction have been used to suggest that the course of psychiatric disorder may best be conceptualized as constituted of several open-linked systems (Strauss and Carpenter, 1974b). Each system, such as work function or symptom type, has several of its own predictors and determinants of its course. The level of cross-correlations between the systems suggests that they also have some, but limited, influence on each other.

Together, these findings indicate that the course of disorder is not only much more varied and flexible than had originally been conceptualized but is far more complex as well. Recent findings regarding the impact of social supports (Hammer, 1981), family environment (Leff and Vaughn, 1980), and life events (Day, 1981) provide further information about the nature and complexity of the course of disorder by indicating that an entire range of individual-environment interactions may influence outcome. Treatment studies, both those showing the value of pharmacologic agents and those indicating the value of psychosocial treatments, provide further data regarding the dynamic and complex characteristics of the course of even the most chronic psychiatric disorders.

Thus, many kinds of research in the last few years have made us lose our innocence regarding the supposed simplicity of prognosis in chronic mental disorders. Many of the previous ways of approaching treatment planning and evaluation of treatment effectiveness have become highly questionable. For example, the view, more often practiced than stated openly, that there is nothing you can do about people with chronic mental illness because they are always going to stay that way, is certainly not justified. The recognition that such an approach is unwarranted and unjust has given rise to volumes like this one and to an international concern about the treatment of persons with such disorders. The World Health Organization, for example, has an entire project focused on assessment and reduction of disability in psychiatric disorders that involves nine research centers in eight countries.

Recognizing the need for attention to the treatment possibilities in chronic mental illness has been a major step forward, and much current research is beginning to suggest ways to approach these possibilities. Several leading projects and their most recent developments are described elsewhere in this volume. The focus of this report is on the implications for treatment and treatment assessment of a study exploring the vicissitudes in chronic mental disorders and possible ways of harnessing the information these vicissitudes provide. One implication of this study is that course of disorder is even more crucial than cross-sectional "outcome" in understanding processes of healing and exacerbation in chronic mental illness.

The data cited previously are a clue to just how complex the course of chronic mental illness might be. One important approach to trying to grasp and define complex processes is to carry out hypothesis-generating research. When a major question has arisen and the crucial variables and processes in it have not been completely defined, flexible hypothesis-generating research can provide the kind of information that is not available from any other approach, even from highly controlled studies (Strauss and Hafez, 1981). In this way, hypothesis-generating research is a crucial complement to controlled studies and is essential to provide guidance for them.

Based on this principle, our research group is conducting the Yale Longitudinal Study (Strauss, 1983), a study aimed primarily at the tasks of hypothesis-generating and development. The Yale Longitudinal Study is an intensive follow-up investigation of patients hospitalized for severe psychiatric disorders. Subjects are included in the study if they are between the ages of 18 and 55, have been recently hospitalized for functional psychiatric disorders, and have no major problem of organic brain syndromes or substance abuse. Since one goal of the project is to study the role of work in the recovery and rehabilitation process, another criterion for entering the study is that the subject has worked at some time during the year before hospitalization. Patients in the study are seen for about five interviews while they are in the hospital. Semistructured interviews are used to obtain basic diagnostic, psychiatric-history, and demographic data. Interviews at this time are also focused on possible ways in which the individuals and their environment have interacted in either a helpful or harmful way before hospitalization.

After the patients are discharged, they are seen every two months in follow-up interviews using a semistructured format. A final interview is done again two years after their hospital discharge. It was amazing to us, in beginning this study, that we could find no previous research of this kind that would allow investigators to note systematically the various paths and factors that influence the course of disorder in an ongoing way. Although certain research on the effects of medication and other treatments has involved frequent follow-up assessments over a brief period or follow-up every six months or so over a few years, this has not been focused on charting the vicissitudes in the patient's condition or on factors that might influence these vicissitudes.

Largely because of the absence of such studies, the concept of the course and outcome of disorder and of treatment effect that is generally used is a static one. Thus (Figure 1), the usual follow-up will have an initial and a later assessment using one general outcome variable which shows either that the patient has improved, stayed the same, or gotten worse. Figure 1 shows a schematic diagram of the overall rating of the course from one subject in our study. Clearly N.E. has stayed about the same during the 12-month follow-up period.

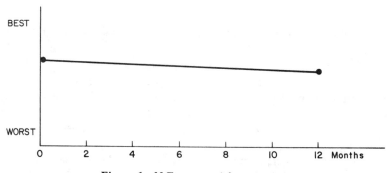

Figure 1 N.E.–general functioning.

If one is interested in understanding the course of disorder, however, such an approach may be grossly inadequate because it neglects two crucial principles:

1. If the state of disorder varies over time, infrequent assessments will give no picture of such vicissitudes. Bimonthly assessments of N.E. showed in fact that she had wide swings in terms of her overall functioning during the 12-month period (Figure 2).

2. The second principle that suggests the inadequacy of the static model is that, because of the multidimensional nature of outcome and its prediction, assessing only one outcome characteristic or a global outcome measure gives very little information about crucial processes. Using a multidimensional (or multi-axial) assessment for N.E. (Figure 3) indicates in fact that she is functioning at very different levels simultaneously in different areas. When she is not severely symptomatic, she is working consistently at a relatively high level. In spite of major changes in both work and symptoms throughout the one-year period, her social-relations functioning remained at a consistently low level until it began to improve in the last two months. Washing out such complexities by infrequent assessments or by assessing only one global measure of functioning may be adequate for some purposes, but a great deal is missed. Because we are still struggling to define the factors, including treatment, that influence the course of psychiatric disorders, systematically ignoring peaks and valleys of symptomatology or of functioning in other areas is likely to cause us to miss crucial cues to interventions that may be most important, or to factors that may be most deleterious.

Based on this kind of bimonthly mapping of several areas of function in a patient's course, we have begun to attempt to define certain general patterns of the evolution of disorder after hospital discharge. In other reports, we have described the various ways people have of controlling their symptoms (Breier and Strauss, in press) and their use of social relations during this period. Here we will focus on a relatively common longitudinal pattern of recovery that we have noted during the posthospitalization period. The pattern will be described in detail because it is particularly relevant for treatment planning and assessment.

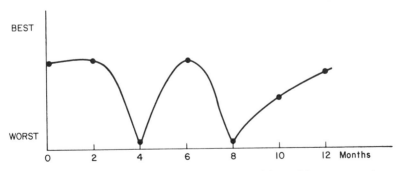

Figure 2 N.E.—general functioning shown in bimonthly assessments.

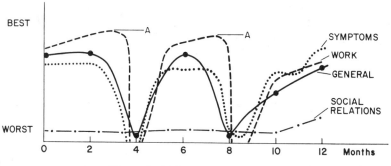

Figure 3   N.E.—areas of function.

After hospital discharge, or sometimes actually beginning during the hospital stay, many patients pass through a "moratorium" period. In this phase, they seem to show little behavioral change, so that patients and clinicians often feel that "nothing is happening." Such experiences may be discouraging for both, and they are particularly frustrating if the treatment program is a high-pressure or total-push program. In fact, rather than "doing nothing" during this phase, many patients seem to be using such a moratorium period for gradually rebuilding their self-esteem, regrouping in their social contacts, and establishing certain basic skills for dealing with people and situations. It is difficult, if not impossible, to measure such processes for evaluation purposes.

After the moratorium period has continued, a "change point" often occurs. At this point, there is movement; perhaps the patient attempts to return to work, to change the living situation, or to increase social contacts. Such attempts at change are often accompanied by at least a minor increase of symptomatology. This increase is alarming to patient, family, and clinician, and often results in actions taken by someone or by all to return the patient to the previous level of functioning. It is our strong impression that these change points may, in fact, have several different outcomes, from major improvement at one extreme to decompensation at the other. In a general way, just as in crisis theory, such a change point may culminate in improvement or dysfunction, and it is often extremely difficult to tell ahead of time, or even in the middle of the phase, which outcome is more likely. It is our strong impression that improvement is far more likely if the moratorium period has helped produce a change in the patient's self-esteem, skills, or social supports.

If the change point has a successful outcome, the person moves up the ladder to the next higher level of functioning. Interestingly, there is practically no research on when such movement ought to take place, how far it should go, and what should happen next. Many of our subjects seemed to go through a series of moratorium-change point sequences, and the first several of these were often successful. Nevertheless, each moratorium period may be discouraging to patient, clinician, and family because, especially for more chronic patients, the length of moratorium that might be required may be interpreted as "resistance," lack of motivation, or permanent disability. This misconception, we believe, has contributed to the previous view that people with chronic mental disorders will be permanently and, without exception, severely disabled.

Finally, after one or more moratoria and change points are successfully accomplished, the person may reach a "ceiling." This ceiling may be defined as the highest point of function the person has reached in the recent past (for example, during the past year). Our impression is that at these ceiling points the person is particularly vulnerable to decompensation.

Patterns in the course of disorder such as these have considerable relevance to treatment and treatment evaluation. A common approach in treatment research, for example, is to think in terms of one treatment for one disorder. Such a viewpoint is greatly assisted by using only a single follow-up assessment of disorder and a single measure of function. If N.E. had started chlorpromazine treatment in the hospital, a single measure of outcome at one-year follow-up might show that she had "not responded." From such a perspective, the complex treatment program shown in Figure 4 might be considered only sloppy (or irrelevant) clinical practice.

If we know, however, that N.E.'s course has had major swings over time, and that her various areas of functioning are at quite different levels, a simple approach to treatment understanding and assessment is seen as likely to provide only the roughest of approximations. It is relatively easy to see, in fact, that several treatments phased in at different times might be beneficial. This does not necessarily mean that practices like polypharmacy are warranted, but only that

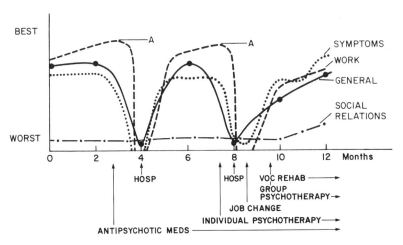

Figure 4 N.E.—treatments and areas of function.

in real treatment situations with real patients, documented by repeated measures of several aspects of functioning, use of medication and various psychosocial approaches at various times may be both common and sound practice. The simpler models of treatment and treatment assessment are ideal for research, but only to the extent they reflect reality. It is often not recognized how much reality such an idealization may sacrifice in order to obtain clarity.

N.E. received several treatments during the course of her disorder. The fact that these were started at various times is easily explained. She started group therapy, for example, after having been in individual psychotherapy because she first refused to be involved in groups and had always been quite isolated and extremely shy and fearful of such situations. After having been in individual psychotherapy, however, she agreed to enter the group (in which her therapist was the leader) and seemed to benefit from the new modality. Following that and certain vocational changes, she began to improve her social relations as reflected by the shifts in that measure at the 12-month-point.

It should also be possible to use an improved understanding of the patterns in the course of disorder to question treatment practices. It seems likely, for example, that anticipating functional "ceilings" is essential, and that treatment during such periods should be highly articulated and focused to meet the patient's particular needs at that time. Many treatment systems, having previously placed an individual in a "program," seem to have an inflexible structure that does not allow increasing the number of sessions, sensitivity to anticipating increased medication needs during such a period, or change in social support systems, all of which might help the person to break through such a barrier. And yet, without such program flexibility and corresponding flexibility of assessment, it seems unlikely that we can do justice at least to this pattern of reality in the recovery process. Thus, more often than not, program inflexibility and an outmoded conceptual base for assessment that uses only one measure or applies it infrequently, may force the recovery process and its complexity into a Procrustean bed and warp the process or even destroy it.

Hypothesis-generating research is necessary to understand the various patterns in the courses of disorders and to establish optimal assessment practices. For considering complex treatment programs, as Leroy Spaniol of Boston University suggests, patient "flow" through treatment modalities and assessment of the modalities themselves may be essential. But even from the data already collected, it seems at the very least that the assessment of treatment efficacy requires an approach based on frequent multidimensional evaluations to give treatment providers and evaluating agencies an adequate approximation of treatment impact on the processes involved in the course of chronic mental illness.

ACKNOWLEDGMENT

This report was supported in part by NIMH Grants MH00340 and MH34365. Figures 1-4 are reprinted by permission of Brunner/Mazel from *Affective and Schizophrenic Disorders: New Approaches to Diagnosis and Treatment*, Michael Zales (ed.), 1983.

REFERENCES

Bleuler, M. 1978. *The Schizophrenic Disorders*. New Haven, CT: Yale University Press.

Breier, A., and Strauss, J. S. in press. Self-control in psychotic disorders. *Arch. Gen. Psychiatry*.

Brockington, I. F., Kendell, R. E., and Leff, J. P. 1978. Definitions of schizophrenia: Concordance and prediction of outcome. *Psychol. Med.* 8: 387-398.

Ciompi, L. 1980. Catamnestic long-term study on the course of life and aging of schizophrenics. *Schizophr. Bull.* 6: 606-618.

Day, R. 1981. Life events and schizophrenia: The "triggering" hypothesis. *Acta Psychiatr. Scand.* 64: 97-122.

Hammer, M. 1981. Social supports, social networks, and schizophrenia. *Schizophr. Bull.* 7: 45-57.

Harding, C. M., and Brooks, G. W. 1980. Longitudinal assessment for a cohort of chronic schizophrenics discharged twenty years ago. *Psychiatric Journal of the University of Ottawa* 5: 274-278.

Leff, J., and Vaughn, C. 1980. The interaction of life events and relatives' expressed emotion in schizophrenia and depressive neurosis. *Br. J. Psychiatry* 136: 146-153.

Phillips, L. 1953. Case history data and prognosis in schizophrenia. *J. Nerv. Ment. Dis.* 117: 515-525.

Schwartz, C. C., Myers, J. K., and Astrachan, B. M. 1975. Concordance of multiple assessments of the outcome of schizophrenia: On defining the dependent variable in outcome studies. *Arch. Gen. Psychiatry* 32: 1221-1227.

Strauss, J. S. 1983. The course of psychiatric disorder: A model for understanding and treatment. Hibbs Award presentation at annual meeting of American Psychiatric Association.

Strauss, J. S., and Carpenter, W. T. Jr. 1972. Prediction of outcome in schizophrenia. I. Characteristics of outcome. *Arch. Gen. Psychiatry* 27: 739-746.

Strauss, J. S., and Carpenter, W. T. Jr. 1974a. Characteristic symptoms and outcome in schizophrenia. *Arch. Gen. Psychiatry* 30: 429-434.

Strauss, J. S., and Carpenter, W. T. Jr. 1974b. Prediction of outcome in schizophrenia. II. Relationships between predictor and outcome variables. *Arch. Gen. Psychiatry* 31: 37-42.

Strauss, J. S., and Hafez, H. 1981. Clinical questions and "real" research. *Am. J. Psychiatry* 138: 1592-1597.

7
Assessment of Client Functioning in Residential Settings

Mark H. Licht

Residential treatment settings for the chronically mentally ill, including mental hospitals, mental health centers, and community residential facilities, provide 24-hour care and treatment. Although this restriction of the clients' freedom allows comprehensive and intensive treatment commensurate with the severity of the clients' disability, it also requires, on both humanitarian and economic grounds, research to increase our understanding of the disorders and our knowledge of effective treatment. Residential treatment requires more complex organization and entails greater risks of abusing the legal and ethical rights of both clients and staff than do outpatient treatment programs. To assure that the multitude of decisions made every day in residential settings for the chronically mentally ill reflect these clinical, managerial, legal/ethical, and scientific considerations, accurate information based on objective and reliable assessment is required. Following the logic and terminology of Mariotto and Paul's (this volume) detailed description of these decisions, the information required to make the decisions, and the criteria for evaluating procedures for obtaining that information (i.e., the "four R's"), this chapter will summarize the assessment approaches typically used to obtain one informational domain, that of client functioning. I shall also describe a new, cost-efficient assessment technology designed to provide replicable and representative information on client functioning relevant to the broad range of decisions required in residential settings for the chronically mentally ill.

TYPICAL METHODS FOR INFORMATION-GATHERING

The three classes of client-functioning variables of importance have been described in this volume by Mariotto and Paul. Assessment of one of these classes of variables, the clients' physical-social life environment, is covered in chapters by Strauss (i.e., the environment outside the residential facility) and by Power (the environment in the residential facility). This chapter will, therefore, deal only with assessment approaches typically used to obtain information on clients' relatively stable personal-social characteristics and problem behaviors.

Relatively Stable Personal-Social Characteristics

Given the relative stability over time and situations of variables in this class, representative information for most decisions can be collected at a single point in time (e.g., demographic and historical variables) or on a periodic but infrequent basis (e.g., opinion, attitude, interest variables, and diagnosis). The information obtained can either be detailed (e.g., hourly wage, number of years of education) or global (e.g., socioeconomic status). Since some decisions require details while others require global information, methods that provide detailed content may be more relevant. Detailed content can then be combined into global units, thus providing information for multiple decisions. In addition, detailed information can typically be collected with greater replicability than can global information, if the detail is not so extreme as to preclude discrimination among separate units of information (Fiske, 1978; Paul et al., in press).

Information on residential clients' relatively stable personal-social characteristics has usually been collected using such unstandardized procedures as unstructured interviews. Various individuals can act as data collectors and as sources of information, gathering the information at any time, anywhere, with any format. Thus, because of their essentially unlimited content coverage, such methods are *potentially* highly relevant and representative. As unstandardized procedures vary on so many dimensions, however, the probability of getting replicable information for any single decision problem, let alone multiple decisions, is extremely low. Thus, these data *actually* have limited relevance and representativeness (Wiggins, 1973). Although relatively inexpensive, the cost of these procedures is really quite high because little of the information is useful.

Assessment procedures that have been standardized for when, what, how, by whom, and from whom data are collected can help assure that replicable and representative information is obtained (Wiggins, 1973). Thus, standardized searches of archival records (Paul and Lentz, 1977; Webb et al., 1981) can provide useful information concerning clients' demographic and historical variables. Information collected with questionnaires, rating scales, and structured interviews (Anthony and Farkas, 1982; Hesselbrock et al., 1982; Luria and Guziec, 1981; Wallace, 1981) can also reveal certain demographic and historical variables among client populations, as well as their attitudes, opinions, interests, and abilities. Recent improvements in the replicability of psychiatric diagnosis have been attributed (Grove et al., 1981) primarily to standardization of how and what data are collected, including: use of more specific and better defined criteria for classification (Endicott et al., 1982; Spitzer et al., 1978); better training of diagnosticians in the use of these criteria (Gibbon et al., 1981); and the use of structured interview techniques for collecting the necessary information, such as the National Institute of Mental Health Diagnostic Interview Schedule (NIMH-DIS;

Robins et al., 1981), the Present State Examination (PSE; Wing et al., 1974), and the Schedule for Affective Disorders and Schizophrenia (SADS; Endicott and Spitzer, 1978). Unfortunately, the level of disability of many chronically mentally ill clients admitted to residential facilities is too great to expect reliable reports of factual information. Assessment procedures with the greatest potential utility for obtaining information on relatively stable personal-social characteristics for this client population consists, therefore, of standardized data sheets and inventories employing archival records and structured interviews with significant others—like staff members or relatives—as information sources.

Problem Behaviors

Clients' problem behaviors constitute the most crucial class of variables in the client domain, because deficits and excesses in functioning determine the clients' continued and recurrent confinement in residential settings (Anthony and Farkas, 1982; Paul, this volume; Strauss and Carpenter, 1981). Information on this class of variables not only allows the making of rational decisions concerning a client's initially identified problems (e.g., placement and disposition, initial treatment plans, and monitoring change in problem areas), but also helps to identify unexpected or undesirable "side effects" of specific psychosocial or biomedical treatments.

Unlike their relatively stable personal-social characteristics, the clients' problem behaviors are less stable over time and situations. In fact, as targets of interventions, problem behaviors are expected to change as a result of treatment. Thus, if this information is to be representative for most decisions made in residential settings, it must be collected on a relatively continuous basis. Assessment methods not amenable to frequent use will fail to provide representative information for most purposes and, thus, fail to be highly relevant. In addition, some decisions require detailed information on an individual's problem behaviors (e.g., problem identification and ongoing monitoring of functioning) while others need information of a more global nature on aggregate groups (e.g., program evaluations). Greater relevance and replicability is most likely to result from procedures that collect detailed information about individuals, later combining these data into global scores for both individual clients and groups.

Traditional methods of assessing clients' problem behaviors include unstructured interviews, staff progress notes, and subjective reports during case review meetings. Like the unstandardized procedures for collecting information on relatively stable personal-social characteristics, these methods do not provide acceptable replicability and representativeness for the decisions to be made in residential settings for the chronically mentally ill. No matter how inexpensive they are in absolute terms, their relative cost is high and their utility low.

Standardized methods that have been employed to assess problem behaviors in residential settings (Paul and Lentz, 1977; Wallace, 1981) have typically included inventories or questionnaires such as the Minnesota Multiphasic Personality Inventory (MMPI; Dahlstrom et al., 1972) or California Psychological Inventory (CPI; Gough, 1975), rating scales like the Nurses Observation Scale for Inpatient Evaluation (NOSIE-30; Honigfeld, 1966) or Brief Psychiatric Rating Scale (BPRS; Overall and Gorham, 1962), and structured interviews like the Inpatient Multidimensional Psychiatric Scale (IMPS; Lorr et al., 1962), PSE (Wing et al., 1973), or SADS (Endicott and Spitzer, 1978). Although these methods provide information potentially useful for decisions involving certain program evaluation and research questions, they also have characteristics that limit their replicability, representativeness, or relevance for measuring client problem behaviors for other decision categories.

With some exceptions, such as the Minimal Social Behavior Scale (MSBS; Farina et al., 1957), most standardized inventories, scales, and interviews obtained directly from clients require levels of functioning beyond that exhibited by chronic patients treated in residential facilities. In addition, most of these methods cannot be employed frequently enough to monitor changes in this relatively unstable class of variables, problem behaviors, without exceptionally high costs. The instruments also fail to provide information detailed enough for many clinical decisions concerning individual clients, which limits their relevance to problems that require multiple decisions. Given the demonstrated and potential susceptibility of these methods to rater biases and to changes over time in raters' criteria (Fiske, 1978; Mariotto and Paul, 1974), their utility might be further limited to decisions that involve relative judgments for a specific group of clients at one time. Thus, these methods have less utility for decisions that require information on absolute level differences, such as comparisons across time and/or client groups. Finally, while these methods produce reasonably replicable information (Gibbon et al., 1981; Mariotto and Paul, 1974), decision makers often fail to determine the degree to which their data are replicable across assessors; thus, they lack the required information for determining the usefulness of the data (Carpenter and Heinrichs, 1981). Among traditional methods, standardized ward rating scales have the greatest potential utility for the chronically mentally ill in residential settings, but their use is limited to program evaluation and research investigations.

Alternative methods with the potential of providing adequate information on certain variables within the class of problem behaviors are standardized event-recording systems and computerized progress notes (Kahn et al., 1981; Redfield, 1979). Although these methods require detailed information to be assessed relatively continuously, their use of clinical treatment staff members as assessors and the need to record all occurrences of specified behaviors limit the number of clients, content, and occasions that can be covered without high costs. The decisions for which these methods can provide representative data are limited; standardized event-recording procedures have their greatest potential utility for ongoing assessment of low-frequency, critical events, like the occurrence of assaults.

Given the accessibility of clients 24 hours a day, seven days a week, and the increasing availability of computer technology, standardized direct observation using independent observers and time-sampling techniques has become a practical method for assessment of clients in residential settings. Direct observational methods can potentially provide cost-efficient, detailed and global data that are both highly replicable across observers and representative for multiple decisions. They are the only approach to assessment that has potential utility for all categories of decision problems for the chronically mentally ill in residential treatment. Several direct observational systems have been used to assess problem behaviors of clients in research projects (Wallace, 1981). To date the most thoroughly developed and evaluated system for obtaining information relevant to the multiple decisions inherent in residential settings for chronic mental patients is the Time-Sample Behavioral Checklist (Licht et al., in press; Power, 1979).

TIME-SAMPLE BEHAVIORAL CHECKLIST (TSBC)

The TSBC uses highly trained technician-level observers who go to the treatment unit in residential settings to observe each client directly—coding the client's behavior during samples of every hour and activity during the entire waking day, seven days a week. Complete coverage of all clients at any time during their residential stay is maintained. As observers record only low-inference, presence/absence judgments, replicability is exceptionally high. Although it may seem to some that "counting behaviors" is a simple-minded approach, the fact is that computer summarization of the óccurrence or nonoccurrence of specific behaviors into higher-level scores produces indexes that account for nearly all of the reliable variance from other assessment procedures. By obtaining both detailed and global scores in this manner, the TSBC provides highly replicable, representative, and relevant information for the multiple decisions to be made in residential settings for chronically mentally ill persons. In addition, both the observers' and the computer-summarized reports provide documentation on both absolute levels and changes in client functioning. The cost-efficiency of the TSBC is enhanced because it frees clinical staff members to spend their time with clients instead of on paperwork. In fact, as a result of the greater efficiency in use of staff time, the TSBC can usually be installed by reallocating existing staff positions rather than adding new positions for observers.

The TSBC was originally developed to assess dependent variables in a long-term comparative treatment study of chronic mental patients in residential settings (Paul and Lentz, 1977). Since then, the feasibility, replicability, and representativeness of the TSBC for widespread implementation has been investigated in multi-institutional studies (Paul, in press; Power, 1979). These efforts have produced evaluative and descriptive/normative TSBC data on more than 1,200 clients representing the complete range of adult treatment programs and populations in public residential facilities. In addition, the TSBC has been incorporated into a computerized Planned Access Information System that combines TSBC, biographical, staff, and program data (see Power, this volume) to provide information for multiple clinical, management, and legal/ethical decisions efficiently and on a continuous, timely basis (Engel and Paul, 1979; Paul, in press).

As part of the Planned Access Information System, a standard format is provided for computer summaries of TSBC information on individuals or groups. Clinical, management, and research staff members are trained to interpret and use the data. Each treatment unit in which the system is installed is equipped with a computer terminal through which individual observations from the previous day are input to a central computer file by clinical staff members while the clients are asleep. The computer summaries then combine the discrete observations for each individual into the standard format for interpretation and documentation. TSBC summaries may be obtained for visual inspection over the terminal's TV tube or as a single sheet of "hard copy," allowing direct entry and documentation in the client's clinical record—thus saving staff time and paper work. Weekly TSBC summary reports are provided regularly for each individual and for each treatment unit (i.e., means and standard deviations over the entire group of clients). Special reports may also be obtained for individuals and subgroups from the continuous data file.

The TSBC summary report format from the Planned Access Information System is presented in Figure 1. The left and middle sections of the TSBC summary, headed INDEX/BEHAVIOR, lists the seven categories and 72 codes employed by observers for each discrete, individual observation. These individual codes cover the incidence of performance of specific appropriate (CONCURRENT ACTIVITIES) and bizarre (CRAZY BEHAVIORS) behaviors, the occurrence or nonoccurrence of both appropriate and inappropriate facial expressions in relationship to apparent stimuli (FACIAL EXPRESSION), and whether the individual's eyes were open or closed at the time of the observation (AWAKE-ASLEEP). Individual codes also reflect whether the individual was alone or with staff, clients, or other people (SOCIAL ORIENTATION), and appropriate and inappropriate physical positions (PHYSICAL POSITION) occurring at the time of observations. Individual codes also indicate the physical location of the individual on each observation, or one of three "control codes" to indicate the reason for the absence of a scheduled observation (LOCATION).

Of course, a single observation has little or no meaning. However, the relative frequency of occurrence or nonoccurrence over multiple observations, or the percentage of time during which each behavior occurs, provides a remarkably thorough picture of an individual's functioning and activities. The three columns of "x.xxx's" in each section of Figure 1 represent numbers provided by the computer program for each TSBC summary. Under the CURNT STATE columns in the left and middle sections, the current status or functioning for the time period

INDEX/BEHAVIOR

POR HOS	CONCURRENT ACTIVITIES:	CURNT STATE	CHANGE FROM ENTRY/L.WK
(AP)	WATCHING OTHERS	X.XXX	X.XXX
(AP)	TALKING TO OTHERS	X.XXX	X.XXX
(AP)	LISTENING TO OTHERS	X.XXX	X.XXX
(AP)	PLAYING A GAME	X.XXX	X.XXX
(AP)	GROUP ACTIVITY	X.XXX	X.XXX
(AW)	READING	X.XXX	X.XXX
(AW)	WRITING	X.XXX	X.XXX
(AW)	HOBBY OR HANDICRAFT	X.XXX	X.XXX
(AW)	HOPKING	X.XXX	X.XXX
(AM)	EATING	X.XXX	X.XXX
(AM)	DRINKING	X.XXX	X.XXX
(AM)	PERSONAL GROOMING	X.XXX	X.XXX
(AE)	SINGING	X.XXX	X.XXX
(AE)	SMOKING	X.XXX	X.XXX
(AE)	LISTENING TO RADIO, PHONO	X.XXX	X.XXX
(AE)	WATCHING TV	X.XXX	X.XXX
(A)	OTHER	X.XXX	X.XXX
	STEREOTYPE(1)/VARIABLE(17)	X.XXX	X.XXX

FACIAL EXPRESSION:

POR HOS		CURNT STATE	CHANGE FROM ENTRY/L.WK
(AP)	SMILING-LAUGHING W/STIM	X.XXX	X.XXX
(AP)	GRIMACING-FROWNING W/STIM	X.XXX	X.XXX
(A)	NEUTRAL NO/STIMULUS	X.XXX	X.XXX
(IS)	NEUTRAL W/STIMULUS	X.XXX	X.XXX
(IC)	SMILING-LAUGHING NO/STIM	X.XXX	X.XXX
(IC)	GRIMACING-FROWNING NO/STIM	X.XXX	X.XXX
	STEREOTYPE(1)/VARIABLE(6)	X.XXX	X.XXX

SOCIAL ORIENTATION:

		CURNT STATE	CHANGE FROM ENTRY/L.WK
(A)	ALONE	X.XXX	X.XXX
(A)	WITH RESIDENTS (PATIENTS)	X.XXX	X.XXX
(A)	WITH STAFF	X.XXX	X.XXX
(A)	WITH OTHERS	X.XXX	X.XXX
	STEREOTYPE(1)/VARIABLE(4)	X.XXX	X.XXX

PHYSICAL POSITION:

		CURNT STATE	CHANGE FROM ENTRY/L.WK
(A)	SITTING	X.XXX	X.XXX
(A)	STANDING	X.XXX	X.XXX
(A)	WALKING	X.XXX	X.XXX
(A)	RUNNING	X.XXX	X.XXX
(A)	DANCING	X.XXX	X.XXX
(IS)	LYING DOWN	X.XXX	X.XXX
	STEREOTYPE(1)/VARIABLE(6)	X.XXX	X.XXX

INDEX/BEHAVIOR

POR HOS	CRAZY BEHAVIORS:	CURNT STATE	CHANGE FROM ENTRY/L.WK
(IS)	ROCKING	X.XXX	X.XXX
(IS)	REPET-STEREOTYPIC MOVEMENT	X.XXX	X.XXX
(IS)	POSTURING	X.XXX	X.XXX
(IS)	SHAKING-TREMORING	X.XXX	X.XXX
(IS)	PACING	X.XXX	X.XXX
(IS)	BLANK STARING	X.XXX	X.XXX
(IC)	CHATTERING-TALKING TO SELF	X.XXX	X.XXX
(IC)	VERB DEL-HALLUC-S.THRT	X.XXX	X.XXX
(IC)	INCOHERENT SPEECH	X.XXX	X.XXX
(IC)	CRYING	X.XXX	X.XXX
(IH)	SCREAMING	X.XXX	X.XXX
(IH)	SWEARING-CURSING	X.XXX	X.XXX
(IH)	VERBAL INTRUSION	X.XXX	X.XXX
(IH)	DESTROYING PROPERTY	X.XXX	X.XXX
(IH)	INJURING SELF	X.XXX	X.XXX
(IH)	PHYSICAL INTRUSION	X.XXX	X.XXX
(I)	OTHER	X.XXX	X.XXX
	STEREOTYPE(1)/VARIABLE(17)	X.XXX	X.XXX

AWAKE-ASLEEP:

		CURNT STATE	CHANGE FROM ENTRY/L.WK
	EYES OPEN	X.XXX	X.XXX
(IS)	EYES CLOSED	X.XXX	X.XXX

LOCATION:

		CURNT STATE	CHANGE FROM ENTRY/L.WK
	CLASSROOM-LOUNGE	X.XXX	X.XXX
	TV ROOM	X.XXX	X.XXX
	CORRIDOR-LOUNGE	X.XXX	X.XXX
	OWN BEDROOM	X.XXX	X.XXX
	OTHER BEDROOM	X.XXX	X.XXX
	ACTIVITY AREA	X.XXX	X.XXX
	LIVING ROOM/DAY ROOM	X.XXX	X.XXX
	OFFICE	X.XXX	X.XXX
	HALLWAY	X.XXX	X.XXX
	DINING AREA	X.XXX	X.XXX
	KITCHEN	X.XXX	X.XXX
	RESTROOM	X.XXX	X.XXX
	BATHING AREA	X.XXX	X.XXX
	LAUNDRY ROOM	X.XXX	X.XXX
	SECLUSION ROOM	X.XXX	X.XXX
(I)	OFF UNIT	X.XXX	X.XXX
	SITTING ROOM	X.XXX	X.XXX
	STEREOTYPE(1)/VARIABLE(20)	X.XXX	X.XXX
(I)	UNAUTH ABS - NO OBSERV	X.XXX	X.XXX
	SICK - NO OBSERVATION	X.XXX	X.XXX
	AUTHORIZED ABS - NO OBSRV	X.XXX	X.XXX

SUMMARY INFORMATION & HIGHER-ORDER SCORES

POR HOS	HIGHER-ORDER SCORES:	CURNT STATE	CHANGE FROM ENTRY/L.WK
(A)	TOTAL APPROPRIATE BEHAVIOR	X.XXX	X.XXX
(AP)	INTERPERSONAL INTERACTION	X.XXX	X.XXX
(AW)	INSTRUMENTAL ACTIVITY	X.XXX	X.XXX
(AM)	SELF MAINTENANCE	X.XXX	X.XXX
(AE)	INDIVIDUAL ENTERTAINMENT	X.XXX	X.XXX
(I)	TOTAL INAPPROPRIATE BEHAV	X.XXX	X.XXX
(IS)	BIZARRE MOTORIC BEHAVIOR	X.XXX	X.XXX
(IC)	BIZARRE FACIAL & VERBALS	X.XXX	X.XXX
(IH)	HOSTILE-BELLIGERENCE	X.XXX	X.XXX
(IX)	ASSAULT FREQUENCY	X.XXX	X.XXX

PROBLEM-ORIENTED RECORDS: BEFORE ENTRY OR REFERENCE, RECORD "T" FOR TEMPORARY PROBS OR PERMANENT PROB NUMBERS IN "POR" COLUMN AND COMPLETE ID BOX BELOW.

THE "HOS" COLUMN REFERS TO CODES THAT ENTER HIGHER-ORDER SCORES. ALL CODES (A-) OR (I-) ENTER "TOTAL" HIGHER-ORDER SCORES. ALL CODES ENTERING (AP) REQUIR A "WITH" SOCIAL ORIENTATION. "PLAYING A GAME" ALONE ENTERS (AE).

TYPE OF SUMMARY:

NUMBER OF PEOPLE SUMMARIZED W/DATA=   TOTAL=
PROPORTION OF OBSERVATIONS WITH DATA =
NUMBER OF OBSERVATIONS WITH DATA... =
NUMBER OF OBSERVATIONS WITHOUT DATA.. =

DATE ADMITTED TO UNIT: /   /
DATES SUMMARIZED:
FACILITY/UNIT:

TSBC ID NUMBER:

RESIDENTS NAME

RESIDENTS ID (DEPT)

FACILITY NAME

UNIT/SUBUNIT   DATE

STAFF SIGNATURE

Figure 1 Format of Time-Sample Behavioral Checklist summary reports from the Planned Access Information System.

of a TSBC summary reflects the proportion of observations or percentage of time during which each coded behavior occurred, ranging from 0.000 to 1.000. For a weekly TSBC summary, current status is typically based on 50 to 100 discrete observations for each individual. Thus, each current state score reflects an absolute level of functioning or activity. For example, a SOCIAL ORIENTATION–alone score of 0.500 indicates that the individual was alone half of the time, or for a group summary, that the average individual was alone half of the time. The last two columns of "x.xxx's" on the TSBC summary provide change scores for on-going monitoring of the detailed changes in individuals or groups. The CHANGE FROM ENTRY column indicates the absolute change in current status from the first week upon entry into the treatment unit, while the CHANGE FROM L.WK column indicates the absolute change in current status from the last week before the time period of the TSBC summary. In addition to the detailed individual codes shown in Figure 1, the left and middle sections of the TSBC summary also include "stereotype(1)/variable(x)" scores for all categories except AWAKE-ASLEEP. These scores reflect the extent to which functioning within a category was limited to a small number of codes or behaviors (i.e., was stereotypical) or ranged across many codes or behaviors (i.e., was variable).

While the left and middle sections of the TSBC summary shown in Figure 1 provide detailed information on discrete codes, the right column includes more global higher-order scores and identifying information necessary for interpretation or documentation. These higher-order scores are parallel to the more global scores that are typically derived from standardized rating scales and structured interviews. However, the TSBC higher-order scores are derived by summing the occurrence of the individual codes over the desired time period. Because the computer file contains continuous data, the higher-order scores can be obtained for any time period desired. Also, the components of the more global scores may be readily identified by the entries in the HOS column of the TSBC summary. Thus, the most global scores shown in the upper right section of the TSBC summary are Total Appropriate Behavior and Total Inappropriate Behavior. Below these total scores are lower-level, or component, appropriate and inappropriate higher-order scores. All lower-level higher-order scores and all discrete codes with an A in the HOS column enter the Total Appropriate Behavior score. Similarly, all lower-level higher-order scores and all discrete codes with an I in the HOS column enter the Total Inappropriate Behavior score. All discrete codes with an AP in the HOS column enter the higher-order score for Interpersonal Interaction, reflecting appropriate social function. In a parallel fashion, the discrete codes entering any of the other lower-level higher-order scores may be retrieved by matching the identifiers in the HOS column. Assault Frequency, obtained through event reporting by clinical staff is also included on the TSBC summary because of the critical importance of this behavior. The remaining columns on the TSBC summary format shown in Figure 1 are those headed POR. These blanks in the POR column are provided for easy integration of the TSBC summary sheet into

Problem-Oriented Records, allowing direct identification and monitoring of progress of target problems and assets.

Replicability and Representativeness of TSBC Data

Information on the quality of TSBC data that is based on several years of data collection is currently available elsewhere (Engel and Paul, 1979; Mariotto, 1979; Paul, 1981; Paul and Lentz, 1977; Power, 1979), with more detailed analyses and presentations to be available in the near future (Paul, in press). Based on available findings, however, it is quite clear that the information obtained from the TSBC is exceptionally trustworthy at both detailed and global levels (e.g., median interobserver reliability of $r = .94$ for individual codes and .97 for higher-order scores). Because of the unpredictable and frequent presence of trained observers, neither clients nor staff members have shown reactive effects of being observed, and the observers have been free of drift and bias caused either by familiarity with clients or the typicality of their behavior.

In addition to being replicable, individual TSBC codes and higher-order scores have been demonstrated to be sensitive to change over time with specified interventions (e.g., based upon a one-week sample, the range of some discrete codes has reflected individual performances from none to 91.7 percent of the time) and able to discriminate among individuals and groups (e.g., among groups with acute-chronic length of hospitalization, good-bad premorbid functioning, various diagnoses). The higher-order scores from the TSBC have also shown exceptional convergent and discriminant validity in both concurrent and predictive studies (e.g., correlations in expected directions ranging from mid-.40s to mid-.80s with event recordings, structured interviews, and standardized ward rating scales—accounting for nearly all of the reliable variance in scores from these scales). Of even greater significance, the TSBC has demonstrated its utility for predicting clients' successful release from residential treatment programs (point biserial $r = .68$ between release and TSBC level of functioning) and for predicting clients' level of functioning in the community after release (rs in the .60s and .70s between ratings of functioning in the community up to 18 months after discharge and TSBC higher-order scores during the week preceding release). Further, cutoff scores have been identified from TSBC normative data to aid in decisions concerning the nature and level of functioning that predict a client's successful discharge to independent functioning and to community placement.

A Sample of the Relevance of TSBC Results

TSBC Standard Weekly Reports (Figure 1) contain information based on all TSBC observations during the immediately preceding week summarized across all times of day and activities. They are provided for each individual and for each ward or treatment unit. By comparing the individual client's current status scores to the normative guidelines, both the detailed and global information required for placement and disposition decisions and for identification of problems and assets is provided, as well as documentation for entry into the individual's clinical record. The change scores provide ongoing monitoring of the client's response to treatment interventions in targeted areas, as well as unexpected side effects in other areas of functioning. This monitoring function is provided for long-term change, through CHANGE FROM ENTRY data, and immediate response, through CHANGE FROM L.WK data. Comparisons of an individual client's functioning to discharge norms provide the legal documentation that treatment could not reasonably be carried out in a less restrictive setting or, conversely, that the client should be considered for discharge or community placement. Similarly, right to receive or refuse treatment issues are addressed by objective data on client improvement or deterioration while receiving or refusing specific interventions. Particularly with the chronically mentally ill who show broad areas of deficits or many excesses in inappropriate behavior, being able to "cut through the forest to see specific trees" is especially helpful in targeting discrete areas for change.

The wardwide standard weekly reports provide the detailed and global information on aggregate groups needed for all categories of decisions. Program evaluation by a unit director is, for example, easily maintained by examination of the higher-order change scores—which reflect whether the unit as a whole is improving, worsening, or staying the same. Comparisons of unit weekly reports between different units allow immediate determination of the absolute levels of functioning of different groups and of the comparative effectiveness on both short- and long-time frames. If differences are shown on higher-order scores, the source of that difference may be examined with the discrete codes. Standard weekly reports on full treatment units allow ongoing treatment to become applied research through appropriate timing of changes in drug regimens, psychosocial programs, specific staff responsibilities, or other structural characteristics. Thus, the standard weekly reports provide precise, detailed, and timely information on the clients' functioning relevant to multiple decision problems in residential settings, concurrent with reducing treatment staff members' paperwork and providing documentation.

Special reports allow a search of the continuous data base to provide TSBC summaries to answer questions of a more precise nature for all categories of decision problems. Assistance in more precise individual problem identification or functional analyses can, for example, be obtained by identifying times, situations, or activities in which a client's particular assets or deficits were observed. Change over different time periods in relationship to specific interventions can greatly assist in individual monitoring. Legal and ethical protection can be obtained in unique circumstances as, for example, in documenting the whereabouts of clients and their activities at any given hour. Special reports can also be obtained on client groups or subgroups to assist with a variety of clinical and management decisions. Differences in functioning of the client population can be examined over different staff shifts, activities, weekends vs. weekdays, or in different locations. Special searches for information on client subgroups can be done on the basis of client characteristics (e.g., sex or legal status), receipt of particular treatments (e.g., specific drugs), or specific staff or treatment team assignments. Over time, special searches of successful and unsuccessful discharges to particular geographic areas or community facilities would help a residential facility to establish local norms to provide more precise guidance for discharge and placement decisions than that already provided by the large normative sample. Although special reports appear in the same format as standard weekly reports, they allow the gathering of even more specific information for all categories of decision problems.

The Planned Access Information System also incorporates TSBC higher-order scores into a series of reports specifically designed for managerial-level decision problems (Engel and Paul, 1979). These quality assurance reports can be provided on a periodic basis (e.g., monthly, quarterly, or annually) or for any time or client group requested. They provide information on aggregate groups of clients within specific functional units (e.g., treatment teams, wards, entire facilities). In fact, information on each of two identified functional units can be presented side-by-side on the same report form for comparative program evaluations. The Planned Access Information System provides three types of quality assurance reports, the first of which is based on client TSBC data.

The format of Quality Assurance Summary No. 1 is presented in Figure 2. This summary report provides information on the global adaptive and maladaptive functioning from the TSBC Total Appropriate, Total Inappropriate, and Assault Frequency data aggregated over clients by movement categories in the functional program units requested (depicted as P-1 and P-2). The information allows evaluation of clients' levels of functioning at entry to each functional unit (labeled PROGRAM ENTRY), at the point in time specified for the beginning of the report (e.g., the beginning of a fiscal year or at the introduction of a new treatment program—labeled START OF PERIOD), and at a later point in time specified for the end of the report (e.g., the end of a fiscal year or two months after the introduction of a new treatment program—labeled END/TERMINATION). In addition, the average length of stay, the change in levels of adaptive and maladaptive functioning, and the percentage of clients improving and becoming worse (both from PROGRAM ENTRY and START OF PERIOD to END/TERMINATION) are provided for evaluation of program effectiveness.

As Figure 2 shows, the information on client functioning and change is presented for the entire group of clients treated within the time period requested for the specified functional units (TOTAL SERVED column) and also for 10 subgroups of clients based on categories of client movement and outcome during that period. The specified functional units (P-1 and P-2) could also be different

FACILITY/UNIT/PROGRAM SUMMARIZED:
P−1=
P−2=

PRODUCTION DATE:
PERIOD SUMMARIZED—START:
END:

QUALITY ASSURANCE SUMMARY NO. 1
TSBC GLOBAL FUNCTIONING & OUTCOME BY CLIENT MOVEMENT

Client Data		Total Served P-1	P-2	Start Perid Continues P-1	P-2	In Period Additions P-1	P-2	End Period Continues P-1	P-2	Dschrg Suc (Days -30) P-1	P-2	Dschrg Fail W/I 30 Days P-1	P-2	Dschrgd to Indep Liv P-1	P-2	Dschrgd by ama/awol/ct P-1	P-2	Dschrgd to Com Plc P-1	P-2	Transferred (Dept/Othr) P-1	P-2	Death P-1	P-2
CLIENTS TOT NUMBR		xxx	xxx	xxx	xxx	xxx	xxx	xxx	xxx	xxx	xxx	xxx	xxx	xxx	xxx	xxx	xxx	xxx	xxx	xxx	xxx	xxx	xxx
% OF TOTAL		xxx.x	xxx.x	xxx.x	xxx.x	xxx.x	xxx.x	xxx.x	xxx.x	xxx.x	xxx.x	xxx.x	xxx.x	xxx.x	xxx.x	xxx.x	xxx.x	xxx.x	xxx.x	xxx.x	xxx.x	xxx.x	xxx.x
ADAPTIVE FUNCTION																							
PROGRAM ENTRY	M	x.xx	x.xx	x.xx	x.xx	x.xx	x.xx	x.xx	x.xx	x.xx	x.xx	x.xx	x.xx	x.xx	x.xx	x.xx	x.xx	x.xx	x.xx	x.xx	x.xx	x.xx	x.xx
	SD	x.xx	x.xx	x.xx	x.xx	x.xx	x.xx	x.xx	x.xx	x.xx	x.xx	x.xx	x.xx	x.xx	x.xx	x.xx	x.xx	x.xx	x.xx	x.xx	x.xx	x.xx	x.xx
START OF PERIOD	M	x.xx	x.xx	x.xx	x.xx	x.xx	x.xx	x.xx	x.xx	x.xx	x.xx	x.xx	x.xx	x.xx	x.xx	x.xx	x.xx	x.xx	x.xx	x.xx	x.xx	x.xx	x.xx
	SD	x.xx	x.xx	x.xx	x.xx	x.xx	x.xx	x.xx	x.xx	x.xx	x.xx	x.xx	x.xx	x.xx	x.xx	x.xx	x.xx	x.xx	x.xx	x.xx	x.xx	x.xx	x.xx
END/TERMINATION	M	x.xx	x.xx	x.xx	x.xx	x.xx	x.xx	x.xx	x.xx	x.xx	x.xx	x.xx	x.xx	x.xx	x.xx	x.xx	x.xx	x.xx	x.xx	x.xx	x.xx	x.xx	x.xx
	SD	x.xx	x.xx	x.xx	x.xx	x.xx	x.xx	x.xx	x.xx	x.xx	x.xx	x.xx	x.xx	x.xx	x.xx	x.xx	x.xx	x.xx	x.xx	x.xx	x.xx	x.xx	x.xx
MALADPTIVE FUNCTION																							
PROGRAM ENTRY	M	x.xx	x.xx	x.xx	x.xx	x.xx	x.xx	x.xx	x.xx	x.xx	x.xx	x.xx	x.xx	x.xx	x.xx	x.xx	x.xx	x.xx	x.xx	x.xx	x.xx	x.xx	x.xx
	SD	x.xx	x.xx	x.xx	x.xx	x.xx	x.xx	x.xx	x.xx	x.xx	x.xx	x.xx	x.xx	x.xx	x.xx	x.xx	x.xx	x.xx	x.xx	x.xx	x.xx	x.xx	x.xx
START OF PERIOD	M	x.xx	x.xx	x.xx	x.xx	x.xx	x.xx	x.xx	x.xx	x.xx	x.xx	x.xx	x.xx	x.xx	x.xx	x.xx	x.xx	x.xx	x.xx	x.xx	x.xx	x.xx	x.xx
	SD	x.xx	x.xx	x.xx	x.xx	x.xx	x.xx	x.xx	x.xx	x.xx	x.xx	x.xx	x.xx	x.xx	x.xx	x.xx	x.xx	x.xx	x.xx	x.xx	x.xx	x.xx	x.xx
END/TERMINATION	M	x.xx	x.xx	x.xx	x.xx	x.xx	x.xx	x.xx	x.xx	x.xx	x.xx	x.xx	x.xx	x.xx	x.xx	x.xx	x.xx	x.xx	x.xx	x.xx	x.xx	x.xx	x.xx
	SD	x.xx	x.xx	x.xx	x.xx	x.xx	x.xx	x.xx	x.xx	x.xx	x.xx	x.xx	x.xx	x.xx	x.xx	x.xx	x.xx	x.xx	x.xx	x.xx	x.xx	x.xx	x.xx
PER CENT ASSAULTIVE																							
PROGRAM ENTRY	%	xx.x	xx.x	xx.x	xx.x	xx.x	xx.x	xx.x	xx.x	xx.x	xx.x	xx.x	xx.x	xx.x	xx.x	xx.x	xx.x	xx.x	xx.x	xx.x	xx.x	xx.x	x.xx
START OF PERIOD	%	xx.x	xx.x	xx.x	xx.x	xx.x	xx.x	xx.x	xx.x	xx.x	xx.x	xx.x	xx.x	xx.x	xx.x	xx.x	xx.x	xx.x	xx.x	xx.x	xx.x	xx.x	x.xx
END/TERMINATION	%	x.x	x.x	xx.x	xx.x	xx.x	xx.x	xx.x	xx.x	xx.x	xx.x	xx.x	xx.x	xx.x	xx.x	xx.x	xx.x	xx.x	xx.x	xx.x	xx.x	xx.x	x.xx
FROM PROGRAM ENTRY																							
LENGTH OF STAY (IN DAYS)	M	xxx	xxx	xxx	xxx	xxx	xxx	xxx	xxx	xxx	xxx	xxx	xxx	xxx	xxx	xxx	xxx	xxx	xxx	xxx	xxx	xxx	xxx
	SD	xxx.x	xxx.x	xxx.x	xxx.x	xxx.x	xxx.x	xxx.x	xxx.x	xxx.x	xxx.x	xxx.x	xxx.x	xxx.x	xxx.x	xxx.x	xxx.x	xxx.x	xxx.x	xxx.x	xxx.x	xxx.x	xxx.x
ADAPTIVE FUNCTION LEVEL CHANGE IMPROVED	%	xx.x	xx.x	xx.x	xx.x	xx.x	xx.x	xx.x	xx.x	xx.x	xx.x	xx.x	xx.x	xx.x	xx.x	xx.x	xx.x	xx.x	xx.x	xx.x	xx.x	xx.x	x.xx
WORSE	%	xx.x	xx.x	xx.x	xx.x	xx.x	xx.x	xx.x	xx.x	xx.x	xx.x	xx.x	xx.x	xx.x	xx.x	xx.x	xx.x	xx.x	xx.x	xx.x	xx.x	xx.x	x.xx
MALADPTIVE FUNCTN LEVEL CHANGE IMPROVED	%	xx.x	xx.x	xx.x	xx.x	xx.x	xx.x	xx.x	xx.x	xx.x	xx.x	xx.x	xx.x	xx.x	xx.x	xx.x	xx.x	xx.x	xx.x	xx.x	xx.x	xx.x	x.xx
WORSE	%	xx.x	xx.x	xx.x	xx.x	xx.x	xx.x	xx.x	xx.x	xx.x	xx.x	xx.x	xx.x	xx.x	xx.x	xx.x	xx.x	xx.x	xx.x	xx.x	xx.x	xx.x	x.xx
TOTAL FUNCTION IMPROVED	%	xx.x	xx.x	xx.x	xx.x	xx.x	xx.x	xx.x	xx.x	xx.x	xx.x	xx.x	xx.x	xx.x	xx.x	xx.x	xx.x	xx.x	xx.x	xx.x	xx.x	xx.x	x.xx
WORSE	%	xx.x	xx.x	xx.x	xx.x	xx.x	xx.x	xx.x	xx.x	xx.x	xx.x	xx.x	xx.x	xx.x	xx.x	xx.x	xx.x	xx.x	xx.x	xx.x	xx.x	xx.x	x.xx
FROM START OF PERIOD																							
LENGTH OF STAY (IN DAYS)	M	xx.x	xx.x	xxx	xxx	xxx	xxx	xxx	xxx	xxx	xxx	xxx	xxx	xxx	xxx	xxx	xxx	xxx	xxx	xxx	xxx	xxx	xxx
	SD	xxx.x	xxx.x	xxx.x	xxx.x	xxx.x	xxx.x	xxx.x	xxx.x	xxx.x	xxx.x	xxx.x	xxx.x	xxx.x	xxx.x	xxx.x	xxx.x	xxx.x	xxx.x	xxx.x	xxx.x	xxx.x	xxx.x
ADAPTIVE FUNCTION LEVEL CHANGE IMPROVED	%	x.xx	x.xx	x.xx	x.xx	xx.x	xx.x	xx.x	xx.x	xx.x	xx.x	x.xx	x.xx	x.xx	x.xx	x.xx	x.xx	x.xx	x.xx	x.xx	x.xx	x.xx	x.xx
WORSE	%	xx.x	xx.x	xx.x	xx.x	xx.x	xx.x	xx.x	xx.x	xx.x	xx.x	xx.x	xx.x	xx.x	xx.x	xx.x	xx.x	xx.x	xx.x	xx.x	xx.x	xx.x	xx.x
MALADPTIVE FUNCTN LEVEL CHANGE IMPROVED	%	x.xx	x.xx	x.xx	x.xx	x.xx	x.xx	x.xx	x.xx	x.xx	x.xx	x.xx	x.xx	x.xx	x.xx	x.xx	x.xx	x.xx	x.xx	x.xx	x.xx	x.xx	x.xx
WORSE	%	xx.x	xx.x	xx.x	xx.x	xx.x	xx.x	xx.x	xx.x	xx.x	xx.x	xx.x	xx.x	xx.x	xx.x	xx.x	xx.x	xx.x	xx.x	xx.x	xx.x	xx.x	xx.x
TOTAL FUNCTION IMPROVED	%	xx.x	xx.x	xx.x	xx.x	xx.x	xx.x	xx.x	xx.x	xx.x	xx.x	xx.x	xx.x	xx.x	xx.x	xx.x	xx.x	xx.x	xx.x	xx.x	xx.x	xx.x	xx.x
WORSE	%	xx.x	xx.x	xx.x	xx.x	xx.x	xx.x	xx.x	xx.x	xx.x	xx.x	xx.x	xx.x	xx.x	xx.x	xx.x	xx.x	xx.x	xx.x	xx.x	xx.x	xx.x	xx.x

PRODUCED BY STATE OF ILLINOIS DEPT OF MENTAL HEALTH & DEVELOPMENTAL DISABILITIES, DIVISION OF INFORMATION SERVICES

Figure 2. Format of Quality Assurance Summary No. 1 from the Planned Access Information System. Source: State of Illinois De-time periods for the same treatment unit, allowing evaluation of changes in populations or effectiveness at different times. Thus, based on Quality Assurance Summary No. 1, administrators, program evaluators, and researchers can examine absolute levels of adaptive and maladaptive functioning, including changes in functioning of clients entering, leaving, and experiencing various outcomes within identified treatment programs during any specified period of time. The other two quality assurance reports provide information on relatively stable personal-social characteristics of clients within the same categories of client movement and outcome as Report No. 1, and information on staff characteristics and treatment procedures, for the same functional units and time periods. Thus, after identifying the nature of clients served and the effectiveness of programs from Report No. 1, Reports 2 and 3 provide the information needed for generating hypotheses about differential effectiveness and for determining the cost-effectiveness of programs. The utility of such objective, standardized information is obvious for decisions concerning initial client placements, staff utilization, program evaluation, legal-ethical-accreditation documentation, and specific research questions (Engel and Paul, 1979; Paul, in press).

In summary, the TSBC provides science-based, cost-effective data that are relevant to a wider range of decision problems in residential treatment settings for the chronically mentally ill than any other system for assessing client functioning of which I am aware. The representativeness of the TSBC for these diverse purposes depends on its high level of interobserver reliability. This exceptional replicability is the result of recording procedures that require only presence/absence judgments of low-inference, discrete behavioral codes and of comprehensive observer training procedures (Fiske, 1979). Systematic observer training procedures have been developed and evaluated (Power et al., 1982) to help assure that, with wider implementation, data collected by all users of the TSBC are highly reliable both within and across residential facilities. Thus, information collected at different sites and at different times can be directly comparable, allowing greater generality and equity in the rational management of residential facilities and greater clarification and confirmation of findings from different research groups, to the ultimate benefit of the chronically mentally ill.

CONCLUSION

A necessary requirement, if decisions are to responsibly reflect the clinical, managerial, legal/ethical, and research considerations inherent in residential treatment of the chronically mentally ill, is representative, replicable, relevant, and cost-efficient assessment of client functioning. The use of standardized structured interviews and rating scales for assessing clients' relatively stable personal-social characteristics and direct observational systems for assessing client assets and problem behaviors can now fulfill this requirement. Incorporation of assessment procedures of known quality, such as the Time-Sample Behavioral Checklist, into computerized information systems allows even greater relevance and lower relative cost in providing necessary information. Improvement in treatment of chronically mentally ill persons confined to residential settings depends, to a great extent, on the application of these types of technical and methodological advancements in assessment.

REFERENCES

Anthony, W. A., and Farkas, M. 1982. A client outcome planning model for assessing psychiatric rehabilitation interventions. *Schizophr. Bull.* 8:13-38.

Carpenter, W. T., and Heinrichs, D. W. 1981. Methodological standards for treatment outcome research in schizophrenia. *Am. J. Psychiatry* 138:465-471.

Dahlstrom, W. G., Welsh, G. S., and Dahlstrom, L. E. 1972. *An MMPI Handbook, vol. 1. Clinical Interpretation* (rev. Ed.). Minneapolis: University of Minnesota Press.

Endicott, J., Nee, J., Fleiss, J., Cohen, J., Williams, J. B. W., and Simon, R. 1982. Diagnostic criteria for schizophrenia. *Arch. Gen. Psychiatry* 39:884-889.

Endicott, J., and Spitzer, R. L. 1978. A diagnostic interview: The Schedule for Affective Disorders and Schizophrenia. *Arch. Gen. Psychiatry* 35:837-844.

Engel, K. L., and Paul, G. L. 1979. Systems use to objectify program evaluation, clinical and management decisions. *J. Behav. Assess.* 1:221-238.

Farina, A., Arenberg, D., and Guskin, S. 1957. A scale for measuring minimal social behavior. *J. Consult. Psychol.* 21:265-268.

Fiske, D. W. 1978. *Strategies for Personality Research.* San Francisco: Jossey-Bass.

Fiske, D. W. 1979. A demonstration of the value of interchangeable observers. *J. Behav. Assess.* 1:251-258.

Gibbon, M., McDonald-Scott, P., and Endicott, J. 1981. Mastering the art of research interviewing. *Arch. Gen. Psychiatry* 38:1259-1262.

Gough, H. S. 1975. *California Psychological Inventory: Manual.* Palo Alto, CA: Consulting Psychologists Press.

Grove, W. M., Andreasen, N. C., McDonald-Scott, P., Keller, M. B., and Shapiro, R. W. 1981. Reliability studies of psychiatric diagnosis. *Arch. Gen. Psychiatry* 38:408-413.

Hesselbrock, V., Stabenau, J., Hesselbrock, M., Mirkin, P., and Meyer, R. 1982. A comparison of two interview schedules. *Arch. Gen. Psychiatry* 39:674-677.

Honigfeld, G. 1966. Nurses observation scale for inpatient evaluation (NOSIE-30). Glen Oaks: Honigfeld.

Kahn, E. M., Ramm, D., and Gianturco, D. T. 1981. TOCRS—the therapy-oriented computer record system. *Behavior Research Methods & Instrumentation* 13:479-484.

Licht, M. H., Power, C. T., and Paul, G. L. in press. Standardized observational systems in service and research. In G. L. Paul (ed.), *Observational Assessment Instrumentation for Institutional Research and Treatment.* Cambridge, MA: Harvard University Press.

Lorr, M., Klett, C. J., McNair, D. M., and Lasky, 1962. Inpatient Multidimensional Psychiatric Scale (IMPS) Manual. Veterans Administration.

Luria, R. E., and Guziec, R. J. 1981. Comparative description of the SADS and PSE. *Schizophr. Bull.* 7:248-257.

Mariotto, M. J. 1979. Observational assessment systems use for basic and applied research. *J. Behav. Assess.* 1:239-250.

Mariotto, M. J., and Paul, G. L. 1974. A multimethod validation of the Inpatient Multidimensional Psychiatric Scale with chronically institutionalized patients. *J. Consult. Clin. Psychol.* 42:495-508.

Overall, J. E., and Gorham, D. R. 1962. The Brief Psychiatric Rating Scale. *Psychol. Rep.* 10:799-812.

Paul, G. L. 1981. Social competence and the institutionalized mental patient. In J. D. Wine and M. D. Smye (eds.), *Social Competence*, pp. 232-257. New York: Guilford Press.

Paul, G. L. (ed.) in press. *Observational Assessment Instrumentation for Institutional Research and Treatment*. Cambridge, MA: Harvard University Press.

Paul, G. L., and Lentz, R. J. 1977. *Psychosocial Treatment of Chronic Mental Patients: Milieu versus Social-Learning Programs*. Cambridge, MA: Harvard University Press.

Paul, G. L., Mariotto, M. J., and Redfield, J. P. in press. The potential utility of different sources and methods of formal assessment. In G. L. Paul (ed.), *Observational Assessment Instrumentation for Institutional Research and Treatment*. Cambridge, MA: Harvard University Press.

Power, C. T. 1979. The Time-Sample Behavioral Checklist: Observational assessment of patient functioning. *J. Behav. Assess.* 1:199-210.

Power, C. T., Paul, G. L., Licht, M. H., and Engel, K. L. 1982. Evaluation of self-contained training procedures for the Time-Sample Behavioral Checklist. *J. Behav. Assess.* 4:223-261.

Redfield, J. 1979. Clinical Frequencies Recording Systems: Standardizing staff observations by event recording. *J. Behav. Assess.* 1:211-219.

Robins, L. N., Helzer, J. E., Croughan, J., and Ratcliff, K. S. 1981. National Institute of Mental Health Diagnostic Interview Schedule: Its history, characteristics, and validity. *Arch. Gen. Psychiatry* 38:381-389.

Spitzer, R. L., Endicott, J., and Robins, E. 1978. Research diagnostic criteria: Rationale and reliability. *Arch. Gen. Psychiatry* 35:773-782.

Strauss, J. S., and Carpenter, W. T. 1981. *Schizophrenia*. New York: Plenum.

Wallace, C. J. 1981. Assessment of psychotic behavior. In M. Hersen and A. S. Bellack (eds.), *Behavioral Assessment: A Practical Handbook*, pp. 328-388. New York: Pergamon Press.

Webb, E. J., Campbell, D. T., Schwartz, R. D., Sechrest, L., and Grove, J. B. 1981. *Nonreactive Measures in the Social Sciences*. Boston: Houghton Mifflin.

Wiggins, J. S. 1973. *Personality and Prediction: Principles of Personality Assessment*. Reading, MA: Addison-Wesley.

Wing, J. K., Cooper, J. E., and Sartorius, N. 1974. *Present State Examination*. London: Cambridge University Press.

8
Assessment of Staff and Programs in Residential Treatment Settings

CHRISTOPHER T. POWER

Of the chronically mentally ill, the most severely debilitated are found in residential treatment settings, in privately operated community extended-care facilities, and publicly supported mental institutions. Because of the seriousness of their problems, these patients receive the most expensive and restrictive form of mental health treatment, typically because less drastic and less comprehensive treatment interventions failed to produce and sustain beneficial effects. As residential treatment is frequently the treatment of last resort for these patients, information on factors that influence treatment outcome is exceptionally important. This is true not only for research purposes, but also for clinical and management decisions if the most effective and cost-efficient treatment procedures are to be discovered and maintained.

Mariotto and Paul (this volume) outlined the range of decisions confronted in mental health services and research and the information required as a rational basis for these decisions. Mariotto and Paul further categorized these informational needs into three domains—client, staff, and time—and provided guides for evaluating the relative utility of methods and instruments for obtaining information. This chapter will focus on the three classes of variables within the staff domain that influence treatment outcome in residential facilities, variables that reflect the treatment environment, the characteristics of the treatment staff, and the treatment itself. Methods for assessing these classes of variables in residential treatment settings will be surveyed briefly, followed by a description of an assessment instrument developed to meet some of the most important needs of residential treatment.

ASSESSMENT APPROACHES TO STAFF DOMAIN VARIABLES

The essence of any decision-making process is the comparison of alternative choices or courses of action. To make such comparisons, comparable information

109

on each alternative is essential as a rational basis for decision-making. Otherwise, decision-making becomes, at best, merely a choice between known aspects of one alternative and unknown aspects of others or, at worst, a choice among unknowns. For this reason, standardized methods of information-gathering that increase the replicability of information and, thus, its comparability, have significant advantages over information-gathering procedures that have not been standardized (Wiggins, 1973).

The Treatment Environment

Standardized approaches to assessing the physical and social treatment environment include the administration of questionnaires, rating scales, and structured interviews to the staff or patients of the facility as well as systematic completion of standardized data sheets through planned examination of facility records or first-hand inspection of the facility. What information is sought and for what purposes should influence the assessment method, assessors, and respondents selected. Some of the work by Robert Ellsworth and his colleagues (1979), intended to identify the distinguishing characteristics of effective psychiatric programs, illustrates the use of multiple sources and methods to obtain information about treatment environments. In this study, in addition to direct inspection of the facility and examination of facility records on the environment of each treatment unit, staff members were interviewed and both staff and patients were asked to complete standardized questionnaires, including the Perception of Ward Scale (Ellsworth et al., 1976) and the Ward Atmosphere Scale (Moos, 1974). A variety of such scales is available (Magnusson, 1981), and similar approaches to assessing treatment environment have been taken in other studies (Lawton and Cohen, 1975). More specialized assessment methods, such as the control graph method Holland et al. (1981) used in their study of the relationship between institutional structure and treatment outcome, may also be necessary for some specific research purposes.

But beyond these special research needs, most of the detailed or global information on the treatment environment necessary for research and service decisions is obtained satisfactorily by a single assessment approach. Although some of the intangible features of the treatment environment, such as reputation, perceived purpose, and degree of support, may require more frequent and alternative assessments for particular information needs, standardized data sheets may provide most or all of the necessary information on treatment environment in a cost-effective manner. As many of the variables descriptive of the treatment environment are easily depicted in nontechnical language, these may be readily listed on data sheets; many aspects of the treatment environment are fixed (e.g., architecture, location) or stable (e.g., available facilities and services), so that assessment done once or infrequently may still provide current, relevant information. Even aspects of the treatment environment likely to require more frequent assessment to provide timely information (e.g., staffing levels) may be recorded and monitored on standardized data sheets with minimal cost or investment of time. With variables descriptive of the treatment environment being so stable, readily apparent, and easy to confirm, replicable information can be obtained on standardized data sheets by facility staff members or outsiders with little investment in their training. Finally, depending on the purposes for which information is sought, items on the data sheet can be selected to ensure representativeness and relevance.

Staff Characteristics

Standardized data sheets are similarly applicable to the second class of variables in the staff domain, the personal and social characteristics of the staff providing treatment. Here again, standardized data sheets, completed either by the staff or by other individuals searching archival records or interviewing staff members, will provide replicable, representative, and relevant information in a cost-effective manner on such staff characteristics as age, gender, race, education, skills, and experience. There are, however, variables in this class—staff morale, attitudes, opinions, and theoretical orientations—that require more frequent and alternative assessment approaches because they are more abstract and more likely to change over time. Questionnaires and rating scales such as the Opinions About Mental Illness scale (Cohen and Struening, 1962), the Job Descriptive Index for job satisfaction (Smith et al., 1969) or the attitude section of the Therapist Orientation Sheet (Paul and Lentz, 1977) have been used to assess such variables. Many studies have examined the relationships between scores on such instruments and various process and outcome characteristics of residential treatment (Lawton and Cohen, 1975). For most research and service purposes, prudent selection of a few scales or questionnaires administered periodically to staff members (e.g., at initial hiring and at 6- to 12-month intervals) would provide information of sufficient representativeness, relevance, and replicability to supplement information obtained on standardized staff biographical data sheets.

Treatment Interventions

Since the primary purpose of residential facilities and staff is treating the mentally disabled, assessment of the third class of variables in the staff domain, therapeutic techniques and interventions, is especially important. Information on these treatment variables is relevant to *all* mental health service decisions discussed by Mariotto and Paul (this volume). Unfortunately, though this is the most important class of variables to be assessed, obtaining useful information on treatment is more difficult than for the other two classes of staff domain variables because of the number and nature of important treatment variables to be considered. Treatment variables are less stable and, in fact, should be changed according to patients' response to treatment. As a result, treatment must be assessed often or continually to provide current information. But in addition to monitoring changes in the administration of such somatic treatments as psychotropic medications, the nature of intended and unintended psychosocial "treatments" patients receive must also be monitored. This is especially important in residential settings, which are distinguished by the intensity and comprehensiveness of the treatment they offer. Patients in residential treatment settings are subject to the influence of the actions and behaviors of staff up to 24 hours a day, regardless of whether such activities are planned as part of a psychosocial intervention or unplanned. Because of this, the actions and behavior of residential treatment staff are powerful variables that have often been ignored (Robinson, 1978), despite their potential for influencing the outcome of any treatment, pharmacological or psychosocial.

Standardized data sheets based on inspection of facility records or interviews with staff members can, at best, provide only global information on the treatment intended or perceived to be dispensed, rather than that actually received by patients. Insufficiently representative information is also the primary shortcoming of standardized questionnaires or rating scales of treatment variables, like the Ward Atmosphere Scale (Moos, 1974), Characteristics of the Treatment Environment (Jackson, 1964, 1969), Perception of the Ward (Ellsworth et al., 1971), or the technique section of the Therapist Orientation Sheet (Paul and Lentz, 1977). Although such instruments may provide less global information on treatment variables than is possible with standardized data sheets, the assessment approach still portrays only the individual's memory, impressions, and perceptions of treatment, rather than the treatment that actually occurred (Edelson and Paul, 1976). This problem is highlighted by demonstrations that score profiles on such scales previously related to outcome could be totally accounted for by differences in ward size and the chronicity of the patients served (Edelson and Paul, 1977), that profiles purported to reflect individual staff effectiveness simply identify staff members who differ in the amount, rather than the nature, of their activity (Engel and Paul, 1981), and by studies that document significant score differences on such scales between different groups of participants in the same treatment program, such as patients vs. staff (e.g., Moos, 1974; Archer and Amuso, 1980). Although information on such differing perceptions of treatment may be useful, accurate knowledge of the treatment actually received by patients is still essential as a rational basis for many clinical and management decisions. Relying on respondents' perceptions, memories, and judgments of the treatment, standardized questionnaires and rating scales reflect the characteristics of respondents as well as those of the treatment. Thus, the utility of these instruments is limited to providing information on the characteristics of the respondents and, at best, only global impressions of the treatment.

Recording treatment activities as they occur or immediately afterward can provide a more accurate measure of the treatment actually dispensed because it relies less on an individual's memory or subjective biases. For discrete somatic treatments, such as the dispensing of psychotropic medications, nursing notes produce an inexpensive record of treatment that can be used to provide detailed or global information that is sufficiently replicable, representative, and relevant for most purposes. A parallel approach can be taken to psychosocial treatment activities. The involvement of patients in specific classes, activities, or forms of interaction with staff can be recorded as they occur. The Clinical Frequencies Recording System (CFRS) is an example of such an event-recording system (Paul and Lentz, 1977; Redfield, 1979). The CFRS, though primarily aimed at assessing patient performance, enables staff members to record systematically and continuously selected aspects of the psychosocial treatment they dispense to patients. Assessment approaches like the CFRS are different from narrative entries into patients' charts in two important respects. By providing a standard format for describing treatment dispensed, approaches like the CFRS facilitate within-program comparisons of the nature and amount of staff and patient participation. Since treatment is recorded as it is dispensed, more detailed and precise information may be obtained while subjective bias caused by retrospection is reduced.

Event recording of treatment is limited, however. To the extent that an event recording system is designed to obtain detailed information on a specific treatment program, its applicability to other programs with differing goals, procedures, activities, and schedules is reduced, thus restricting opportunities for cross-program comparisons. Even within a single treatment program, this approach provides information only on planned treatment activities and is of no help in monitoring unstructured activities that may also influence treatment outcome. Further, there is a limit to the extent staff members can record their treatment activities without interfering with or affecting the quality of the treatment itself and, thus, a limit to the representativeness and relevance of information obtained by this method. Staff members could be asked to record additional details following treatment, but this introduces retrospection and opportunities for bias. Besides, staff members often find it difficult to reflect about and describe many aspects of their behavior with patients and are typically predisposed to view their actions in terms of patient or staff approval, rather than treatment goals (Robinson, 1978).

Direct observation by nonparticipatory observers provides several advantages as a method for obtaining information about the behavior and treatment activities of staff members. The increased replicability possible with the direct recording of observable behaviors and events has led Fiske (1978, 1979) to propose it as the only practical means of assessment of persons that can approach the objectivity of measurement in the natural sciences. In addition, by using nonparticipatory observers, the representativeness and relevance of the information gathered can be ensured by scheduled observational sampling of behaviors, events, times, places, persons, or situations of interest for particular purposes. Use of nonparticipatory observers allows assessment of all aspects of treatment, planned or unplanned, and standardization of the direct observational methods permits valid cross-program comparisons. The recent availability of affordable computer technology has established this assessment approach as practical for mental health services. Computer technology allows the extensive and detailed information obtainable through direct observation to be efficiently stored and retrieved. For such purposes as research, legal/ethical documentation, or concrete, specific feedback for staff training and development, time-place-person-specific observations can be quickly retrieved by using computers while, for purposes that require more global information such as program description, evaluation, and monitoring, multiple observations can be computer-summarized to provide useful indexes. This expanded range of relevance, combined with the superior quality of the information this assessment approach provides as a basis for decisions, serves to reduce its relative cost and enhance its potential utility for mental health services.

An example of this assessment approach is the Staff-Resident Interaction Chronograph (SRIC). Although initially developed for research and staff training purposes (Paul and Lentz, 1977), the SRIC seems to be the most developed and promising instrument currently available for meeting the multiple informational needs of residential treatment facilities (Licht et al., in press). A description of the SRIC and its utility will serve to further illustrate the advantages of this approach to assessing treatment interventions.

THE STAFF-RESIDENT INTERACTION CHRONOGRAPH (SRIC)

The SRIC is a standardized observational instrument based on the fact that the common ground of all psychosocial treatments and the psychosocial influence on biological treatments involve staff-patient interactions of specific types, form, and content. As a result, the SRIC is applicable to all residential treatment programs, regardless of content, aim, or theoretical orientation; standardization of the SRIC allows cross-program comparisons within and among different treatment facilities.

SRIC data are obtained by trained, technician-level, nonparticipatory observers. For each SRIC observation, an observer systematically records all the interactions with patients of a single, targeted staff member during a 10-minute observation period. Interactions are recorded for each minute within a matrix of five columns and 21 rows, with 10 such matrices completed during the 10-minute observation period. The five columns of the matrix specify the nature of the patient behavior the staff member is responding to (appropriate, inappropriate failure, inappropriate crazy behaviors, or requests) or staff initiations of interactions (neutral). The 21 rows categorize the nature of the staff member's behavior, verbal and nonverbal, toward residents. Detailed definitions for these categories are provided elsewhere (Paul et al., in press), but it should be noted that the 21 staff behavior categories encompass a broad range of techniques derived from various psychosocial theoretical orientations, such as Rogerian reflec-

tions, psychodynamic interpretations, and behavioral verbal and material reinforcement, as well as noninteractive staff activity, which may be coded as
announcements, other job-relevant activity (e.g., attending to or observing patients, paperwork), or job-irrelevant activity (e.g., personal phone calls, reading
a novel).

Each staff interaction or activity is coded by recording in one or more of
the cells of the 5 x 21 matrix the initials or code number of the patient or patient
group contacted. For example, if a patient named Alice Smith asked the observed
staff member to light her cigarette and the staff member provided the light,
"A.S." would be recorded in the cell identified by the intersection of the patient
REQUEST column and the staff behavior DOING FOR row.

SRIC observers also record information on other aspects of the observed
activity. The numbers of patients the observed staff member is responsible for,
directly and as shared responsibility with other staff, and the number of patients
contacted individually and as part of a group are tallied and noted. The time of
observation, staff member observed, activity and its location are also recorded.

Adequate representation of a treatment program is obtained by combining
multiple SRIC observations. Carefully constructed observational schedules of 10
to 16 discrete SRIC observations per day provide an unbiased sampling of staff
and treatment activities. In addition, the frequent and unannounced appearances
of observers on the unit, combined with training observers to be unobtrusive,
minimize staff reactivity to the observational process. Even when used explicitly
for staff evaluations, the SRIC has proved to be a nonreactive mode of assessment
when applied as a component of treatment programs (Hagen et al., 1975); surprisingly little staff reactivity was encountered even in 10-day trials of SRIC implementation in 36 treatment programs.

SRIC observations are summarized by first tallying the number of interactions in each cell of the 5 x 21 matrix. For efficiency, these data are then entered
into computer files to facilitate summarization of all SRIC observations for a
given time period and treatment program, or summarization of specific staff,
activities, locations, times, or other treatment factors.

The extensiveness of the information provided by the SRIC can be seen in
the sample computer output shown in Figure 1. NO.-1 and NO.-2 on this print-
out reflect the ability of this summary output form to present two different
summaries on a single sheet for comparisons of programs, staff, or changes over
time. The top portion provides identifying information and descriptions of the
data base. The central portion displays detailed information on the specific staff-
patient interactions observed, paralleling the five-column by 21-row matrix used
to record the interactions. The last five columns provide hourly rates for each
type of interaction; the last two columns and bottom three rows provide totals
of staff and patient (or resident) behavior categories, both in hourly rate and
percentage formats. The bottom portion provides information on the average

STAFF RESIDENT INTERACTION CHRONOGRAPH (SRIC): GROUP SUMMARY

PRODUCTION DATE:
REQUESTED BY:
SRIC-ID NO.: NO.-1:
              NO.-2:

TYPE OF SUMMARY:

DATES SUMMARIZED: NO.-1: (/ /) (/ /)   FACILITY/UNIT: NO.-1:   NO. STAFF: NO.-1:
                  NO.-2: (/ /) (/ /)   NO.-2:   NO.-2:

NO. OF SRICS SUMMARIZED: NO.-1:   AVG INCIDENCE/HR FOR A SINGLE OCCURRENCE WITH THIS NO. OF SRICS & STAFF IS: NO.-1: X.XX
                         NO.-2:   NO.-2: X.XX

AVERAGE HOURLY INSTANCES OF STAFF ACTIVITY (MEAN)

CATEGORY OF STAFF BEHAVIOR	CATEGORY OF RESIDENT BEHAVIOR TO WHICH STAFF RESPONDED										TOTAL STAFF BEHAVIOR		% OF INTERACTION		CATEGORY OF STAFF BEHAVR
	APPROPRIATE (AP)		INAPPROPRIATE FAILURE (INF)		INAPPROPRIATE CRAZY (INC)		REQUEST (R)		NEUTRAL (N)						
	NO.-1	NO.-2	NO.-1	NO.-2	NO.-1	NO.-2	NO.-1	NO.-2	NO.-1	NO.-2	NO.-1	NO.-2	NO.-1	NO.-2	
POSITIVE VERBAL	XX.XX	XX.XX	XX.XX	XX.XX	XX.XX	XX.XX	XX.XX	XX.XX	XX.XX	XX.XX	XX.XX	XX.XX	XX.XX	XX.XX	(POS VERBAL)
NEGATIVE VERBAL	XX.XX	XX.XX	XX.XX	XX.XX	XX.XX	XX.XX	XX.XX	XX.XX	XX.XX	XX.XX	XX.XX	XX.XX	XX.XX	XX.XX	(NEG VERBAL)
POS NONVERBAL	XX.XX	XX.XX	XX.XX	XX.XX	XX.XX	XX.XX	XX.XX	XX.XX	XX.XX	XX.XX	XX.XX	XX.XX	XX.XX	XX.XX	(POS NONVERB)
NEG NONVERBAL	XX.XX	XX.XX	XX.XX	XX.XX	XX.XX	XX.XX	XX.XX	XX.XX	XX.XX	XX.XX	XX.XX	XX.XX	XX.XX	XX.XX	(NEG NONVERB)
POS NONSOCIAL	XX.XX	XX.XX	XX.XX	XX.XX	XX.XX	XX.XX	XX.XX	XX.XX	XX.XX	XX.XX	XX.XX	XX.XX	XX.XX	XX.XX	(POS NONSOC)
NEG NONSOCIAL	XX.XX	XX.XX	XX.XX	XX.XX	XX.XX	XX.XX	XX.XX	XX.XX	XX.XX	XX.XX	XX.XX	XX.XX	XX.XX	XX.XX	(NEG NONSOC)
POS STATEMENT	XX.XX	XX.XX	XX.XX	XX.XX	XX.XX	XX.XX	XX.XX	XX.XX	XX.XX	XX.XX	XX.XX	XX.XX	XX.XX	XX.XX	(POS STATMT)
NEG STATEMENT	XX.XX	XX.XX	XX.XX	XX.XX	XX.XX	XX.XX	XX.XX	XX.XX	XX.XX	XX.XX	XX.XX	XX.XX	XX.XX	XX.XX	(NEG STATMT)
POSITIVE PROMPT	XX.XX	XX.XX	XX.XX	XX.XX	XX.XX	XX.XX	XX.XX	XX.XX	XX.XX	XX.XX	XX.XX	XX.XX	XX.XX	XX.XX	(POS PROMPT)
NEGATIVE PROMPT	XX.XX	XX.XX	XX.XX	XX.XX	XX.XX	XX.XX	XX.XX	XX.XX	XX.XX	XX.XX	XX.XX	XX.XX	XX.XX	XX.XX	(NEG PROMPT)
POS GRP REFERENCE	XX.XX	XX.XX	XX.XX	XX.XX	XX.XX	XX.XX	XX.XX	XX.XX	XX.XX	XX.XX	XX.XX	XX.XX	XX.XX	XX.XX	(POS GP REF)
NEG GRP REFERENCE	XX.XX	XX.XX	XX.XX	XX.XX	XX.XX	XX.XX	XX.XX	XX.XX	XX.XX	XX.XX	XX.XX	XX.XX	XX.XX	XX.XX	(NEG GP REG)
REFLECT/CLARIFY	XX.XX	XX.XX	XX.XX	XX.XX	XX.XX	XX.XX	XX.XX	XX.XX	XX.XX	XX.XX	XX.XX	XX.XX	XX.XX	XX.XX	(REFL/CLARIF)
SUGGEST ALTRNATIV	XX.XX	XX.XX	XX.XX	XX.XX	XX.XX	XX.XX	XX.XX	XX.XX	XX.XX	XX.XX	XX.XX	XX.XX	XX.XX	XX.XX	(SUGGEST ALT)
INSTRUCT/DEMONSR	XX.XX	XX.XX	XX.XX	XX.XX	XX.XX	XX.XX	XX.XX	XX.XX	XX.XX	XX.XX	XX.XX	XX.XX	XX.XX	XX.XX	(INSTRUC/DEM)
DOING WITH	XX.XX	XX.XX	XX.XX	XX.XX	XX.XX	XX.XX	XX.XX	XX.XX	XX.XX	XX.XX	XX.XX	XX.XX	XX.XX	XX.XX	(DOING WITH)
DOING FOR	XX.XX	XX.XX	XX.XX	XX.XX	XX.XX	XX.XX	XX.XX	XX.XX	XX.XX	XX.XX	XX.XX	XX.XX	XX.XX	XX.XX	(DOING FOR)
PHYSICAL FORCE	XX.XX	XX.XX	XX.XX	XX.XX	XX.XX	XX.XX	XX.XX	XX.XX	XX.XX	XX.XX	XX.XX	XX.XX	XX.XX	XX.XX	(PHYS FORCE)
IGNORE/NO RESPONS	XX.XX	XX.XX	XX.XX	XX.XX	XX.XX	XX.XX	***	***	***	***	XX.XX	XX.XX	XX.XX	XX.XX	(IGNORE/NO R)
ANNOUNCE	***	***	***	***	***	***	***	***	***	***	XX.XX	XX.XX	XX.XX	XX.XX	(ANNOUNCE)
ATTEND/RECORD/OBS	***	***	***	***	***	***	***	***	***	***	XX.XX	XX.XX	***	***	(A/R/O)
TOTAL INTERACTION	XX.XX	XX.XX	XX.XX	XX.XX	XX.XX	XX.XX	XX.XX	XX.XX	XX.XX	XX.XX	XXX.XX	XXX.XX	XXX.XX	XXX.XX	TOTAL INTERAC
% OF INTERACTIONS	XX.XX	XX.XX	XX.XX	XX.XX	XX.XX	XX.XX	***	***	***	***	***	***	***	***	% OF INTERACT
TOTAL ACTIVITY	***	***	***	***	***	***	***	***	***	***	XXX.XX	XXX.XX	***	***	TOTAL ACTIVIT

NOTE: "% OF INTERACTIONS" COLUMN FOR (ANNOUNCE) (A/R/O) AND "TOTAL INTERACTIONS" REFLECT % OF TOTAL ACTIVITY INSTEAD OF INTERACTIONS. "(IGNORE/NO R)-(N)" CODES ARE NOT INCLUDED IN "% OF INTERACTION FIGURES".

AVG RESIDENTS PRESENT: NO.-1: XX.X   CONTACTS/HOUR/RESIDENT: INDIVIDUALLY: NO.-1: X.XX   IN A GROUP: NO.-1: X.XX   TOTAL: NO.-1: X.XX
                       NO.-2: XX.X   NO.-2: X.XX   NO.-2: X.XX   NO.-2: X.XX
                       AVG INTERACTIONS/CONTACT: NO.-1: X.XX   AVG ATTENTION RECVD BY INDIVIDUAL RESIDENT: NO.-1: XX.XX
                                                 NO.-2: X.XX   NO.-2: XX.XX

AVG FUNCT RESPONSIBLE: NO.-1: XX.X   CONTACTS/HOUR/RESIDENT: INDIVIDUALLY: NO.-1: X.XX   IN A GROUP: NO.-1: X.XX   TOTAL: NO.-1: X.XX
                       NO.-2: XX.X   NO.-2: X.XX   NO.-2: X.XX   NO.-2: X.XX
                       AVG INTERACTIONS/CONTACT: NO.-1: X.XX   AVG ATTENTION RECVD BY INDIVIDUAL RESIDENT: NO.-1: XX.XX
                                                 NO.-2: X.XX   NO.-2: XX.XX

Figure 1 Format of Staff-Resident Interaction Chronograph Summary. Source: State of Illinois Department of Mental Health and Developmental Disabilities, Division of Information Services.

number of patients staff members were responsible for as well as number of contacts, interactions per contact, and total attention received by the average patient on an hourly basis.

As part of a multi-institutional study, the feasibility and reliability of the SRIC were tested in 36 treatment programs for mentally ill, retarded, and substance abuse clients. Programs in public mental institutions (state and Veterans Administration hospitals, mental health centers) as well as privately operated community extended-care facilities were sampled, covering open and locked units ranging in size from eight to 120 beds. The SRIC proved to be practical in all settings and programs with all populations. Observers were able to code staff-patient interactions reliably, with inter-observer reliability correlation coefficients averaged across all categorized interactions (matrix cells) exceeding $r = 0.990$ for each observer pair at all data collection sites.

The development and use of the SRIC as a standardized instrument for multi-institutional data collection also provided full-week samples of treatment programs for the establishment of normative tables. The SRIC data obtained in 30 treatment programs sampled in public mental institutions show the sensitivity of SRIC indexes to differences among psychosocial treatments. But besides demonstrating the ability of the SRIC to discriminate among treatment programs, the normative data also reveal wide differences among programs. Overall staff activity, interactive and noninteractive, in the most active treatment program (513.64 instances per hour) was, for example, more than five times that observed in the least active program (91.46). Actual staff-patient interactions ranged from a low of 42.66 interactions per hour to a high more than ten times that number, 459.23 interactions per hour. Average observed staff members were found to be responsible for as few as 4.31 patients in some programs and as many as 32.96 in others. Not surprisingly, such large differences in responsibility and activity produce a similarly large range in the amount of attention a program's average patient receives, ranging from fewer than two staff interactions per hour to almost 25 per hour. Such ranges were obtained with other SRIC indexes as well (Licht, 1979).

The Utility of SRIC Information

The information provided by the SRIC is largely value-free; that is, the desirability of specific types of interactions is not predetermined but must be established from theories, legal and ethical guidelines, or empirical documentations of effectiveness. This enhances the instrument's primary purpose: detailed documentation of the psychosocial treatment actually received by patients, rather than treatment planned or intended, or merely global aspects of the treatment perceived to have occurred.

The utility of the information provided by the SRIC has been documented in both research and mental health services, and several other applications have been suggested (Engel and Paul, 1979; Licht, 1979; Mariotto, 1979; Paul and Lentz, 1977). The SRIC has served as an objective criterion of effectiveness in evaluating staff training and development (Paul et al., 1973), and to monitor and document programmatic procedures in group therapy (Paden et al., 1974). As a feedback mechanism for staff, use of the SRIC has fostered not only a fourfold increase in staff-patient interactions but also limited the "error rates" of non-programmatic interactions to less than one-half of one percent in two programmatically different treatment programs staffed by the same personnel (Paul and Lentz, 1977). The results of such low error rates were that nonprofessional floor staff members, who had the greatest amount of contact with patients, were functioning as "therapists," providing psychosocial treatment consistent with that given by the professional staff. By documenting the nature and amount of staff attention patients actually receive, the SRIC has also provided legal/ethical protection to staff members, individually and as a group. The availability of SRIC information has served to defuse unjustified complaints or concerns about treatment, while allowing monitoring of clinical staff members to identify and remediate undesirable staff actions quickly. Applicable to any residential treatment program, the SRIC has been recommended as a means of assuring taxpayers that additional rehabilitative programming is indeed occurring in community extended-care facilities that receive incentive funding to provide more than custodial care (Kohen and Paul, 1976).

For research purposes, the SRIC has been useful for documenting differing treatment histories of patients selected for studies of the effects of previous treatment on specific tasks (Montgomery et al., 1974; Lentz, 1975; Theobald and Paul, 1976). SRIC information has also helped to define psychological environments and situations in studies of the contribution of person and situation variables to the behavior of chronic mental patients (Mariotto and Paul, 1975; Mariotto, 1978). An especially important use has been to describe and monitor the psychosocial environment during psychopharmacological interventions (Paul et al., 1972). Such documentation of planned *and* unplanned psychosocial activities that are the context of any psychopharmacological intervention can strengthen findings from drug studies.

Perhaps the most exciting potential use of the SRIC is as a "bootstrap" mechanism for improving treatment effectiveness. When the SRIC was used to document relationships between specific classes of staff-patient interactions and patient functioning and improvement, the data showed that how staff members interact with patients is more important than how much they interact (Paul and Lentz, 1977). The ability of the SRIC to differentiate among treatment programs provides several additional means for specifying in positive terms what staff members can do to improve treatment. The available normative data provide information on how an identified program differs from others, providing initial guidance for improving the program in question. But additional suggestions for improvement can be derived by comparing and contrasting SRIC summaries of programs, staff, or time periods within a single program, so that features of the psychosocial treatment associated with greater effectiveness or efficiency may be identified. SRIC observations of an exceptionally effective staff member can, for example, be summarized and contrasted to those obtained on other staff members to identify the distinguishing features of the effective staff member's interactions with patients.

Development of the SRIC continues. It has been incorporated into a larger, computer-based Planned Access Information System designed to consolidate information on staff and patient demographics, program characteristics and costs, psychopharmacological treatment, psychosocial treatment as assessed by the SRIC, and patient functioning as assessed by the Time-Sample Behavioral Checklist (TSBC, Licht, this volume). In addition, TSBC observations of staff are included to provide an accounting of how clinical staff members spend their time while on duty. In the implementation of this Planned Access Information System, SRIC summaries in the format illustrated in Figure 1 are produced weekly, summarizing all treatment activities and staff for the entire week to provide overall, week-to-week monitoring. Staff TSBC summaries that reflect how staff members spend their time are also produced each week, both as group means and as individual summaries distributed to each clinical staff member to encourage self-monitoring. Special, additional SRIC or staff TSBC summaries can be obtained at any time on specific staff members or staff subgroups based on demographic characteristics, activities, times, locations, or other parameters by accessing and responding to a series of questions sequentially presented on remote cathode-ray computer terminals located on each unit.

In addition, global-level SRIC and TSBC data on staff, staff and patient demographic information, staff and patient program census and movement data, and information on absolute levels and changes in patient functioning are presented in a series of Quality Assurance Summaries, with additional space available for information on psychopharmacological treatments and program costs. This information is presented in a side-by-side format to facilitate identification of significant differences between more and less effective or efficient programs, facilities, or time periods for a single program. Thus, in addition to objective monitoring of the significant aspects of residential treatment, this computer-based system is designed to provide information needed to improve treatment in residential facilities. In fact, the development of such comprehensive information systems should not only facilitate research but also advance the clinical and management practices of residential mental health services to a level approaching that of applied science.

With the quality of the information provided by the SRIC and its extensive range of utility, the relative cost of this assessment instrument is potentially quite low. Materials and procedures for training observers in reliable SRIC data collection, with minimal reliance on experienced personnel, have been developed and evaluated (Licht et al., 1980). Though most SRIC observers employed thus far have been high school graduates functioning in clerk-, technician-, or aide-level positions, the reliance of the SRIC on nonparticipatory observers is the largest cost of the instrument. Using the same observer staff to obtain additional data on patient functioning with the TSBC (Licht, this volume) reduces the cost. Even further savings are possible if the information provided by the SRIC is used to improve the management and utilization of clinical staff. The resulting increased efficiency could allow the Planned Access System to be implemented in most facilities we have examined by judicious reallocation of staff positions, rather than adding staff members. The primary determinant of the relative cost of instruments like the SRIC, however, is the value placed on obtaining current, accurate, and objective information on how mentally ill patients are actually treated in residential facilities; no other assessment approach provides the detailed information necessary for describing, improving, and monitoring staff activities that affect treatment outcome for the chronically mentally ill.

CONCLUSION

Although obtaining information on the characteristics of the environment or staff of residential treatment facilities by standardized data sheets and questionnaires or rating scales is suitable for most purposes in mental health services, such assessment approaches are inadequate for obtaining information on the most important aspect of these facilities—the actual treatment of patients. Direct observational assessment is the only approach capable of capturing the detailed and global information on all psychosocial treatment activities, planned as well as unplanned, that is necessary for rational decision-making in residential treatment. Observational assessment instruments like the SRIC provide a continuous guide for evaluating and improving treatment practices. The increasing availability of inexpensive computer technology now makes this assessment approach practical for mental health services.

ACKNOWLEDGMENTS

The research on the Staff-Resident Interaction Chronograph reported in this chapter was supported in part by Public Health Service grants MH-15553 and MH-25464 from the National Institute of Mental Health and by grants from the Illinois Department of Mental Health and Developmental Disabilities, the Joyce Foundation, and the MacArthur Foundation.

REFERENCES

Archer, R. P., and Amuso, K. F. 1980. Comparison of staff's and patients' perceptions of ward atmosphere. *Psychol. Rep.* 46:959-965.
Cohen, J., and Struening, E. L. 1962. Opinions about mental illness in the personnel of two large mental hospitals. *J. Abnorm. Soc. Psychol.* 64:349-360.

Edelson, R. I., and Paul, G. L. 1976. Some problems in the use of "attitude" and "atmosphere" scores as indicators of staff effectiveness in institutional treatment. *J. Nerv. Ment. Dis.* 162:248-257.

Edelson, R. I., and Paul, G. L. 1977. Staff "attitude" and "atmosphere" scores as a function of ward size and patient chronicity. *J. Consult. Clin. Psychol.* 45:874-884.

Ellsworth, R. B., Collins, J. F., Casey, N. A., Schoonover, R. A., Hickey, R. H., Hyer, L., Twemlow, S. W., and Nesselroade, J. R. 1979. Some characteristics of effective psychiatric treatment programs. *J. Consult. Clin. Psychol.* 47: 799-817.

Ellsworth, R. B., Maroney, R., Klett, W., Gordon, H., and Gunn, R. 1971. Milieu characteristics of successful psychiatric treatment programs. *Am. J. Orthopsychiatry* 41:427-441.

Engel, K. L., and Paul, G. L. 1979. Systems use to objectify program evaluation, clinical and management decisions. *Journal of Behavioral Assessment* 1:221-238.

Engel, K. L., and Paul, G. L. 1981. Staff performance: Do attitudinal "effectiveness profiles" really assess it? *J. Nerv. Ment. Dis.* 169:529-540.

Fiske, D. W. 1978. *Strategies for Personality Research*. San Francisco: Jossey-Bass.

Fiske, D. W. 1979. A demonstration of the value of interchangeable observers. *Journal of Behavioral Assessment* 1:251-258.

Hagen, R. L., Craighead, W. E., and Paul, G. L. 1975. Staff reactivity to evaluative behavioral observations. *Behavior Therapy* 6:201-205.

Holland, T. P., Konick, A., Buffum, W., Smith, M. K., and Petchers, M. 1981. Institutional structure and resident outcomes. *J. Health Soc. Behav.* 22:433-444.

Jackson, J. 1964. Toward the comparative study of mental hospitals: Characteristics of the treatment environment. In A. F. Wessen (ed.), *The Psychiatric Hospital as a Social System*, pp. 35-87. Springfield, IL: Thomas.

Jackson, J. 1969. Factors of the treatment environment. *Arch. Gen. Psychiatry* 21:39-45.

Kohen, W., and Paul, G. L. 1976. Current trends and recommended changes in extended-care placement of mental patients: The Illinois system as a case in point. *Schizophr. Bull.* 2:575-594.

Lawton, M. P., and Cohen, J. 1975. Organizational studies of mental hospitals. In M. Guttentag and E. L. Struening (eds.), *Handbook of Evaluation Research*, vol. 2, pp. 201-238. Beverly Hills: Sage Publications.

Lentz, R. J. 1975. Changes in chronic mental patients' interview behavior: Effects of differential treatment history and explicit impression management prompts. *Journal of Behavior Therapy and Experimental Psychiatry* 6:192-199.

Licht, M. H. 1979. The Staff-Resident Interaction Chronograph: Observational assessment of staff performance. *Journal of Behavioral Assessment* 1:185-197.

Licht, M. H., Paul, G. L., Power, C. T., and Engel, K. L. 1980. The comparative effectiveness of two modes of observer training on the staff-resident interaction chronograph. *Journal of Behavioral Assessment* 2:175-205.

Licht, M. H., Power, C. T., and Paul, G. L. in press. Standardized observational systems in service and research. In G. L. Paul (ed.), *Observational Assessment Instrumentation for Institutional Research and Treatment*. Cambridge: Harvard University Press.

Magnusson, D. (ed.) 1981. *Toward a Psychology of Situations: An Interactional Perspective*. Hillsdale, NJ: Erlbaum.

Mariotto, M. J. 1978. Interaction of person and situation effects for chronic mental patients: A two-year follow-up. *J. Abnorm. Psychol.* 87:676-679.

Mariotto, M. J. 1979. Observational assessment systems use for basic and applied research. *Journal of Behavioral Assessment* 1:239-250.

Mariotto, M. J., and Paul, G. L. 1975. Persons versus situations in the real-life functioning of chronically institutionalized mental patients. *J. Abnorm. Psychol.* 84:483-493.

Montgomery, G. K., Paul, G. L., and Power, C. T. 1974. Influence of environmental contingency history on acquisition of new discriminations by chronic mental patients. *J. Abnorm. Psychol.* 83:339-347.

Moos, R. H. 1974. *Evaluating Treatment Environments: A Social Ecological Approach*. New York: Wiley.

Paden, R. C., Himelstein, H. C., and Paul, G. L. 1974. Video-tape vs. verbal feedback in the modification of meal behavior of chronic mental patients. *J. Consult. Clin. Psychol.* 42:623.

Paul, G. L., and Lentz, R. J. 1977. *Psychosocial Treatment of Chronic Mental Patients: Milieu versus Social-Learning Programs*. Cambridge: Harvard University Press.

Paul, G. L., Licht, M. H., Engel, K. L., and Power, C. T. in press. The Staff-Resident Interaction Chronograph Observer Manual. In G. L. Paul (ed.), *Observational Assessment Instrumentation for Institutional Research and Treatment*. Cambridge: Harvard University Press.

Paul, G. L., McInnis, T. L., and Mariotto, M. J. 1973. Objective performance outcomes associated with two approaches to training mental health technicians in milieu and social learning programs. *J. Abnorm. Psychol.* 82:523-532.

Paul, G. L., Tobias, L. L., and Holly, B. L. 1972. Maintenance psychotropic drugs in the presence of active treatment programs: A "triple-blind" withdrawal study with long-term mental patients. *Arch. Gen. Psychiatry* 27:106-115.

Redfield, J. 1979. Clinical frequencies recording systems: Standardizing staff observations by event recording. *Journal of Behavioral Assessment* 1:211-219.

Robinson, V. M. J. 1978. The behavior of staff: An ignored variable in programme evaluation. *Soc. Sci. Med.* 12:175-182.

Smith, P. C., Kendall, L. M., and Hulin, C. L. 1969. *The Measurement of Satisfaction in Work and Retirement*. Chicago: Rand McNally.

Theobald, D. E., and Paul, G. L. 1976. Reinforcing value of praise for chronic mental patients as a function of historical pairing with tangible reinforcers. *Behavior Therapy* 7:192-197.

Wiggins, J. S. 1973. *Personality and Prediction: Principles of Personality Assessment*. Reading: Addison-Wesley.

III
Biology and the Psychopharmacological Treatment of Chronic Mental Illness

9
Efficacy of Drug Treatment for Chronic Schizophrenic Patients

NINA R. SCHOOLER AND JOANNE B. SEVERE

The purpose of this paper is to examine several issues that are relevant to treatment of chronic schizophrenic patients with drugs.

Specifically, these issues are:

1. The effectiveness of antipsychotic drugs for the specific treatment of psychopathology as opposed to the prevention of subsequent relapse.

2. The role of compliance with medication-taking in understanding the effectiveness of antipsychotic drug treatment for chronic schizophrenic illness.

3. The development of newer strategies for antipsychotic drug administration designed to enhance drug efficacy and minimize risks associated with long-term treatment.

A number of other important topics that could have been treated in this chapter have had to be excluded. The relationship of drug and psychosocial treatments is discussed in other chapters in this volume. The role of other drug classes in the treatment for schizophrenia, either instead of antipsychotic drugs or adjunctively, has been receiving increasing attention (Donaldson et al., 1983). The interested reader may find relatively recent reviews of the role of antidepressants (Siris et al., 1978) and anxiolytics (Nestoros, 1980) of interest. Finally, tardive dyskinesia, the late-appearing neurologic syndrome, represents a significant risk to patients receiving antipsychotic drugs for extended periods of time. Studies have begun to define the extent of this risk (Kane et al., 1982). A recent monograph (Jeste and Wyatt, 1982) provides a balanced review of current information on this topic.

EFFICACY OF ANTIPSYCHOTIC DRUGS IN THE LONG-TERM TREATMENT OF PSYCHOPATHOLOGIC SYMPTOMS

The evidence regarding the effectiveness of maintenance antipsychotic drug treatment in preventing relapse in schizophrenic patients is powerful—persuading both the clinician and researcher that these drugs do indeed prevent the recurrence of flagrant symptomatic episodes. Davis (1975) reviewed 24 double-blind maintenance studies in which patients were randomly assigned to either an antipsychotic drug or a placebo for more than one month. He found that in *all* these studies, which involved both chronic inpatients and outpatients, relapse rates were higher in the group treated with placebo than drug, in most cases statistically significantly higher. This finding is consistent across all the studies. On the average, based on figures provided by Davis, 20 percent of 1,858 patients treated with drugs relapsed, compared to 52 percent of 1,337 patients randomized to treatment with placebo.

Thus, we do not seek to challenge the data that show the effectiveness of drugs for the prevention of relapse or rehospitalization but rather to expand the question to encompass effects on symptoms and social adjustment. Although many reports of studies often include assessment of outcomes other than relapse, we have not found a review in the literature that attempts to integrate these data to provide a summary of the effectiveness of antipsychotic drugs for long-term treatment of specific symptoms and other aspects of social functioning that is comparable to that just described for relapse. Such a review is particularly pertinent because of recent renewed interest in subclassification of schizophrenic symptomatology. Crow (1980) proposed a typology in which Type I schizophrenia is characterized by "positive" symptoms and responsiveness to neuroleptic drugs. Type II is characterized by "negative" symptoms and lack of responsiveness to neuroleptic drugs. There is also frequent reference in the literature (e.g., Strauss, Carpenter, and Bartko 1974) that drugs are effective for reduction and prevention of the occurrence of such positive symptoms but not for the more pervasive negative symptoms or defects.

Our method is as follows: For each study identified in the 1975 review by Davis we determined whether or not, either in the paper cited or in another paper based on the same study, data were presented regarding symptomatology as well as relapse. Data regarding symptomatology are available for 14 of the 24 studies cited. In addition, two studies that had such data available—one conducted after the Davis review (Rifkin et al., 1977) and one excluded by Davis (Paul et al., 1972)—were included in our review of a total of 16 studies. Twelve of the studies involved inpatients; four studied outpatients treated in their communities.

Before turning to an examination of the data regarding symptomatology, perhaps we should exonerate the reviewers who failed to integrate data reporting on symptoms from many studies in the same way that they summarized data on relapse. First, although there may be differences among investigations in the criteria used to define relapse, such differences are minor compared to differences among rating scales, definitions of symptoms, etc. Further, a relapse or rehospitalization, however defined, represents a single outcome for each case. In examining ratings of psychopathology, each patient may receive multiple ratings at any given time and such ratings may be repeated many times during the course of a study. The differences among symptoms at a given time are precisely what interests us, but the multiplicity of time points presents a methodological problem. Strauss (this volume) provides graphic evidence that ignoring the variability in a patient over time may lead to inaccurate interpretation of the course of the illness. He advocates longitudinal evaluation. The caveats he offers with respect to interpretation of the course of illness without attention to variability over time are equally if not more relevant in ascertaining the effectiveness of treatment (Schooler and Levine, 1983).

The data from the 16 studies under review do not in general have a true longitudinal perspective. In most cases they provide information about symptoms at the end of the study course; in some, additional cross-sectional "snap shots" are provided at earlier time points. Evaluating the effect of antipsychotic drugs on symptoms is further complicated by the inclusion in some studies of data from patients whose symptom evaluations were made at the time the patients were being withdrawn from treatment because of relapse. In these individuals decompensation may overwhelm differences in symptomatic response; when data from such patients are pooled with data from patients who have not relapsed, the effect of a treatment on symptoms may appear less positive than if patients who relapsed were excluded from analysis or had been evaluated during the period before relapse.

Inpatient Studies

Table 1 lists the 12 studies conducted with inpatients. These studies lasted between four and seven months and were all carried out before 1972. As may be seen from the table, these studies do differ in whether or not symptom evaluations included ratings made at the time of relapse. This would be the case, for instance, if analyses of symptom data at the *end* of a seven-month study included the last or relapse evaluation of patients who relapsed before the end of the study. Since the impact of including these relapse or termination evaluations on the results of a study depends on the percentage of patients who relapsed before study end, Table 1 includes the percentage of patients who relapsed in the placebo-treated group. In general, patients in these studies were chronically institutionalized. As indicated in Table 1, in more than half of the studies patients had been hospitalized for more than ten years on the average.

The last two columns of Table 1 list symptoms that do and do not show differences between drug- and placebo-treated groups. Fewer differences are seen at evaluations made at three months or earlier during the study course. As would be expected, studies that included patients at termination and had substantial numbers of relapsing patients were more likely to report symptom differences between drug and placebo than those that either excluded relapsers from analyses of symptoms or had very few relapsers. Even so, in studies that looked at patients at more than one time point, significant differences were more likely to appear after six rather than three months of placebo substitution. In studies that

Table 1 Treatment Effects on Symptoms of Psychopathology and Social Functioning in Inpatient Studies

Study (subjects included)	N	Continuous Hospitalization	Study Length (months)	Placebo Patients' Relapse Rate	Drug vs. Placebo — No Difference	Drug vs. Placebo — Differences
Good et al. (1958) (all patients)	112	2 mos-3 yrs	6	0	@ 3 months: ward morbidity score, psychiatric interview	@ 6 months: ward morbidity score; hallucinations, delusions, incoherence, disorientation
Shawver et al. (1959) (patients at termination)	120	8 yrs (MDN)	6	17.5%	@ 3 months: activity level, mental disorganization, interpersonal relations	@ 6 months: activity level, mental disorganization, interpersonal relations @ 3 and 6 months: anxiety level, activity abnormality
Diamond and Marks (1960) (patients at termination)	40	6 & 16 yrs	6	55%	@ 3 months: improvement in psychopathology and hospital adjustment	@ 6 months: improvement in psychopathology and hospital adjustment
Schiele et al. (1961) (all patients)	80	10 yrs	4	5%		@ 2 months and 4 months: ward behavior, improvement in psychopathology
Adelson and Epstein (1962) (all patients)	288	2-10 yrs	4	0		Total morbidity score
Freeman and Alson (1962) (no data provided)	96	12 yrs	6	31%		@ 6 months: total morbidity score; symptoms such as inappropriate affect, apathy, withdrawal, hostility, fears and delusions

Study	N	Age		%		
Caffey et al. (1964)	348	10 yrs	4	45%	@ 4 months: 11 of 14 symptoms; e.g., excitement, hostile-belligerence, grandiosity, motor disturbance	@ 4 months: (non-relapsed) 3 of 14 symptoms; conceptual disorganization, thinking disorganization, agitated depression
Marjerrison et al. (1964)	88	12-20 yrs	7	6%	@ 1,2,3, and 4 months: ward behavior score	@ 5,6, and 7 months: ward behavior score
Garfield et al. (1966)	27	10 yrs	5	22%	@ 5 months: perceptual and thinking distortion, schizophrenic disorganization	
Prien and Cole (1968)	838	14.5 yrs	6	39%	@ 6 months: grandiosity, anxious intropunitiveness, retardation and apathy of social interest	@ 6 months: excitement, hostile-belligerence, paranoid projection, disorientation, perceptual distortion, motor disturbance, all ward ratings except social interest
Prien et al. (1969)	360	15 yrs	6	45%		@ 6 months: ward ratings, psychiatric interview
Paul et al. (1972)[1]	52	17 yrs	4	0	@ 4 months: psychiatric ratings, ward ratings, Bizarre Behavior Index	

[1]Not included in Davis (1975) paper.

reported symptom differences, such differences did not appear in all symptoms, particularly in studies that excluded relapsers.

The study by Caffey et al. (1964) provides the most complete data for examining differences between antipsychotic drugs and placebo in the development of symptoms, limited only by the four-month duration of study. These investigators reported results separately for relapsing and nonrelapsing patients. Among the nonrelapsed patients only three of 14 symptom criteria—conceptual disorganization, thinking disorganization, and agitated depression—distinguished the drug from placebo groups. Among the relapsed patients all the symptom criteria rated by ward personnel reflected increases in symptomatology but only some of the ratings based on clinician interview. Hostility, paranoia, grandiosity, perceptual distortion, and anxious intropunitiveness did not increase even among relapsing patients on both drug and placebo. Three of these same symptoms—paranoia, perceptual distortion, and anxious intropunitiveness—improved in the placebo-treated patients who did not relapse. The symptoms that did worsen among the relapsing patients (retardation and apathy, disorientation, motor disturbance, and conceptual disorganization) span the range of symptoms that define schizophrenia and drug action. In this study, there is no evidence that negative symptoms such as retardation and apathy are not affected by drug. These negative symptoms improve in patients who receive medication and do not relapse and get worse in patients who relapse, on or off medication. Similar findings were reported by Goldberg et al. (1965) in a six-week study of phenothiazine-treated, acutely ill schizophrenic patients. These investigators reported significantly greater reduction in apathy and motor retardation among drug- than placebo-treated patients.

Results in the present series of inpatient withdrawal studies are not consistent in terms of positive and negative symptoms. Among the longer studies, however, negative symptoms are less likely to show differences between the drug- and placebo-treated groups (e.g., Prien and Cole, 1968).

Outpatient Studies

When we turn to the outpatient studies presented in Table 2 we note that they are fewer in number (only four), more recent (only one was completed before 1970), and of longer duration (the shortest is nine months long). Finally, three of the four have examined symptom outcome for nonrelapsed patients, making it possible to evaluate drug effects that are not simply a reflection of the exacerbation associated with relapse.

The most detailed description of a population of patients withdrawn from medication and followed over a nine-month period is provided by Stevens (1973) based on the patients in the Hirsch et al. (1973) study. Symptomatic behavior increased significantly in patients receiving placebo, reflecting the 60-percent relapse rate seen in this study. However, social withdrawal and depressed mood, which were at high levels at the beginning of the study, did not change signifi-

Table 2 Treatment Effects on Symptoms of Psychopathology and Social Functioning in Outpatient Studies

Study (subjects included)	N	Length of Illness	Study Length (months)	Placebo Patients' Relapse Rate	Drug vs. Placebo	
					No Difference	Differences
Engelhardt et al. (1967) (nonrelapsers only)	24	—	12	NA		Ideas of persecution: drug pts. improved, placebo pts. worsened. Other symptoms: drug pts. improved, placebo pts. no change)
Hirsch et al. (1973) Stevens (1973) (patients at termination)	81	80% more than 11 years	9	60%	Self-neglect, social withdrawal, depressed mood, leisure time activities	Relative's judgment of psychotic behavior, embarrassing behavior, sociability
Hogarty et al. (1974 a and b) (nonrelapsers only)	112	19.5 months	24	80%	@ 6,12,18 and 24 mos: social functioning, psychopathology, mood	For men @ 12 months: apathy and retardation, schizophrenic disorganization, hostile paranoia, severity of illness
Rifkin et al. (1979)[1] (nonrelapsers only)	36	3.2 years	12	68%	@ 3,6 and 9 mos: leisure activities, friends, heterosexual adjustment, role performance	

[1]Not included in Davis (1975) paper.

cantly in either drug- or placebo-treated patients during the course of the study. Sociability as distinct from social withdrawal did suffer among the placebo-treated patients. These data are consistent with the idea that negative symptoms or a defect state are not responsive to antipsychotic drugs. They do not, however, support the hypothesis that drug withdrawal has a beneficial effect on such symptoms.

In the other three outpatient studies, a variety of strategies were used to examine treatment effects relatively independently of relapse. Rifkin et al. (1979) matched drug and placebo nonrelapsers on a number of background variables. Using measures of social and vocational functioning they found no differences between these matched drug- and placebo-treated patients who did not relapse during the first eight months of their 12-month trial. There were too few nonrelapsed placebo patients at 12 months for comparison. Engelhardt et al. (1963) also used a matching procedure to select 12 pairs of drug- and placebo-treated patients who had severe ratings of psychopathology at the start of the study and who had not relapsed for at least the first 12 months of the trial. The 24 patients included in this report are thus a subset of the 294 patients included in the study (Engelhardt et al., 1967) cited by Davis (1975). Those patients treated with drug improved significantly in 10 of 20 symptoms. The most improvement on drug was seen in ideas of reference, incoherent speech, delusions, and withdrawal. In placebo-treated patients, only incoherent speech improved and ideas of persecution worsened.

Hogarty et al. (1974b) found no consistent differences between nonrelapsed chlorpromazine- and placebo-treated schizophrenic patients at six, 12, 18, and 24 months. The placebo nonrelapsed group, however, only included 20 percent of those originally assigned to treatment by the end of the 24-month study. There were differences in drug effects that depended upon the patient's sex. After 12 months, men treated with placebo who did not relapse were rated as having less apathy and retardation, less schizophrenic disorganization and hostile paranoia, and being less severely ill than nonrelapsing men treated with drug. Further, men on placebo were rated as showing better overall role performance than men on drug at both 12 and 18 months. On these same symptoms, in contrast, women had improved more on drug than placebo but the differences were smaller than those for men. At 24 months among the nonrelapsed patient group, men had still improved more on placebo than drug while women had improved more on drug than placebo in such symptoms as thinking disturbance, paranoid projection, and schizophrenic disorganization. Most differences reflected psychopathologic symptoms rather than social or vocational functioning. In the latter areas, only the overall role performance of men was affected and placebo was better than drug. These sex-specific differences in drug effects must be seen in the context of relapse (Hogarty et al., 1974a). The relapse rate for males was double that for women on drug during the two-year study period (63 percent vs.

37 percent). The relapse rates on placebo were comparable for the sexes (82 percent and 80 percent).

Conclusion

The studies reviewed here are not consistent in showing drug effects only on positive symptoms and having little effect on negative symptoms or a defect state. How can we account for this? One potentially important factor is chronicity. If symptoms of withdrawal and apathy in the relatively acute state are responsive to antipsychotic drug treatment as shown by Goldberg et al. (1965) and unresponsive later in the course of illness, then the more chronic the population the more likely is it that there will be no differences between the effects of drug and placebo treatment on these symptoms. In general, this is the case in the studies reviewed here. Studies with patients who have a chronic history as indexed by length of hospitalization in the inpatient studies and length of illness in outpatient studies do tend to show less drug responsiveness of these symptoms (e.g., Prien and Cole, 1968; Stevens, 1973; Freeman and Alson, 1962). As all those studies were cross-sectional rather than prospective, it is not possible to conclude that individual patients who were drug-responsive early in the course of their illness became less so as their illness progressed. Further, not all patients who are treated acutely go on to develop a chronic course, so that this change in the composition of the sample could also contribute to differences between samples of patients drawn from populations early and late in the course of illness.

THE ROLE OF COMPLIANCE

In the previous section of this paper we focused on the efficacy of antipsychotic drugs in schizophrenia. Although we reviewed ample evidence indicating that drugs are significantly more effective than placebo in preventing relapse, there is still a substantial reported relapse rate on medication. In a study with outpatients, Leff and Wing (1971) reported a 33-percent relapse rate during nine months. Hogarty et al. (1974a) reported that the 30-percent relapse rate of patients receiving chlorpromazine in the first year after discharge rose to 48 percent by the end of the second year. Particularly with outpatients, it has been observed that such reported rates are not a true estimate of the effectiveness of medication in preventing relapse because not all patients were taking medication as prescribed. Patient noncompliance is often implicated clinically as contributing to the relapse of patients for whom medication is prescribed.

The development of long-acting injectible forms of antipsychotic drugs (specifically fluphenazine enanthate and fluphenazine decanoate) offered the hope that reducing patients' reliance on daily medication-taking by administering injections at two- or three-week intervals would significantly reduce relapse by improving compliance. Two lines of evidence suggested this might be a useful strategy. First, clinical reports suggested that relapsing patients or their families often reported noncompliance with oral medication during the period preceding relapse. When medication has to be taken orally, it is not possible to disentangle the true sequence of events: Did a patient in remission stop taking medication and subsequently develop an exacerbation of symptoms? Or did cessation of medication follow the development of symptoms? This is an additional manifestation of the loss of insight about the relationship of medication to control of the illness. Second, in retrospective cohort studies of patients treated with long-acting depot medication, reduction of up to 50 percent in frequency of relapse and number of days spent in hospital was compared to previous experience (e.g., Denham and Adamson 1971; Johnson and Freeman, 1972; Marriott and Hiep, 1976). These mirror image studies encouraged the belief that noncompliance with medication-taking did indeed play a substantial role in the discouragingly high rates of relapse seen in schizophrenic patients ostensibly being maintained on antipsychotic drugs.

A series of controlled studies conducted in a range of patient populations in the United States, Great Britain, and France sought to test the noncompliance hypothesis directly (Crawford and Forrest, 1974; Del Giudice et al., 1975; Rifkin et al., 1977; Falloon et al., 1978; Simon et al., 1978; Hogarty et al., 1979; Schooler et al., 1980). In all studies listed in Table 3, the delivery of medication via long-acting depot injections as opposed to oral administration was the variable under investigation. Del Giudice et al. (1975), in a sample of American veterans, found fluphenazine enanthate to be significantly superior

Table 3   Prospective Studies Comparing Long-Acting Depot Fluphenazine and Oral Antipsychotic Drugs

Study	Patient Population	N	Study Length (months)	Depot Patients' Relapse Rate
Crawford and Forrest (1974)	stable outpatients	29	10	14%
Del Giudice et al. (1975)	newly discharged	88	16	NA
Rifkin et al. (1977)	remitted outpatients	73	12	8%
Falloon et al. (1978)	newly discharged	41	12	40%
Simon et al. (1978)	inpatients	181	18	NA
Hogarty et al. (1979)	newly discharged	105	24	40%
Schooler et al. (1980)	newly discharged	214	12	24%

to fluphenazine hydrochloride in preventing relapse, during periods of up to 15 months. In a sample of stable reliable outpatients, Crawford and Forrest (1974) found no statistically significant difference between groups receiving fluphenazine decanoate or trifluoperazine hydrochloride. Rifkin et al. (1977), studying carefully defined patients in remission, found no significant difference in rates of relapse between groups receiving fluphenazine decanoate or fluphenazine hydrochloride. Falloon et al. (1978) found no differences in rates of relapse among groups receiving fluphenazine decanoate or pimozide, an oral nonphenothiazine neuroleptic, in a 12-month study of newly discharged schizophrenic patients. In an 18-month study, Simon et al. (1978) found no differences in clinical status among chronic schizophrenic outpatients treated with fluphenazine decanoate, with pipothiazine palmitate (another long-acting depot neuroleptic), or with the physician's choice of an oral neuroleptic. Relapse was not a criterion studied. Hogarty et al. (1979), in a two-year study (the longest prospective trial), found no differences in rates of relapse or in levels of psychopathology and adjustment between patients treated with fluphenazine decanoate and those treated with fluphenazine hydrochloride, but found relatively high relapse rates for both, up to 40 percent over two years. Schooler et al. (1980), in the most recent and largest of these studies, found no significant differences in relapse rates during a one-year period following hospital discharge. The relapse rate on fluphenazine decanoate was 24 percent.

The general conclusion from these studies is that guaranteeing administration of medication does not significantly reduce the patient's risk of relapse. The clinical applicability of these findings has been questioned on the grounds that patients willing to enter a clinical trial in the first place are not the kinds of patients whom one would expect to be noncompliant. We have shown (Schooler, 1980) that, if we assumed that all the patients who refused to participate in our group's 1980 study had been included in that trial, and that if all refusers assigned to oral treatment had relapsed and the refusers assigned to depot medication had relapsed at the same rate as the patients included in the study, the difference in relapse rate between oral and injectible medication still would not have been significant.

The role of depot administration of neuroleptics cannot, therefore, be seen as providing a direct solution to the problem of the noncompliant patient. Rather, administration of long-acting depot drugs serves two "diagnostic" functions in clinical use. First, the patient who relapses while receiving a depot neuroleptic is clearly identified as one for whom antipsychotic medication does *not* prevent relapse although it may have delayed or reduced the severity of the symptom exacerbation. Although such a patient may refuse injections as part of the developing relapse, the refusal can be separated from the development of the illness, and the limitation of medication in future maintenance treatment for that patient is known. Those responsible for the clinical management of the patient will not attribute the course of the illness to problems with compliance. They may explore other treatment options and at the very least blame for the relapse will no longer reside with the patient for not taking medication or with the family for not monitoring him or her more closely.

Second, covert noncompliance cannot occur. The patient who accepts prescriptions for oral medication and does not take the medication or takes it irregularly will, if the medication is changed to depot fluphenazine, receive medication regularly based on a once-in-three-weeks schedule, or the patient will refuse injections outright so that the noncompliance will be immediately detected. In this situation, in contrast to the first case, what might have been judged as a relapse on medication can be judged as a case of noncompliance.

Results from the studies of depot neuroleptics provide evidence regarding the magnitude of the difference in relapse rates between the situation when compliance can be controlled as opposed to inferred or judged clinically. The studies also provide the most accurate evidence available of the magnitude of relapse under controlled guaranteed conditions. Table 3 presents the relapse or rehospitalization rates reported in each of the six studies of depot treatment. As the data in this table show, these rates differ from study to study but they can be interpreted as representing accurate estimates of the minimum risk of relapse for the population represented in each study.

NEWER STRATEGIES FOR ANTIPSYCHOTIC DRUG ADMINISTRATION

Recognizing the limits of efficacy of drug treatment has served to focus recent research on treatment strategies to increase the efficacy in terms of relapse and effects on specific symptoms. The risk of tardive dyskinesia (Kane et al., 1982) has also led researchers and clinicians to seek ways of using antipsychotic drug treatment that will minimize that risk.

The major current thrust of research regarding drug treatment strategies has been in the direction of reducing the amount of medication patients receive, either through dosage reduction or by using drugs episodically during periods of symptom exacerbation rather than continuously. The work that will be described next is ongoing research—drug treatment studies of the 80s with few definitive results as yet. However, these studies point to important new directions for the treatment of schizophrenia.

Low-Dose Treatment

The earliest reported study of low-dose treatment (Goldstein et al., 1978) was motivated initially by a desire to conduct a placebo-controlled study of phenothiazines and family therapy in the period immediately following a patient's brief hospitalization at a community mental health center. Unable to use placebo, the researchers settled for an extremely low dosage of injectible fluphenazine enanthate, 6.25 mg every two weeks, and randomly assigned patients to receive either that dosage or the standard dosage of 25 mg every two weeks. Patients were also randomly assigned to either family therapy or not. The family therapy was brief (six weekly sessions), pragmatic, and it focused on several issues: recognition of a schizophrenic illness in the patient, the importance of medication in the treatment of that illness, the identification of specific stressors leading to symptom exacerbation, and some general principles of stress management (Goldstein and Kopeikin, 1981). After the six-week study course, and persisting for six months, no patients who had received both the standard dosage of medication combined with the family therapy sessions had relapsed. Patients who had received standard dosage alone or had received family therapy in combination with the low dosage held an intermediate position; among patients who received the low dosage without family therapy, 25 percent had relapsed within six weeks, the number rising to almost 50 percent in six months. No statistically significant effects of dosage level on specific symptoms were seen during the six-week treatment period although symptoms of withdrawal were greater among the standard-dosage-treated patients. A significant reduction in withdrawal symptoms was seen, however, among patients who received family therapy. Of particular interest is the fact that patients who had received both standard drug treatment and family therapy showed a sustained reduction in withdrawal symptoms after six months.

A study directly investigating a low-dosage treatment strategy was conducted by Kane et al. (1983): Their patient population was restricted to remitted or clinically stable outpatients. Patients were treated with either low doses (1.25 to 5 mg biweekly) or standard doses (12.5 to 50 mg biweekly) of fluphenazine decanoate for one year. Preliminary results of the study show a 56-percent relapse rate with the low-dosage treatment, significantly higher than the 7-percent rate seen with the standard dosage in this study. Detailed data regarding symptomatic outcome from this study are not yet available so that we cannot assess whether or not the lower doses offer an advantage in terms of development of withdrawal symptoms. Early analyses of ratings of social adjustment and functioning indicate, however, that despite the greater likelihood of relapse, patients treated with the lower doses were rated significantly better than standard-dose patients in social and leisure activities (may we speculate that they are less withdrawn?), general adjustment, and a family member's rating of satisfaction with the patient. Another noteworthy finding from this study is that patients receiving low-dose treatment showed less increase of symptoms associated with tardive dyskinesia. Although scores for both groups were extremely low and could not be considered evidence of tardive dyskinesia, the fact that any difference could be detected suggests that this strategy may have potential importance in reducing the incidence of tardive dyskinesia.

A definitive answer regarding the role of low-dosage antipsychotic drug treatment is not available. The data from the Kane et al. (1983) study are not all in, particularly with regard to symptoms of psychopathology and social adjustment, crucial variables in assessing the value of treatments over long periods. To our knowledge, two other controlled experimental studies of low vs. standard dosage treatment with neuroleptics are currently being conducted in the United States. Both studies also use injectible fluphenazine decanoate but with somewhat different dosage schedules. Steven Marder, at the Brentwood Veterans Administration Hospital, is comparing a fixed-dose 5-mg biweekly injection with 25 mg in a sample of male schizophrenic veterans. Gerard E. Hogarty, at the University of Pittsburgh, is comparing two formulations, one offering 5 mg per cc of vehicle and one offering 25 mg per cc of vehicle, and allowing clinical titration of the number of cc's injected biweekly. Patients entering this study must be clinically stabilized. No data on patient outcome are as yet available from either study. However, the set of investigations should, over the next several years, provide details regarding the role that the strategy of reducing dosage can play in the long-term treatment of schizophrenia.

Intermittent or Targeted Medication Treatment

A second treatment strategy under investigation is that of intermittent or targeted medication. This strategy is based on the assumption that there are schizophrenic patients who do not need medication continuously; the illness in this case is conceptualized as one with a relapsing course. In such patients continuous administration of medication has been used only because that is the only way to insure that when patients *do* need it they will receive it.

With the intermittent or targeted medication strategy it becomes crucial to be able to identify the potential of symptom exacerbation early enough so that medication can be introduced before the patient becomes sufficiently ill to require rehospitalization. Strategies for such identification of prodromal symptoms vary but they require development of a therapeutic relationship that involves frequent contact with the patient and an understanding by the patient of the need to identify prodromal symptomatology. Two investigators, Carpenter at the University of Maryland and Herz at the University of Buffalo, are pursuing this strategy independently.

Carpenter et al. (1982) hypothesize that good candidates for this approach are patients who are in clinical remission, have a history of positive response to drug treatment, and develop prodromal signs of impending relapse so that intervention can be started. Patients are included in the study if they have a diagnosis of schizophrenia and are judged clinically to be good candidates for antipsychotic medication. They are randomly assigned to either continuous or targeted medication and are followed for two years. Preliminary six-month results indicate that the strategy is feasible—patients assigned to targeted medication received medication for an average of 8.8 weeks of the first six-month period compared to 25.2 weeks for those assigned to continuous medication. Despite this substantial reduction in drug exposure, there are no differences between the two groups in either number of hospitalizations or number of days in hospital.

Herz and Melville (1980) hypothesize that, to use an intermittent treatment strategy effectively, early signs of illness or symptom exacerbation need to be identified. The researchers found substantial agreement both among patients and among patients and their families in the reports of which symptoms were prominent in the development of an episode. Most frequently mentioned were "being tense and nervous" (reported by more than 70 percent of patients), followed by other signs of dysphoria such as trouble sleeping (60 percent), restlessness (50 percent), loss of interest (59 percent), reduced enjoyment (60 percent). In structured interviews, only about half of the patients reported that the pattern of symptom development was the same for each episode.

Herz et al. (1982) designed an intermittent medication study with schizophrenic outpatients who were in relative remission of psychotic symptoms, had been on a stable dosage of antipsychotic medication for at least six months, and lived with or in close proximity to a significant other person. In an open study involving 19 subjects they found that 14 could be effectively discontinued from medication. Five of these patients experienced prodromal signs that were successfully treated with medication. The study is currently being replicated with a double-blind protocol. Results from the controlled comparison are not yet available.

Conclusive data comparing either reduced dosage but continuous medication or intermittent medication to standard drug treatment are not yet available, so the merits of neither strategy can be stated unequivocally in comparison to general current practice. Further, as we have indicated, these two treatment strategies are based on clearly different sets of assumptions regarding the nature of antipsychotic drug effects in the long-term treatment of schizophrenic patients. A direct test of these assumptions is not currently being made because the treatment strategies are not being directly compared to one another in any completed or current research. Thus the comparison of reduced dosage and targeted medication strategies to standard-dose continuous treatment represents the next step in our continuing effort to understand the drug-treatment needs of chronic schizophrenic patients.

NOTE

The views expressed in this paper are those of the authors and do not necessarily reflect those of the National Institute of Mental Health.

REFERENCES

Adelson, D., and Epstein, L. J. 1962. A study of phenothiazines with male and female chronically ill schizophrenic patients. *J. Nerv. Ment. Dis.* 134:543-554.

Caffey, E. M., Diamond, L. S., Frank, T. V., Grasberger, J. C., Herman, L., Klett, C. J., and Rothstein, C. 1964. Discontinuation or reduction of chemotherapy in chronic schizophrenics. *J. Chron. Dis.* 17:347-358.

Carpenter, W. T., Stephens, J. H., Rey, A. C., Hanlon, T. E., and Heinrichs, D. W. 1982. Early intervention vs continuous pharmacotherapy of schizophrenia. *Psychopharm. Bull.* 18:21.

Crawford, R., and Forrest, A. 1974. Controlled trial of depot fluphenazine in outpatient schizophrenics. *Br. J. Psychiatry* 124:385-391.

Crow, T. J. 1980. Molecular pathology of schizophrenia; more than one disease process? *Br. Med. J.* 280:66-68.

Davis, J. M. 1975. Overview: Maintenance therapy in psychiatry: I. Schizophrenia. *Am. J. Psychiatry* 132:1237-1245.

Del Giudice, J., Clark, W. G., and Gocka, E. F. 1975. Prevention of recidivism of schizophrenics treated with fluphenazine enanthate. *Psychosomatics* 16:32-36.

Denham, J., and Adamson, L. 1971. The contribution of fluphenazine enanthate and decanoate in the prevention of readmission of schizophrenic patients. *Acta Psychiatr. Scand.* 47:420-430.

Diamond, L. S., and Marks, J. B. 1960. Discontinuance of tranquilizers among chronic schizophrenic patients receiving maintenance dosage. *J. Nerv. Ment. Dis.* 131:247-251.

Donaldson, S., Gelenberg, A. J., and Baldessarini, R. J. 1983. The pharmacologic treatment of schizophrenia: A progress report. *Schizophr. Bull.* 9:504-527.

Engelhardt, D. M., Freedman, N., Hankoff, L. D., Mann, D., and Margolis, R. 1963. Long term drug-induced symptom modification in schizophrenic outpatients. *J. Nerv. Ment. Dis.* 137:231-241.

Engelhardt, D. M., Rosen, B., Freedman, D., and Margolis, R. 1967. Phenothiazines in the prevention of psychiatric hospitalization. *Arch. Gen. Psychiatry* 16:98-101.

Falloon, I., Watt, D. G., and Shepherd, M. 1978. A comparative controlled trial of pimozide and fluphenazine decanoate in the continuation therapy of schizophrenia. *Psychol. Med.* 8:59-70.

Freeman, L. S., and Alson, E. 1962. Prolonged withdrawal of chlorpromazine in chronic patients. *Dis. Nerv. Syst.* 23:522-525.

Garfield, S. L., Gershon, S., Sletten, I., Neubauer, H., and Ferrel, E. 1966. Withdrawal of ataractic medication in schizophrenic patients. *Dis. Nerv. Syst.* 27:321-325.

Goldberg, S. C., Klerman, G. L., and Cole, J. O. 1965. Changes in schizophrenic psychopathology and ward behavior as a function of phenothiazine treatment. *Br. J. Psychiatry* 111:120-133.

Goldstein, M. J., and Kopeikin, H. S. 1981. Short- and long-term effects of combining drug and family therapy. In M. J. Goldstein (ed.), *Developments in Interventions with Families of Schizophrenics*, pp. 5-26. Washington: Jossey-Bass.

Goldstein, M. J., Rodnick, E. H., Evans, J. R., May, P. R. A., and Steinberg, M. R. 1978. Drug and family therapy in the aftercare treatment of acute schizophrenics. *Arch. Gen. Psychiatry* 35:1169.

Good, W. W., Sterling, M., and Holtzman, W. H. 1958. Termination of chlorpromazine with schizophrenic patients. *Am. J. Psychiatry* 115:443-448.

Herz, M. I., and Melville, C. 1980. Relapse in schizophrenia. *Am. J. Psychiatry* 137:801.

Herz, M. I., Szymanski, H. V., and Simon, J. C. 1982. Intermittent medication for stable schizophrenic outpatients: An alternative to maintenance medication. *Am. J. Psychiatry* 139:918.

Hirsch, S. R., Gaind, R., Rohde, P. D., Stevens, B. C., and Wing, J. K. 1973. Outpatient maintenance of chronic schizophrenic patients with long-acting fluphenazine: Double-blind placebo trial. *Br. Med. J.* 17:633-637.

Hogarty, G. E., Goldberg, S. C., Schooler, N. R., and Ulrich, R. F. 1974a. Drug and sociotherapy in the aftercare of schizophrenic patients: II. Two-year relapse rates. *Arch. Gen. Psychiatry* 31:603.

Hogarty, G. E., Goldberg, S. C., and Schooler, N. R. 1974b. Drug and sociotherapy in the aftercare of schizophrenic patients: III. Adjustment of non-relapsed patients. *Arch. Gen. Psychiatry* 31:609-618.

Hogarty, G. E., Schooler, N. R., Ulrich, R., Mussare, F., Ferro, P., and Herron, E. 1979. Fluphenazine and social therapy in the aftercare of schizophrenic patients: Relapse analyses of a two-year controlled trial. *Arch. Gen. Psychiatry* 36:1283-1294.

Jeste, D. V., and Wyatt, R. J. 1982. *Understanding and Treating Tardive Dyskinesia*. New York: Guilford Press.

Johnson, D. A. W., and Freeman, H. 1972. Long-acting tranquilizers. *Practitioner* 208:395-400.

Kane, J. M., Rifkin, A., Woerner, M., Reardon, G., Sarantakos, S., Schiebel, D., and Ramos-Lorenzi, J. 1983. Low dose neuroleptic treatment of outpatient schizophrenics: I. Preliminary results for relapse rates. *Arch. Gen. Psychiatry* 40:893-896.

Kane, J. M., Woerner, M., Weinhold, P., Wegner, J., and Kinon, B. 1982. A prospective study of tardive dyskinesia development: preliminary results. *J. Clin. Psychopharmacol.* 2:345-349.

Leff, J. P., and Wing, J. K. 1971. Trial of maintenance therapy in schizophrenics. *Br. Med. J.* 2:599-604.

Marjerrison, G., Irvine, D., Stewart, C. N., Williams, R., Matheu, H., and Demay, M. 1964. Withdrawal of long-term phenothiazines from chronically hospitalized psychiatric patients. *Can. J. Psychol.* 9:190-298.

Marriott, P., and Hiep, A. 1976. A mirror image out-patient study at a depot phenothiazine clinic. *Aust. N.Z. J. Psychiatry* 10:163-167.

Nestoros, J. N. 1980. Benzodiazepines in schizophrenia: A need for reassessment. *International Journal of Pharmacopsychiatry* 15:171-179.

Paul, G. L., Tobias, L. L., and Holly, L. 1972. Maintenance psychotropic drugs in the presence of active treatment programs. A "triple-blind" withdrawal study with long-term mental patients. *Arch. Gen. Psychiatry* 27:106-115.

Prien, R. F., and Cole, J. O. 1968. High dose chlorpromazine therapy in chronic schizophrenia: Report of the National Institute of Mental Health-Psychopharmacology Research Branch Collaborative Study Group. *Arch. Gen. Psychiatry* 18:482-495.

Prien, R. F., Levine, J., and Cole, J. O. 1969. High dose trifluoperazine therapy in chronic schizophrenia. *Am. J. Psychiatry* 126:53-61.

Rifkin, A., Quitkin, F., Kane, J., Klein, D. F., and Ross, D. 1979. The effect of fluphenazine upon social and vocational functioning in remitted schizophrenics. *Biol. Psychiatry* 14:499-508.

Rifkin, A., Quitkin, F., Rabiner, C. J., and Klein, D. F. 1977. Fluphenazine decanoate, fluphenazine hydrochloride given orally, and placebo in remitted schizophrenics: I. Relapse rates after one year. *Arch. Gen. Psychiatry* 344:43-47.

Schiele, B. C., Vestre, N. D., and Stein, K. E. 1961. A comparison of thioridazine, trifluoperazine, chlorpromazine, and placebo: A double-blind controlled study on the treatment of chronic, hospitalized, schizophrenic patients. *Journal of Clinical and Experimental Psychopathology* 22:151-162.

Schooler, N. R. 1980. How generalizable are the results of clinical trials? *Psychopharm. Bull.* I, 16:29-31.

Schooler, N. R., and Levine, J. 1983. Strategies for enhancing drug therapy of schizophrenia. *Am. J. Psychotherapy* 37:521-532.

Schooler, N. R., Levine, J., Severe, J. B., Brauzer, B., DiMascio, A., Klerman, G. L., and Tuason, V. B. 1980. Prevention of relapse in schizophrenia. *Arch. Gen. Psychiatry* 37:16-24.

Shawver, J. R., Gorham, D. R., Leskin, L. W., Good, W. W., and Kabnick, D. E. 1959. Comparison of chlorpromazine and reserpine in maintenance drug therapy. *Dis. Nerv. Syst.* 20:452-457.

Simon, P., Fermanian, J., and Ginestet, D., Goujet, M. A., and Peron-Magnan, P. 1978. Standard and long-acting depot neuroleptics in chronic schizophrenia. *Arch. Gen. Psychiatry* 35:893-897.

Siris, S. G., van Kammen, D. P., and Docherty, J. P. 1978. Use of antidepressant drugs in schizophrenia. *Arch. Gen. Psychiatry* 35:1368-1377.

Stevens, B. 1973. Role of fluphenazine decanoate in lessening the burden of chronic schizophrenics on the community. *Psychol. Med.* 3:141-158.

Strauss, J. S., Carpenter, W. T. Jr., and Bratko, J. 1974. Speculations on the processes that underlie schizophrenia signs and symptoms. *Schizophr. Bull.* 2:61-69.

10
Neuroleptic Blood Level Monitoring in Maintenance Studies of Schizophrenic Outpatients

CYRUS SAJADI, ROBERT C. SMITH, ALLA SHVARTSBURD, VONA MORTON, JACK R. GORDON, AND MOSHEN MIRABI

The value of maintenance therapy with neuroleptic drugs to reduce the risk of relapse in schizophrenic patients is well documented (see review by Davis, 1975; Goldberg et al., 1979; Hogarty et al., 1974). Schizophrenic patients maintained on placebo have two to three times higher relapse rates than do similar patients treated with standard neuroleptic medications.

Although the value of neuroleptic medication for the prevention of schizophrenic relapse is established, two important clinical research questions remain to be addressed: Is the patient's neuroleptic dosage related to the efficacy of maintenance therapy for schizophrenia and are minimum dosages as effective as high dosages? Are blood levels of neuroleptics related to the efficacy of maintenance therapy?

Different patients treated with the same dosage of neuroleptics demonstrate widely varying drug blood levels. For a few neuroleptics, recent studies indicate that a relationship may exist between acutely psychotic hospital patients' plasma or red blood cell (RBC) levels of the drugs and the patients' clinical response. For butaperazine, haloperidol, and fluphenazine this relationship fits into an apparent "therapeutic window," the best response occurring in patients who have blood levels in the middle range (Garver et al., 1977; Casper et al., 1980; Smith et al., 1982; Dyskin et al., 1981).

Does the same therapeutic window exist for schizophrenic outpatients maintained on these neuroleptics? No well-controlled published studies have addressed the blood-level question concerning outpatient treatment for schizophrenics. Davis and Baldessarini (1980) made a cross-sectional comparison of dosages in a series of outpatient studies of neuroleptics, most of which did not include two

143

neuroleptic dosages in the same study. They concluded that there was no significant difference between relapse rates among patients treated with dosages in the range of 100 ng to 2000 ng of chlorpromazine equivalents per day. A few controlled studies have begun to address the dosage question. Kane and associates (1980) have recently shown that patients on low-dose fluphenazine decanoate (1.25 to 5.0 mg biweekly) had significantly higher relapse rates than did patients on more standard dosages (12.5 to 50 mg biweekly). Lehman and associates at McGill University (unpublished manuscript) also gathered data that suggested slightly higher relapse rates and significantly higher Brief Psychiatric Rating Scale (BPRS) scores among schizophrenic outpatients maintained on a relatively low dosage (50 mg/day) of chlorpromazine compared to standard or high dosages. Brown and associates (1982) suggested that schizophrenic outpatients who had low blood levels of neuroleptics (assessed by radioreceptor assay) during maintenance therapy had a higher rate of relapse. Our results come from a preliminary study of drug blood levels of schizophrenic patients maintained on haloperidol and thioridazine and the relationship of fluctuations in drug blood levels to fluctuations in clinical status.

METHOD

Participants were outpatients in the TRIMS adult psychiatric clinic who had a Research Diagnostic Criteria-assessed diagnosis of schizophrenia or schizoaffective psychosis and gave informed written consent for participation in the study (Table 1). For some purposes, comparisons were made to blood level studies done with schizophrenic hospital patients treated with fixed dosages of neuroleptics who were participating in a related blood level and clinical response study (Smith et al., 1982; Shvartsburd et al., 1983).

The present study was designed originally to maintain patients at preset blood level ranges. Patients were randomly assigned to haloperidol or thioridazine, except for patients who were maintained on the same medication if they had

Table 1 Characteristics of Patient Sample

	Haloperidol	Thioridazine	Total
Number of Patients	8	12	20
Age (mean ± S.D.)	35.8 + 2.8	31.4 + 7.3	33.2 + 4.4
(range)	(23-52)	(20-42)	(20-52)
Sex			
Male	2	3	5
Female	6	9	15
Diagnosis (RDC)			
Schizophrenia	8	10	18
Schizoaffective Psychosis	0	2	2

had a good response to either drug, and patients who had had severe side effects from either haloperidol or thioridazine and were assigned to the alternate medication. Patients were randomly assigned to two dosage groups, low or moderate. During four weeks of fixed treatment with these initial dosages, the patients' neuroleptic plasma levels were monitored. If their drug blood levels fell into predetermined ranges (Table 2), they were maintained on the same dosage; if their mean plasma levels were above or below the indicated range, their dosage was increased or decreased to bring them into the appropriate range. During the course of subsequent treatment, the patients' dosage was adjusted if their blood levels fell consistently outside the predetermined ranges of the blood level group to which the patients had been randomly assigned.

Table 2   Dosage Assignments and Blood Level Ranges

(a) Split random assignment— haloperidol	
low blood level range	high blood level range
initial dose 3 to 5 mg/ day haloperidol	initial dose 15 to 20 mg/ day haloperidol
After first month, adjust dosage to reach appropriate blood level range:	
2 to 6.5 ng/ml plasma	9 to 14 ng/ml plasma

(b) Split random assignment— thioridazine	
low blood level assignment	high blood level assignment
initial dose thioridazine 25 to 75 mg/day	initial dose thioridazine 200 to 400 mg/day
After first month, adjust dosage to reach appropriate blood level range:	
50 to 150 ng/ml plasma thioridazine*	300 to 650 ng/ml plasma thioridazine

*Range was 30 to 70 ng/ml earlier in study.

Patients were seen weekly or biweekly during the first two months and monthly thereafter. At each visit they participated in 15- to 30-minute sessions of supportive psychotherapy and were evaluated with the Brief Psychiatric Rating Scale, the interview form of the New Haven Schizophrenia Index (NHSI), the Side Effect Checklist (SEC), and the Simpson Angus Scale (SA). The BPRS scores will be described in this report.

Relapse and prodromal worsening were defined as follows: Relapse—$\geqslant$ 15-point increase in the BPRS score on any single rating and/or rehospitalization of the patient; prodromal worsening—$\geqslant$ 10-point increase on the BPRS during a two- to three-week period.

**Table 3   Procedures for Dosage Change If Relapse
or Prodromal Worsening Occurs**

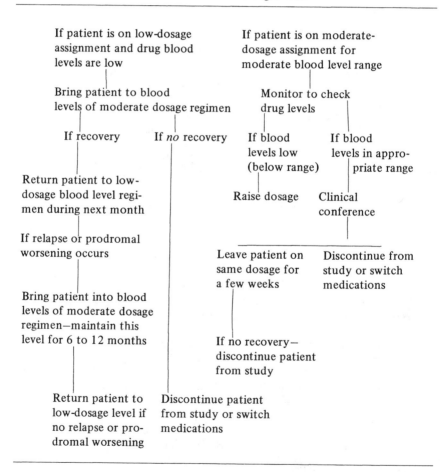

If patients met criteria of prodromal worsening or relapse, their neuroleptic dosage could be altered to get them into a new blood level range according to procedures outlined in Table 3. Recovery from relapse or prodromal worsening was defined as a return of the patient's BPRS score to within two points of the BPRS baseline before the onset of the current relapse or prodromal worsening episode. If the patient recovered from the exacerbation of psychosis, he or she was returned to the original blood level range as shown in Table 2, after three to six months.

Blood was drawn during each clinic visit, at a similar time of day for each patient (e.g., 2 to 3 p.m., 9 to 10 a.m.). Patients skipped their morning dose on the day of the visit. Blood samples were processed, stored, and later analyzed by a gas-liquid chromatographic (GLC) nitrogen detector technique described in our previous publications (Shvartsburd et al., 1983; Shvartsburd et al., in press; Smith et al., 1982). Here we present our study of plasma levels of haloperidol, thioridazine and its metabolite, mesoridazine.

Patients' ingestion of medication was monitored by several procedures: patients' self-reports, special daily pill dispensers for some patients, pill counts, phone calls to patients, and reports from relatives.

RESULTS

Neuroleptic Plasma Levels

During periods of fixed-dosage treatment with neuroleptics, the schizophrenic outpatients showed considerable variations in plasma levels of haloperidol, thioridazine, and mesoridazine, variations much greater than we had found previously in hospitalized schizophrenics. Figures 1 and 2 show plasma haloperidol levels in schizophrenic inpatients and schizophrenic outpatients; Figures 3 and 4 show representative plasma thioridazine levels in these two groups of patients. In the hospital patients, plasma mesoridazine levels were somewhat more variable than those of the parent compound thioridazine, but outpatients treated with thioridazine had shown even greater variation in plasma mesoridazine levels. When we measured plasma levels in the same patients during their hospitalization and before or during outpatient maintenance treatment, we found that their haloperidol and thioridazine plasma levels (Figures 5 and 6) were much more stable during inpatient than outpatient treatment. A few of the schizophrenic outpatients did, however, have relatively stable neuroleptic blood levels.

In most cases the large variability in neuroleptic blood levels did not seem to be caused by poor compliance with the drug regimen. Although a few patients whose neuroleptic plasma levels fluctuated widely had a history of noncompliance, several others whose medication ingestion was reliable—as indicated by pill counts, ingestion records, and the patients' own reports—showed equally large variability. One patient, whose thioridazine levels varied greatly during

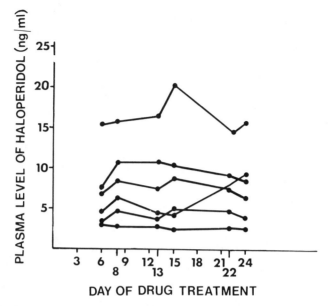

Figure 1   Day-to-day variation of steady-state plasma haloperidol levels in schizo-phrenic hospital patients treated with fixed dosages.

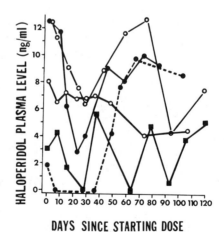

Figure 2   Intrapatient variation in plasma haloperidol levels in schizophrenic out-patients during period of fixed-dosage treatment.

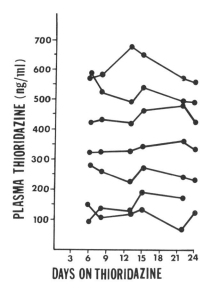

Figure 3 Day-to-day variation of plasma thioridazine levels in schizophrenic hospital patients treated with fixed doses.

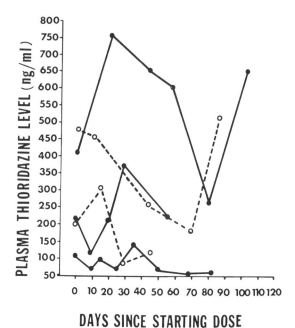

Figure 4 Intrapatient variation of plasma thioridazine levels in schizophrenic outpatients during period of fixed-dosage treatment.

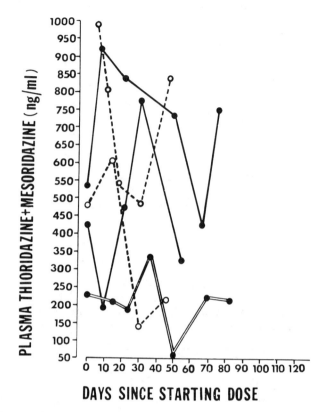

Figure 5   Intrapatient variation in gas-liquid chromatography-assayed total plasma levels (thioridazine plus mesoridazine) in schizophrenic outpatients treated with fixed dosages.

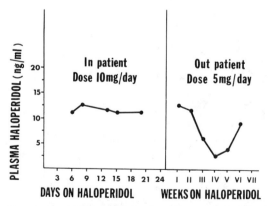

Figure 6   Comparison of variation of haloperidol levels in the same patient during inpatient and outpatient fixed-dosage treatment.

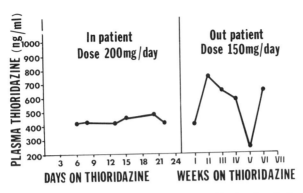

Figure 7 Comparison of variation of plasma thioridazine levels in the same patient during inpatient and outpatient fixed-dosage treatment.

fixed-dosage treatment, lived in a halfway house where a nurse checked medication ingestion closely (Figure 7).

Neuroleptic Blood Levels and Clinical Response

Are the large fluctuations of neuroleptic plasma levels we found in schizophrenic outpatients related to similar variations in their psychiatric status and psychopathology scores? In the relatively small number of patients in our study to date three relationship patterns were evident. In one or two patients, fluctuation in their BPRS scores followed a pattern of fluctuation in plasma neuroleptic levels (Figure 8). A few other patients showed a possible "threshold" effect

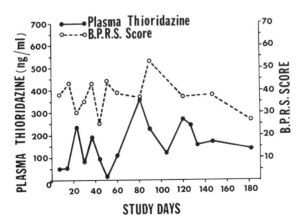

Figure 8 Representative example of fluctuations of plasma thioridazine levels and BPRS scores.

of neuroleptic blood levels; at most plasma levels, these patients' fluctuations in drug levels and BPRS scores seemed unrelated, but their BPRS scores increased when their drug levels dropped very low. An example of this pattern in a patient is illustrated in Figure 9. The majority of patients, however, showed a third pattern—no clear relationship between BPRS scores and plasma neuroleptic levels. These patients had either relatively stable BPRS scores despite wide fluctuations in week-to-week neuroleptic levels, or fluctuations in BPRS scores and neuroleptic levels that did not covary in a systematic or predictable way (Figure 10).

Were dosages or blood levels of haloperidol and thioridazine related to psychotic relapse? Two of seven patients treated with haloperidol, and six of 13

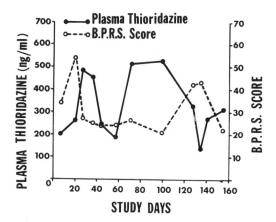

Figure 9   Representative record of patient whose BPRS scores were high at same times his thioridazine plasma levels were relatively low.

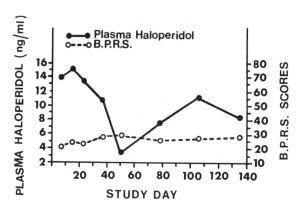

Figure 10   Representative record of patient whose BPRS scores remained stable despite wide fluctuations in his plasma haloperidol levels.

patients treated with thioridazine, fulfilled the criteria for relapse or prodromal worsening defined above. Four patients required rehospitalization and five patients had more than one relapse. There were no significant differences in the initial blood level group dosage assignment between patients who relapsed and those who did not (Tables 4 and 5). The two haloperidol-treated patients who relapsed were assigned to the low blood level group, yet for thioridazine-treated patients there were slightly more relapses in the moderate blood level dosage assignment group than in the low blood level assignment group. Relapsing patients did not consistently have low neuroleptic levels or plasma levels below the apparent therapeutic range. Only two of seven patients who relapsed while on

Table 4   Relationship Between Relapse on Haloperidol and Initial Blood Level Group Assignment

| | *Haloperidol Initial Blood Level Assignment* | |
	Patients in initial moderate blood level assignment group	Patients in initial low blood level assignment group
Relapse	0	2
No relapse	3	2

Fisher Exact Test $p = 0.295$

Table 5   Relationship Between Relapse on Thioridazine and Initial Blood Level Group Assignment

| | *Thioridazine Initial Blood Level Assignment* | |
	Patients in initial moderate blood level assignment group	Patients in initial low blood level assignment group
Relapse	4	2
No relapse	2	5

Fisher Exact Test $p = 0.209$

thioridazine, for example, had drug plasma levels below 250 ng/ml at the time of relapse, and only three of the seven had steady-state plasma thioridazine levels below 250 ng/ml. The rest of the patients' thioridazine blood levels were above 250 ng/ml (Table 6). Both patients who relapsed on haloperidol had blood levels above 7 ng/ml at time of relapse; our research with actively ill, hospitalized schizophrenic patients indicates that this drug blood level is within the therapeutic window for haloperidol. During the course of treatment, only one of the two patients had mean haloperidol plasma levels below 7 ng/ml (Table 6). Three of four thioridazine-treated patients who had a second relapse had drug blood levels at that time which were lower than their plasma levels at the first relapse (Table 7). In some of these patients, plasma levels decreased even though the thioridazine dosage had been raised. As Table 7 shows, the four patients who relapsed twice all had plasma thioridazine levels below 250 ng/ml at the time.

DISCUSSION

The wide fluctuations of drug blood levels in schizophrenic outpatients suggest that a single blood sample is not a useful indicator of average or steady-state neuroleptic plasma levels in outpatients treated with haloperidol or thioridazine. Factors accounting for the higher intrapatient variability of thioridazine, mesoridazine, and haloperidol plasma levels in the schizophrenic outpatients we studied are unclear. Differences in blood sampling time or medication compliance do not fully explain the higher blood level fluctuations in outpatients as compared to inpatients. In our study, each patient's blood was drawn at about the same time of day, and we attempted to avoid fluctuations in steady-state blood levels caused by drug absorption and distribution kinetics by having patients skip their morning dose on the day of blood sampling. Although the clinical histories of one or two patients suggested poor compliance with medication ingestion, this fact cannot explain the wide intrapatient blood level variations in most of our participants. Self-report records of most patients, as well as pill counts, indicated good compliance. Even the patient whose medication was administered by a nurse showed very wide variation in thioridazine blood levels.

Factors like variations in diet and physical activity, which are likely to be much less uniform in schizophrenic outpatients than hospital patients, merit further investigation. More research is needed also to determine the relative importance of strict compliance with a prescribed schedule of medication ingestion as an influence on the variability of neuroleptic blood levels. A study by Schooler and associates (1980) found no difference in relapse rates among patients taking fluphenazine orally and intramuscularly, which suggests that adherence to strict medication schedules may not be as important as has been believed in maintaining remission in neuroleptic-treated schizophrenic outpatients.

Our preliminary results, based on a small number of patients, indicate that dosage and blood levels of neuroleptics do not consistently covary with changes

Table 6 Drug Levels in Patients Who Relapsed or Had Prodromal Worsening

Patient	Dosage (mg/day)	Plasma Levels at Time of Relapse		Mean Plasma Level (ng/ml) at this Dosage	
		Drug	Total	Drug	Total
Thioridazine: Initial Moderate Blood Level Assignment					
1	200	20	84[1]	163	316
2	300	266	938[1]	350	545
3	150	153	423[1]	306	603
4	150	472	659[1]	555	705
Thioridazine: Initial Low Blood Level Assignment					
5	50	465	730[1]	183	330
6	50	264	264[1]	226	410
Haloperidol: Initial Low Blood Level Assignment					
7	5	7.8		8.5	
8	4	12.7		6.3	

[1]Thioridazine + mesoridazine.

Table 7   Drug Levels of Recurrently Relapsing Patients

Patient	Dosage at First Relapse (mg/day)	Level at First Relapse (ng/ml)	Dosage at Second Relapse	Level at Second Relapse
		Thioridazine		
1	200	20	200	226
2	300	266	500	137
5	50	465	50	230
6	50	264	75	201
		Halperidol		
8	4	12.7	2	7.2

in BPRS scores or relapse rates, and that these factors may not be strongly related to the maintenance of remission or the degree of clinical response by schizophrenic outpatients. The relatively high intrapatient variation of neuroleptic plasma levels in our sample may suggest, however, that our study design may be less appropriate for addressing some of these questions. Our original design was to adjust neuroleptic dosages to maintain drug levels in a predetermined range. If drug levels vary widely from week to week, however, a single blood level will not indicate steady-state plasma levels in a specific patient. Adjustment of dosage according to drug blood levels may not, therefore, be an effective design for this kind of study. We are currently investigating the issues of neuroleptic dosages and blood levels in maintenance of schizophrenic outpatients, using a multiple fixed-dosage design, to determine more precisely how blood levels vary during fixed-dosage treatment, and whether or not very low dosages of neuroleptics are as effective as moderate or moderately high ones in treating schizophrenic outpatients.

ACKNOWLEDGMENT

The research was supported, in part, by grant MH 34692 from the National Institute of Mental Health, Robert C. Smith, M.D., Ph.D., principal investigator.

REFERENCES

Brown, W. A., Laughren, J., Chrisholm, E., and Williams, B.W. 1982. Low serum neuroleptic levels predict relapse in schizophrenic patients. *Arch. Gen. Psychiatry* 39:998-1000.

Casper, R., Garver, D. L. Dekirmenjian, H., Chang, S., and Davis, J. 1980. Phenothiazine levels in plasma and red blood cells. *Arch. Gen. Psychiatry* 37:301-305.

Davis, J.M. 1975. Overview: Maintenance therapy in psychiatry: I. Schizophrenia. *Am. J. Psychiatry* 132:1237-1245.

Davis, J.M., and Baldessarini, R.J. 1980. What is the best maintenance dose of neuroleptics? *Psychiatry Research* 3:115-122.

Dyskin, M.W., Javaid, J.I., Chang, S.S., Schaffer, C., Shabid, A., and Davis, J.M. 1981. Fluphenazine pharmacokinetics and therapeutic response. *Psychopharmacology* 73:205-210.

Garver, D.L., Dekirmenjian, H., Davis, J.M., Casper, R., and Ericksen, S. 1977. Neuroleptic drug levels and therapeutic response: Preliminary observations with red blood cell-bound butaperazine. *Am. J. Psychiatry* 134:304-307.

Goldberg, S.C., Schooler, N., Hogarty, G.E., and Roper, M. 1977. Prediction of relapse in schizophrenic outpatients treated by drugs and sociotherapy. *Arch. Gen. Psychiatry* 34:171-184.

Hogarty, G.E., Goldberg, S.C., Schooler, N.R., and Ulrich, R.F. 1974. Drugs and sociotherapy in the after care of schizophrenic patients. *Arch. Gen. Psychiatry* 31:603-618.

Kane, J.M., Ritkin, A., Woerner, M., and Reardon, G. 1980. Low-dose neuroleptics in outpatient schizophrenics. *Psychopharmacol. Bull.* 18:20-21.

Schooler, H., Levine, J., Severe, J., Brauzer, B., DiMascio, H. Klerman, G.L., and Tuasen, V.B. 1980. Prevention of relapse in schizophrenia: An evaluation of fluphenazine decanoate. *Arch. Gen. Psvchiatry* 37:16-24.

Shvartsburd, A., Dekirmenjian, H., and Smith, R. C. 1983. Blood levels of haloperidol in schizophrenic patients. *Journal of Clinical Psychopharmacology* 3:7-12.

Shvartsburd, A., Nwokeafor, V., and Smith, R. C. in press. Red blood cell and plasma levels of thioridazine and mesoridazine in schizophrenic patients. *Psychopharmacology*.

Smith, R.C., Vroulis, G., Shvartsburd, A., Allen, R., Lewis, N., Schoolar, J.C., Chojnacki, M., and Johnson, R. 1982. RBC and plasma levels of haloperidol and clinical response in schizophrenia. *Am. J. Psychiatry* 139:1054-1056.

11
Long-Term Maintenance Pharmacotherapy in Recurrent and Chronic Affective Disorders

ROBERT F. PRIEN

This review deals with the pharmacologic treatment of recurrent and chronic depressive disorders, areas that have been relatively neglected in the research literature. I will focus first on the use of drugs for the long-term maintenance treatment of patients with recurrent major depressions, then discuss briefly the sparse data available on maintenance pharmacotherapy of chronically depressed patients.

MAINTENANCE DRUG THERAPY IN RECURRENT MAJOR DEPRESSION

Studies of the drug treatment of affective disorders are usually restricted to the acute episode and are limited to a three- to eight-week period. A survey of antidepressant drug trials published in the North American psychiatric literature between 1976 and 1978 (Prien, 1981) shows that only 15 percent of the trials lasted beyond eight weeks and fewer than 5 percent longer than 12 weeks; the mode was six weeks. Unfortunately, most major depressions last longer than six weeks and many have long-term complications in the form of waxing and waning of symptomatology, recurrences, and residual impairment. Maintenance pharmacologic treatment aimed at preventing the reemergence of symptoms and the occurrence of new episodes has been studied far less adequately than treatment directed at the acute episode. As a result, there are many gaps in our knowledge as to how to treat affective disorders following the initial control of the patient's acute symptoms.

Course of Depressive Illness

To understand the effects of pharmacologic treatment on the clinical course of major depressive disorder, it is first necessary to have knowledge about the natural course of the disorder. One important question is how long depressive episodes can be expected to last. Hamilton (1979), reviewing studies on the natural course of affective illnesses, reported that the mean length of depressive episodes in patients with unipolar and bipolar disorders is four and a half months, with about 30 percent of episodes lasting longer than six months. In a current five-hospital study of the course of depressive illness (the NIMH Collaborative Study of the Psychobiology of Depression) researchers report that only 2 percent of patients with major depressive disorders recover after two months and only 14 percent after three months (R.B. Hirschfeld, 1982, personal communication). The findings from these and other surveys suggest that clinical trials of antidepressant drugs should not be restricted to a six- to eight-week period.

One question posed in almost every epidemiological or clinical study of the natural course of depression is whether or not major depression is a recurring disorder. The risk of a subsequent episode is of obvious importance in determining whether one should initiate a program of long-term therapy following the patient's recovery from a depressive episode. There is considerable disparity among studies in the proportion of patients who experience more than one episode. Zis and Goodwin (1979) reviewed the 10 largest and most frequently quoted studies of the natural course of depressive illness and found recurrence rates ranging from 42 to 97 percent. Differences in patient populations, criteria for identifying episodes, and length of observation periods account for much of the variance among studies. In all studies, however, there is general agreement that major depression has a strong tendency to recur. A conservative estimate is that at least half the individuals who have an initial episode of major depression will have one or more recurrences (DSM-III, 1980; Klerman, 1978). There is also general agreement that with each successive episode, recurrences tend to occur more frequently. For a significant number of patients, affective illness is both episodic and chronic. From 20 to 40 percent of patients with a major depressive disorder have a chronic course between episodes characterized by persistent symptomatology and/or significant social impairment (Weissman, 1979; Rounsaville et al., 1980; Keller and Shapiro, 1982). Thus, the clinical course of depression can best be described in terms of recurrences, remissions, and chronicity—a highly legitimate focus for long-term pharmacotherapeutic approaches.

Types of Maintenance Therapies

Two types of maintenance therapy will be discussed: continuation therapy and long-term preventive therapy. Continuation therapy refers to the continuation of drug treatment for the patient, after initial control of acute symptomatology, for the purpose of maintaining control over the episode. Long-term preventive therapy refers to pharmacologic treatment administered over long periods to prevent further episodes or to reduce their severity and duration. These two types of maintenance therapy, though distinguishable in theory (Quitkin et al., 1976), are often blurred in clinical practice. It may be extremely difficult to determine when continuation therapy ends (i.e., when the episode is over) and when preventive therapy begins. The two therapies will be discussed separately, however, because they serve different functions in modifying the course of depressive disorders.

Continuation Maintenance Therapy

Major depressive episodes do not necessarily end with the drug-induced control of the patient's acute symptoms. Continued administration of antidepressant drugs may be required for months following the initial suppression of symptoms. The use of continuation therapy is based on the assumption that antidepressants suppress the symptoms of depression without altering the course of the postulated underlying disorder; medication must be continued until the underlying illness runs its natural course. Several studies show that when medication is discontinued immediately following drug-induced remission of symptoms, a significant proportion of patients relapse, often within a few weeks.

Placebo-controlled studies. Table 1 shows the results of placebo-controlled studies of continuation treatment. In each study, an antidepressant drug was used to control acute symptomatology, after which about half of the patients were switched to placebo and the other half continued to receive antidepressant medication. Patients were observed for two to eight months. The high relapse rate for patients receiving placebo illustrates their continued vulnerability for months following their apparent recovery and provides strong support for the need of continuation therapy.

It is possible that patients who relapse after they stop taking antidepressants may be manifesting a new rather than a continuation of the old episode. This is probably not the case with most patients, however. Most relapses occur relatively rapidly after withdrawl of medication. In the studies cited in Table 1, most relapses occurred within two to 10 weeks following the switch to placebo. Also, the reemergence of symptoms after withdrawal of medication seems to be independent of the patient's previous frequency of episodes. Patients with long intervals between episodes relapse as quickly as patients with relatively short intervening periods of recovery (Mindham et al., 1973; Prien et al., 1973, 1980; Klerman et al., 1974; Coppen et al., 1978; Stein et al., 1980).

Duration of continuation therapy. The clinician may be faced with a difficult decision in determining how long to continue maintenance treatment after the acute symptoms have been controlled. Ideally, continuation therapy should be maintained for as long as the episode is expected to last. A major problem is that, when continuation therapy is successful, it may be difficult to determine when the episode is over. This may cause the clinician either to withdraw the drug prematurely, thereby subjecting the patient to a relapse, or prolong treatment unnecessarily, thereby exposing the patient to uncomfortable and potentially dangerous cardiovascular or anticholinergic side effects.

Table 1   Continuation Therapy Studies

Investigator	Treatments	N	Relapse Rate (%)
Seager and Bird,	Imipramine	12	17
1962	Placebo	16	69*
Mindham et al.,	Amitriptyline		
1973	or Imipramine	50	22
	Placebo	42	50*
Prien et al.,	Lithium	45	27
1973	Imipramine	38	37[a]
	Placebo	39	67
Klerman et al.,	Amitriptyline	50	12
1974	Placebo/no pill	49	29*
Coppen et al.,	Amitriptyline	13	0
1978	Placebo	16	31*
Stein et al.,	Amitriptyline	29	28
1980	Placebo	26	69*
Prien et al.,	Imipramine +		
1980	Lithium	35	9
	Placebo	33	39*
Total	Active Drug	272	20
	Placebo/no pill	221	48*

*$p < 0.05$ by Fisher's Exact Probability Test
[a]lithium vs. placebo $p < 0.05$
imipramine vs. placebo $p < 0.05$
lithium vs. imipramine $p > 0.05$

Studies of the natural course of depressive illness are only of limited help in estimating episode length. A study of the natural course of depressive disorders conducted by Angst and coworkers (1973) indicates that the duration of episodes tends to remain constant or lengthen slightly with each new episode. Thus, the length of the preceding episode may serve as the lower estimate of the duration of the next one. The problem is that effective drug treatment of the previous episode may have made the episode appear shorter than it was.

Work with such biological variables as rapid eye movement (REM) sleep activity (Kupfer, 1980), levels of cortisol secretion (Carroll, 1978), desamethasone suppression (Brown, 1979; Carroll, 1982), thyroid-stimulating hormone blunting (Kirkegaard and Smith, 1978), and other measures of neuroendocrine secretory patterns ultimately may provide a biological marker of episode length. The most promising work has been done with the dexamethasone suppression test (DST). Evidence suggests that the DST may be a better indicator of episode length than clinical symptomatology. Several small uncontrolled trials (Brown, 1979; Gold et al., 1980; Goldberg, 1980; Greden et al., 1980; Amsterdam et al., 1981) report that the return of a normal dexamethasone suppression pattern in patients with an abnormal DST may indicate that it is safe to discontinue antidepressant drug therapy.

Two major collaborative multihospital trials of maintenance drug therapy for depressed patients provide yet another clue for determining when the episode is over. A recently completed five-hospital study (the NIMH Collaborative Study of Maintenance Drug Therapy in Depression) indicates that the probability of relapse after withdrawal of antidepressant medication is related to the length of time the patient was symptom-free before the drug was discontinued (Prien et al., 1980). Patients who were symptom-free for more than 10 weeks before therapy was discontinued showed no higher relapse rate (13 percent) than did patients who continued to receive medication (12 percent). By contrast, patients who were symptom-free for fewer than 10 weeks before continuation therapy was stopped had an extremely high relapse rate (65 percent); patients who were symptom-free for fewer than 10 weeks but continued to receive medication has a low relapse rate (6 percent).

The findings from the NIMH study suggest that every attempt should be made to continue treatment until the patient has had no symptoms for two or three months. The results also indicate the need for focusing on mild as well as moderate and severe symptomatology in determining continued need for medication. The presence of mild symptoms not characteristic of the individual's usual functioning between previous episodes is as predictive of relapse as more severe symptomatology.

Results of the NIMH study correspond to those reported from an eight-center study conducted by the Medical Research Council in England (Mindham et al., 1973). Patients with residual symptomatology at the time continuation therapy was stopped had a significantly higher relapse rate than did patients who showed no symptoms at withdrawal.

Finally, Keller et al. (1982), who analyzed possible predictors of relapse in 75 patients recovering from an acute episode, reported that the presence of an underlying chronic depression predicted a statistically significant increase in the incidence of relapse.

Long-Term Preventive Therapy

After successful continuation drug therapy, the clinician must decide whether or not to continue the maintenance drug regimen to prevent the patient from developing further episodes. Most research on long-term preventive therapy has been conducted with lithium, imipramine, or amitriptyline in patients with a history of frequent and severe episodes of primary major depression or mania. Other treatments and populations have not been well studied.

The most critical questions relating to long-term preventive drug therapy are who should receive treatment, what drug should be used, and how long treatment should be continued.

Who should receive treatment. Several factors determine whether or not long-term preventive therapy should be started: (1) the likelihood of a recurrence in the near future; (2) the severity and abruptness of previous episodes and the potential impact of a subsequent episode on the patient, family, job, and therapeutic relationship; (3) the patient's willingness to commit himself or herself to indefinite maintenance treatment; (4) the presence of possible contraindications to long-term treatment; (5) the patient's response to previous psychopharmacologic regimens; and (6) the family's insight into the illness and capacity to recognize and report the first signs of a recurrence.

Most clinicians believe that a patient should have had at least two or three well-defined episodes requiring psychiatric intervention before he or she is treated with long-term preventive pharmacotherapy. Patients who have only a single attack, mild attacks, or a long interval between episodes (e.g., more than five years) should probably not receive long-term treatment. An exception is the patient for whom a second episode would be life-threatening or highly disruptive to career or family functioning. For patients with regular seasonal episodes, preventive drug treatment might be considered only for vulnerable periods (Ban and Hollender, 1981).

Support for initiating long-term preventive treatment after two or three episodes comes from surveys on the natural course of depressive illness. Angst and coworkers (1973) clearly demonstrated the relationship between episode frequency and risk of recurrence. As may be seen in Table 2, cycle length (the period between the onset of one episode and that of the next) tends to decrease with successive episodes through the first four or five episodes and then remain stable. Average cycle length ranges from 33 to 37 months for the first cycle to 20 to 22 months for the second and 11 to 13 months for the fifth. The progressive decrease in cycle length is attributed to a shortening of the interval between episodes rather than to a decrease in the length of the episode. Assuming that the average acute episode lasts for an average of four to five months, the average interval between episodes shrinks from about two and a half years after one episode to about half a year after five episodes. Thus, patients with multiple episodes are at high risk for an early recurrence and are suitable candidates for preventive pharmacotherapy.

Survey data are of limited usefulness for determining the risk of recurrence for individual patients. Group statistics presented in many survey reports fail to reflect the great variability in course of illness among individual patients. After the initial episode, some patients may remain episode-free for many years, whereas others may have their second episode within a few months. Even patients who

Table 2   Relationship between Number of Episodes
and Mean Cycle Length

Number of Episodes	Mean Cycle Length (months)	
	Unipolar	Bipolar
1	37	33
2	22	20
3	18	16
4	13	13
5	13	11
6	12	11
7	11	10
8	11	11
9	9	9
10	9	8

Adapted from Angst et al., 1973.

have two or three episodes in a two year-period are not necessarily destined for a recurrence during the next two years. Surveys indicate that as many as a third of patients who have two episodes during a two-year period do not have a recurrence during the following two years (Grof et al., 1979). Unfortunately, research has not provided predictors for identifying this subgroup of patients.

Choice of drug. The choice of medication for long-term preventive therapy is limited to lithium or a tricyclic antidepressant. Other drugs have not been adequately evaluated for this purpose, although there have been isolated trials of two tetracyclic antidepressants (mianserin and maprotiline) (Coppen et al., 1976, 1978), carbamazepine (Okuma et al., 1981), and flupenthixol (Ahlfors et al., 1981). These trials involved small numbers of patients and, except for the study of carbamazepine, did not have placebo controls.

Most long-term drug trials are analyzed separately for bipolar and unipolar patients. Evaluations of the effectiveness of lithium and the antidepressants for bipolar and unipolar groups are summarized in Table 3.

Bipolar disorder. Lithium is the recommended long-term treatment for patients with bipolar disorder. In the six studies comparing lithium against placebo (Table 3), lithium was significantly superior to placebo in reducing the frequency of recurrences (statistical significance is based on the $p = 0.05$ level as determined by Fisher's Exact Probability Test). Summed across studies, 33 percent of the lithium-treated patients had a recurrence, compared to 81 percent of the placebo-treated patients. Separating the results according to manic and depressive recurrences shows lithium to be significantly superior to placebo in preventing both types of recurrences. Manic recurrences occurred among 22

Table 3 Long-Term Preventive Therapy Studies

Investigator	Treatment	Unipolar Relapse Rate N	Unipolar Relapse Rate %	Bipolar Relapse Rate N	Bipolar Relapse Rate %
Baastrup et al., 1970	lithium	17	0	28	0
	placebo	17	53*	22	55*
Coppen et al., 1971	lithium	11	9	17	18
	placebo	15	80*	21	100*
Cundall et al., 1972	lithium	4	75	12	33
	placebo	4	50	12	83*
Prien et al., 1973b	lithium			101	43
	placebo			104	80*
Prien et al., 1973a	lithium	27	48	18	28
	imipramine	25	48[c]	13	77[d]
	placebo	26	92	13	77
Fieve et al., 1976	lithium	14	57	17	59
	placebo	14	64	18	94*
Coppen et al., 1976	lithium	12	25		
	maprotiline	8	75*		
Coppen et al., 1978	lithium	15	0		
	mianserin	13	54*		
Kane et al., 1981	lithium			38	21
	li + imi			37	32
Glen et al., −1[a] 1981	lithium	12	33		
	amitriptyline	7	57[e]		
	placebo	9	89		
2[b]	lithium	56	64		
	amitriptyline	47	65		
Kane et al., 1982	lithium	11	27		
	imipramine	11	73		
	li + imi	14	14[f]		
	placebo	13	85		

*$p < 0.05$ by Fisher's Exact Probability Test
[a]Patients had one previous episode.
[b]Patients had two or more previous episodes.
[c]lithium vs. placebo and imipramine vs. placebo−$p < 0.05$
[d]lithium vs. imipramine and lithium vs. placebo−$p < 0.05$
[e]lithium vs. placebo−$p < 0.05$; other comparisons−$p > 0.05$
[f]lithium vs. imipramine, lithium vs. placebo, lithium + imipramine vs. imipramine, lithium + imipramine vs, placebo−$p < 0.05$; other comparisons−$p > 0.05$

percent of the lithium-treated patients and 60 percent of the placebo-treated patients. Corresponding figures for depressive recurrences were 16 percent for lithium-treated patients and 33 percent for those who received placebo. These findings were the basis for the Food and Drug Administration's 1974 decision to approve the use of lithium for the long-term maintenance treatment of patients suffering from bipolar disorders.

Imipramine, the only antidepressant to be evaluated for patients with bipolar illness, has demonstrated little effectiveness against manic attacks. The Veterans Administration–National Institute of Mental Health Collaborative Study of Lithium Therapy (Prien et al., 1973a) reported that 54 percent of imipramine-treated bipolar patients developed a manic episode, compared to 11 percent of lithium-treated patients. There was no major difference between lithium and imipramine in the occurrence of depressive episodes. Kane and coworkers (1981) showed no advantage of the combination of lithium and imipramine over lithium alone for either manic or depressive recurrences.

Unipolar disorders. The issue of the effectiveness of lithium and the tricyclic antidepressants for the long-term treatment of patients with recurrent unipolar disorders is a subject of debate. Two multihospital collaborative studies (Prien et al., 1973a; Glen et al., 1981), show that lithium, imipramine, and amitriptyline are equally effective for unipolar patients and that all three treatments are more effective than placebo. Other studies report that lithium is more effective than imipramine (Kane et al., 1982), maprotiline (Coppen et al., 1976), and mianserin (Coppen et al., 1978). Neither lithium nor the antidepressants are approved for the long-term treatment of unipolar disorder by the Food and Drug Administration. The FDA contends that further study is needed. Some clinicians disagree (Schou, 1979), at least with respect to lithium, arguing that the evidence is sufficient to justify use of lithium for the long-term preventive treatment of patients for unipolar disorder.

Effectiveness of drugs in modifying course of illness. Both the physician and patient must have realistic expectations regarding long-term preventive drug therapy. Neither lithium nor the antidepressants are panaceas for unipolar or bipolar disorders. Failure rates for lithium in bipolar populations and for lithium and imipramine in unipolar populations average 30 to 40 percent (in most studies, failure is defined as the appearance of an episode that requires either hospitalization or treatment with a psychopharmacologic agent other than the medication under study).

Even with responsive patients, one does not know whether lithium and the antidepressants actually prevent the occurrence of major episodes or merely dampen the episode sufficiently to prevent a full attack. Research findings suggest that the drugs may act in both ways, depending on the individual case. Despite differing opinions as to how the drugs modify the course of illness, there is general agreement that only a minority of patients achieve complete normalization during treatment. Schou (1982), for example, indicates that only about one-fifth of the patients who are suitable candidates for lithium treatment can be expected to have no recurrences during long-term treatment with the drug. The remaining four-fifths will manifest varying frequencies and severities of recurrence ranging from rare and mild attacks to frequent and severe episodes.

Need for further research. Clinicians need more options in choosing drugs for the long-term treatment of patients for both unipolar and bipolar disorders. For unipolar disorder, there are a wide range of newer antidepressants (e.g., maprotiline, trazodone, bupropion, mianserin) that may offer advantages over lithium, imipramine, or amitriptyline. Monoamine oxidase inhibitors need to be evaluated as long-term treatments for patients who respond positively to these drugs during acute episodes. Long-term management of patients after electroconvulsive shock therapy requires careful study. For patients with bipolar disorder, antidepressants other than imipramine may be effective in preventing depressive recurrences. These drugs also may involve less risk of mania. Carbamazepine, which offers promise as an alternative to lithium for the treatment of acute mania, warrants evaluation on a long-term basis, particularly with patients who are prone to manic recurrences. Neuroleptic drugs, alone or in combination with lithium, may be beneficial for selected patients. A long-term trial with neuroleptics seems more justifiable for patients with manic episodes who do not respond to lithium.

Duration of treatment. A critical decision for the practitioner is how long to continue long-term maintenance drug therapy. Although there is no evidence that preventive drug therapy cures recurrent affective illness, recurrences may cease spontaneously after many years of illness. Angst (1978) reported that one of three unipolar patients and one of eight bipolar patients over 65 years of age stopped having episodes of illness. Thus, patients who were ill for a long time but have been free of abnormal mood swings for several years may no longer require medication. The only way to determine whether or not a patient still requires medication is to discontinue it and carefully monitor the patient for signs of an emerging episode.

CHRONIC DEPRESSION

Most studies of long-term maintenance therapy use samples consisting of patients who have a history of well-defined episodes with intervening periods of good recovery. No well-controlled study of maintenance pharmacotherapy has been directed specifically at patients who have chronic depression or frequent subacute mood swings. This is not a small population. Weissman and Myers (1978) conducted a mental health survey in an urban community and found that 6 percent of the sample suffered from chronic or intermittent depressive symptomatology that had persisted for at least two years without a period of sustained relief. The symptomatology was often accompanied by impairment in social functioning, work performance, marital relations, and child-rearing.

Classification of Chronic Depressions

There have been many conceptualizations and classifications of chronic depression. Chronic depression has been described by several overlapping, but not necessarily synonymous, terms, including depressive personality, chronic characterological depression, dysthymic disorder or dysthymic personality, chronic minor depression, chronic intermittent depressive disorder, and neurotic depression. A currently popular classification subdivides the chronic depressions into early- and late-onset disorders (Weissman, 1979; Akiskal et al., 1980; Klerman, 1980). Early-onset depressions usually appear in childhood or adolescence and develop in the context of significant neurotic or characterological pathology. Patients with early-onset chronicity are at high risk for developing a major episode. Weissman (1979) estimated that 75 percent of these patients will have an acute depressive episode at some time in their lives. Late-onset depressions usually follow an acute major depression and represent either an incomplete remission of the patient's episode or a depression secondary to a preexisting nonaffective disorder. Akiskal and coworkers (1981) further divided early-onset characterological depressions into "subaffective (i.e., subsyndromal) dysthymia" and "character spectrum disorder." They claim that subaffective dysthymia shares many of the features of primary affective illness and responds well to tricyclic antidepressants and lithium. Character spectrum disorder, by contrast, represents a heterogeneous mixture of personality disorders with inconsistent depressive features that respond poorly to pharmacologic treatment. The efficacy of drug therapy for patients with these subtypes has not been studied adequately. Data from Akiskal's (1981) open trials suggest however, that subtypes most responsive to antidepressant drug therapy are early-onset subaffective dysthymia and late-onset depression resulting from incomplete remission of an acute episode.

Double Depression

Keller and Shapiro (1982) coined the term "double depression" to represent the state in which a major depressive episode is superimposed upon an underlying chronic depression. The investigators found that 26 percent of 101 patients meeting the Research Diagnostic Criteria (RDC) (Spitzer et al., 1978) for major depressive disorder also had a diagnosis of chronic depression. Patients were considered chronically depressed if they satisfied the RDC for chronic minor depressive disorder or intermittent depressive disorder of two years or longer. These diagnostic categories are roughly equivalent to the *DSM-III* category of dysthymic disorder. The investigators evaluated the patients with chronic depression for a year and found a high rate of recovery from the acute depression (89 percent) but a low recovery rate (31 percent) when recovery included the chronic as well as acute disorder. The effects of specific treatments were not reported. Overall results suggested, however, that the chronic condition may be difficult to control with pharmacotherapy.

Other studies using RDC classifications also report a high incidence of patients with double depression. In the NIMH Collaborative Study of Maintenance Drug Therapy in Depression (Prien, unpublished data, 1982) we screened more than 2,000 inpatients and outpatients satisfying the RDC for recurrent unipolar major depression and found that 20 percent also met the criteria for chronic minor disorder or intermittent depressive disorder; 6 percent had an RDC diagnosis of cyclothymic personality, and 3 percent a diagnosis of labile personality. Another 22 percent had a history of impaired social, familial, and vocational functioning between episodes, often accompanied by periodic mild depressive symptomatology that did not meet the criteria for either minor depression or intermittent depressive disorder. The latter patient subgroup was included in the study and showed a much slower rate of recovery from the major depression than did patients who had a history of good functioning between episodes. Outcome results for maintenance therapy for these patients are not yet available.

Rounsaville and coworkers (1980) studied 64 consecutively admitted patients who satisfied RDC for major depressive disorder: 36 percent had an intermittent depressive disorder, 14 percent a cyclothymic personality, and 16 percent a labile personality. There was no significant difference between patients with chronic depression and those without chronic depression in their response to a four-week trial of antidepressant drugs.

The pharmacologic treatment of patients with double depression has not been well studied. One reason is that those with chronic depression have been excluded from most long-term maintenance drug therapy studies or have been ignored in analyses of data. In addition, most studies do not use outcome measures that are designed to evaluate changes in subsyndromal depressive states, personality functioning, or social adjustment.

There is a need for systematic trials to evaluate short-term and long-term treatment outcome with antidepressants and lithium in these subgroups: patients who have recurrent major depression (RMD) with underlying chronicity vs. those who have RMD without underlying chronicity, and those who have RMD with late-onset chronicity vs. those with RMD and chronicity of early onset. This research should focus on both the acute and chronic components of illness.

Drugs and Psychotherapy

The value of combining psychotherapeutic approaches with drug therapy for chronically depressed patients should be explored in carefully controlled trials. Psychotherapy may be of particular value in ameliorating impairment in social performance, family functioning, and coping with problems of living that may result from frequent and severe episodes (Davenport et al., 1976; Weissman,

1978; DiMascio et al., 1979; Blackburn et al., 1981; Jamison, 1982). Psychotherapeutic approaches may also be useful in treating patients for early-onset characterological depressions before the appearance of the first acute episode (Weissman, 1979). It has also been suggested that long-term group psychotherapy or structured psychological support may enhance the patients' drug compliance and acceptance of long-term drug therapy programs (Shakir et al., 1979). Unfortunately, the combination of pharmacotherapy and psychotherapy has not been evaluated in systematic fashion over a prolonged period. Well-controlled studies are needed to evaluate the responsiveness of both the acute and chronic components of the patient's depressive disorder to various modalities of treatment. Such trials should devote special attention to the diagnosis of chronic depression, using appropriate control groups and treatment outcome measures sensitive to changes in both acute depressive symptoms and in characteristics associated with chronic depression.

REFERENCES

Ahlfors, U. G., Baastrup, P. C., Dencker, S. J., Elgen, K., Lingjaerde, O., Pedersen, V., Schou, M., and Aaskoven, O. 1981. Flupenthixol decanoate in recurrent manic-depressive illness: A comparison with lithium. *Acta Psychiatr. Scand.* 63:226-237.

Akiskal, H. S., Rosenthal, T. L., Haykal, R. D., Lemmi, H., Rosenthal, R. H., and Scott-Strauss, A. 1980. Characterological depressions—Clinical and sleep EEG findings separating sub-affective dysthymias from character spectrum disorders. *Arch. Gen. Psychiatry* 37:777-783.

Akiskal, H. S., King, D., Rosenthal, T. L., Robinson, D., and Scott-Strauss, A. 1981. Chronic depressions. Part I. Clinical and familial characteristics in 137 probands. *Journal of Affective Disorders* 3:297-315.

Amsterdam, J. D., Winokur, A., and Caroff, S. 1981. Dexamethasone suppression test as a prognostic tool: Two case reports. *Am. J. Psychiatry* 138: 979-980.

Angst, J. 1978. The course of affective disorders: II. Typology of bipolar manic-depressive illness. *Arch. Psychiatr. Nervenk.* 226:65-73.

Angst, J., Baastrup, P., and Hippius, W. 1973. The course of monopolar depression and bipolar psychoses. *Psychiatric Neurologie et Neurochirurgie (Amst.)* 76:489-500.

Baastrup, P. C., Poulson, J. C., Schou, M., Thomsen, K., and Amdisen, A. 1970. Prophylactic lithium: Double-blind discontinuation in manic-depressive and recurrent disorders. *Lancet* 2:326-440.

Ban, T. A., and Hollender, M. H. 1981. *Psychopharmacology for Everyday Practice.* Basel, Switzerland: Karger.

Blackburn, I. M., Bishop, S., Glen, A. I. M., Whadley, L. J., and Christie, J. E. 1981. The efficacy of cognitive therapy in depression: A treatment trial using cognitive therapy and pharmacotherapy, each alone and in combination. *Br. J. Psychiatry* 139:181-189.

Brown, W. 1979. The 24-hour dexamethasone suppression test in a clinical setting: Relationship to diagnosis, symptoms, and response to treatment. *Am. J. Psychiatry* 136:413-423.

Carroll, B. J. 1978. Neuroendocrine function in psychiatric disorders. In M. A. Lipton, A. DiMascio, and K. F. Killam (eds.), *Psychopharmacology: A Generation of Progress*, pp. 487-497. New York: Raven Press.

Carroll, B. J. 1982. The dexamethasone suppression test: New applications. Presented to American Psychiatric Association, Toronto.

Coppen, A., Chose, K., and Rao, R. 1978. Mianserin and lithium in the prophylaxis of depression. *Br. J. Psychiatry* 133:206-210.

Coppen, A., Montgomery, S. A., Gupta, R. K., and Bailey, J. E. 1976. A double-blind comparison of lithium carbonate and maprotiline in the prophylaxis of the affective disorders. *Br. J. Psychiatry* 128:479-485.

Coppen, A., Montgomery, S., Rao, V. A. R., Bailey, J., and Jorgensen, A. 1978. Continuation therapy with amitriptyline in depression. *Br. J. Psychiatry* 133:28-33.

Coppen, A., Noguera, R., Bailey, J., Burns, B. H., Swani, M. S., Hare, E. H., Gardner, R., and Maggs, R. 1971. Prophylactic lithium in affective disorders. *Lancet* 2:275-279.

Cundall, R. L., Brooks, P. W., and Murray, L. G. 1972. Controlled evaluation of lithium prophylaxis in affective disorders. *Psychol. Med.* 3:308-311.

Diagnostic and Statistical Manual of Mental Disorders, Third Ed. 1980. Washington, DC: American Psychiatric Association, p. 216.

DiMascio, A., Weissman, M. M., Prusoff, B. A., Neu, C., Zwilling, M., and Klerman, G. L. 1979. Differential symptom reduction by drugs and psychotherapy in acute depression. *Arch. Gen. Psychiatry* 36:1450-1456.

Davenport, Y. B., Ebert, M. H., Adland, M. L., and Goodwin, F. K. 1976. Couples group therapy as an adjunct to lithium maintenance of manic patients. *Am. J. Orthopsychiatry* 47:495-502.

Fieve, R. R., Kumbarachi, T., and Dunner, D. L. 1976. Lithium prophylaxis of depression in bipolar I, bipolar II and unipolar patients. *Am. J. Psychiatry* 133:925-929.

Glen, A. I. M., Johnson, A. L., and Shepherd, M. 1981. Continuation therapy with lithium and amitriptyline in unipolar depressive illness: A controlled clinical trial. *Psychol. Med.* 11:409-416.

Gold, M. S., Pottash, A. L. C., Extein, I., and Sweeney, D. R. 1980. Dexamethasone suppression tests in depression and response to treatment (letter). *Lancet* 1:1190.

Goldberg, I. K. 1980. Dexamethasone suppression test as indicator of safe withdrawal of antidepressant therapy (letter). *Lancet* 2:376.

Greden, T. F., Albala, A. A., Haskett, R. F., James, N. M., Goodman, L., Steiner, M., and Carroll, B. J. 1980. Normalization of dexamethasone test: A laboratory index of recovery from endogenous depression. *Biol. Psychiatry* 15:449-458.

Grof, P., Angst, J., Karasek, M., and Keitner, G. 1979. Patient selection for long-term lithium treatment in clinical practice. *Arch. Gen. Psychiatry* 36:894-897.

Hamilton, M. 1979. Mania and depression: Classification, description, and course. In E. S. Paykel and A. Coppen (eds.), *Psychopharmacology of Affective Disorders*, pp. 1-13. New York: Oxford University Press.

Jamison, K. 1982. Psychological issues in bipolar affective illness. Presented to American Psychiatric Association, Toronto.

Kane, J. M., Quitkin, F. M., Rifkin, A., Ramos-Lorenzi, J. R., Saraf, K., Howard, A., and Klein, D. F. 1981. Prophylactic lithium with and without imipramine for bipolar I patients: A double-blind study. *Psychopharmacol. Bull.* 17: 144-145.

Kane, J. M., Quitkin, F. M., Rifkin, A., Ramos-Lorenzi, J. R., Nayak, D. P., and Howard, A. 1982. Lithium carbonate and imipramine in the prophylaxis of unipolar and bipolar II illness. *Arch. Gen. Psychiatry* 39:1065-1069.

Keller, M. B., and Shapiro, R. W. 1982. Double depression: Superimposition of acute depressive episodes on chronic depressive disorders. *Am. J. Psychiatry* 139:438-442.

Kirkegaard, C., and Smith, E. 1978. Continuation therapy in endogenous depression controlled by changes in the TRH stimulation test. *Psychol. Med.* 8: 501-503, 1978.

Klerman, G. L. 1978. Long-term treatment of affective disorders. In M. A. Lipton, A. DiMascio, and K. F. Killam (eds.), *Psychopharmacology: A Generation of Progress*, pp. 1303-1312. New York: Raven Press.

Klerman, G. L. 1980. Other specific affective disorders. In H. I. Kaplan, A. M. Freedman, and B. J. Sadock (eds.), *Comprehensive Textbook of Psychiatry*, Third Ed., pp. 1332-1338. Baltimore: Williams & Wilkins.

Klerman, G. L., DiMascio, A., Weissman, M., Prusoff, B., and Paykel, E. S. 1974. Treatment of depression by drugs and psychotherapy. *Am. J. Psychiatry* 131:186-191.

Kupfer, D. J. 1980. Sleep and neuroendocrine abnormalities in affective disorders: New findings. Presented to American College of Neuropsychopharmacology, San Juan, Puerto Rico.

Mindham, R. H., Howland, C., and Shepherd, M. 1973. A evaluation of continuation therapy with tricyclic antidepressants in depressive illness. *Psychol. Med.* 3:5-17.

Okuma, T., Inanaga, K., Otsuki, S., Sari, K., Takahashi, R., Hazama, H., Mori, A., and Watanabe, S. 1981. A preliminary double-blind study on the efficacy of carbamazepine in prophylaxis of manic-depressive illness. *Psychopharmacology* 73:95-96.

Prien, R. F. 1981. Survey of antidepressant drug use. Presented to the International Seminar on Epidemiological Impact of Psychotropic Drugs, Milan.

Prien, R. F., Caffey, E. M., and Klett, C. F. 1973b. Prophylactic efficacy of lithium carbonate in manic-depressive illness. *Arch. Gen. Psychiatry* 28: 337-341.

Prien, R. F., Klett, C. H., and Caffey, E. M. 1973a. Lithium carbonate and imipramine in prevention of affective episodes. *Arch. Gen. Psychiatry* 29: 420-425.

Prien, R. F., Kupfer, D. J., Mansky, P. M., Small, J., Tuason, V., and Voss, C. 1980. Continuation therapy in depression: Preliminary findings from the National Institute of Mental Health-Pharmacologic and Somatic Treatments Research Branch Collaborative Study of Long-term Maintenance Drug Therapy in Affective Illness. Presented to American College of Neuropsychopharmacology, San Juan, Puerto Rico.

Quitkin, F., Rifkin, A., and Klein, D. F. 1976. Prophylaxis of affective disorders. *Arch. Gen. Psychiatry* 33:337-346.

Rounsaville, B. J., Sholomskas, D., and Pruskoff, B. A. 1980. Chronic mood disorders in depressed outpatients. *Journal of Affective Disorders* 2:73-88.

Schou, M. 1979. Lithium as a prophylactic agent in unipolar affective illness: Comparison with cyclic antidepressants. *Arch. Gen. Psychiatry* 36:849-851.

Schou, M. 1982. Lithium in recurrent affective illness. Presented to American Psychiatric Association, Toronto.

Seager, C. P., and Bird, R. L. 1962. Imipramine with electrical treatment in depression—a controlled trial. *J. Ment. Sci.* 108:704-707.

Shakir, S. A., Volkmar, F. R., Bacon, S., and Pfefferbawn, A. 1979. Group psychotherapy as an adjunct to lithium maintenance. *Am. J. Psychiatry* 136:455-456.

Spitzer, R. L., Endicott, J., and Robins, E. 1978. The research diagnostic criteria. Biometrics Research, New York State Department of Mental Hygiene.

Stein, M. K., Rickels, K., and Weisse, C. C. 1980. Maintenance therapy with amitriptyline: A controlled trial. *Am. J. Psychiatry* 137:370-371.

Weissman, M. M. 1978. Psychotherapy and its relevance to the pharmacotherapy of affective disorders: From ideology to evidence. In M. A. Lipton, A. DiMascio, and K. F. Killam (eds.), *Psychopharmacology: A Generation of Progress*, pp. 1313-1322. New York: Raven Press.

Weissman, M. M. 1979. Acute and chronic depressions and depressive personality. Presented to the Conference on Clinical Depressions: Diagnostic and Therapeutic Challenges, San Juan, Puerto Rico.

Weissman, M. M., and Myers, J. K. 1978. Affective disorders in a United States community: The use of research diagnostic criteria in an epidemiologic survey. *Arch. Gen. Psychiatry* 35:1304-1311.

Zis, A. P., and Goodwin, F. K. 1979. Major affective disorder as a recurrent illness: A critical review. *Arch. Gen. Psychiatry* 36:835-839.

12
Drug-Psychosocial Interactions in the Treatment of Schizophrenia

ROBERT PAUL LIBERMAN, IAN R. H. FALLOON, AND CHARLES J. WALLACE

Our view is that schizophrenia can be found, not in the affected person, but among the interactions and interstices of the person's environment, biological substrate, and behavior. The phenomenology of schizophrenia is fluid and dynamic, changing and in flux (the schizophrenic is not psychotic 24 hours a day!) because the underlying interactions are also in flux. Schizophrenia remains ultimately a clinical entity, with its pathognomonic signs and symptoms serving as flimsy and changing barometers of interacting biological and social processes.

Schizophrenia can be defined as a group of characteristic signs and symptoms in thought disturbance (delusions, passivity, incoherence), perception (hallucinations), affect (anhedonia, flat or inappropriate), and motor activity (catatonia). Beyond symptoms, schizophrenia pervades almost all areas of an individual's functioning. There may be impairments in social relations (withdrawal, avoidance), in work (distractibility, apathy), in cognitive processing (poor vigilance, sensory overload), and in self-care (poor grooming, eating and sleeping problems).

MULTIDIMENSIONAL INTERACTIVE MODEL OF SCHIZOPHRENIA

If we view the symptoms and impairments that comprise the schizophrenic experience and syndrome as being in equilibrium with biological and environmental determinants, what processes mediate the impact of the biological and environmental events on the person? The appearance or increase in characteristic schizophrenic symptoms may occur in a susceptible individual when:

1. the underlying biological diathesis or vulnerability increases;
2. stressful major life events overwhelm the individual's coping skills in social and instrumental roles;

175

3. the individual cannot cope with minor stressors or life tension because
social problem-solving skills either have never been learned, or if the individual previously had them in his/her repertoire, they wither as a result
of disuse, reinforcement of the sick role, or loss of motivation;
4. the individual's social support network weakens or diminishes.

Neuroleptic medication reduces a schizophrenic's vulnerability to relapse
and protects the person from the stressful impact of life events and pathological
family relationships (Leff et al., 1973; Vaughn and Leff, 1976; Leff and Vaughn,
1981); however, the modulation of biological vulnerability by drugs cannot fully
mitigate a vulnerable individual's susceptibility to relapse through stressors, loss
of social support, or diminution in problem-solving skills. This helps to explain
why, even with reliable ingestion of neuroleptics, about 40 percent of newly discharged schizophrenic patients relapse within a year (Hogarty et al., 1979).

From this vantage point, an increase or reappearance of symptoms in a person vulnerable to schizophrenia is an outcome of the balance or interaction between the number of life stressors and the problem-solving capacities of the
individual and his/her support network (Liberman et al., 1980).

A somewhat simplified interactive model of schizophrenic symptom formation is presented in Figure 1. The model has four levels of variables—those in the
external environment, enduring vulnerability characteristics, transient intermediate states, and outcome indicators. The first class of variables are the *social
stressors* and *nonsupportive social network* that increase the probability of relapse. Social stressors include life events as well as exposure to critical and
emotionally overinvolved family members. Loss or estrangement of friends,
relatives, neighbors, co-workers, and help-givers all reduce the supportiveness of
the social network. The effects of social stressors and social network variables
are assumed to interact; for example, the death of a loved one may be compounded by the lack of other social support or may be minimized by the presence of other supportive figures. Vulnerable individuals may experience stress
from even minor everyday events and interactions—like shopping, preparing a
meal, casually talking with a relative—that challenge underdeveloped or under-
used life skills.

The second level of variables includes the individual's *enduring, traitlike
characteristics* that may reflect vulnerability and biological diathesis. Presumed
central nervous system traits may be manifested by dysfunctions in information-
processing and arousal. There is some evidence that first-degree relatives of
schizophrenics also show these anomalies (Dawson et al., 1981). These dysfunctions may be relatively permanent but latent, and they become detectable only
when the individual is unduly stressed. In other cases, the underlying vulnerability, genetic loading, and psychological dysfunctions may be so great that even
minor life events or small losses of social support may tip the balance into psychosis. In either case, the pre-existing vulnerability makes the individual susceptible to symptom formation.

An Interactional Model for Schizophrenia

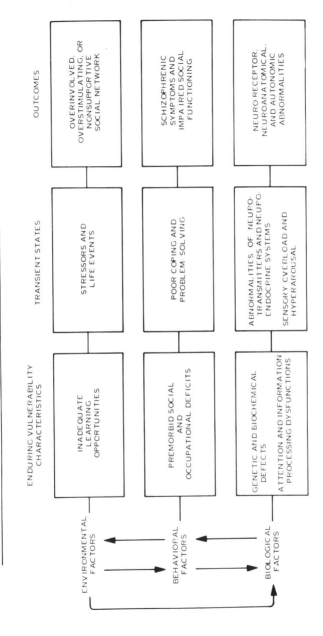

Figure 1   An interactional model for understanding the nature of schizophrenia. From Liberman, 1982b. Reprinted with permission of *Schizophrenia Bulletin*.

On the third level of variables are the *transient intermediate states* of "sensory overload and hyperarousal" and "deficient processing of social stimuli." These intermediate states occur when the vulnerable individual is stressed beyond a certain threshold. The activation of these intermediate states can produce a chain reaction resulting in damage to the individual's family and social support systems. A vicious cycle is created as the person's inability to cope exacerbates external stressors, which in turn contribute to the worsening of schizophrenic symptoms.

The appearance of schizophrenic symptoms, impaired social and occupational functioning, and perhaps rehospitalization are the *outcome indicators* in the interactive model of schizophrenia. Some schizophrenic individuals with good interpersonal problem-solving skills might be able to reduce environmental stressors and recruit greater social support. The schizophrenic with good premorbid social and vocational adjustment, for example, may have resources to mitigate the negative impacts of social stressors, sensory overload, and hyperarousal, thereby breaking the vicious cycle and minimizing or alleviating symptomatology (Liberman, 1982a).

In summary, a diathesis-stress interactive model of the formation of schizophrenic symptoms consists of noxious social events that combine with pre-existing vulnerability to produce intermediate states of sensory overload, hyperarousal, and impaired processing of social stimuli. These intermediate states and their behavioral concomitants generate even more stressors, leading to the appearance of schizophrenic symptoms and impaired functioning. The model suggests points of entry for treatment intervention. Strategies for drug treatment, for example, might include increased dosages or intermittent prescription of neuroleptics timed to coincide with periods of increased stress or early warning signals of symptom exacerbation. Psychosocial therapies might be designed to affect those socioenvironmental stressors, personal coping skills, and social support linkages implicated in the pathogenesis of symptom formation.

RATIONALE FOR COMBINED DRUG AND PSYCHOSOCIAL TREATMENT

It is almost a truism among eclectic clinical psychiatrists that neuroleptic and psychosocial therapy should play supplementary and not competing roles in the comprehensive management of schizophrenic patients. Despite hopes and expectations, neuroleptic drugs have not provided a wholly satisfactory treatment for schizophrenia. Relapse and rehospitalization rates for schizophrenic patients on medication and released to the community indicate that about 40 percent and 60 percent cannot sustain community adaptation for one and two years respectively (Hogarty et al., 1979; Linn et al., 1979). Three to five years after discharge, only 25 to 35 percent of patients have not required readmission (Kohen and Paul, 1976). Patterns of recidivism can be even more disturbing than sustained chronicity and can lead to widespread demoralization of patients, families, and treatment personnel. This demoralization, in itself, has an adverse impact upon therapeutic efforts.

Neuroleptic drugs cannot be counted on as a sole treatment for schizophrenia for another reason. Almost all clinical trials of neuroleptics find that 15 to 30 percent of schizophrenic patients do as well on placebos. Although we cannot yet identify the characteristics that predict good response in the absence of drug therapy, it is suspected that the premorbid social competence of the individual, supportive elements in the treatment setting, and the family's emotional climate may be important factors.

Two other related factors—side effects and noncompliance—limit the applicability of neuroleptic drug therapy and point to the need for effective psychosocial interventions. Noxious side effects of neuroleptics, especially akinesia, akathisia, and the extrapyramidal syndrome, contribute significantly to the patient's reluctance to adhere reliably to a medication regimen and may even provoke symptomatic relapse (Van Putten, 1974; Hogarty et al., 1979). Drugs do not teach living and coping skills, nor do they improve the quality of an individual's life, except indirectly, by removing symptoms. Most schizophrenic patients need to learn or relearn social and personal skills for surviving in the community.

Most experienced clinicians view neuroleptic therapy as accomplishing reconstitutive and prophylactic goals. In ameliorating the cognitive disorganization and disabling symptoms of psychosis, drugs enable the patient to make effective contact with the environment and engage in a therapeutic alliance with a therapist or psychosocial program. Continuity of care that integrates both maintenance medication and pursuit of personal, social, and instrumental role goals has the best chance of restoring the individual with schizophrenia to a functional existence and reasonable quality of life (May, 1976).

Neuroleptic agents should not be viewed simplistically as tranquilizers or antipsychotics, but rather as chemicals that exert influences on cognitive processes, attentional and arousal mechanisms, information flow, and learning capacities. Drugs affect the onset and offset of signal detection and thresholds for discrimination and generalization of environmental input. In laboratory animals, neuroleptics interfere with the conditioned avoidance response, thereby modulating the effects of stressful stimuli. In short, drugs change the sensitivity and reactivity of the nervous system to inner and external stimuli. Behavioral pharmacologists have assessed brain reactions to neuroleptics through the conditioned avoidance response.

With rare exceptions, most studies of the effects of neuroleptics on cognitive and attentional tasks in clinical populations point to the drugs' enhancement of psychological processes. In one exception to this conclusion, untreated, actively psychotic schizophrenic patients showed no impairments in temporal processing of information while patients on neuroleptics showed significant deficits (Goldstone et al., 1979). On the other hand, phenothiazines and related neuroleptics were found to produce significantly improved performance on psychological tests of attention and signal detection which were correlated with clinical improvements, especially in paranoid schizophrenic patients (Spohn et al., 1977). Using a digit span test of distractibility, schizophrenics did strikingly better while on medication than when retested after a two-week drug withdrawal (Oltmanns et al., 1978). Baro and Dom (1976) found that neuroleptics, as opposed to placebos, improved schizophrenic patients' leaning of visual-motor, mechanical, and associative tasks and that the addition of reinforcers (cigarettes, sweets, money) enhanced these drug-induced learning effects. The few studies in this area suggest that neuroleptics improve the performance of schizophrenics on cognitive, attentional, and learning tasks that are presumed to reflect core psychological deficits in schizophrenia.

CLINICAL EVIDENCE FOR DRUG-PSYCHOSOCIAL INTERACTIONS

Only clinical research data can satisfactorily answer the question, How do antipsychotic drugs and psychosocial interventions interact to affect the course of schizophrenia? The question, significant to contemporary psychiatry because of its clinical, training, and fiscal implications, can be more clearly rephrased in five subquestions:

Does psychosocial treatment add nothing to the benefits of neuroleptics?

Do neuroleptics add nothing to the beneficial effects of psychosocial treatment?

Does psychosocial treatment reduce the benefits produced by neuroleptic drugs?

Do neuroleptic drugs impair the beneficial outcomes produced by psychosocial treatment?

Do neuroleptic drugs and psychosocial treatments provide additive or synergistic benefits to schizophrenic patients?

Before attempting to drain this swamp of often conflicting results and views, it would be wise to dispose of a few lurking alligators that would interfere with the task. The alligators, well camouflaged, have muddied the waters and interfered with our understanding the conflicting outcomes reported in the literature. These alligators represent variables that have not always been recognized for their confounding potential; when taken into account, they can help us disentangle seemingly disparate findings and see their convergence. When reviewing the studies on drug-psychosocial interactions, then, we will do well to keep in mind how the nature of the interactions is affected by the type or subtype of schizophrenic patient (young/old, male/female, acute/chronic, recently hospitalized or long-stay, good/poor premorbid, paranoid or nonparanoid); the type of psychosocial treatment (psychodynamic, behavioral); the type of setting or environment in which the drugs and psychosocial treatment are offered (state hospital, community mental health center, day hospital, outpatient clinic); the type of assessment measures used for outcome determinations; the time at which outcome is assessed (or, stated another way, the duration of the treatment methods); and the characteristics of the therapist providing drug or psychosocial treatment (experience, overinvolvement, personality).

Early in the psychopharmacotherapy era, some research psychiatrists, who carried out pathfinding studies that documented the strikingly beneficial effects of phenothiazines, reported clearcut and statistically significant differences in the therapeutic outcomes as a function of the ward milieu (Rathod, 1958; Hamilton et al., 1960, 1963; Goldsmith and Drye, 1963). Inpatient wards that had occupational therapy or group therapy were associated with better drug outcomes. Although these authors agreed uniformly that drug effects were related to qualitative aspects of the treatment environment, the field of psychiatry largely ignored this caveat and its implications. Many clinicians embraced instead the conclusion that the schizophrenic patient must be treated with drugs and that their failure to do so was unethical. In the last 15 years, studies have clearly elucidated that drugs are not administered nor responded to in an environmental vacuum.

Does Psychosocial Treatment Add Nothing to Drug Effects?

Two landmark studies, of the late 1950s and early 1960s, concluded that psychodynamic psychotherapy did not add anything of significant value to the beneficial outcomes attributable to phenothiazines. At Camarillo State Hospital May and his colleagues (May, 1976; May and Tuma, 1976; Tuma et al., 1978) randomly assigned recently admitted, subacute patients to drug, psychotherapy, drug + psychotherapy, milieu, and electroconvulsive therapy. The psychotherapy was "ego supportive and reality defining" and was provided by psychiatrists or psychiatry residents with six months to six years' experience who were supervised by qualified psychoanalysts. Using multiple outcome criteria, the drug-treated patients did significantly better than those not receiving drugs, and there was no interaction between the psychotherapy and drug treatments. A slight benefit appeared, however, for patients receiving both psychotherapy and drugs in reduced cost of treatment during one year after discharge and in reduced number of hospital days over a five-year follow-up period.

In a companion study with distinctly more chronic, long-stay schizophrenics, Grinspoon and his colleagues (1967, 1972) compared neuroleptics vs. placebo in the context of an active milieu program on a small university research unit with intensive analysis-oriented psychotherapy provided by experienced analysts. When patients were switched from drug to placebo, they deteriorated rapidly even with continued psychotherapy. Patients showed maximal benefit from their combined drug-psychotherapy treatment during the first 10 to 12 weeks of treatment despite the fact that the treatments were continued intensively for two years. The absence of further benefits from long-term psychotherapy provided indirect evidence that psychotherapy did not add anything of significance to the drug therapy.

Hogarty and his colleagues (1973, 1974, 1975, 1979), studying newly discharged outpatient schizophrenics, found that sociotherapy (social casework and vocational rehabilitation), added to administration of oral or long-acting injectable phenothiazines, did not affect the patients' relapse rates nor social adjustment during the first year of treatment. Follow-ups after 18 and 24 months of treatment did, however, reveal the beneficial effects of adding sociotherapy to drug therapy.

Reviewing all controlled studies of nonpharmacologic therapies in schizophrenia up to mid-1973, May (1976) rated them on a Design-Relevance Scale to obtain the "weight of the evidence" in favor of a particular treatment. It was found that inpatients receiving individual or group psychotherapy did not improve more than did controls who, by and large, were receiving neuroleptic medication only. On the other hand, outpatients receiving neuroleptics showed added benefits from group therapy.

Do Neuroleptic Drugs Fail to Improve Effects of Psychosocial Treatment?

In a quasi-experimental, post-hoc study of 49 schizophrenic patients treated for four months on a National Institute of Mental Health research unit, Carpenter and his colleagues (1977) found that mean outcome scores did not distinguish the 22 patients treated with phenothiazines from the 27 kept drug-free. Both groups had been indistinguishable at admission in terms of prognostic and psychopathological features. The only difference between the groups was the greater likelihood of postpsychotic depression among patients treated with drugs. It is important to describe the rather special inpatient milieu associated with these good findings for nondrug treatment. Patients were seen in psychoanalytically oriented psychotherapy two to three times a week. All patients participated in group psychotherapy once a week and most also had family therapy once weekly. Therapeutic sessions focused on self-understanding and integration of the psychotic experience into the individual's life. Therapists were senior residents or postresidency fellows supervised by senior psychoanalysts. The milieu, richly staffed with nurses, occupational and recreational therapists, emphasized social adaptation, clarifying behavioral communications, helping the patient assess his effect on others, and exploring appropriate expressions of impulses and feelings. Since this study was not designed for treatment outcome comparisons between drug and placebo (e.g., patients were not randomly assigned to treatment conditions), the results should be viewed as evocative and not definitive.

Studies of the schizophrenic patient's family climate, while not explicating treatment factors, can contribute to the overall context of drug-environment interactions. An American and two British studies have shown, in rigorous replications, that symptomatic relapse is much more likely if a schizophrenic patient lives with relatives who are characterized as being high on "expressed emotion"

(Vaughn et al., 1982). High expressed emotion reflects critical, hostile, and over-protective attitudes toward the patient. Low expressed emotion, on the other hand, marks relatives who are tolerant, supportive, and accepting of the patient and his/her illness and impairments. In each of these studies, the relapse rate for patients coming from families low on expressed emotion was 16 to 17 percent over a nine-month period following discharge from the hospital, compared to 48 to 58 percent for those from families high on expressed emotion. Neuroleptic medication did not affect the relapse rates of patients living with more tolerant and supportive relatives, but it did have a statistically significant protective effect against relapse for patients from critical or overprotective families.

In a well-controlled, "triple blind" study of hard-core, residual, long-stay chronic psychotic patients from a state hospital, Paul and his colleagues (1972) assigned patients matched on level of functioning and bizarre behavior to two intensive psychosocial treatment units in a regional hospital—one a therapeutic community, the other a social learning program based on a token economy. All patients had been receiving moderate doses of maintenance neuroleptic drugs. On each ward, one group continued taking the medication while the other was abruptly withdrawn and switched to placebo. All patients showed significant improvements in ward functioning, psychopathology, and bizarre behavior, those in the social learning unit making greater improvements. After 17 weeks, patients on drug and those on placebo had improved equally; the medication had not provided advantages over and above those produced by psychosocial treatment. There was evidence, in fact, that during the initial month or two of living in their new, intensive therapeutic milieus, the patients on placebo actually learned to function in prosocial fashion more quickly than those who remained on neuroleptics. If this finding could be replicated, it would be one of the few pieces of evidence that, for selected patients, neuroleptics retard learning and impair the beneficial effects of proper psychosocial settings.

Paul and his colleagues worked with 106 of the most chronic and regressed patients still residing in the state hospital system after efforts at deinstitutionalization had failed to move them. The results, most of which came only after two years or more of intensive therapy, were remarkable (Paul and Lentz, 1977). Ninety-seven percent of the social-learning patients and 71 percent of the therapeutic community patients attained enduring (18 months to five years) community placement after they had experienced significant reductions in maladaptive behavior and improvements in adaptive capacity during their inpatient treatment. This amazing rate of enduring discharges was paralleled by significant improvements in clinical and behavioral status as determined by a multilevel battery of evaluation instruments. *By the end of the second year of programming, fewer than 25 percent of the patients in either psychosocial treatment unit were on maintenance neuroleptic drugs, compared to the 100 percent at the start of the program.* This proportion was further reduced to below 11 percent after four years of treatment on the social-learning unit. The conclusion was that older chronic mental patients engaged in active psychosocial treatment have little or no need for long-term neuroleptic drugs. This conclusion has been echoed by Gardos and Cole (1976) who, based on a review of the literature, predicted that 50 percent of all medicated *chronic* schizophrenic outpatients would do as well clinically without medication.

Working with similarly regressed and custodial schizophrenic patients, we have accumulated evidence that also supports the conclusion that withdrawal of drugs in patients who remain bizarre and symptomatic despite adequate trials of neuroleptics does not lead to an increase in psychopathology. This work has been conducted for 12 years on the Camarillo/UCLA Clinical Research Unit at Camarillo State Hospital, a unit that is richly staffed and employs intensive behavior therapy and recreational activities. Systematically varying reinforcement contingencies and phenothiazines or introducing reinforcement methods while keeping drug dosage constant, we have demonstrated that delusional and hallucinatory speech can be reduced, bizarre behavior eliminated, aggressive behavior brought under control, and cognitive performance improved more as a function of the behavior therapy interventions than of the presence or dosage of the phenothiazines (Liberman et al., 1973; Liberman and Davis, 1975; Liberman, 1976).

Do Neuroleptic Drugs Impair Psychosocial Treatment Effects?

There is no evidence from large, well-controlled studies that drugs interfere with the beneficial effects of psychosocial treatment, aside from the data pertaining to lowered rate of improvement in chronic inpatients reported by Paul and his colleagues and described above. There are, however, some clinical guidelines that may help psychiatrists to avoid misusing drugs in situations that could iatrogenically produce poorer outcomes than expected in psychosocial treatment settings. Drugs produce neurological, autonomic, and sedative side effects, especially at high dosages, that may interfere with the patient's engagement in therapeutic relationships and in therapeutic activities. When patients are "snowed" with drugs, they can hardly react in positive ways to the cues, stimuli, and feedback of psychosocial treatments.

Drugs may also produce paradoxical and central nervous system (CNS) toxic effects that mimic psychotic symptoms. There is a controversy among experts, for example, over the nature of the apathy syndrome noted in many patients on neuroleptic drugs. Van Putten and May (1978) describe two types of drug-induced syndromes—"postpsychotic depression" consisting of subjective feelings of sadness, hopelessness, gloom, and despondent mood; "pseudo-depression" consisting of silence, apathy, emotional unresponsiveness, and indifference to surroundings. Some view these syndromes as variants of drug-induced depression and others as extrapyramidal symptoms-linked akinesia; there is general agreement, however, that at least some of these pathological clinical pictures are drug-induced. Some experts in psychopharmacology recommend antiparkinson drugs to reverse the "depression-like" behavior, but there are no controlled studies on the efficacy of this antidote.

Neuroleptics can produce other CNS-toxic and paradoxical effects that mimic psychotic symptoms and behavior. Pseudo-catatonic states (Gelenberg and Mandel, 1977), exacerbations of psychotic symptoms, and "supersensitivity psychosis" (Chouinard and Jones, 1980) have been reported. A paradoxical aggressive reaction to neuroleptics was reported (Liberman et al., 1981) in which a chronic schizophrenic patient served as his own control as drugs were systematically withdrawn and reintroduced and again withdrawn. The patient was observed for both threatening and assaultive behavior while undergoing a behavior therapy program of differential reinforcement for nonbelligerent behavior and time-out from reinforcement for assaultive behavior. It was only when he was in nondrug periods that his threats and assaults could be controlled by the behavioral interventions. This would be a clear example of neuroleptic drug interfering with the benefits of psychosocial treatment.

A variety of mechanisms, all speculative, might explain paradoxical effects of neuroleptics. For one, the neuroleptics produce uncomfortable and subtle neuromuscular side effects, such as akathisia, muscle tension, and dystonias. Many patients describe such symptoms as "inner turmoil" that can "drive them up the wall." Coping with extrapyramidal symptoms may result in levels of agitation and acting out which can simulate psychotic excitement and, in any event, seriously compromise the value of psychosocial treatment. Additional explanations for drug-related flare-ups of symptoms may come from the disinhibitory phenomenon seen most typically with alcohol, or the blurring of patients' ability to discriminate the social deviance of their behavior. A final possible explanation may be that neuroleptics, in certain individuals, interfere with a patient's learning from his/her environment. This may have accounted for the faster improvement noted by Paul and his colleagues (1972) among patients who were withdrawn from drugs before being transferred to a social-learning program.

Does Psychosocial Treatment Impair Drug Effects?

While the early studies comparing drugs and psychotherapy showed no advantages to adding psychotherapy to drug treatment, neither did they find any disadvantages accruing from the combined treatment. Goldberg and his colleagues (1977) have found, however, that adding social casework and vocational rehabilitation services to drugs poses a hazard for some patients. Those for whom sociotherapy hastened relapse suffered from greater and continuing symptom severity than did patients who were in reasonable remission and who benefited from the addition of sociotherapy. It was felt that sociotherapy, in encouraging patients to expand their goals, acted as a stressor for patients still vulnerable to relapse because of residual psychopathology. Without the cognitive capacity to cope with the extra stimulation of sociotherapy, symptomatic patients were more likely to relapse.

Studies in England and the USA have documented the re-emergence of florid schizophrenic symptoms in long-stay, hospitalized patients who were exposed to demanding, total-push, rehabilitation efforts (Wing, 1978). A study of foster homes in five different states revealed that deterioration in the behavior of the schizophrenic residents was associated with more activity in the home, frequent leisure activities, and more intensive supervision of the resident by the sponsor or the visiting social worker (Linn et al., 1980). Similar findings came from a multihospital study of day treatment plus drugs vs. drugs alone for schizophrenic outpatients (Linn et al., 1979).

These findings support the concept of over- and understimulation in defining the relationship between clinical state and environment. Understimulating environments produce the clinical poverty syndrome with deficit, negative symptoms of schizophrenia predominating. Overstimulating environments or psychosocial treatments, particularly with vulnerable, residually symptomatic patients, can produce flare-up of florid, positive symptoms of schizophrenia. Finding the golden mean for any particular patient is not unlike walking a tightrope.

Are Neuroleptic Drugs and Psychosocial Treatment Additive?

Much evidence from many studies supports the conclusion that properly designed psychosocial treatments, combined with rationally prescribed neuroleptic drugs, offer greater protection against relapse and higher levels of social adjustment than drugs or psychosocial treatment alone. These studies are summarized in other publications (Keith and Mathews, 1982; Mosher and Keith, 1979; McCreadie et al., 1978; Schooler, 1978; Hogarty et al., 1976; Heinrichs and Carpenter, 1982) and only some of their clinical implications will be presented here. The overall consensus of these studies is that neuroleptic drugs have a primary effect on cognitive disorganization and symptoms and are associated only secondarily and with less impact with improvements in psychosocial functioning. The opposite seems to be the case with social and psychosocial therapies. In combination, their beneficial impact on the comprehensive needs of the schizophrenic patient is additive. We offer the following propositions as clinical advice crystallized from the results of many studies, but our views are state-of-the-art "wisdom" rather than scientifically replicated truths.

1. Psychosocial treatment is most helpful for patients who are in reasonably good states of partial or full remission from florid symptoms and have reached stable levels of maintenance medication. Psychosocial treatment during acute flare-ups of symptomatology should be aimed at calming the patient, reducing levels of social and physical stimulation, and assisting the patient to integrate and understand the symptoms as part of an illness process.

2. The most effective psychosocial treatment—whether provided by individual therapy, group or family therapy, day hospital or inpatient milieu therapy—contains elements of practicality, concrete problem-solving of everyday challenges, low-key socialization and recreation, engagement in attainable tasks, and specific goal-orientation.

3. A continuing positive relationship is central in the overall strategy for treating the schizophrenic patient, no matter how much drug or psychosocial treatment contributes to the overall plan. This relationship may be with the prescribing psychiatrist or with a paraprofessional case manager.

4. The critical time to offer psychosocial treatment is during the after-care period when the patient needs assistance in surmounting the problems and stressors of readjusting to family and community.

5. Psychosocial treatment should be long-term. Its benefits do not become apparent before 12 months and are even greater at two years. It is likely that indefinite, if not lifelong, psychosocial support, guidance, and training are optimal for most chronic schizophrenic patients. As neuroleptic drugs are most effective in maintaining *symptomatic* improvement when continued indefinitely, it is not surprising that *psychosocial* rehabilitation efforts are similarly optimized by continuity.

6. Psychosocial treatment should focus on stressors in the environment and deficits in personal characteristics that seem to play specific roles in relapse and community maladjustment. Schizophrenic relapse, at least in the first year after discharge, is not adequately explained by drug noncompliance. Nor is there any evidence that a patient's level of manifest psychopathology at hospitalization or discharge predicts subsequent relapse. The best explanation, based on converging lines of evidence from studies over the past ten years, is that the patient's characteristics and social environment—type of psychosocial therapy as well as natural living milieu—are the most powerful influences on relapse, even in the face of reliably administered maintenance medication.

Incorporating lessons learned from research on combined drug and psychosocial therapies, recently completed studies have aimed at greater operational specificity in formulating psychosocial intervention strategies. Developed under the aegis of the Mental Health Clinical Research Center for the Study of Schizophrenia—co-sponsored by the UCLA department of psychiatry, USC-LA County Medical Center, Camarillo State Hospital, and the Los Angeles VA Medical Center—these interventions have employed behavioral principles in structured, intensive programs intended to bring about desirable changes in the social competence of patients and in the family's emotional climate.

RATIONALE FOR SOCIAL SKILLS TRAINING AND FAMILY THERAPY

One working hypothesis for explaining at least some of the determinants of schizophrenic symptom formation is that psychopathology erupts when a person is overwhelmed by situational and social challenges he or she does not have the interpersonal, problem-solving resources to cope with. Correlations between premorbid social inadequacy and symptomatic outcome/rehospitalization have been recognized for many years (Zigler and Phillips, 1962; Kazdin, 1979). A study of schizophrenic patients placed in foster homes after brief psychiatric hospitalizations found that relapse rates at one year after discharge were significantly higher among patients who had prerelease deficiencies in social skills (Linn et al., 1982). Schizophrenic persons demonstrate major deficits in discrete social skills and problem-solving ability when facing interpersonal challenges (Spivack, et al., 1976; Liberman et al., 1980). When exposed to systematic social skills training, schizophrenics have shown an ability to improve their molecular conversational skills (eye contact, fluency, verbal expressiveness), to improve their assertiveness and appropriate affect, and to generalize these improvements to novel situations and conversational partners (Liberman et al., 1980). With neuroleptic medication dosage kept constant, significant differences in social competence emerged between groups trained in social skills and their controls (Wallace et al., 1980).

Another documented problem area for schizophrenics is the emotional climate of the patient's family. Evidence has accumulated from studies in London and Southern California that among the most powerful predictors of relapse in schizophrenia is the level of "expressed emotion" in relatives of schizophrenic patients (Vaughn et al., 1982). High "expressed emotion" (e.g., excessive criticism or emotional overinvolvement) is three to four times as likely to predict relapse than low "expressed emotion" (e.g., tolerant, supportive, and accepting attitudes). While physical separation of the schizophrenic patient from relatives high on expressed emotion is one possible intervention strategy, reducing the amount of face-to-face contact is easier said than done. Many of the highly emotional families and their schizophrenic member are "glued" together by years of mutual dependency and gratifications. An alternative approach, described below, is to provide family therapy aimed at reducing criticism and overinvolvement by training family members in communication and problem-solving skills.

SOCIAL SKILLS TRAINING CLINICAL TRIAL

Twenty-eight, male schizophrenic patients who met DSM-III criteria for schizophrenia (elicited by the Present State Examination) and most of whom had had multiple hospitalizations and were living with relatives found to be high on "expressed emotion" were admitted to the Camarillo/UCLA Clinical Research Unit for a 10-week therapy program. Social skills training sessions were held in groups of three patients and two co-therapists for two hours a day, five days a week. The cognitive problem-solving methods used are described elsewhere

(Wallace et al., 1980; Wallace, 1982). Social skills training consisted of 200 interpersonal situations that were rehearsed—hospital and community problems, family problems, friendship and peer interactions—using instructions, cueing, modeling, videotape feedback, positive reinforcement, and generalization programming. The training encompassed three aspects of interpersonal problem-solving: perceiving incoming messages and meanings accurately, generating reasonable alternatives for responding and considering the potential consequences of each alternative, and effectively delivering a chosen response using verbal and nonverbal skills (Liberman et al., 1982).

One night a week for two hours, three patients and their parents and siblings met with three co-therapists for educational discussions and behavioral rehearsal of family situations. In the first two of nine sessions, the leaders provided information on schizophrenia, its course and treatments. The remaining sessions consisted of training in such specific communication skills as expressing positive feelings, giving positive feedback, making requests of others, listening actively, and expressing anger or dissatisfaction. Each skill was taught in the context of family problem situations in which the patient and relatives learned to pinpoint problems in living, develop options for dealing with the problem, weigh the pros and cons of the options, choose a reasonable option for implementation, provide mutual support for implementation, and re-evaluate the problem after the chosen action was carried out.

The training was a controlled clinical trial with a randomly assigned comparison group of patients who received equally intensive holistic health therapy (jogging, meditation, yoga, art therapy) and insight-oriented family therapy. The same therapists rotated between leading social skills training and holistic health sessions. Individually titrated neuroleptic medication was provided to patients in both treatment conditions. A quasi-control group of 28 male schizophrenic patients, diagnosed similarly and living with high "expressed emotion" relatives, served as a standard of reference for hospital "as usual" treatment.

Patients were evaluated before, during, and for two years after the inpatient treatment period. Aftercare was not controlled but was closely monitored and did not differ from the two initial treatment conditions. The assessment battery incorporated questionnaire inventories, interviews, and naturalistic observations aimed at tapping symptomatic status, social skills, cognitive problem-solving skills, community and family adjustment, and rehospitalization rates. Relapse judgments were made "blindly" from symptoms elicited by the Present State Examination (Wing et al., 1974) administered "blindly" by a psychiatrist at times of symptomatic exacerbation. Psychopathology ratings also were made on the Psychiatric Assessment Scale (Krawiecka et al., 1977), an eight-item instrument that is particularly suited for use with symptom data elicited by the Present State Examination.

Results of the Clinical Trial

Relapse judgments arrived at by "blind" ratings of symptoms elicited by the two instruments revealed after one year that 21, 50, and 56 percent of the patients in the social skills training, holistic health, and standard hospital treatment groups, respectively, had relapsed. Relapse rates for the latter two groups were almost identical to those found for similarly diagnosed schizophrenics living with relatives high on "expressed emotion" in two studies done in London, 10 years apart (Vaughn and Leff, 1979). During the two-year follow-up period, the patients in the holistic health group spent many more days in the hospital than did those in the social skills training group. This statistically significant difference in rehospitalization held up even after covarying an index of compliance with neuroleptic medication during the aftercare period, namely, "total days off medication," as reported by patients and relatives to the aftercare social worker. The average time to first relapse also distinguished the two treatment conditions—417 days for patients who received social skills training and 296 days for those who received holistic health therapy.

In addition to better outcomes in psychopathology, community tenure, and rehospitalization, the patients in social skills training showed significantly better acquisition, durability, and generalization of social skills measured before, after, and at nine months following hospitalization. Four ratings of social adjustment made by relatives nine months after discharge also revealed statistically significant differences in favor of the patients who had received social skills training. The problem-solving approach offered to patients and relatives in social skills training seemed to result in more families' being able to reduce their expressed emotionality from high to low (Snyder and Liberman, 1981). Because the clinical trial incorporated both social skills training and family therapy as a "packaged" intervention, however, it was not possible to attribute the benefits to either of the two psychosocial treatment components. For this reason, a study was designed to assess the impact of behaviorally oriented family therapy alone. Since hospital-based treatment—as provided in the social skills training trial—had limited impact on the crucial aftercare period, the family therapy was designed for outpatients over a two-year period of gradually declining contact.

BEHAVIORAL FAMILY THERAPY FOR PREVENTING
SCHIZOPHRENIC RELAPSE

In a trial of a type of family therapy similar to that used in the social skills training trial, 36 young adult schizophrenics, who were living at home in families either high on "expressed emotion" or showing signs of tension and burden, were randomly assigned to in-home family therapy or clinic-based individually supportive therapy (Falloon et al., 1982). Before entering the study all patients had attained a stable baseline of symptoms and had complied with one month of neuroleptic therapy.

Regardless of treatment condition, all patients followed the same treatment schedule: weekly visits during the first three months, biweekly visits for the next six months, and monthly visits thereafter. In addition, all patients were seen monthly at the clinic by a psychiatrist or clinical pharmacist who was blind to the type of therapy and responsible for maintaining optimal neuroleptic dosages. Those not compliant with oral medication were switched to long-acting depot injections. Along with monthly ratings of target symptoms, Brief Psychiatric Rating Scale (BPRS) scores, and side effects, blood specimens for assay of prolactin and plasma medication levels were obtained at the monthly clinic visits.

The family therapy, based on a behavioral orientation (Falloon and Liberman, 1983). began with sessions about the nature, course, and treatment of schizophrenia. The notion that families could "cause" schizophrenia was refuted, but it was pointed out that families could contribute to improving the course of the illness. The rationale for continuing neuroleptic medication, even in the face of symptom remission, was discussed at length.

Beyond education, the family sessions were devoted to reducing tensions by improving the families' coping skills. They rehearsed behaviors, modeling, feedback, social reinforcement, and did homework on communication skills where these were deficient. Table 1 outlines the problem-solving and communication skills that were the focus of the family therapy.

Table 1   Problem-Solving and Communication Skills as Targets of Family Therapy

Problem-Solving	Communication
Pinpointing a problem or stressor	Empathic listening
Sharing or "owning" the problem	Making positive requests for behavioral change
Generating alternative solutions	
Examining pros and cons of alternatives	Initiating positive statements and giving positive feedback
Choosing the "best" alternative	
Deciding how to implement the chosen alternative	Acknowledging positives
Reevaluating progress on implementation and praising for approximations	Expressing negative feelings directly and "owning" them
	Responding to unexpected and irrational behavior

The comparative effectiveness of the family therapy and individual therapy programs was assessed by a battery of outcome measures which included severity of schizophrenic symptoms, community tenure, social functioning, family burden, and cost-effectiveness. Table 2 depicts the differences in outcome for the two psychosocial therapies plus the medication used by patients in the two groups.

Statistically significant advantages of family therapy were noted in each of the outcome dimensions. While only 6 percent of the family-treated group suffered an exacerbation of schizophrenic symptoms during the first nine months of treatment, 44 percent of the individually treated patients did so. This compares with the replicated findings of about 55 percent relapses among

Table 2   Results Comparing Behavioral Family Therapy and Individual Therapy in the Management of Chronic Schizophrenics

	Patients*		Significance Level
	Family	Individual	
Clinical exacerbations			
nine months	1	8	$p < 0.01$
two years	2	15	$p < 0.01$
Target symptom rating			
pretreatment	2.22±0.95	2.15±0.94	
maximum level during first nine months	2.25±0.99	4.10±1.81	$p < 0.01$
maximum level nine months-two years	2.55±1.19	4.75±1.23	$p < 0.01$
Symptom remission			
at nine months	10	4	$p < 0.05$
at two years	12	4	$p < 0.01$
Community tenure			
mean no. hospital days during first nine months	0.83	8.39	—
mean no. hospital days per year for two years	1.8	11.3	—
no. patients admitted			
first nine months	2	9	$p < 0.05$
two-year period	4	10	$p < 0.05$
no. total admissions			
first nine months	2	14	—
two-year period	5	22	

*18 patients participated in each treatment

patients from families high on "expressed emotion" during nine-month follow-ups. Not only were 56 percent of the family-treated patients in excellent remission at the nine-month point, many of them were functioning at "normal" levels in their social and vocational spheres.

Two years after treatment had begun, the relapse rates for the two treatment conditions were 11 percent for those in family therapy and 83 percent for those in individual therapy. For patients hospitalized during the two-year treatment period, the average number of days spent in hospital for the family therapy and individual therapy patients were 1.8 days/year and 11.3 days/year respectively.

At first glance, the results suggest a major breakthrough in the treatment of schizophrenic patients. Another interpretation might be, however, that family therapy may have merely enhanced medication compliance. An analysis of compliance suggests that somewhat more regular tablet-taking did indeed occur in the family group. Two-thirds of the patients in family therapy took their medication reliably during the first nine months of treatment, compared to 50 percent of those in individual therapy. Even in the family-treated group, the only relapsed patient was irregular in medication use. Even if this type of family therapy only enhanced compliance with medication, it would represent an advance in managing patients with a disorder for which long-term drug therapy is the mainstay. Yet the amount of medication actually ingested (as judged from tablet counts, self-reports, relatives' reports, and plasma levels) by patients in the two conditions does not explain the differential treatment outcomes by medication use alone. Using chlorpromazine-equivalent dosages, the patients in the family therapy programs were prescribed and actually ingested about 100 mg per day *less* than their counterparts in individual therapy.

Together with the results of three long-term drug studies which showed that exacerbations are not prevented by pharmacotherapy alone (Falloon et al., 1978; Hogarty et al., 1979; Schooler et al., 1980), our results cannot be explained solely by the efficacy of drug therapy. Instead, we might postulate that the enhanced problem-solving capacity of the patients and their relatives in the family therapy program blunted the pathogenic impact of stressors on the schizophrenic disorder, and enabled the patients to remain out of the hospital longer on less medication.

Neuroleptics Plus Behavioral Therapy: A Breakthrough?

The combination of optimal neuroleptic drug therapy with innovative psychosocial interventions—behavioral family therapy and/or social skills training—has become a popular "united front" in the battle against the ravages of schizophrenia. Psychopharmacologists and behavioral psychotherapists at a number of centers are testing this truly eclectic treatment approach. In addition, clinical trials are being conducted at the Medical Research Council Social Psychiatry

Unit in London (Leff et al., 1982), at the University of Pittsburgh (Anderson et al., 1981), and at Brown University/Providence VA Medical Center (Monti et al., 1982).

Table 3 shows the preliminary results achieved by pooling nine- or twelve-month postdischarge outcomes from studies in London, California, and Pittsburgh. The results, given the inevitable variations in subjects and treatment and assessment methods among centers, are remarkably favorable for combining psychosocial treatments and drugs. The approximately 50-percent relapse rates in schizophrenics from high expressed-emotion families have been reported several times (Vaughn and Leff, 1976; Brown et al., 1972; Vaughn et al., 1982); thus the reduction of relapse to below 15 percent represents a considerable achievement. If these results are confirmed when the various studies have been completed, we may enter an era of optimism for the treatment of schizophrenia.

To temper the enthusiasm for these new treatment approaches somewhat, we must remember that reducing relapse, as defined by return or exacerbation of florid symptoms of schizophrenia, is only one slice of the total outcome "cake." Negative symptoms, social functioning, occupational status, independent living, and quality of life must be evaluated as well, even though they are more difficult to measure.

PSYCHOSOCIAL INTERVENTIONS TO IMPROVE ADHERENCE TO NEUROLEPTICS

Obtaining compliance with neuroleptic drug regimens remains a lacuna in the pharmacotherapist's armamentarium. Even when drug administration is assured by injectable, long-acting neuroleptics, the patient must still journey voluntarily

Table 3   Relapse Rate for Schizophrenic Patients at Risk for Relapse Because of Living in High Expressed-Emotion Families

	No. Patients	No. Relapses (9 mos.-1 year)	Percentage Relapsed
Family Therapy and/or Social Skills Training	71	9	12.7
Controls	52	26	50

Comparison between patients treated with optimal neuroleptic medication plus family therapy and/or social skills training vs. medication plus standard aftercare.

The data represent pooled results from four studies: Maudsley Hospital, London (N=23); Camarillo State Hospital (N=28); USC-LA County Medical Center (N=36); Western Pennsylvania Psychiatric Institute (N=44).

Chi square = 20.52, $p < 0.01$.

to the clinic or hospital to receive the medication (or must remain voluntarily at home to see the visiting nurse). Compliance with neuroleptics, like that with medication for other chronic disorders, has been reported to range between 40 to 60 percent (Blackwell, 1972; Wilcox et al., 1965).

Adherence to medication is a behavioral response that must be learned by each patient, and the learning opportunities are meager. Patients enter the hospital in a psychotic state and are rapidly medicated without much education or even explanation regarding the drugs. During the hospital period, nurses deliver the medication on a rigorous once to thrice daily schedule, loudly reminding the patient to take it. In a few weeks the patient is discharged with a few days' supply of medication and a prescription, still with little rationale and clarification of the effects and side effects of the medication. Although the nurses and physician strongly urge the patient to "take your medication," the patient soon stops taking the pills—medicine labels him as "crazy," "sick," or "weak"; it produces unpleasant side effects without any subjective benefits; is a bothersome routine; is difficult to remember when cognitive and behavioral disturbances occur; and it makes a significant dent in an already strained budget. Even after skipping the medication, the patient continues to feel quite well because the antipsychotic effects last longer than the side effects. This "honeymoon period" only serves to reinforce the cessation of medication use, making future stoppages more likely. Within 1 to 12 months, the patient's psychotic behavior returns as the medication is slowly metabolized and excreted, and stressful life events accumulate. Once again the patient requires hospitalization and the revolving door keeps turning.

Despite these interfering factors, the prescribing therapist may help the patient learn regular drug-taking with some straightforward strategies.

Behavioral Analysis of Drug-Taking

Adherence to long-term drug-taking is a complex phenomenon. There are a multitude of explanations for reduced compliance. In addition to reviewing the drug-taking pattern of each patient carefully, it may be important to explore his attitudes and feelings towards the prescribed regimen. Although best conducted at the beginning of therapy, the behavioral analysis may need to be reviewed throughout the period of treatment. Potential problems may be apparent at an early stage, and intervention at this point may forestall the development of noncompliance.

The drug-taking patterns of individual patients differ, but the issues in low compliance are shared by many patients. These include:

Aftercare clinic attendance. Clearly, the patient must show up for clinic appointments to receive his prescribed tablets or injections. Nonattendance at aftercare clinics in the first month after discharge from hospital is, however, the most common cause of interrupted drug therapy. The first reason for this, and the most obvious, is that the patient (and his community caregivers) are not given clear instructions about the need for clinic attendance, or even told such other basic facts as the precise location of the clinic or appointment time. Often patients are told to arrange their own appointments. Such simple administrative defects should not be overlooked: patients recovering from a schizophrenic episode are seldom free from deficits of information-processing at the time they are discharged, and special care is required to ensure their subsequent clinic attendance.

Another, usually overlooked, problem regarding clinic attendance is the social anxiety of many schizophrenic patients. Leff and Wing (1971) described the anxiety many patients experience sitting in crowded clinic waiting rooms as a possible reason for the patients' nonattendance. Efforts to make the clinic milieu nonthreatening and welcoming and to avoid long waiting periods may help the socially anxious schizophrenic patient. One approach that has been demonstrably effective is to bring the patient to the aftercare clinic and introduce him to the staff, thereby bridging the gap between hospital and clinic and reducing the patient's fear of the unknown. More severely ill patients may require specific anxiety management programs to treat their social phobias.

For better-functioning patients, another obstacle is taking time off from work. Returning to work after a period of disability, most people are reluctant to ask for frequent time off to attend clinics. Although most aftercare clincs are open outside the usual working hours to serve such people, many patients lack the assertive skills to discuss this issue frankly with their employers. Brief role-playing and modeling, with the therapist taking the part of the employer, may show the patient how to ask for time off. Efficient clinic operation, which reinforces the patients' timely attendance by not keeping them waiting, avoids the issue of excessive time off from work.

Attendance is facilitated when patients are given appointments, reminded by mail or telephone calls, when waiting time is minimized, contact with clinic staff (both clerical and professional) is nonthreatening, and clinics are open at hours that meet the needs of the patient population. In some programs volunteers and community workers take patients to their first clinic appointments; other clinics have created a recreational milieu in which food and low-key socialization is available (Liberman and Davis, 1975). Socially anxious patients, however, may be threatened even more by group settings in which they are expected to perform in front of people, and they may find recreational settings even more anxiety-provoking.

Finally, when patients do not attend the clinic despite prompting, assertive outreach may be needed. A clinic nurse visits the patient, investigates the reasons for nonattendance, ensures that a supply of medication is available, and attempts to establish regular attendance. It should be remembered that, even with long-acting intramuscular preparations, nonattendance at the clinic is a frequent cause of treatment failure. Patients afraid of injections are likely to avoid having them as often as prescribed. The visiting nurse is an important resource in ensuring the patient's continued treatment with both oral and parenteral drugs.

Forgetfulness and cognitive problems. Not all poor compliance is caused by resistance to the medication; a more common reason is forgetfulness. This is magnified in conceptually disorganized patients. One patient would forget whether or not she had taken her tablets, while at other times a hallucinatory voice would tell her not to take them, or, subsequently, not to attend the clinic.

In the hospital, drug compliance is maintained by nursing staff with patients taking a passive role. This does not train patients to take control of their own drug-taking when they return home. In the VA Medical Center's "self-meds" program, patients are given their own bottles of tablets while still in the hospital. Although fraught with difficulties from the ward management viewpoint, this makes it possible to evaluate the patient's drug-taking ability and to devise strategies to remedy deficiencies.

To learn more about and promote medication adherence of psychiatric patients who require long-term maintenance drug therapy, we evaluated seven patients on the clinical research unit at Camarillo State Hospital for their compliance with self-administration of an inactive protein placebo (Marshall et al., 1979). Five patients were low-functioning chronic schizophrenics, one had pathological obesity of the Prader-Willi syndrome, and one had a chronic non-psychotic organic brain syndrome secondary to trauma. All seven patients had spent an average of five years in hospitals.

We wanted to develop interventions that would motivate patients to take their medications regularly and independently. As a first step, we made baseline observations of the patients' use of a placebo placed at their plate on the dining table during meals.

We prepared individual pill bottles marked with each patient's name and the instruction to take one pill before each meal. The patients were shown pill bottles and were told there would be a bottle containing one pill next to their place each time they sat down to eat. They were instructed to take one pill before each meal and to turn the bottle in at the end of the meal. They were to report to the staff any experience they attributed to the pill. Other medications were continued as before.

Placebos were distributed at 332 mealtimes, and patients took them at 303 meals, a 91 percent compliance rate. Individual compliance ranged from 81 to 100 percent. There was no evidence of cheeking, spitting out, or hiding the pills.

In a previous study on the Clinical Research Unit, we had instructed patients to request their medications at a specific time each day. They were prompted daily with a reminder card four hours before they were to ask for their medications. Thirty-six percent of the medications were requested as a result of the reminder, and 75 percent when the requests were reinforced with tokens. This contrasts with 91-percent compliance when pills were visibly accessible at meals but no other prompts or rewards were given.

Although the two studies are not entirely comparable, they do suggest that the reinforcement of drug compliance may be less effective than the powerful stimulus control provided by attendance at meals and the presence of individual pill bottles. Incorporation of natural cues for taking medications, such as having them with meals, may increase the chronic mental patient's reliability in taking medications. Moreover, the taking of medication at meals more closely resembles the real-life circumstances of medication use at home or in community residential facilities.

The forgetful patient may benefit from prompting procedures as well as from a simplification of the drug-taking regimen. Once-daily doses of tablets may help. A wide range of prompting strategies may be developed to suit each patient's circumstances. One patient, who often forgot to take her tablets in the evening, nearly always brushed her teeth morning and evening. She was taught to place a tablet next to her toothpaste when she brushed her teeth at night. Her mother was able to check unobtrusively that the tablet was in place during the day and had been taken at night.

If possible, patients should take responsibility for their tablet-taking. Irritating nagging by concerned parents or other household members is usually counterproductive and only gives emotional reinforcement to noncompliance. Family members can be instructed in effective, supportive prompting procedures.

Some patients use plastic containers that hold medication dosages for each day. This is a simple self-monitoring aid; the medication can be carried in purse or pocket if it needs to be taken at work or away from home. Packaging of tablets in daily doses, a format that has been particularly effective for oral contraceptives, is not yet available for schizophrenic patients.

Unpleasant effects. The psychomotor effects of akathisia and akinesia have been most clearly linked to poor compliance (Van Putten, 1974). Yet it seems that patients' subjective, unpleasant experiences of the drugs are more closely associated with reduced ingestion rather than the more overt behavioral side effects.

Patients find it difficult to describe clearly the nature of these subtle, unpleasant feelings and, as a result, they are frequently overlooked. Patients notice that when they do not take their medication they feel better and, quite logically, believe that the drugs are harmful. Another unwanted effect is the interaction between neuroleptics and alcohol. Patients often skip doses when they drink or attend social gatherings to avoid the potentiating effect of the drugs on the alcohol. Misinformed patients stop taking their neuroleptics when prescribed antibiotics, analgesics, and other drugs for medical complaints.

Patients and their household members can be educated about the side effects they may expect from the drugs, and strategies for coping with the side effects should be explained. Such educational efforts are associated with the beneficial effects of social skills training and behavioral family therapy described above.

Patients may receive specific strategies to deal with specific side effects. One patient with persistent akathisia was trained in deep-muscle relaxation and noted considerable relief. Patients are encouraged to describe their grievances about their drugs in a clear, descriptive manner. At times, the physician may use role-playing and assertion-training to teach clear expression of the unpleasant experiences.

Patient and family attitudes. Patients who share positive attitudes about the benefits of the drugs with household members seem likely to adhere to long-term drug therapy, and the reverse is true as well.

Some negative attitudes commonly expressed are:

1. Drugs should not be taken for a long time because they lead to dependence and addiction.

2. If you feel well and are coping, you should not need drugs. "If I need drugs, I must be sick."

3. Taking drugs is a sign of a weak character. These attitudes can be changed by educating the patient and his household members about the nature of schizophrenia, the expected benefits from regular medication, the nature of the medication and its mode of action, and the potential risks and problems associated with the medication (Boyd et al., 1981). The goal is to help the patient and his support network to become informed consumers with a sufficient knowledge base to participate actively in monitoring the effects of the medication. These goals are similar to those of teaching diabetic patients about insulin.

Maintaining compliance. Good compliance, once established, will not necessarily be sustained over a long period by a patient who remains symptom-free for months. Even when he experiences no dysphoric feelings from the neuroleptics, he has little motivation to continue taking regular medication.

Several behavioral strategies have been employed to deal with this maintenance problem.

Incentives. A systematic incentive program that rewards tablet-taking is like the strategy parents of young children often use when they give their child a piece of candy after the child takes the medicine. In a similar manner, a schizophrenic patient improved his compliance when he received a chocolate bar or ice cream treat immediately after he had taken his tablets after dinner, coupled with praise. After the primary reinforcer (food) was withdrawn, the secondary social reinforcement (praise) was enough to maintain excellent compliance. Tablet-taking became a positive experience instead of an unpleasant daily event. In general, the use of praise by family members contingent upon tablet-taking is effective in shaping and maintaining tablet-taking, whereas focusing on missed doses with nagging and coercion is seldom effective. Attention and praise from the prescribing physician for reported drug compliance is powerful reinforcement for many patients. Conversely, when the physician seldom asks whether or not the patient is taking his medicine regularly, the patient begins to think it is not important.

In a community-based reinforcement program aimed at increasing the reliability of medication-taking among former mental patients, thirty ex-patients were visited on a regular, time-interval schedule by rehabilitation workers who tested their urine for the presence of phenothiazine metabolites. Positive urine tests resulted in the receipt of credits that could be used immediately or saved for the purchase of desirable items from a reinforcement menu. After the individual was "hooked" on the reinforcers, the visits faded to a variable-interval schedule with increasing periods between visits. This change in the schedule of reinforcement produced more reliable and durable taking of medication and a decrease in rehospitalization. After one year of evaluation, a cost-effectiveness study found that the community incentive program saved $15,000 over a more conventional medical check by a physician (Turner, 1973).

Plasma level estimations of neuroleptics are another avenue of feedback to the physician and patient. When medication compliance can be monitored in this manner, the physician should praise the patient who shows sustained "therapeutic" drug levels and not merely watch for "subtherapeutic" results. Physician and patient can develop mutual interest in the levels and their relationship to compliance. In addition, physicians will be able to reduce dosages to very low levels if adequate plasma levels show that the risk of excessive reduction is minimal.

Cognitive structuring. The patient, his family, and his physician may all contribute to enhanced drug compliance by repeatedly rehearsing the rationale for continued drug therapy. This will have been clearly outlined in initial education of the patient and his family, but it requires repeated discussion. Despite adequate drug-taking, considerable doubts of the merits of continued medication may remain. This lack of faith in the treatment leads eventually to reduced compliance. In such cases, specific cognitive structuring may be useful. In one case, a patient who was a heavy smoker was instructed to make a card that fitted into his cigarette pack and to write on it three reasons for continuing to take medication regularly; he wrote:

"I take regular medication because:
1. It makes me calm
2. It stops me hearing voices
3. It helps me sleep."

He was asked to pull out the card each time he took a cigarette and to read it three times before he lit up. His compliance, albeit somewhat irregular, was maintained.

A simple rationale for continued drug-taking involves the "insurance policy" analogy. Patients are instructed to consider regular neuroleptics as insurance to guard against the high risk of relapse, rehospitalization, and the associated social disruption of their lives. Patients who have been taught to expect relapses, even when perfectly compliant with drug-taking, are better prepared to cope with a recrudescence of symptoms without losing respect for the treatment.

DECISION TREE FOR CLINICAL MANAGEMENT OF SCHIZOPHRENICS

It is possible to construct a flow chart that provides decision points for taking clinical actions in the long-term management of schizophrenic patients. The decision tree, depicted in Figure 2, is meant as a starting point for rational clinical management of schizophrenic patients and is expected to be revised and updated as new information accumulates on matching characteristics of patients with selectively effective treatment methods. It is hoped that the flow chart/ decision tree can aid clinicians in their struggle to provide the best quality of care to individuals suffering from schizophrenic disorders.

Initial Treatment of Acute Psychotic Episode

The flow chart begins with patients who are displaying florid symptoms of schizophrenia, principally the so-called positive symptoms of hallucinations, delusions, thought interference, and thought disorder. It is to be expected, however, that florid exacerbations of the positive symptoms will almost always be accompanied or followed by negative symptoms or impairments.

When faced with a patient who is floridly ill, the clinician first ascertains whether or not the patient falls into a small subgroup that merits consideration for a drug-free trial of treatment. This should be done before plunging into the standard treatment of neuroleptic drug therapy and psychosocial treatment. Patients who might respond well to a drug-free treatment approach, however, would have to meet the stringent criteria of (1) having a first or second acute onset of symptoms with prominent affective components and clear precipitating events (Vaillant, 1962); (2) having a good premorbid social/occupational adjustment; (3) living with relatives who are low on expressed emotion; (4) nonparanoid status (Goldstein, 1970) which has been reported, in tandem with good premorbid status, to predict favorable outcome on placebo; (5) phenomenological experiences such as racing thoughts, confusion, and timelessness (Buckley, 1982); realistic, integrative, and insightful attitudes toward one's illness (McGlashin and Carpenter, 1981); and (6) dysphoric subjective response to a test dose of a neuroleptic (Van Putten et al., 1981) which predicts poor compliance with medication. These characteristics, which have been suggested as being potential markers for drug-free treatment of schizophrenia, require a great deal of additional research before their predictive value to clinicians can be confirmed. The availability of a thorough psychiatric evaluation, the suffering of the patient, and issues of dangerousness and safety must be considered in deciding to embark on a drug-free trial period.

Furthermore, beyond the favorable characteristics of the patient, the success of a drug-free trial requires special treatment relationships and environments.

Therapists at all levels of the interdisciplinary mental health team need to be specially selected and trained for working in a drug-free context with acutely disturbed schizophrenics. The treatment environments can be in traditional hospital settings as well as in the community (Carpenter et al., 1977; Rappaport et al., 1978; Mosher and Menn, 1978). It cannot be overemphasized how much effort and preparation must be invested in developing a milieu that permits drug-free treatment of acute schizophrenic patients; it seems unlikely that such treatment can become widespread.

For the vast majority of patients, the first treatment decision will be neuroleptic drug therapy combined with goal-oriented, practical psychosocial treatment. As outlined above, the major thrust of psychosocial treatment is crisis intervention, re-integrative and supportive. The objectives of pharmacotherapy are to achieve the best symptomatic improvement with the lowest possible drug dosage and profile of side effects.

Whether or not the initial, ordinarily brief period of acute treatment takes place in a hospital, day treatment center, or in a home-based or community-based framework will depend on the availability of nonhospital settings and resources and the supportive capacity of the family. This treatment period usually occurs between two weeks to two months for reasonable reconstitution of most patients' acute symptoms and cognitive disorganization.

Second Stage Interventions: Rehabilitation

Once acute symptoms have subsided, it is time to move toward more active psychosocial interventions aimed at restoring function and drug tactics aimed at prevention of relapse. This forces the clinician to abandon notions of cure and, instead, to emphasize environmental modification for prosthetic effects, and building the patient's skills for community survival. The clinician uses modest levels of medication consistent with the patient's active participation in rehabilitation programs. With florid symptoms held in check by medication, more definitive rehabilitation can proceed without risking overstimulation and its attendant exacerbation.

Decisions regarding arenas for rehabilitation should flow naturally from assessment of the patient's deficits: Lack of social competence, conversational skills, and instrumental role skills should lead to social and life skills training; lack of occupational skills should trigger referrals to vocational rehabilitation and sheltered and transitional employment opportunities; relationships with family members who are high on expressed emotion, and in families in which tension is high and problem-solving low, should impel educational and behavioral approaches to family therapy. Rehabilitation strategies can be designed to improve the patient's independent functioning through acquisition of skills and strengthening behavioral repertoires (Wallace et al., 1980) or to compensate for functional deficits by providing social prostheses in the form of case managers, better residential care homes in the community, or interdisciplinary rehabilitation teams (Stein and Test, 1978).

What is to be done if the patient's symptoms don't subside quickly? Because a patient's initial refractoriness to neuroleptic drugs may reflect absorption problems, systematic evaluation of dose-response, using repeated measures of psychopathology (Liberman and Davis, 1975), should be done. But if, despite the best techniques of modern psychopharmacotherapy, the patient's psychotic symptoms remain high and hamper his or her ability to participate in re-learning programs, longer structured treatment with realistically low performance expectations should be considered. Since refractoriness to drug treatment may stem from stressful family or community environments, it may be useful to consider the "retreat" and "asylum" functions of the hospital for this continued treatment period. If the patient's symptoms still don't reach an acceptable level of remission even after prolonged neuroleptic therapy, other somatic interventions should be considered.

These may include the use of another class of neuroleptic or the addition of other psychotropic agents; for example, lithium for patients whose affective symptoms are prominent; antidepressants for those whose depression is unyielding to neuroleptic dosage increases; antiparkinsonian drugs for patients whose akinesia, akathisia or other extrapyramidal symptoms interfere with their psychosocial rehabilitation; tegratol when cerebral dysrhythmias are present; propranolol for increasing levels of neuroleptic drugs at brain receptors without risking increased extrapyramidal symptoms or tardive dyskinesia; and recently benzodiazepines, at extraordinarily high dosage levels, for previously refractory schizophrenic patients. Tolerance, dependency, and withdrawal seizures may complicate treatment with benzodiazepines which, in schizophrenia, needs replication. Despite its recent eclipse by the neuroleptics, electroconvulsive therapy should be considered for patients who do not respond to neuroleptics, especially if catatonic symptoms are present.

Long-Term Maintenance and Treatment-Refractory Patients

For the large proportion of patients, about 60 to 70 percent in most studies, who remain in relative remission for a year after their last relapse and hospitalization, an important clinical decision becomes how long to continue medication. This is currently at issue since recent studies have found no longer remissions among patients maintained on long-acting injectable neuroleptics vs. those on oral medications, which suggests that long-term compliance with medication is not as important as previously believed. It is becoming increasingly apparent that neuroleptic drugs delay but rarely prevent relapse; hence, it may be fruitful, and helpful in reducing the hazards of tardive dyskinesia and other long-term side effects, to consider guidelines for reducing or discontinuing neuroleptics in the maintenance of schizophrenic patients.

If the patient is living with tolerant, supportive, accepting relatives or residential care sponsors, there may be fewer risks in switching to drug-free, low-dosage, or intermittent drug therapy than continuing the patient on conventional dosages. Two-year follow-ups of patients in London suggest that low expressed emotion in relatives continues to confer some degree of protection against relapse, but this may require at least intermittent or low-dose neuroleptics to protect the patient from succumbing to major life events (Leff and Vaughn, 1980, 1981).

Some investigators have found that intermittent schedules or low-dosage neuroleptic therapy may keep risk of relapse acceptably low (Kane and Rifkin, 1982; Herz et al., 1982). If the patient on intermittent drug therapy and his relatives become alert to the early warning signals of impending relapse (insomnia, difficulty concentrating, suspiciousness, loss of appetite, social withdrawal), they can return to the psychiatrist for consultation and possible readministration of medication to abort a relapse. Once the symptoms are controlled, the patient-relative-physician "team" jointly decide on the timing for phasing down and discontinuing the drug. If the patient and his/her significant others are knowledgeable collaborators in the maintenance phase of treatment, the hazards of indefinite neuroleptic therapy can be significantly reduced by interconnected psychosocial rehabilitation and judicious, targeted use of medication. Since the use of low or intermittent dosages of neuroleptics does increase the risk of relapse, the consequences of relapse need to be considered in deciding to use these methods. For some patients—for example, a wage earner who is head of a family—raising the risk of relapse is unacceptable, while for others—marginally functioning, publicly assisted individuals—the risk is nil.

Noncompliance with neuroleptic medication may still be a major roadblock in the pathway to successful maintenance of patients in the community. The flow chart in Figure 2 describes what can be done with a patient who fails to adhere to his/her medication regimen. Long-acting depot neuroleptics can be helpful in some cases where medication is effective but isn't being taken. Most important is educating the patient and his/her relatives about the effects and side effects of neuroleptics and conducting a careful behavioral analysis of the reasons for noncompliance. The analysis can generate one or more tactics for improving reliability of drug-taking.

While plasma levels of neuroleptics and their many metabolites have not yet been demonstrated to correlate with clinical response, it may be informative to perform a plasma level if only to determine whether or not the patient is taking the medication at all. As pharmacokinetics and plasma levels of neuroleptics become better standardized against clinical response, we shall be able to use laboratory tests for improving our calibration of dose-response in schizophrenia.

For the chronic schizophrenic patients who do not respond to the above efforts at treatment and rehabilitation, the only strategy left is intensive behavior therapy, such as a ward-wide token economy and social learning program. This approach has been shown to be highly effective in remediating pathological behaviors and in significantly increasing the release of patients to the community and their survival in the community (Paul and Lentz, 1977; Liberman et al., 1974, 1976; Liberman, 1976; Fichter et al., 1976). These methods are expensive because they usually require high staff-to-patient ratios and rigorous training, coordination, and supervision of the interdisciplinary staff. Frequent behavioral observations and interventions must be carefully programmed into a highly responsive and contingently therapeutic environment to overcome the inertia and refractoriness of patients' long-standing behavioral deficits and excesses. These behavioral methods are often found to diminish the amount of medication needed to control bizarre, aggressive, and disorganized chronic patients.

Beyond the drug and social therapies available to schizophrenic patients from mental health professionals, clinics, and hospitals, a new force for maintaining patients in the community has emerged that relies more on advocacy, self-help, and nonprofessional intervention. Community support programs, disseminated by the NIMH after such model psychosocial rehabilitation programs as Fountain House had become popular and effective, provide a variety of resources in the community to enable patients to live in dignity and with less threat to their survival. Social clubs, transitional living arrangements such as halfway homes and foster homes, day centers, sheltered workshops, and transitional employment all combine to serve as protective buffers for individuals susceptible to life stressors (Mosher and Keith, 1980; Keith and Mathews, 1982). From the theoretical standpoint of the stress/diathesis model of schizophrenia, we hypothesize that supportive social processes and neuroleptic drugs combine to make schizophrenic patients less vulnerable to stress-induced exacerbations.

SUMMARY

Clinicians who work with schizophrenic persons and their families have left the old ideological battlefields where advocates of drug vs. psychotherapeutic approaches once jousted. We have outgrown the "either drugs or psychotherapy" dialectic. Modern treatment of schizophrenic patients requires both, depending on the patient's characteristics, the point in the patient's course of disorder, the characteristics of the family and treatment environments, the pharmacokinetics and dose-response of neuroleptic drugs of each patient, and the availability of psychosocial interventions that are more specific than the psychotherapies of decades ago. It is time for modern treatment of schizophrenia to catch up with current concepts of the nature of the disorder, which include both biological and psychosocial contributions.

Although neuroleptic drugs generally seem to improve the patient's cognitive performance and information-processing, they also produce side effects and paradoxical exacerbations of symptoms that may interfere with a patient's learn-

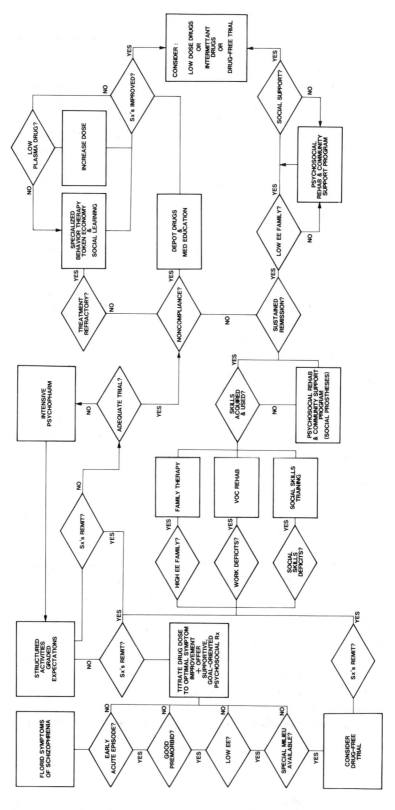

Figure 2 Flow chart for guiding clinical decision-making regarding types and timing of neuroleptic drug and psychosocial treatments for schizophrenic patients.

ing from his or her environment. There are points in the course of patients' schizophrenic disorders—as in older patients who have lived through many years of institutional and drug treatment—at which drugs seem to have little or no value when structured, active treatment is available in the social milieu. On the other hand, there are psychosocial influences that do not seem to facilitate the therapeutic actions of neuroleptics—psychoanalytic therapy or overstimulating environments in which expectations for change may be unrealistically high. One must remember that drugs are always given to patients who respond to the biochemical effects in the context of living environments. These environments, whether they exert favorable, unfavorable, or neutral influences on the drug-responding patient, are a fact of life and need to be considered as part of the patient's total treatment and rehabilitation.

A major limitation of neuroleptic drug therapy comes from the noncompliance of many patients. Psychosocial methods, mostly stemming from social learning principles, may be successfully used to overcome the reasons for patients' failure to adhere to their pharmacotherapy. Just as neuroleptic drugs require consistent and indefinite use to maintain their therapeutic and prophylactic effects, so do psychosocial treatments require consistency and long-term application. Remediating psychological and social deficits in patients with schizophrenic disorders involves the same persistent application of the environment as remedying the patient's neurochemical disturbances with medication.

REFERENCES

Anderson, C. M., Hogarty, G., and Reiss, D. J. 1981. The psychoeducational family treatment of schizophrenia. In M. Goldstein (ed.), *New Directions for Mental Health Services: New Developments in Interventions with Families of Schizophrenics*. No. 12. San Francisco: Jossey-Bass.

Baro, F., and Dom, R. 1976. The interaction between neuroleptic treatment and sociotherapeutic approach in chronic schizophrenics. *Acta Psychiatr. Belg.* 76:735-758.

Blackwell, B. 1972. The drug defaulter. *Clin. Pharmacol. Ther.* 14:378-381.

Boyd, J. L., McGill, C. W., and Falloon, I. R. H. 1981. Family participation in the community rehabilitation of schizophrenics. *Hosp. Community Psychiatry* 32:629-632.

Brown, G., Birley, J. L. P., and Wing, J. K. 1972. Influence of family life on the course of schizophrenia. *Br. J. Psychiatry* 121:241-258.

Buckley, P. 1982. Identifying schizophrenic patients who should not receive medication. *Schizophr. Bull.* 8:429-432.

Carpenter, W. T., McGlashin, T. H., and Strauss, J. S. 1977. The treatment of acute schizophrenia without drugs. *Am. J. Psychiatry* 134:14-20.

Chouinard, G., and Jones, B. D. 1980. Neuroleptic-induced supersensitivity in psychosis: Clinical and pharmacological characteristics. *Am. J. Psychiatry* 137:16-21.

Dawson, M. E., Nuechterlein, K. H., and Liberman, R. P. 1981. Relapse in schizophrenic disorders: Possible contributing factors and implications for behavior therapy. In M. Rosenbaum, C. M. Franks, and Y. Jaffee (eds.), *Perspectives on Behavior Therapy in the Eighties*. New York: Springer.

Falloon, I. R. H., Boyd, J. L., McGill, C. W., Razani, J., Moss, H. B., and Gilderman, A. M. 1982. Family management in the prevention of exacerbations of schizophrenia. *N. Engl. J. Med.* 306:1437-1440.

Falloon, I. R. H., and Liberman, R. P. 1983. Behavioral family interventions in the management of chronic schizophrenia. In W. McFarlane, and C. Beels (eds.), *Family Therapy of Schizophrenia*. New York: Guilford Press.

Falloon, I. R. H., Watt, D. C., and Shepherd, M. 1978. The social outcome of schizophrenic patients in a trial of continuation therapy. *Psychol. Med.* 8: 265-274.

Fichter, M., Wallace, C. J., Liberman, R. P., and Davis, J. R. 1976. Improving social interaction in a chronic psychotic using "nagging" (discriminated avoidance). Experimental analysis and generalization. *J. Appl. Behav. Anal.* 9:377-386.

Gardos, G., and Cole, J. O. 1976. Maintenance antipsychotic therapy: Is the cure worse than the disease. *Am. J. Psychiatry* 133:32-36.

Gelenberg, A. J., and Mandel, M. R. 1977. Catatonic reactions to high potency neuroleptic drugs. *Arch. Gen. Psychiatry* 34:947-950.

Goldberg, S. C., Schooler, N. R., Hogarty, G. E., and Roper, N. 1977. Prediction of relapse in schizophrenic patients treated by drug and sociotherapy. *Arch. Gen. Psychiatry* 34:171-184.

Goldsmith, J., and Drye, R. 1963. Milieu as a variable in clinical drug research. *Dis. Nerv. Syst.* 24:742-745.

Goldstein, M. J. 1970. Premorbid adjustment, paranoid status, and patterns of responses to phenothiazine in acute schizophrenia. *Schizophr. Bull.* 1:24-37.

Goldstone, S., Nurnberg, H. G., and Chamon, W. T. 1979. *Psychopharmacology* 65:119-124.

Grinspoon, L., Ewalt, J. R., and Shader, R. 1967. Long term treatment of chronic schizophrenia. *Int. J. Psychiatry* 4:116-128.

Grinspoon, L., Ewalt, J. R., and Shader, R. I. 1972. *Schizophrenia Pharmacotherapy and Psychotherapy*. Baltimore: Williams & Wilkins.

Hamilton, M., Smith, A. C., Lapidus, H. E., and Cadogen, E. P. 1960. A controlled trial of thiopropazate, chlorpromazine, and occupational therapy in chronic schizophrenics. *J. Ment. Sci.* 106:40-55.

Hamilton, M., Horden, A., Waldrop, F. N., and Lofft, J. 1963. A controlled trial on the value of prochlorperazine, trifluoperazine, and intensive group treatment. *Br. J. Psychiatry* 109:510-522.

Heinrichs, D. W., and Carpenter, W. T. 1982. The psychotherapy of the schizophrenic disorders. In L. Grinspoon (ed.), *Psychiatry: 1982 Annual Review*, pp. 154-165. Washington: American Psychiatric Press.

Herz, M. I., Szymanski, H. V., and Simon, J. 1982. An intermittent medication approach for stable schizophrenic outpatients: An alternative to maintenance medication. *Am. J. Psychiatry* 139:918.

Hogarty, G. E., Goldberg, S. C., and the Collaborative Study Group 1973. Drugs and sociotherapy in the aftercare of schizophrenic patients. One year relapse rates. *Arch. Gen. Psychiatry* 28:54-64.

Hogarty, G. E., Goldberg, S. C., and the Collaborative Study Group 1974. Drugs and sociotherapy in the aftercare of schizophrenic patients, II & III. *Arch. Gen. Psychiatry* 31:603-618.

Hogarty, G. E., Goldberg, S. C., and Schooler, N. R. 1975. Drug and sociotherapy in the aftercare of schizophrenia: A review. In M. Greenblatt (ed.), *Drugs in Combination with Other Therapies*, pp. 1-12. New York: Grune & Stratton.

Hogarty, G. E., Ulrich, R., Goldberg, S., and Schooler, N. 1976. Sociotherapy and the prevention of relapse among schizophrenic patients. In R. L. Spitzer and D. F. Klein (eds.), *Evaluation of Psychological Therapies*, pp. 285-293. Baltimore: Johns Hopkins University Press.

Hogarty, G. E., Schooler, N. R., Ulrich, R., Mussare, F., Ferro, P., and Herron, E. 1979. Fluphenazine and social therapy in the aftercare of schizophrenic patients. *Arch. Gen. Psychiatry* 36:1283-1295.

Kane, J., and Rifkin, A. 1981. Low dose neuroleptics in the treatment of outpatient schizophrenics: A preliminary report. Paper presented to New Clinical Drug Evaluation Unit Conference, Key Biscayne, FL, May 26, 1981.

Kazdin, A. E. 1979. Sociopsychological factors in psychopathology. In A. S. Bellack and M. Hersen (eds.), *Research and Practice in Social Skills Training*, pp. 41-74. New York: Plenum Press.

Keith, S. J., and Mathews, J. M. 1982. Group, family and milieu therapies and psychosocial rehabilitation in the treatment of the schizophrenic disorders. In L. Grinspoon (ed.), *Psychiatry: 1982 Annual Review*, pp. 166-177. Washington: American Psychiatric Press.

Kohen, W., and Paul, G. L. 1976. Current trends and recommended changes in extended care placements of mental patients. *Schizophr. Bull.* 3:24-27.

Krawiecka, M., Goldberg, D., and Vaughn, M. 1977. A standardized psychiatric assessment scale for rating chronic psychotic patients. *Acta Psychiatr. Scand.* 55:299-308.

Leff, J. P., and Vaughn, C. E. 1980. The interaction of life events and relatives' expressed emotion in schizophrenia and depressive neurosis. *Br. J. Psychiatry* 136:146-153.

Leff, J. P., and Vaughn, C. E. 1981. The role of maintenance therapy and relatives' expressed emotion in relapse of schizophrenia: A two year follow-up. *Br. J. Psychiatry* 139:102-104.

Leff, J. P., and Wing, J. K. 1971. Trial of maintenance therapy in schizophrenia. *Br. Med. J.* 3:599-604.

Leff, J. P., Hirsch, S. R., Gaind, R., Rolides, P. O., and Stevens, B. S. 1973. Life events and maintenance therapy in schizophrenic relapse. *Br. J. Psychiatry* 123:659-668.

Leff, J. P., Kuipers, L., Berkowitz, R., Eberlein-Vries, R., and Sturgeon, D. 1982. A controlled trial of social intervention in the families of schizophrenic patients. *Br. J. Psychiatry* 141:121-134.

Liberman, R. P. 1976. Behavior therapy for schizophrenia. In L. J. West and D. Flinn (eds.), *Treatment of Schizophrenia*, pp. 175-206. New York: Grune & Stratton.

Liberman, R. P. 1982a. Social factors in schizophrenia. In L. Grinspoon (ed.), *Psychiatry 1982: Annual Reviews*, pp. 97-111. Washington: American Psychiatric Press.

Liberman, R. P. 1982b. What is schizophrenia? *Schizophrenia Bull.* 8:435-437.

Liberman, R. P., and Davis, J. 1975. Drugs and behavior analysis. In M. Hersen, A. S. Bellack, and P. Miller (eds.), *Progress in Behavior Modification*, pp. 307-330. New York: Academic Press.

Liberman, R. P., Davis, J., Moon, W., and Moore, J. 1973. Research design for analyzing drug-environment-behavior interactions. *J. Nerv. Ment. Dis.* 156: 432-439.

Liberman, R. P., McCann, M., and Wallace, C. J. 1976. Generalization of behavior therapy with psychotics. *Br. J. Psychiatry* 129:490-496.

Liberman, R. P., Wallace, C. J., Vaughn, C. E., Snyder, K. S., and Rust, C. 1980. Social and family factors in the course of schizophrenia: Toward an interpersonal problem-solving therapy for schizophrenics and their relatives. In J. Strauss, S. Fleck, M. Bowers et al. (eds.), *Psychotherapy of Schizophrenia: Current Status and New Directions*, pp. 21-54. New York: Plenum Press.

Liberman, R. P., Wallace, C. J., Tiegen, J., and Davis, J. 1974. Behavioral interventions with psychotics. In K. S. Calhoun, H. E. Adams, and E. M. Mitchell (eds.), *Innovative Treatment Network in Psychopathology*, pp. 323-412. New York: Wiley.

Liberman, R. P., Marshall, B. D., Jr., and Burke, K. L. 1981. Drug and environmental interventions for aggressive psychiatric patients. In R. B. Stuart (ed.), *Violent Behavior: Social Learning Approaches to Prediction, Management and Treatment*, pp. 227-264. New York: Brunner/Mazel.

Liberman, R. P., Nuechterlein, K. H., and Wallace, C. J. 1982. Social skills training and the nature of schizophrenia. In J. P. Curran and P. M. Monti (eds.), *Social Skills Training: A Practical Handbook for Assessment and Treatment*. New York: Guilford Press.

Linn, M. W., Caffey, F. M., Klett, J., Hogarty, G. E., and Lamb, H. R. 1979. Day treatment and psychotropic drugs in the aftercare of schizophrenic patients. *Arch. Gen. Psychiatry* 36:1055-1066.

Linn, M. W., Klett, J., and Caffey, E. M. 1980. Foster home characteristics and psychiatric patient outcome. *Arch. Gen. Psychiatry* 37:129-132.

Linn, M. W., Klett, C. J., and Caffey, E. M. 1982. Relapse of psychiatric patients in foster care. *Am. J. Psychiatry* 139:778-783.

Marshall, B. D., Wallace, C. J., and Liberman, R. P. 1979. Assessing psychiatric patients' compliance in taking medication. *Hosp. Community Psychiatry* 30:125.

May, P. R. A. 1976. When, what & why? Psychopharmacotherapy and other treatments in schizophrenia. *Comp. Psychiatry* 17(6):683-693.

May, P. R. A., and Tuma, A. H. 1976. A followup study of the results of the treatment of schizophrenia. In A. L. Spitzer and D. F. Klein (eds.), *Evaluation of Psychological Therapies*, pp. 256-284. Baltimore: Johns Hopkins University Press.

McCreadie, R. G., Main, C. J., and Dunlop, R. A. 1978. Token economy pimozide and chronic schizophrenia. *Br. J. Psychiatry* 133:179-181.

McGlashin, T. H., and Carpenter, W. T. 1981. Does attitude toward psychosis relate to outcome? *Am. J. Psychiatry* 138:797-801.

Monti, P. M., Corriveau, D. P., and Curran, J. P. 1982. Social skills training for psychiatric patients: Treatment and outcome. In J. P. Curran and P. M. Monti (eds.), *Social Skills Training: A Practical Handbook for Assessment and Treatment*, pp. 185-223. New York: Guilford Press.

Mosher, L. R., and Keith, S. J. 1979. Research on the psychosocial treatment of schizophrenia: A summary report. *Am. J. Psychiatry* 136:623-631.

Mosher, L. R., and Keith, S. J. 1980. Psychosocial treatment: Individual, group, family and community support approaches. *Schizophr. Bull. Special Report*: 127-158.

Mosher, L. R., and Menn, A. Z. 1978. Community residential treatment for schizophrenia: Two year follow-up. *Hosp. Community Psychiatry* 29:715-723.

Oltmanns, T. F., Ohayn, J., and Neale, J. M. 1978. The effect of antipsychotic medication and diagnosis criteria on distractibility in schizophrenia. *J. Psychiatr. Res.* 14:81-91.

Paul, G. L., and Lentz, R. J. 1977. *Psychosocial Treatment of the Chronic Mental Patient.* Cambridge: Harvard University Press.

Paul, G. L., Tobias, L. T., and Holly, B. L. 1972. Maintenance psychotropic drugs in the presence of active treatment programs: A "triple blind" withdrawal study with long-term mental patients. *Arch. Gen. Psychiatry* 27:106-115.

Rappaport, M., Hopkins, H. D., and Hall, K. 1978. Are there schizophrenics for whom drugs may be necessary or contraindicated? *Int. Pharmacopsychiatry* 13:100-111.

Rathod, N. H. 1958. Tranquilizers and patients' environments. *Lancet* 1:611-613.

Schooler, N. 1978. Antipsychotic drugs and psychological treatment in schizophrenia. In M. A. Lipton, A. Dimascio, and K. F. Killam (eds.), *Psychopharmacology: A Generation of Progress*, pp. 1155-1168. New York: Raven Press.

Schooler, N. R., Levine, J., Severe, J. B., Brauzer, B., DiMascio, A., Kleeman, G. L., and Tuason, V. B. 1980. Prevention of relapse in schizophrenia: An evaluation of fluphenazine decanoate. *Arch. Gen. Psychiatry* 37:16-24.

Snyder, K. S., and Liberman, R. P. 1981. Family assessment and intervention with schizophrenics at risk for relapse. In M. J. Goldstein (ed.), *New Directions for Mental Health Services (No. 12)*, pp. 49-60. San Francisco: Jossey-Bass.

Spivack, G., Platt, J. J., and Shure, M. B. 1976. *The Problem Solving Approach to Adjustment.* San Francisco: Jossey-Bass.

Spohn, H. E., Lacoursiere, R. B., Thompson, R., and Lolafoye, C. 1977. Phenothiazine effects on psychological and psychophysiological dysfunction in chronic schizophrenics. *Arch. Gen. Psychiatry* 34:633-644.

Stein, L. I., and Test, M. A. (eds.) 1978. *Alternatives in Mental Hospital Treatment.* New York: Plenum Press.

Tuma, A. H., May, P. R. A., Yale, C., and Forsythe, A. B. 1978. Therapist experience: General clinical ability and treatment outcome in schizophrenia. *J. Consult. Clin. Psychol.* 46:1120-1126.

Turner, A. J. 1973. *Programs and Evaluations: Annual Report.* Huntsville-Madison County Community Mental Health Center, Huntsville, AL.

Vaillant, G. E. 1962. The prediction of recovery in schizophrenia. *J. Nerv. Ment. Dis.* 135:534-543.

Van Putten, T. 1974. Why do schizophrenic patients refuse to take their drugs? *Arch. Gen. Psychiatry* 31:67-72.

Van Putten, T., and May, P. R. A. 1978. "Akinetic depression" in schizophrenia. *Arch. Gen. Psychiatry* 35:1101-1107.

Van Putten, T., May, P. R. A., Marder, S. R., and Wittman, L. 1981. Subjective response to antipsychotic drugs. *Arch. Gen. Psychiatry* 38:187-190.

Vaughn, C. E., and Leff, J. P. 1976. The influence of family and social factors on the course of psychiatric illness. *Br. J. Psychiatry* 129:125-137.

Vaughn, C. E., Snyder, K. S., Freeman, W., Jones, S., Falloon, I. R. H., and Liberman, R. P. 1982. Family factors in schizophrenic relapse: A replication. *Schizophr. Bull.* 8(2):425-426.

Wallace, C. J. 1982. The social skills training program of the Mental Health Clinical Research Center for the Study of Schizophrenia. In J. P. Curran and P. M. Monti (eds.), *Social Skills Training: A Practical Handbook For Assessment and Treatment*, pp. 57-89. New York: Guilford Press.

Wallace, C. J., Nelson, C. J., Liberman, R. P. Aitchison, R. A., Lukoff, D., Elder, J. P., and Ferris, C. 1980. A review and critique of social skills training with schizophrenic patients. *Schizophr. Bull.* 6:42-64.

Wilcox, D. R. C., Gillan, R., and Hare, E. H. 1965. Do psychiatric patients take their drugs? *Br. J. Medicine* 2:790-792.

Wing, J. K. 1978. The social context of schizophrenia. *Am. J. Psychiatry* 135: 1333-1339.

Wing, J. K., Cooper, J. E., and Sartorius, N. 1974. *The Measurement and Classification of Psychiatric Symptoms*. London: Cambridge University Press.

Zigler, E., and Phillips, L. 1962. Social competence and outcome in mental disorder. *J. Abnorm. Psychol.* 63:264-271.

IV
Psychosocial Treatment
of Chronically Mentally Ill Patients

13
Vocational Rehabilitation
of the Psychiatrically Disabled

WILLIAM A. ANTHONY, JOANNE HOWELL,
AND KAREN S. DANLEY

One would have to be culturally blind not to recognize the value placed on work and worklike activity in America. Besides its obvious function of providing a way to earn a living, work is believed to be important for many other reasons, some of the most obvious being: work keeps oneself occupied, overcomes boredom, increases self-respect, and provides a social outlet.

Pithy phrases and sentences abound concerning the value of work. Some allude to the religious quality of work: "Blessed is he who has found his work; let him ask no other blessedness" (Carlyle), or to its effect on our emotions: "Can anything be sadder than work left unfinished? Yes; work never begun" (Pollard). Other statements attest to the belief that work is better than the alternatives: "Better to work and fail than to sleep one's life away" (Jerome), or "You can't eat for eight hours a day nor drink for eight hours a day nor make love for eight hours a day—all you can do for eight hours a day is work" (Faulkner). Some quotes reflect the fact that pleasure and leisure are promised only to those who work: "It is impossible to enjoy idling thoroughly unless one has plenty of work to do" (Jerome), or "Work is the meat of life, pleasure the dessert" (Forbes).

In spite of the many seeming advantages accrued to a worker, historically the mental health system has been something short of enthusiastic about the psychiatrically disabled person's work behavior. Evidence to be presented indicates that we have not been very successful at teaching clients the skills that will help them be workers. But we have been very successful at teaching clients how to be clients! Unfortunately, the skills of the worker are very different from the skills of the client. In this decade Americans as a group are experiencing difficulty in obtaining and maintaining employment. Of course, disabled clients have always had problems in this area, and psychiatrically disabled clients seem to have additional barriers. In 1979 the National Institute of Handicapped Research concluded: "Although mentally disabled clients make up the largest number of cases eligible for vocational rehabilitation services, they have the least probability of success before and after rehabilitation."

Earlier reviews of employment data suggested that, during the year after discharge, about 20 to 30 percent of former patients either worked full-time throughout the year or were employed at the one-year follow-up date. Studies of the last ten years show (Anthony et al., 1972, 1978; Anthony and Nemec, 1983) a 10- to 20-percent employment rate, with some follow-up studies reporting no employment for patients targeted for deinstitutionalization.

Although explanations for this decrease might conceivably focus on the greater severity of illness of the population being discharged, or on hard economic times, evidence indicates that employment rates of other groups of severely disabled persons have actually increased. The Rehabilitation Services Administration reports, for example, that between 1973 and 1977 the number of spinal-cord injured persons who were vocationally rehabilitated increased 400 percent. During the same period there was a three-percent decrease in the number of persons primarily disabled by mental illness who were successfully rehabilitated (Skelley, 1980).

Ciardello (1981) noted that psychiatrically disabled clients now predominate in many sheltered workshops, despite the fact that most workshops were originally designed to meet the needs of the mentally retarded and physically disabled. A U.S. Department of Labor analysis of sheltered workshops shows that "mentally ill" clients made an average of 45 cents per hour doing piece work in workshops, compared to $1.05 per hour for other disabled persons.

Psychiatrically disabled clients who attempt to compete for jobs often confront the negative attitudes of employers, more so than any other disabled group (Betven and Driscoll, 1981). The "psychiatric" label seems most harmful when the person's awkward interpersonal behaviors and lack of interviewing skills reinforce a popularly held stereotype of psychiatrically disabled persons (Anthony, 1979).

Unfortunately, persons with psychiatric disabilities have a poor chance of becoming vocationally rehabilitated, even though their need to work is so great. In addition to the obvious prejudices of employers, the client is confronted with a mental health/rehabilitation system that has never given a high priority to the vocational rehabilitation of severely psychiatrically disabled clients. Attempts to provide these services to psychiatric patients are not perceived as high-status, important work; the mental health professionals engaged in vocational rehabilitation are often the lowest paid mental health workers. The implicit assumption is that vocational rehabilitation activities are routine, intellectually simplistic, and easy. Vocational outcome figures indicate otherwise. In addition, clients seem to be caught between two philosophies: Mental health service providers believe that clients need to work so that they can get well, while the vocational rehabilitation people operate on the assumption that clients must be well in order to work.

Actually, the complexities involved in rehabilitating the psychiatrically disabled for a work environment are immense. Consider these facts:

1. Successful adjustment to a work environment does not correlate significantly with adjustment in one's living or learning environments. Each environment must be addressed separately.

2. Clients often lose their jobs, not because of their inability to perform job tasks, but because of deficits in interpersonal skills. Interpersonal functioning must be assessed and treated as part of the vocational program.

3. Clients who have lost their jobs often do not possess the skills necessary to obtain a similar job. They often need to be taught job-seeking skills.

4. Clients who are no longer interested in jobs for which they have previous experience or training often do not know how to choose a new vocational objective. They often need career counseling.

5. Hospital-based work therapy settings and competitive employment settings are not alike. The work behavior of the psychiatrically disabled client is situationally specific, so that clients need to be trained in environments similar to the ones in which they are expected to work.

6. Disincentives to working, such as loss of social security benefits, Medicaid, and food stamps, cannot be ignored. The advantages *and* disadvantages of obtaining employment must be addressed directly with clients. Issues of *why* to work as well as *what* work to choose need to be discussed.

Such problems and complexities make the process of vocational rehabilitation anything but routine. Yet in the field of mental health the vocational rehabilitation of the psychiatrically disabled has been approached as if it were simple. A common mistake is waiting until the treatment process is nearly complete before vocational rehabilitation issues are even considered. Or worse yet, the mental health practitioner may perceive the vocational rehabilitation process to be simply a matter of finding a job for the client and placing the client in it, thereby totally misunderstanding the time and problems involved. "Dumping" a client in a job is apt to produce the same outcome as "dumping" clients into the community.

Our thesis is that vocational rehabilitation of the psychiatrically disabled is an application of a comprehensive psychiatric rehabilitation approach.

AN OVERVIEW OF PSYCHIATRIC REHABILITATION

The overall goal of psychiatric rehabilitation is to assure that the person who has a psychiatric disability can perform the physical, emotional, or intellectual skills needed to live, learn, and work in his or her own community, with the least possible amount of support from agents of the helping professions (Anthony, 1979). Major methods of reaching this goal involve either teaching clients the specific skills they need to function effectively in their lives and/or developing the community and environmental resources needed to support or strengthen clients' present level of functioning (Anthony et al., 1983).

Psychiatric rehabilitation is modeled on the physical rehabilitation approach. A physical therapist, for example, focuses on improving hemiplegic clients' functional abilities by helping them to use their existing skills, teaching them new skills, and obtaining environmental resources that will accommodate and boost the clients' functional skills (Anthony, 1982).

Similarly, the rehabilitation of psychiatrically disabled persons also focuses on improving their skills and environmental resources. A person's skills and community supports are more related to rehabilitation outcome than are his or her symptoms (see research reviews, Anthony, 1979; Anthony et al., 1978). Research has shown repeatedly that clients can learn a variety of physical, emotional, and intellectual skills regardless of their present symptoms.

Psychiatric rehabilitation interventions are always specific to the environment. The goal of a single intervention is either to maintain the client in a present environment or to prepare the client to move to a new one. Teaching interventions are not developed to instruct the client in "conversational skills"; rather, they are designed to teach the conversation skills required by a specific living, learning, or working environment. Examples of these skills might be conversing with the family at dinner or talking with co-workers during breaks at work.

The Psychiatric Rehabilitation Process

The three phases of psychiatric rehabilitation are the diagnostic phase, the planning phase, and the intervention phase. This diagnostic, planning, and intervention process (DPI process) is grounded in the philosophy and principles of physical rehabilitation (Wright, 1960) and is integrated with various elements of the psychotherapeutic approach (Carkhuff, 1969). But because the psychiatric rehabilitation approach focuses on skills and environment, the rehabilitation *diagnosis* differs significantly from the typical psychiatric diagnosis. The former neither attempts to label nor categorize the clients' symptomatology but to yield behavioral and descriptive information about the disabled clients' current skills and the skill level demanded by the community in which they wish to live, learn, and work. Such information enables the practitioner and clients to develop treatment *plans* designed to increase the clients' strengths and assets, decrease or compensate for their deficits, and/or modify the clients' environments to make them more suitable to the clients' level of functioning. Client- and environmental-focused *interventions* based on this plan lead to the clients' improved ability to reach their personal rehabilitation goals.

Rehabilitation diagnosis. In developing a rehabilitation diagnosis, the clients must accept the diagnosis as valid, because they will later be expected to take action based on understanding their present functioning. In traditional psychiatric treatment, clients have never been deliberately helped to understand their diagnostic labels, even though with the development of *DSM-III*, diagnoses have become more behaviorally descriptive. The inclusion of psychosocial stressors and highest level of functioning reflects movement toward including a rehabilitation philosophy in the psychiatric diagnostic system. In contrast to a *DSM-III* psychiatric diagnosis, however, the psychiatric rehabilitation diagnosis assumes that all clients have their own unique assets and deficits that cannot be grouped by type of illness or personality. Although formulating a rehabilitation diagnosis is time-consuming, it assures that the clients' own perspective, skill assets, skill deficits, and environmental resources are being addressed in relation to each environmental goal.

Table 1 is an example of a rehabilitation diagnosis for a client who is attempting to move from an inpatient setting to a halfway house. Table 2 shows the diagnosis for the same client in relation to a work goal. The diagnosis indicates that the client has two distinct but interrelated rehabilitation goals and that both involve moving from a present to a future environment. In both instances, the diagnosis contrasts the client's present skill level with the one he will need to function in each of the new environments. Note that some of the clients' skills are strengths (+) while some are deficits (−).

A similar assessment specifies the type and level of resources available in the client's environment. Table 3 shows a sample of environmental strengths and deficits that might be critical to a client's rehabilitation outcome. Such an extensive list might not be made for each client, but Table 3 provides some common examples of environmental strengths and deficits.

Rehabilitation plan. Once the diagnosis has been established, an individual plan is developed to identify each client's appropriate and necessary rehabilitation interventions: how personal and/or environmental resources must be changed to achieve the client's own living, learning, and/or working goals; what interventions must occur for the client and/or environmental resources to move from current to required levels. Specifically, the rehabilitation plan specifies how client skills or environmental resources will be developed and which practitioners must implement the interventions (Cohen et al., 1980).

Rehabilitation interventions. Client skill development may be achieved by one or a combination of two methods: direct skill teaching and skill programming.

Direct skill teaching requires more of a practitioner than modeling the skill for the client or reinforcing approximate skill behaviors. Skill teaching involves planning *what* and *how* to teach, involving clients in the instructional process, and monitoring the clients' skill use in the environment (Danley et al., 1982).

When clients possess the needed skills but cannot use them in the needed environment, the practitioner employs *skill programming*. This consists of planning how the client will use his or her skills to achieve identified goals in specific

Table 1   Skill Assessment Chart for Client with Rehabilitation Goal[1]

Rehabilitation Problem 1: No housing upon hospital discharge
Rehabilitation Goal 1:   To live successfully in a halfway house

Relevant Environment	Skill Type (PEI)	+/−	Defined Skill Behavior	Level of Functioning	
				Present	Needed
Halfway House					
Hygiene	P	−	% of time client washes self once a day	60	100
	P	+	% of time client brushes teeth at least once a day	100	100
Nutrition	I	+	# of foods in each basic food group client can list	8	5
	I	−	% of trials client can develop a menu representing a balanced meal	60	80
Responsibility	P/E	+	% of time client does chores when asked	90	80
		−	without being asked	60	80
Relationships	E	+	# of times per day client can appropriately initiate social conversation with house members	5	3
	E	+	% of time client makes supportive statements to others when sadness or discomfort is expressed	80	70
CMHC					
Support Seeking	E	+	% of time client requests emotional assistance when anxiety level is high	100	100
Assistance Awareness	I	−	# of names and phone numbers client can list for potential support people	0	3

environments. The skill program states steps the client needs to take, building on strengths and decreasing deficits. The skill program includes time lines and reinforcements that may be needed to help the client to perform the steps in the program (Anthony et al., 1983).

The second primary psychiatric rehabilitation intervention is *resource development*. This may involve programming or skill teaching with the client's family or close associates. Resource development involves helping clients select the

Table 2   Skill Assessment Chart for Client with Rehabilitation Goal 2

Rehabilitation Problem 2: No employment
Rehabilitation Goal 2:   Work in sheltered workshop

Relevant Environment	Skill Type (PEI)	+/−	Defined Skill Behavior	Level of Functioning Present	Needed
Halfway House Responsibility	I	+	% of trials client can set alarm clock for given time	90	80
	P	−	# of days per week client has prepared clean clothes to wear in a.m.	3	5
	P	−	# of days/week client gets out of bed at specified time on own initiative	2	5
Sheltered Workshop Dependability	I	+	% of trials client can accurately repeat, from memory, the absence report phone number at workshop	90	80
	P	−	# of days/week client can arrive at job site on time	0	5
	P	−	# of days per year client misses work due to illness	>30	<12
Getting Along	E	−	% of time client can accept correction from supervisor without swearing	75	100
Task Performance	E	−	Consecutive amount of time client can stay on task without talking or reacting to voices	50 min.	90 min.
	P	−	# of minutes client can go between smoking breaks at work	50	90

people, places, things, or activities that will increase their ability to function effectively in the desired living, learning, or working environment. Examples of this type of intervention might be helping a client choose a person to help with getting a job, a new place to live, a reliable mode of transportation, or a social activity. If no environmental resources are available that are commensurate with a client's present level of functioning, the intervention might involve creation of new resources. A sheltered apartment might have to be developed, for example, or a new social activity group created.

Table 3   Environmental Assessment Chart

Rehabilitation Problem:	No employment
Rehabilitation Goal:	Sheltered workshop employment

Relevant Environment	Person	+/-	Defined Environmental Factors	Level of Functioning	
				Present	Needed
Sheltered Workshop					
	Director	+	# of work slots director will make available by needed date	1	1
	Supervisor	+	% of times supervisor will give praise to client when job performance meets or exceeds expectations	100	100
	Workers	–	# of workers available to orient client to worksite social routine	0	2
	Bus Driver	–	# of minutes bus driver waits for client to come from house to bus after sounding horn	2	3
Halfway House					
	Manager	–	# of times per week manager will check to see if client is out of bed by needed time (during first month)	0	5
	House-mate(s)	–	Average # of times per day housemates give positive support in relation to client working in sheltered workshop	0	2
CMHC					
	Counselor	+	Level of programming skills counselor has to plan, monitor, and support client progress	high	high
	Day Treatment Staff	–	% of skill teaching programs staff has for remediating essential client skill deficits	75	100

PSYCHIATRIC VOCATIONAL REHABILITATION

Although at first glance the vocational rehabilitation process for psychiatric clients seems straightforward, practitioners and clients often become confused by the assortment of assessment methods, intervention strategies, and vocational environments from which to choose. In one Massachusetts urban area, for example, employment settings range from full-time competitive jobs through transitional sheltered workshops, to prevocational and activities-in-daily-living training in hospitals—14 possibilities in all. Placement in work environments is meaningless to clients, however, unless the purpose of the placement is clear. During early stages of the process, a work environment might produce a vocational assessment through experiences such as diagnostic interviewing, work samples, interest and aptitude testing, situational assessment, and job site evaluations. At another point, the same environment might be used to engage the client in vocational exploration, career decision-making, career planning, work values clarification, and job skills training. At still another point, the same environment might be useful for work adjustment training. Because of the wealth of available assessment methods, intervention strategies, and alternative work environments, clients and practitioners need a well-defined vocational rehabilitation model that enables everyone to know, at any given point in time, what is happening to the client and why.

A Vocational Rehabilitation Model

A model of the vocational rehabilitation process (Table 4) organizes assessment, intervention, and environmental variables into a matrix that juxtaposes the psychiatric rehabilitation process with all phases of vocational rehabilitation.

Table 4   Psychiatric Rehabilitation Process and Its Relationship to Vocational Rehabilitation Phases

| | | Rehabilitation Process | | |
		diagnose	plan	intervene
	choose			
Vocational Rehabilitation Phases	get			
	keep			

Vocational rehabilitation begins, as does the general psychiatric rehabilitation process, with determination of a vocational rehabilitation goal based on the client's perspective. This step seems obvious, yet it is often neglected. Too often it is the practitioner's goal *for* the client, and not the client's personal goal, that is identified. A vocational rehabilitation goal must be clearly explored, understood, and owned by the client before the vocational rehabilitation process can proceed with any meaning or direction.

As shown in Table 4, the vocational rehabilitation process is, in its most basic form, the process of assisting clients in choosing, getting, and keeping a job. This model can help clients to understand that (1) they will be involved in an *assessment* or diagnosis of their ability to choose, get, and keep a job; (2) they will develop a *plan* that will increase their ability to do this; (3) they will be part of an *intervention* based on the plan designed to help them do these three things. Any vocational environment can be understood in this context. Practitioners can use this model to simplify the vocational rehabilitation process for clients. The model also illustrates the comprehensiveness of the vocational rehabilitation process; each or all of the three phases can be addressed in depth depending on the specific phase or phases in which the client needs assistance.

Table 5 presents typical client work-related deficits categorized by the three vocational rehabilitation phases. Not all psychiatrically disabled clients have deficiencies in all phases, though many do.

Table 6 portrays the relationship between the three vocational rehabilitation phases and the four major vocational rehabilitation interventions used to overcome client deficits in choosing, getting, and keeping a job. Psychiatrically disabled clients may become involved in some or all of the intervention components, depending on their diagnosed strengths and deficits. Clients who cannot effectively choose a job need *career counseling* to develop a realistic occupational objective and to make career plans based on their interests, values, and the requirements of the world of work. These clients also need *occupational skills training* so that they can gain job-specific skills (e.g., typing, programming, waiting on tables) that are necessary to do the job they want. Clients who cannot get a job need *career placement* services to develop the ability to seek out possible jobs and to be hired. Clients who cannot keep a job need *work adjustment training* to remediate the deficits in various job-related skills (e.g., getting to work on time, conversing with co-workers). A psychiatric rehabilitation practitioner who is skilled in the methods and strategies involved in the four vocational intervention components, as well as in the practices of psychiatric rehabilitation, can identify precisely the specific vocational rehabilitation phases with which the client needs assistance. With continual active involvement of the client, the practitioner develops a plan that specifies how the needed vocational interventions will be carried out.

The classification scheme depicted in Table 6 offers the rehabilitation

Table 5 Typical Work Deficits Categorized by the Three Vocational Rehabilitation Phases

Choosing a Job	Getting a Job	Keeping a Job
Cannot identify own interests	Cannot identify job-related assets	Cannot dress appropriately for work
Cannot identify own abilities	Cannot identify own employment sources	Cannot use public public transportation
Does not know what occupations relate to interests	Does not use sources of employment information	Cannot be punctual
Does not know what occupations relate to abilities	Does not look for work frequently enough	Cannot control temper at work
Does not evaluate occupational alternatives based on own values (decision-making skills)	Cannot write a resume	Cannot make friends at work
	Cannot fill out an application	Cannot accept criticism
Cannot list more than one work alternative	Cannot explain job skills	Cannot follow directions
	Cannot use stigma-reduction skills with interviewer	Cannot give directions
Lacks career plan to achieve career objective	Cannot attend and respond to interviewer	Cannot work for extended periods
Cannot identify deficits which are hindering career plan	Cannot dress appropriately for interview	Cannot evaluate own work performance
	Cannot ask questions of interviewer	
	Cannot explain career plans to an interviewer	
	Cannot perform specific job skills (i.e., cooking, typing, programming)	

Table 6   Relationship between Vocational Rehabilitation Phases
and Major Vocational Interventions

Vocational Interventions

	choose	career counseling
Vocational Rehabilitation Phases	get	occupational skills training career placement
	keep	work adjustment training

practitioner a concept of typical vocational deficits and possible interventions. Obviously, in the actual practice of vocational rehabilitation, there is much overlap in the performance of services related to these intervention categories. Many agencies and practitioners provide all four, while others might provide only one. Some vocational counseling centers might help clients develop an occupational objective and a career plan, but ignore the clients' placement and work adjustment needs. Other agencies may provide training or assistance in vocational placement for clients who already have career plans and work adjustment skills. Some less knowledgeable facilities might go so far as to provide placement services whether or not the client has an adequate career plan or can demonstrate adequate levels of work adjustment.

The intervention strategies used by agencies also differ in their orientation to the psychiatric rehabilitation approach. Agencies that provide vocational interventions with an emphasis on rehabilitation will attempt to teach clients the skills they need. Agencies that lack such an orientation may merely walk the client through the vocational rehabilitation process while offering little or no skill development. Clients may, for example, select an occupational objective, develop a career plan, or even obtain a job primarily through the efforts of their counselor. These clients will never learn from the practitioner how to implement the vocational development process themselves. More comprehensive rehabilitation practices actively teach the client to overcome deficits and ensure environmental support for the use of these skills.

Choosing a Job—Career Counseling

The first step of psychiatric vocational rehabilitation is the choice of a realistic occupational objective that enables clients to obtain their goal. A client may want to work full time, for example, but may be unable to state the type of work he/she wants to do. Perhaps the job the client wants seems unattainable to the practitioner or, conversely, objectives offered by the practitioner may be unacceptable to the client.

When the client's occupational objective seems unclear or inappropriate, career counseling is the proper intervention. It promotes clients' exploration of their own interests and value systems and develops their understanding of the relationship between their unique set of values and interests and those demanded by employers in various occupations.

For many psychiatrically disabled clients, vocational "choice" is unheard of. Hospital and community settings promote neither client choice nor risk-taking. Furthermore, a history of failure steers many individuals away from choosing and committing themselves to a course of action. Psychiatrically disabled persons are often passive recipients of aftercare or day treatment, even though studies do show the usefulness of posthospital treatment when it is willingly attended (Anthony et al., 1978). Compounding the clients' problems with vocational choice are mental health and rehabilitation practitioners who sometimes limit themselves to standardized interest, aptitude, or needs assessment tools or recommend vocational options based mainly on computerized profiles. Skillful career counseling can help clients become aware of and understand their choices and improve the practitioners' use of vocational intervention tools.

Many severely psychiatrically disabled persons had well-developed job skills before they became ill. Partly because of the disability and the passage of time their skills may have deteriorated and their interests and values changed. Unfortunately, their occupational choices after the onset of disability are often based on their former values and skills rather than on a comprehensive, current picture. A common fallacy is that clients cannot develop new interests and values. The truth is that they *can* when they are stimulated by new knowledge and experience gained in the rehabilitation process.

Career counseling begins, as does all psychiatric rehabilitation, with a diagnosis of the clients' skills and resources in relation to the task of choosing the occupational objective. Typical skill deficits in choosing a job are shown in column 1 of Table 5. Typical resource deficits include someone to administer an aptitude test, a place to gain work experience, or a college or high school transcript. Once skill and resource needs are identified, an intervention plan most likely to result in job success and satisfaction can be developed. Typical career counseling interventions include reading about occupations, talking with people on the job, and instruction in decision-making skills.

Getting a Job—Occupational Skills Training and Career Placement

Getting a job requires that the client have the basic skills and resources needed to perform occupational tasks plus the skills and resources needed to obtain employment. These two types of requirements will indicate which vocational interventions are needed—career placement or occupational skills training.

Occupational skills training. The goal of an occupational skills training program is for the client to acquire the physical, emotional, and intellectual skills needed to perform a particular job. The client who wants to be a carpenter needs to know tools, be able to identify types of wood, ask questions when instructions are unclear, and be able to reduce personal stress on the job. Occupational skills training usually occurs after career counseling and before career placement, but job-specific skills training may be done along with work adjustment training.

Occupational skills training can take place in almost any vocational environment, including hospitals, formal training schools, or on the job. Occupational skills training takes place in environments that can be scaled according to their similarity to competitive work settings (Hursh & Anthony, 1983). Table 7 illustrates such a scale. On levels 2 and 3 are traditional hospital and sheltered workshops. Level 4 sites are in industry but have sheltered workshop status and are usually connected to a rehabilitation agency. In Level 5 training sites clients are employed by business and industry but are receiving additional supervision and training by agency staff or are attending peer support groups.

Career placement. Career placement skills include behaviors needed to locate and gain access to job possibilities as well as skills involved in presenting oneself to an employer in writing and in person (see Table 5, column 2). Career placement resources may include transportation or appropriate interview and work clothing (Pierce et al., 1980).

Data support the notion that clients can be trained to improve their career placement abilities (Azrin and Philip, 1979; Keil and Barber, 1973; Prazak, 1969; Safieri, 1970) and that these skills have a significant impact on rehabilitation outcome (Anderson, 1968; Keith et al., 1977; McLure, 1972; Pumo et al., 1966). Nevertheless, job placement has been shunned by many mental health

Table 7   Skills Training Environments Scaled According to Their Proximity to a Competitive Employment Environment

Level 6 — Competitive employment environment
Level 5 — Competitive employment environment with supportive services
Level 4 — Competitive employment environment with sheltered components
Level 3 — Segregated work site — prototype workshop
Level 2 — Institutional (hospital/ward) work duties
Level 1 — No institutional work demands

and rehabilitation practitioners who feel uncomfortable relating to the business world, do not have adequate time to visit and understand local industry, and see placement activities as an undesirable part of their job. They often fail to understand the need to develop job options that reflect the clients' interests and values. Improved career placement technology (Azrin and Philip, 1979; Weslowski, 1981) has, however, helped to make the teaching of career placement skills a more credible professional activity.

Career placement is appropriate for psychiatrically disabled clients who need to learn how to identify *what* they have to offer to employers, locate *where* they can offer it, and market themselves in writing and in person.

Keeping a Job—Work Adjustment Training

Work adjustment training programs are designed for clients who lack the general work-related and social skills needed to maintain a job (Neff, 1968). These include behaviors known as "work habits," whose relative importance varies greatly from setting to setting. Being punctual, for example, may be extremely important to one employer and not to another. The practitioner must understand the specific environmental requirements for each client if the diagnosis of work adjustment is to lead to successful rehabilitation. Similarly, resources like clothes needed to keep a job vary widely.

Many severely disabled adults either never acquired work habits or lost them. Although work habits are the main focus of work adjustment training, social skills training is essential also because of the intense interpersonal interaction demanded by many work environments.

Effective work adjustment training is conducted in an *in vivo* setting in which the client learns to handle gradually increasing demands and tasks (Anthony, 1979). It is a concrete instructional program with explicit skill goals which involves psychiatrically disabled clients in their own vocational rehabilitation process. It is not simply shaping client behavior by such reinforcement techniques as token economies. Such programs may modify present behavior but are unlikely to foster generalization to other work environments.

In addition, work adjustment training provides the practitioner with observable data on clients' natural work behavior in the work environment. This information is valuable for feedback to clients and as a basis for program modification.

In essence, work adjustment training attempts to teach clients the skills needed to "get along" in the job and to be "dependable."

VOCATIONAL INTERVENTION OUTCOME RESEARCH

Many vocational outcome studies that have investigated a single intervention have focused on career placement (Anderson, 1968; Azrin et al., 1975, 1979; McLure, 1972; Stude and Pauls, 1977; Ugland, 1977; Wesolowski, 1980). First promoted by the Minnesota Rehabilitation Center (Anderson, 1968), and the subject of later studies, career placement has become a credible intervention in both rehabilitation and mental health settings. Evidence of this new emphasis can be found in the excellent comparison of six current career placement programs by Wesolowski (1981).

Occupational skills training often occurs concurrently with some type of work adjustment training. Perhaps the most notable intervention of this kind occurred at the Vermont State Hospital (Brown, 1970) and was summarized by Rubin and Roessler (1978):

> Via utilization of existing hospital facilities, training programs for farm hands, maintenance men, cook helpers, and general maids were developed under the Manpower Development and Training Act of 1962. Program activities deviated from typical mental hospital patient work routines in that competitive work environment conditions such as quality standards and time deadlines were stressed. Work experiences were complemented by social development activities such as group therapy, gripe sessions, and field trips to restaurants. Program participants ranged in age from 16 to 57 years with an average hospitalization of 7½ years. Only patients who were considered good candidates for discharge were selected for the program. Thirty-seven of the 40 patients who entered the program completed it. At the time of the report of program results, 22 of the completers were holding jobs, and 6 either were taking further training or were in school (p. 72).

A later study by Ciardello (1981) gives evidence that occupational skills training offered in many current sheltered workshop settings is often inappropriate for psychiatric clients. Many of the production tasks involved in most sheltered workshop settings require the very skills in which psychiatric clients are consistently deficient.

Most of the literature is critical of the environment in which the training is carried out. Sheltered work adjustment training situations are criticized because they often prepare the client for a sheltered work placement and not for competitive work. As (Anthony, 1979) wrote:

> One of the greatest challenges facing work adjustment training programs is the blending of a therapeutic environment with a competitive working environment. That is, if the goal is to help the client function as independently as possible, and at the same time to teach appropriate work habits, a sensitive balance between treatment and work must be attained. This balance may be achieved by maintaining competitive employment expectations while at the same time providing opportunities for clients to explore with each other their deficits, strengths, difficulties, and how

to function more effectively in the work environment. Although work adjustment programs attempt to approximate a working environment, practitioners must not lose sight of the fact that such settings are created in order to rehabilitate (p. 139).

Career counseling interventions are rarely reported in the literature, even though the psychiatrically disabled are often deficient in work experience (Ciardello and Bingham, 1982). The element of career choice for the severely psychiatrically disabled apparently seems foreign to many practitioners and researchers. Yet Rogan (1980) presented case studies of the use of career decision-making skills which eventually resulted in successful employment.

In a small quasi-experimental study, Kline and Hoisington (1981) investigated the impact of a work values group which met for 1½ hours per week for 12 weeks. More than half of the work values group members obtained employment whereas, in the comparison group, only 10 percent did so. This result suggests the potential impact of career counseling on vocational outcome.

Some interesting research questions are apparent: Does each of the four major types of vocational interventions truly affect vocational outcome? What client characteristics contribute to outcome? Does a comprehensive approach that uses all four types of interventions, and is based on an assessment of client needs, really achieve higher levels of success than any single approach (e.g., career placement)?

The field of psychiatric vocational rehabilitation is beset by questions and lacks answers. The process of psychiatric vocational rehabilitation described here may be a guide for practitioners and their clients as they attempt to achieve positive vocational outcome. It may also be useful to researchers as they investigate the field.

SUMMARY COMMENTS

Mental health programs have typically focused on decreasing clients' personal discomfort and lessening their dependence on the mental health system itself (e.g., deinstitutionalization). Yet, outcome data indicate that merely reducing a person's symptoms or decreasing dependence does not automatically lead to an improvement in client functioning (Anthony, 1977). As a matter of fact, dependence on support systems can be healthy in that reliance in one area, such as a supportive living situation, can enhance the clients' functioning in their vocational environment (Anthony et al., 1983).

The two predominant systems concerned with the vocational rehabilitation of the severely psychiatrically disabled are state departments of mental health and state divisions of vocational rehabilitation. Although their collaboration is essential, it is hindered by a number of barriers (Cohen, 1981), and the planned integration of local services is found in very few places. A recent conference on vocational rehabilitation/mental health collaboration noted the following:

> The VR and MH systems have unique capabilities for offering work-related services to some common client subgroups within the [chronically mentally ill] population. A systematic plan for the integration of the services provided by both the MH and VR systems to the shared client population needs to be jointly developed. The plan needs to specify the shared target population, desired client outcomes, unique MH/VR practitioner activities, inservice and preservice training, and work-related rehabilitation system and policies (Cohen, 1981).

For this kind of collaboration to operate effectively, however, a number of issues must be faced. First and foremost, if the vocational rehabilitation needs of the severely psychiatrically disabled are ever to be met, then the mental health field must move toward providing more vocational rehabilitation services. State divisions of vocational rehabilitation simply do not have the staffing nor the mandate to provide the level of vocational rehabilitation services needed by severely psychiatrically disabled persons. Mental health programs need to expand their treatment and role to include the tasks of diagnosing, planning, and intervening in the vocational area of functioning.

Mental Health Departments

For mental health professionals to carry out the vocational rehabilitation process they must receive additional training in rehabilitation. There is great danger in the possibility that mental health professionals will approach the vocational rehabilitation process from a treatment orientation, by focusing on work as a means for decreasing the client's psychiatric symptomatology and increasing the client's personal insight. This mistaken emphasis is apt to occur despite the fact that behavioral symptoms and therapeutic insights have not been shown to relate to vocational outcome and that the type of treatment interventions that have been shown to affect vocational outcome are rehabilitative (Anthony, 1979).

The symptoms of psychosis are more relevant to the cause of the vocational dysfunction than they are to its treatment. The vocational area is problematic not so much because of the client's symptomatology, but because the psychiatric disability has impeded the client's personal and vocational development. Severely psychiatrically disabled clients are "vocationally immature" because they lack many normal life experiences and life roles that are the foundation of one's vocational identity. As a result, their knowledge of themselves, including their own skills, interests, and values in relation to the world of work is minimal; their ability to test the reality of self-knowledge against the demands of the working world is often deficient, and their general knowledge of the world of work is sparse.

The vocational rehabilitation approach used with the psychiatrically disabled is basically not so different from the vocational intervention approach used with other persons, disabled or not. The important differences are in emphasis. *More time* is needed to go through the process, because of the clients' vocational immaturity. *More energy* is needed to form a collaborative relationship with clients who are used to having things done *to* and *for* them rather than *with* them. *More alternative vocational environments* are needed to allow clients opportunity for reality-testing and exploration. *More strategies* are needed for dealing with *stigma* against the psychiatrically disabled clients. *More effort* must be devoted to a deliberate refocusing of the helping process on the client's needed *skills* and environmental *supports* rather than focusing on client pathology.

The vocational rehabilitation of the severely psychiatrically disabled is a lengthy and complex process—but it is certainly not a medical process. Expertise in psychiatric diagnosis and treatment does not seem to be necessary nor sufficient for rehabilitation to occur. Treatment specialists must realize that psychiatric vocational rehabilitation is *not* another treatment designed to make the client well. Rather, it is an attempt to enable the client to fulfill an important life role and to reap the accompanying psychological and material benefits.

Vocational Rehabilitation Divisions

In contrast to mental health professionals who identify work as a means of helping clients get "well," many vocational rehabilitation practitioners want clients "well" so that they can help them get work! More vocational rehabilitation practitioners need to realize that symptomatic clients can be rehabilitated (Anthony and Margules, 1974), and that they needn't wait until treatment is finished to become involved. Local state rehabilitation agencies need to be more involved with mental health programs to help psychiatrically disabled clients become "rehabilitation-ready."

Weekly meetings between mental health and vocational rehabilitation agencies create the opportunity for professionals on both teams to identify client needs that are not being met, and to make recommendations for new services that might fill that gap. The modification or creation of community resources, designed to meet the needs of this population, is a major step toward designing an effective service delivery system for clients and away from struggling to fit the client into the entrance criteria of existing programs that do not reflect clients' needs.

Local coordination between mental health and vocational rehabilitation agencies is also needed to catch recidivists before they lose their jobs. Although state vocational rehabilitation agencies offer post-employment services, many psychiatrically disabled individuals do not reach out for assistance by calling their former rehabilitation counselors. Mental health providers who know of the client's difficulty, however, must immediately inform the appropriate rehabilitation practitioner for crisis intervention. The probability that this will happen increases with a joint vocational rehabilitation/mental health approach to rehabilitation.

State agency administrators need to support the activities of their service delivery personnel. One of the most difficult aspects of rehabilitating psychiatrically disabled individuals is the time it takes to move them through diagnosis, planning, and appropriate career interventions. Mental health systems are designed to serve the long-term client; state rehabilitation programs are not. In vocational rehabilitation, standards exist for the number of months it takes for a "typical client" to move through the process. Because the psychiatrically disabled individual is not the "typical client" in terms of the time needed for rehabilitation, these standards often inhibit access to and services from VR agencies. State vocational rehabilitation administrators need to acknowledge this and allow practitioners to gear service delivery to the clients' personal time frames, so long as those clients are constructively participating in their own rehabilitation.

Practitioner Attitudes

One essential attitude of practitioners is the belief that psychiatrically disabled individuals can participate in their own rehabilitation. Diagnoses and plans are not developed solely to fulfill government funding requirements or to track a client population. Their most important purpose is to assist clients in understanding their own strengths and deficits, to choose goals based on their own needs and interests, and to plan programs in which the clients are motivated to participate.

Psychiatrically disabled clients have value as individuals. Their own personal needs and goals must be attended to, even if deemed "unrealistic" or "unattainable" by practitioners. If they are not, the chance that they will understand and accept their own strengths and deficits is minimal and the likelihood that they will actively participate in programs designed to assist them will be slim.

Lastly, psychiatrically disabled persons have the right to vocational rehabilitation services. Studies have shown that even schizophrenics, whose symptoms appear outwardly psychotic, can work (Anthony et al., 1978). If mental health workers wait until symptoms decrease, if hospitals shut off work opportunities for hospitalized patients, if state rehabilitation facilities deny these clients services because they do not seem to fit into their system, then we are denying these clients their rights to rehabilitation.

A Final Word

This paper began with quotations describing the benefits and advantages of work. Unfortunately, employment base rate data indicate that severely psychiatrically disabled clients are not likely to be reaping employment benefits. Even the meager benefits of unemployment are now being stripped away from many clients by the Social Security Administration (Anderson, 1982).

A line from a poem by Robert Frost succinctly illustrates the psychiatrically disabled person's employment situation. In *The Death of a Hired Hand*, Frost describes a worker who is not dependable, has difficulty getting along with co-workers, and possesses few job skills. "He has nothing to look backward on with pride, nothing to look forward to with hope." This bleak picture is the fundamental challenge of psychiatric vocational rehabilitation.

REFERENCES

Anderson, J.A. 1968. The disadvantaged seek work—through their efforts or ours? *Rehabilitation Record* 9:5-10.

Anderson, J.R. 1982. Social security and SSI benefits for the mentally disabled. *Hosp. Community Psychiatry* 33:295-298.

Anthony, W.A. 1977. Psychological rehabilitation: A concept in need of a method. *Am. Psychol.* 32:658-662.

Anthony, W.A. 1979. *The Principles of Psychiatric Rehabilitation*. Baltimore: University Park Press.

Anthony, W.A. 1982. Explaining "psychiatric rehabilitation" by an analogy to "physical rehabilitation." *Psychosocial Rehabilitation Journal* 5:61-66.

Anthony, W.A., and Margules, A. 1974. Toward improving the efficacy of psychiatric rehabilitation: A skills training approach. *Rehabilitation Psychology* 21:101-105.

Anthony, W.A., and Nemec, P. 1983. Rehabilitation. In A.S. Bellack (ed.), *Treatment and Care for Schizophrenia*. New York: Grune & Stratton.

Anthony, W.A., Buell, G.J., Sharratt, S., and Althoff, M.E. 1972. The efficacy of psychiatric rehabilitation. *Psychosocial Bulletin* 78:447-456.

Anthony, W.A., Cohen, M.R., and Cohen, B.F. 1983. The philosophy, treatment process and principles of the psychiatric rehabilitation approach. *New Directions in Mental Health*, pp. 67-69.

Anthony, W.A., Cohen, M.R., and Vitalo, R. 1978. The measurement of rehabilitation outcome. *Schizophr. Bull.* 4:365-383.

Azrin, N. J., and Philip, R. A. 1979. The job club method for the job handicapped: A comparative outcome study. *Rehabilitation Counseling Bulletin* 23:144-155.

Azrin, N.H., Flores, T., and Kaplan, S.J. 1975. Job finding club: A group assisted program for obtaining employment. *Behav. Res. Ther.* 13:17-27.

Betven, N.L., and Driscoll, J.H. 1981. The effects of past psychiatric disability on employer evaluation of a job applicant. *Journal of Applied Rehabilitation Counseling* 12:50-55.

Brown, J.K. 1970. Mental patients work back into society. *Manpower* 2:20-25.

Carkhuff, R. R. 1969. *Helping and Human Relations*, vols. 1 and 2. New York: Holt, Rinehart and Winston.

Ciardello, J.A. 1981. Job placement success of schizophrenic clients in sheltered workshop programs. *Vocational Evaluation and Work Adjustment Bulletin* Fall:125-128.

Ciardello, J.A., and Bingham, W.C. 1982. The career maturity of schizophrenic clients. *Rehabilitation Counseling Bulletin* December:3-9.

Cohen, M. 1981. *Improving Interagency Collaboration between Vocational Rehabilitation and Mental Health Agencies: A Conference Summary Report.* Boston: Center for Rehabilitation Research and Training in Mental Health.

Cohen, M.R., Vitalo, R.V., Anthony, W.A., and Pierce, R.M. 1980. *The Skills of Community Service Coordination. Psychiatric Rehabilitation Practice Series: Book 6.* Baltimore: University Park Press.

Danley, K., Ridley, D., and Cohen, M. 1982. *Review of Skill Teaching Guides.* Boston: Center for Rehabilitation Research and Training in Mental Health.

Hursh, N.C., and Anthony W.A. 1983. The vocational preparation of the psychiatric patient in the community. In I. Barofsky and R. Budson (eds.), *The Chronic Psychiatric Patient in the Community: Principles of Treatment.* New York: Spectrum.

Keil, E. L., and Barbee, J. R. 1973. Behavior modification and training the disadvantaged job interviewee. *Vocational Guidance Quarterly* September: 50-56.

Keith, R.D., Engelkes, J.R., and Winborn, B.B. 1977. Employment seeking preparation and activity: An experimental job placement training model for rehabilitation clients. *Rehabilitation Counseling Bulletin* 21:159-165.

Kline, A., and Hoisington, B. 1981. Placing the psychiatrically disabled: A look at work values. *Rehabilitation Counseling Bulletin* 25:365-369.

McLure, D. P. 1972. Placement through improvement of clients' job seeking skills. *Journal of Applied Rehabilitation* 3:188-196.

National Institute of Handicapped Research 1979. Past employment services aid mentally disabled clients. *Rehab Brief* August:1-4.

Neff, W. 1968. *Work and Human Behavior.* New York: Atherton Press.

Prazak, J.A. 1969. Learning job seeking interview skills. In I. Krumboltz and C. Thoreson (eds.), *Behavioral Counseling*, pp. 414-424. New York: Rinehart and Winston.

Pumo, B., Sehl, R., and Cogan, F. 1966. Job readiness: Key to placement. *J. Rehabil.* 32:18-19.

Rogan, D. 1980. Implementing the rehabilitation approach in a state rehabilitation agency. *Rehabilitation Counseling Bulletin* 24:49-60.

Rubin, S.E., and Roessler, R.T. 1978. Guidelines for successful vocational rehabilitation of the psychiatrically disabled. *Rehab. Lit.* 39:70-74.

Safieri, D. 1970. Using an educational model in a sheltered workshop program. *Mental Hygiene* 54:140-143.

Skelley, T.J. 1980. National developments in rehabilitation: A rehabilitation services administration perspective. *Rehabilitation Counseling Bulletin* 24:22-33.

Stude, E.W., and Pauls, T. 1977. The use of a job seeking skills group in developing readiness. *Journal of Applied Rehabilitation Counseling* 8:115-120.

Ugland, R.P. 1977. Job seekers' aids: A systematic approach for organizing employer contacts. *Rehabilitation Counseling Bulletin* 22:107-115.

Wesolowski, M.D. 1980. JOBS (Job Obtaining Behavior Strategy) in VR agencies. The effects of attendance and disincentives. *Int. J. Rehab. Res.* 3:531-532.
Wesolowski, M.D. 1981. Self directed job placement in rehabilitation: A comparative review. *Rehabilitation Counseling Bulletin* November:80-89.
Wright, B. 1960. *Physical Disability: A Psychological Approach.* New York: Harper.

14
Residential Treatment Programs and Aftercare for the Chronically Institutionalized

GORDON L. PAUL

Residential treatment settings for the chronically mentally ill consist of such institutions as mental hospitals, mental health centers, and community extended-care facilities. Their defining feature is that clients reside in the facility 24 hours per day to receive treatment. Although, in current practice, admissions to residential treatment facilities are often based on other grounds, their reason-for-being is that the clients' disturbance and functioning is too burdensome or too dangerous to allow treatment in a less restrictive setting (Paul, in press, a). Thus, the primary goal of residential treatment should be to provide effective programs for the most severely disabled of the mentally ill. Intramural residential programs should improve the clients' functioning to a level allowing their return to less restrictive community settings. Integrated extramural or community programs should provide effective treatment for the less severely disabled persons who do not require residential treatment. These programs should also maintain and further improve functioning of those returned from residential treatment settings—at least to a level that does not require their readmission to residential treatment (HHS Steering Committee, 1980; Paul, 1978).

The preceding chapters in this volume document the woeful inadequacy of current practices of residential treatment and aftercare. Figures for 1982 show more than 40 percent of public mental hospital beds to be occupied by patients chronically institutionalized for a year or more, reflecting the failure of current residential treatment practices. Rising hospital admissions, with readmission rates that have climbed from 25 to 60-70 percent, reflect the failure of short-term intramural crisis stabilization, chemotherapy, and current aftercare programs to improve or maintain the functioning of significant numbers of patients with shorter residential stays. Up to 90 percent of chronically institutionalized patients do not respond to chemotherapeutic treatment. Among the "revolving-door" group readmitted several times to residential facilities and who initially respond to neuroleptic drugs, only 20 to 25 percent do not experience toxic side effects or relapse. Only 0 to 25 percent of those who remain in the community return to productive employment, and many who are transferred to nursing homes continue to be severely disabled.

The great majority of the chronically mentally ill depend on the public sector for treatment, either because they are poor or are rapidly depleting their own insurance, personal funds, and those of their families. Hospital treatment is the most expensive of all mental health services, with daily costs in 1982 having averaged more than $87 per resident (nearly $32,000/year) in Texas state hospitals—the most poorly funded of the large states. The minimum requirements for rational decision-making based on treatment effectiveness are absent in most public mental institutions. In fact, bureaucratic, administrative, and political obstacles in the public sector operate not only to maintain the status quo but actively discourage improvements in accountability and treatment effectiveness (HHS Steering Committee, 1980; Paul, 1978). Keisler (1982) noted that even though community-based treatment has been the stated goal of the public mental health system for nearly two decades, *de facto* and *de jure* policies have actually continued to support expensive and ineffective institutional treatment facilities as the major recipients of public funds.

Given this sorry state of affairs, many mental health professionals and consumers question the desirability of maintaining residential treatment facilities at all. The problems of the chronically mentally ill must be seen as interactive, involving the patients' social and physical environment as well as individual factors (Paul, 1981). As I have noted elsewhere (Paul, 1978), this, rightly, leads many people to question the reasonableness of attempting to change patients' condition in the artificial setting of a residential facility, in view of the attendant problems of generalization to a community environment in which improved functioning must ultimately be maintained. Others question the dehumanization and potential infringement on individual rights attendant upon residence in any "total institution." The ineffectiveness of prolonged hospitalization during which only traditional biological and psychosocial procedures are employed has been documented innumerable times (e.g., Anthony et al., 1972; Erickson, 1975; Kirshner, 1982; Paul, 1969a; in press, a). All of these factors, combined with the extraordinary expense of residential treatment for a relatively small proportion of the total group of chronically mentally ill persons (Goldman et al., 1981; HHS Steering Committee, 1980), lead many to endorse Mendel's indictment of mental institutions as "always expensive and inefficient, frequently anti-therapeutic, and never the treatment of choice" (1974, p. 8).

The negative attitudes toward mental hospitals as most currently operate are clearly justified, and "hospitals" *per se* with their associated focus and structure do seem to be the least desirable settings for treating the chronically mentally ill (Paul, 1978). Residential treatment—whether in a hospital or another facility—must, however, remain a reality for the foreseeable future for institutionalized chronically mentally ill patients who are so severely disturbed and low-functioning that they cannot be moved elsewhere. These people have no place to go until effective treatment can prepare them to return to the community with tenure and to survive in less restrictive environments.

In this chapter I hope to familiarize the reader with the nature of the problems of the chronically institutionalized and some promising alternatives to changing their plight.

MAJOR REASONS FOR THE FAILURE TO MAINTAIN COMMUNITY TENURE

Several years ago I reviewed the literature to see if any consistent bases could be identified from different studies to account for the failure of the chronically mentally ill to remain in the community once they were discharged from mental institutions (Paul, 1969a). Three major factors emerged—deficits, excesses, and an absence of community bridging and support functions. More specifically:

Deficits in cognitive, social, and instrumental functioning, including:
—self-care and self-maintenance
—appropriate interpersonal interaction and communications
—being "on time" and remaining "on task"
—routine housekeeping, money management, and transportation activities
—obtaining/maintaining training or work
Excesses in extreme bizarre behavior, including:
—dangerous, threatening, or aggressive acts
—expressions of personal distress, suicidal thoughts
—verbalized delusions, hallucinations
—inappropriate expressions of affect, incoherent speech
—unusual and peculiar observable actions
Absence of resources in the community to provide:
—continuity of supportive interpersonal/social relationships at re-entry
—knowledgeable brief crisis intervention without hospitalization
—continuous supportive interpersonal/social relationships
—affordable housing/living arrangements
—appropriate training/vocational positions

As earlier chapters in this volume have shown, these three problem areas continue to appear in nearly any investigation that includes assessment of relevant variables. The terminology used to describe them often varies with the orientation and discipline of the investigators, but the influence of both deficits and excesses in functioning in relapse and rehospitalization continues to be documented in recent reports by sociologists and epidemiologists as well as workers in rehabilitation, psychology, and psychiatry (e.g., Andreasen and Olsen, 1982; Anthony and Farkas, 1982; Curran and Monti, 1982; Herz and Melville, 1980; Marsh et al., 1981; Möller et al., 1982; Paul, in press, b; Paul and Lentz, 1977; Strauss and Carpenter, 1978, 1979; Tessler and Manderscheid, 1982). The deficits in cognitive, social, and instrumental functioning are variously referred to as "skills deficits," "low social competence," "deficit syndrome," or "negative symptoms" of psychosis. The deficits in functioning are among the most important to long-term outcomes for the mentally ill and among the most neglected in current psychiatric research (Carpenter and Heinrichs, 1981). The excesses in extreme bizarre behavior are variously referred to as "behavioral problems," "crazy behavior," "inappropriate or maladaptive behavior," "florid symptoms," or "positive symptoms" of psychosis. They are clearly important and have been the primary focus of drug research and treatment. Although such excesses may often trigger patients' rehospitalization, the problems are partially independent of deficits in functioning, and less pervasive for all but the most severely disabled patients.

While deficits and excesses in functioning are important behavioral problems for the chronically mentally ill themselves, the absence of resources in the community is equally important to both short-term and long-term outcome of treatment (Bachrach, 1981; HHS Steering Committee, 1980; Hull and Thompson, 1981; Tessler et al., 1980). The importance of supportive social relationships has been a particular emphasis of recent work (Beels, 1978; Vaughn and Leff, 1981). The difficulties of community re-entry are especially severe for the chronically institutionalized or other chronically mentally ill person who is likely to be vulnerable to stress. Supportive interpersonal relationships have been shown to reduce stress or insulate vulnerable people from its effects in a variety of stressful situations (Caplan, 1982; Price, 1981).

A sad commentary on the ineffectiveness of current residential treatment programs and aftercare procedures is that the best predictors of a patient's rehospitalization (beyond the absence of supportive social relationships in the community) continue to be the length and number of previous hospitalizations and his or her level of social competence before entry to residential treatment. The extent to which these factors, rather than posttreatment measures, continue to predict outcomes for both acutely and chronically disabled persons reflects the lack of positive impact of current practices.

SEVERITY OF THE PROBLEM FOR THE
CHRONICALLY INSTITUTIONALIZED

As I indicated earlier, we have few choices other than residential treatment for chronically institutionalized individuals who are so severely disabled and low-functioning that they have no place to go until effective intramural programs can at least prepare them to participate in community treatment programs. We might suspect that these individuals would come from what Goldman et al. (1981) call the "long-stay" group who have been continuously hospitalized for a year or more, and from the "new young chronic" or "revolving-door" group who have experienced multiple admissions of shorter duration (Bachrach, 1982).

To examine the nature of the problem of these groups, data were abstracted from the Time-Sample Behavioral Checklist (TSBC) normative sample of more than 1,200 residential clients (Light, this volume; Power, 1979; Paul, in press, b). Excluding those with diagnoses of mental retardation, alcohol or substance abuse, three samples of patients were drawn from the 18- to 65-year-old age group in public mental hospitals: a chronically institutionalized group with a year or more of continuous hospitalization; a chronically "revolving-door" group who had four or more hospitalizations all of less than a year; and an acute and prechronic sample of patients who had less than a year's hospitalization and three or fewer admissions.

These groups' average hourly incidence of both appropriate and inappropriate functioning during one week is displayed in Figure 1, along with the "pretreatment" functioning of a sample of chronically institutionalized people who participated in new psychosocial treatment programs that I shall describe later. Ages of members in the psychosocial group ranged from 18 to 55 years; all had been hospitalized at least two years. Their average duration of hospitalization was about 17 years. All were diagnosed as schizophrenic and all had been rejected for community placement in aggressive deinstitutionalization efforts. Figure 1 shows both the severity of their deficits in adaptive-appropriate behavior and the extreme excesses in bizarre-inappropriate behavior. None could have survived outside of an institutional setting at the time of assessment (Paul and Lentz, 1977). The dark bars and lower scale in Figure 1 reveal a systematic increase in the level of bizarre behavior as institutional chronicity moves up from the acute and prechronic sample, through the revolving-door and long-stay groups. Note that both long-stay groups at the top of the figure are far from the "burned out" psychotic patients of the pre-deinstitutionalization era—their incidence of bizarre behavior averaged more than 60 and 90 percent, respectively, every waking hour for a full week! In a parallel fashion, the lighter bars and top scale in Figure 1 reveal a systematic decrease in the level of total competent functioning with increasing institutional chronicity. The acute and prechronic sample averaged about 2.85 incidents of competent performance per hour—a level adequate for community functioning. In contrast, the two long-stay groups at the top of Figure 1 show an average level of appropriate-competent performance at or below that of severe and profound mentally retarded groups who have been institutionalized for nearly their entire lives (Paul, in press, b).

Further clarification of the severity of deficits in cognitive, social, and instrumental functioning of chronically institutionalized persons can be seen in Figure 2. Here data from the Clinical Frequencies Recording System (CFRS; Paul, in press, b; Redfield, 1979) provide more precise information on the group who

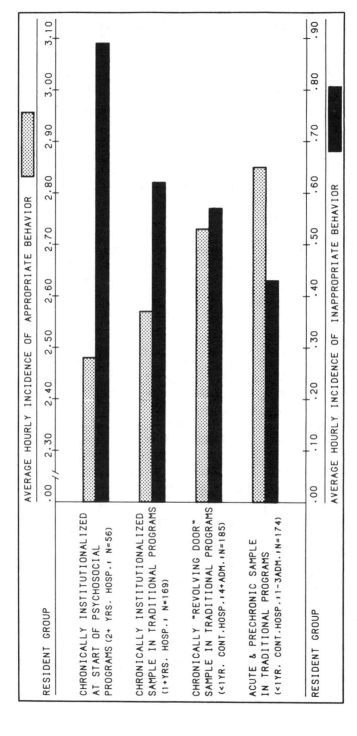

Figure 1 Average incidence of discrete appropriate and inappropriate behavior of mentally ill groups differing in chronicity of institutionalization. (Data from Time-Sample Behavioral Checklist for one week [Paul, in press, b]).

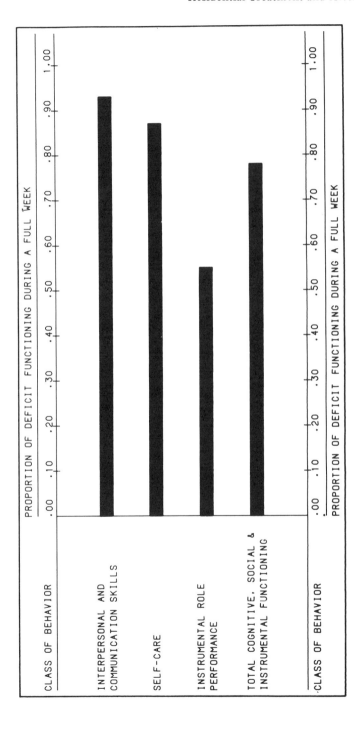

Figure 2 Average deficits in competence for the chronically institutionalized who remain after deinstitutionalization. (Data from Clinical Frequencies Recording System for Milieu and Social-Learning groups in comparative study at program entry, N=56 [Paul and Lentz, 1977]).

later became engaged in new psychosocial treatment programs. During an entire week, with multiple opportunities each day, the group averaged less than 10 percent normal competence in interpersonal and communication skills—a high proportion were simply mute, and the majority failed to make sense when they did talk. Similarly, more than 85 percent of opportunities for self-care activities—normal eating, bathing, dressing, and grooming—were failures. The lowest level of deficits were seen in instrumental role performance, but failures still occurred here for more than half of the opportunities. The primary basis for success in this area was that some patients could follow a schedule. For total competent performance, the group averaged nearly 80 percent deficits.

The major point I wish to make with these data is that we see very different levels of functioning, even among the institutionalized chronically mentally ill. With continued tracking of the resident groups shown in Figure 1, fewer than 12 percent of the chronically institutionalized persons sampled in traditional programs successfully returned to the community within six months of the assessment, and they already had spent an average of about 10 years in continuous hospitalization. Similarly, about a third of persons in the revolving-door sample went on to become continuous long-stay patients, as did about 14 percent of the acute and prechronic sample. Patients who were or became chronically institutionalized were clearly discernible by TSBC assessments, showing high levels of deficits and/or extreme levels of disturbance and bizarre behaviors. Few members of society—in fact, few professionals in the mental health field—appreciate the severity of problems in the subgroup of chronically institutionalized patients. Unless one has seen a loved one in this condition or has worked in a state hospital or state school for the retarded, one is unlikely to have encountered people like these. They are the severely disabled, chronically institutionalized mentally ill for whom effective residential treatment programs must be found.

NECESSARY FOCUS (MINIMAL GOALS) OF RESIDENTIAL PROGRAMS

My earlier analysis of the major reasons for the failure of the chronically mentally ill to maintain community tenure, and the severity of the problems of the chronically institutionalized, logically led to the development of targets for residential treatment programs (Paul, 1969a, 1980). Four areas of focus were identified as minimal goals for residential treatment programs if they are to have any chance of returning the chronically institutionalized to the community with continuing tenure. The first three are specific targets for change in the clients themselves, while the fourth target focuses on interactions with the extramural community:

Resocialization—including the establishment of minimal competence in self-care, interpersonal interaction, and communication skills and their components.

Instrumental role performance—including the establishment of salable vocational and housekeeping skills; minimally, the "on time"/"on task" components necessary to participate in community training programs.

Reduction or elimination of extreme bizarre behavior—including appropriate changes in frequency, intensity, or timing of cognitive, affective, and motor events or acts that are consensually identified as distressing.

"Bridging the gap" from residential programs to community functioning—including training for generalization to natural support systems; establishment of living arrangements, training or vocational positions, and at least one supportive "significant other" in the community before re-entry; provision of aftercare consultants who are knowledgeable about the individuals and follow them from residential programs to establishment in the community through scheduled contacts on a declining basis.

COMPARATIVE INVESTIGATION OF RESIDENTIAL PROGRAMS

After determining the necessary focus required for intramural programs, the literature was searched further to see if any principles, procedures, or programs offered any promise at all for the chronically institutionalized (Paul, 1969a). Two approaches seemed promising, although neither had yet been subjected to an adequately controlled evaluation to determine cause-effect outcomes for total comprehensive programs. Both were psychosocial approaches that emphasized the importance of clear communication, resident responsibility, problem-solving and skills training, and particular types of staff-resident interaction. Their basic principles, concepts, program structure, and nature of staff-resident interactions were, however, very different. Therefore, my colleagues and I developed two comprehensive intramural programs on the basis of the promising approaches, specifically focusing on the minimal goals identified earlier. The Milieu Therapy Program emphasized a therapeutic community structure and based the nature and content of staff-resident interaction on communication theory and principles derived from social-psychological research. The Social Learning Program emphasized a token-economy structure and based the nature and content of staff-resident interactions on social-learning theory and empirical principles of instrumental and associative learning. Both programs were "high technology" psychosocial treatments in the sense of requiring very precise staff-behavior-by-resident-behavior-by-setting specification to allow staff training, replication, and implementation elsewhere, should either prove to be effective (Paul and Lentz, 1977).

Rather than attempting a large-scale clinical trial in which the sheer weight of numbers carries the day, psychosocial treatment evaluations require critical analytical designs in which the precision of equation, measurement, and control allows establishment of cause-effect relationships between treatment procedures and change in client functioning (Paul, 1969b). We, therefore, undertook a longitudinal investigation to determine whether or not either of the comprehensive psychosocial programs had any generalizable effects on the chronically institutionalized mental patient. Space limitations preclude a detailed presentation of either procedures or findings. Since these are available elsewhere (Paul and Lentz,

Table 1 Summary of Design from Comparative Residential Treatment Study

Procedures	Treatment Programs		
	Traditional Hospital	Milieu Therapy	Social Learning
Pre-transfer assessment & equation:			
Rating scales, str. interviews, demogr.	X	X	X
Transfer, orientation, habituation	X	X	X
Ongoing clinical program development and intramural treatment	as usual ~6 years	specified principles & procedures 4½ years	specified principles & procedures 4½ years
Ongoing assessments:			
(a) Rating scales/str. interviews:			
Post-transfer	X	X	X
Every 6 mos.	X	X	X
Pre-release	X	X	X
(b) Time-Sample Behavioral Checklist:	(hourly, 1 wk. sample)	hourly	hourly
(c) Clinical Frequencies Recording System:		moment-to-moment	moment-to-moment
(d) Staff-Resident Interaction Chronograph:		hourly	hourly
Declining contact aftercare for 6 to 24 mos.: (independent) or 18 mos. (comm. placement):	X	X	X
Ongoing assessments:			
Rating scales/str. interviews: Pre-release	X	X	X
Every 6 mos.	X	X	X
Re-admission	X	X	X

Note: Same staff conducted both psychosocial programs, with daily counterbalanced rotation (see Paul and Lentz, 1977).

1977; Rhoades, 1981), I will present only the highlights of design and overall outcome of our research and development efforts as they relate to practical treatment decisions for the future.

The overall experimental design, shown in Table 1, involved three treatment programs conducted concurrently—a traditional hospital comparison to evaluate the state of affairs in the absence of new treatments and the two new psychosocial programs. Initially, three patient groups of 28 each were equated by random assignment from stratified blocks on three measures of functioning from ward rating scales and structured interviews, with additional equation on 13 demographic variables—in essence, all variables that might be related to prognosis. The three groups were then randomly assigned to receive traditional hospital programs or one of the psychosocial programs. The patients were then transferred to the treatment sites and received orientation to their new treatment settings; post-transfer assessments insured continued equation of groups. "New" patients were admitted to each group from the chronically hospitalized population to maintain 28 inpatients in each program, with new patients selected so as to maintain group equation at the entry assessment. The intramural programs were conducted concurrently for 4½ years, both psychosocial programs following specified principles and procedures. The traditional hospital program was conducted "as usual," with our staff monitoring and assessing function only. Hospital monitoring continued for another year and a half after termination of the psychosocial units, so that the hospital had six years in which to treat the original patient group, while psychosocial programs were limited to a maximum of 4½ years. Intramural assessments by means of ward rating scales and structured interviews were conducted for patients in all three groups before and after entry to study programs, every six months thereafter, and immediately before release, with reliability checks for all measures. In addition, the observational instruments described earlier in this volume by Licht and Power (b, c, and d in Table 1) were continuously maintained on both psychosocial programs. A one-week sample of the traditional hospital program was obtained on the Staff-Resident Interaction Chronograph (SRIC) to provide more detailed information on the hospital's psychosocial procedures. Staff attitudes and personality characteristics were also measured.

During the closed intramural period, a discharge criterion of independent functioning with self-support was maintained. Patients were rehospitalized, when necessary, in the program from which they had been discharged. At the end of the intramural period, community placement that allowed patients to be discharged to room-and-board facilities without independent self-support or, at best, employment in a sheltered-workshop was offered once again. All patients had been rejected for such placement at the time of the initial assessment. As the lower portion of Table 1 indicates, aftercare was provided to those discharged from all three groups according to the minimal goals described. Aftercare was conducted by our trained psychosocial staff, because the major evaluative questions concerned the intramural programs' comparative effectiveness. Assessments were done at prerelease and every six months after the patients' discharge in the community, or at readmission when necessary. Patients discharged to independent functioning and self-support were followed for at least 24 months, with systematic declining contact for a minimum of six months, and as needed thereafter. Patients in community placements were followed for at least 18 months before the project ended.

The patient groups' severity of problems was described earlier (Figures 1 and 2). Half of the patients were male, 13 percent were black, 80 percent were never married or divorced. All were of low socioeconomic status with poor premorbid competency, had hospital diagnoses of schizophrenia, and had previously received neuroleptic drugs. Their average age was about 45 years with an average of about 17 years of hospitalization that included past histories of electroconvulsive shock for 45 percent and insulin shock for 30 percent. All in all, they were the most severely disabled group of mental patients who had been the subject of systematic investigation, whether based on prognostic indicators, actual deficits in functioning, or extremes of bizarre behavior.

Some additional highlights of staff and program characteristics are presented in Table 2. The psychosocial programs were housed in identical, adjacent 28-bed units of a mental health center; for comparison, 28 beds were maintained in the treatment service of a state hospital. Staff-client ratios and staffing levels of the psychosocial programs were set to be equal to those of the state hospital, and all staff members were employed by the same civil service system. Although these staffing levels are terribly low (and somewhat dependent on the physical plant), we purposely established the staffing of the psychosocial programs to be practical for widespread implementation, should either program prove to be effective. We were not interested in finding out whether or not chronically institutionalized patients could be helped if each had the full-time attention of a physician or psychologist, because no public system could ever support such a treatment program. Thus, the staffing ratios were not only low, but 80 percent of staff members were high-school level personnel. Moreover, the same staff conducted both psychosocial programs, alternating between units every half day (day shift) or daily (evening and night shifts) to equate time and exposure. Such staff equation with ongoing assessment is a crucial design feature if we are to know that treatment effects are the result of the programs rather than of personality characteristics of the staff.

Although many detailed differences between treatment programs were established through SRIC assessments—and they turn out to be the crucial differences for treatment of effectiveness—Table 2 reflects some of the overall differences in activity and orientation. "Other job-related activity" indicates about equal amounts of meetings, paperwork, and the like for staff members in all three programs. The psychosocial programs, however, averaged more than two to three times the sheer amount of staff/client interaction of the traditional program.

Table 2   Staff and Program Characteristics from Comparative
Residential Treatment Study

	Treatment Programs		
Characteristics	Traditional Hospital	Milieu Therapy	Social Learning
Size	28 beds	28 beds	28 beds
Avg. staff/client ratio	0.557	0.566	0.566
Avg. percentage of non-professionals	80.9%	79.8%	79.8%
Majority staff gender	female	female	female
Majority staff personality	honest stable-extrov.	honest stable-extrov.	honest stable-extrov.
Preferred attitude/orientation	medical-custodial	re-educ.-active	re-educ.-active
Avg. staff/client interaction	102.56/hr.	348.89/hr.	264.71/hr.
Avg. other job-related activity	47.22/hr.	48.70/hr.	48.74/hr.
Avg. job-irrelevant activity	14.69/hr.	0.08/hr.	0.06/hr.
Psychosocial treatment sched.	4.9% (2.9%) waking hrs.	85.2% waking hrs.	85.2% waking hrs.
Neuroleptic drug use—before	89.3%	96.4%	89.3%
Neuroleptic drug use—after	100.0%	17.9%	10.7%

Note: Same staff conducted both psychosocial programs, with daily counterbalanced rotation (see Paul and Lentz, 1977).

Similarly, participants in the psychosocial programs regularly received active psychosocial treatment during more than 85 percent of their waking hours, and the use of neuroleptic drugs was drastically reduced. In the traditional program, in contrast, the use of neuroleptic drugs was increased; only 4.9 percent of the patients' waking hours were scheduled for psychosocial treatment, and it was carried out during only 2.9 percent of the patients' waking hours.

As Strauss (this volume) pointed out in discussing outpatient treatment, clients do not change in a steady progression over time or within different components of functioning. The moment-to-moment and hourly assessments by the observational instruments (Time-Sample Behavioral Checklist, Clinical Frequencies Recording System, and SRIC) provide intramural programs with precise measures of change in different components of functioning, in the patterns of change for individual clients, and in the relationship of change in client functioning to specific components of intervention procedures for both psychosocial and drug treatment. With such precise measurements it was possible to identify individuals who did not respond to drugs and to maintain those who did respond to drugs in the active psychosocial programs at the lowest possible dosage levels so as to minimize the risk of side effects. Maintenance-level neuroleptic drugs were still required by 11 to 18 percent of the chronically institutionalized clients who participated in the psychosocial programs, but the remainder showed no benefits from neuroleptic drugs in the presence of comprehensive psychosocial treatment.

Client functioning during the intramural period of the comparative investigation varied considerably in response to identifiable events (Paul and Lentz, 1977). For present purposes, however, the major practical outcomes can be gleaned by examining change in critical areas of focus from program entry to discharge or program termination. Figure 3 shows the average decrease in excessive, bizarre behavior—one of the crucial treatment targets for the chronically institutionalized. The dark bars in Figure 3 show that the Social Learning Program was very effective in reducing or eliminating the excesses in bizarre behavior or "florid symptoms" of psychoses. All components show significant reductions, the average reduction from incidence at entry exceeding 60 percent for every class of maladaptive functioning for the Social Learning Program. This program was particularly effective in eliminating belligerence and dangerous and aggressive acts— an average reduction of 97 percent, which reflects elimination of dangerous and aggressive acts for all but one person whose physical condition precluded participation in procedures that were known to be effective. The Milieu Therapy Program was ineffective in reducing dangerous and aggressive acts by this severely disturbed population. The Milieu Therapy Program significantly reduced the incidence of every other class of maladaptive behavior, but not as well as the Social Learning Program. In fact, the only area of functioning in which the Milieu Therapy Program was ultimately as effective as the Social Learning Program was in reducing Cognitive Distortion—those bizarre verbal statements and inappropriate facial expressions that indicate thought disorders. Even for this class of maladaptive behavior, the Social Learning Program was more efficient.

Differential effectiveness of the two psychosocial programs was even greater with regard to overcoming deficits in cognitive, social, and instrumental functioning—the minimal treatment targets focused on in resocialization and instrumental role performance. The lighter bars in Figure 4 show the Milieu Therapy Program to have produced only about a 25-percent average increase in total competent functioning. In contrast, the dark bars in Figure 4 show the remarkable effectiveness of the Social Learning Program in overcoming the patients' severe deficits. The increase in competent interpersonal and communication skills is particularly impressive, since this increase would extend over about four pages if the bar were extended on the same scale.

Considering all clients treated, the Social Learning Program produced significant improvement in *every* individual who was physically capable of participating, including those who had failed to improve in the Milieu Therapy Program. Although the majority were still functioning at marginal levels, even after significant improvement, 25 percent had improved to levels that were indistinguishable from the "normal" population. Compared to the number of patients who

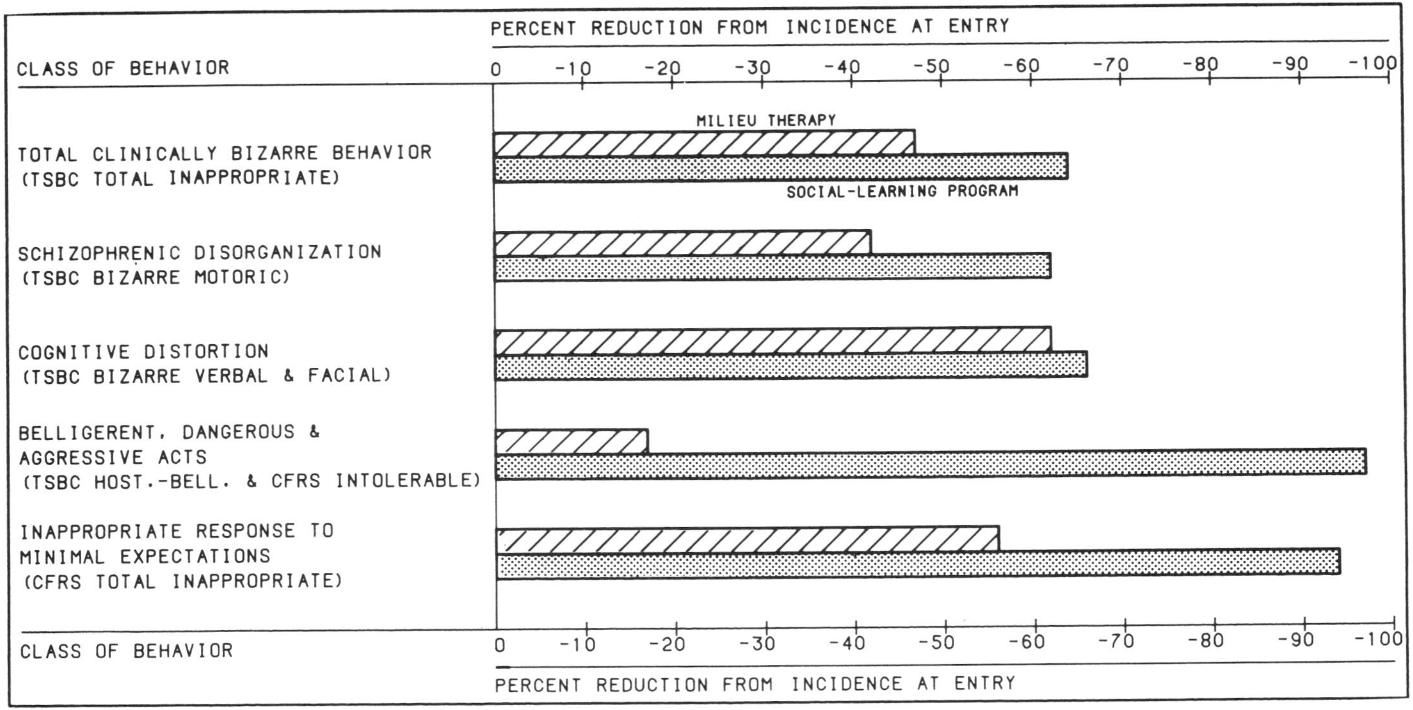

Figure 3 Average decrease in maladaptive behavior from program entry to release or program termination for original equated groups in two psychosocial programs (N=28 each). (Data from Time-Sample Behavioral Checklist and Clinical Frequencies Recording System [Paul and Lentz, 1977]).

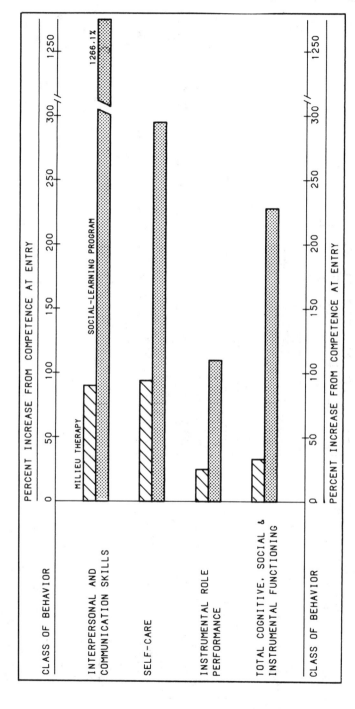

Figure 4 Average increase in competent functioning from program entry to release or program termination for original equated groups in two psychosocial programs (N=28 each). (Data from Clinical Frequencies Recording System [Paul and Lentz, 1977]).

improved in the Social Learning Program, only 55 percent in the Milieu Therapy Program sustained their improvement, while only a third of that number improved in the traditional hospital program. Hospital practices were not related to change in patient functioning, whereas the relationship of staff/client interactions measured by the SRIC clearly documented the principles and procedures of the Social Learning Program to be effective ingredients—even for the majority of improvements obtained in the Milieu Therapy Program. No further improvements were taking place in either the hospital or milieu programs, but in nearly all classes of functioning, clients in the Social Learning Program were continuing to improve.

The practical outcomes must, of course, be based on the ultimate community tenure achieved by clients in different programs, rather than on their improved intramural functioning alone. Early on it became clear that social-learning principles were the most promising on which to base aftercare consultations. Therefore, the declining-contact procedures described earlier as a necessary focus for "bridging the gap" from residential programs to community functioning were provided to residents released from all three intramural programs employing social-learning principles and technology. Of the original groups, 10.7 percent of social learning, 7.1 percent of milieu therapy, and none of the hospital program participants achieved an independent release with self-support and no rehospitalizations. Given their initial level of disability I believe any such outcome is remarkable. The remaining patients were discharged to community room-and-board facilities with, at best, employment in a sheltered workshop. The declining-contact aftercare procedures employing social-learning principles were exceptionally effective on an absolute level; they prevented rehospitalization for more than 97 percent of discharged patients, without differences between the effectiveness of aftercare procedures for those coming from different intramural programs. The outcome status at final follow-up, presented in Table 3, is nearly the same as that obtained at termination of the psychosocial programs. All those returned to the community had maintained continuing tenure for a minimum of 18 months with the exception of two from the traditional program who were not discharged until the end of the follow-up period. Some participants in the psychosocial programs had been functioning continuously in the community for more than five years at final follow-up. The observational assessments in the institution (TSBC and CFRS) not only predicted successful discharge, but also the level of continuing functioning in the community up to 18 months after discharge (Paul, 1981).

I noted earlier that the numbers and levels of staff in the psychosocial programs were set to be equal to those in the traditional hospital so that the findings could be implemented by other public mental health services. Since the Social Learning Program treated more individuals during the same period of time in the same number of beds, used fewer drugs, and was more effective, we might expect

Table 3   Outcome Status at Final Follow-Up for All Clients Treated by Traditional Hospital and Two Psychosocial Programs

Treatment Program	No.	Never Returned to Community or Returned/Rehospitalized	Returned to Community with Continuing Tenure
Traditional Programs	31	51.6%	48.4% (3 mos. minimum)
Milieu Therapy	31	29.0%	71.0% (18 mos. minimum)
Social Learning	40	7.5%	92.5% (18 mos. minimum)

Adapted from Table 40.1, Paul and Lentz (1977)

Table 4   Comparative Per-Case Costs and Savings to Taxpayers during Project
Period for Traditional Hospital and Two Psychosocial Programs

Comparison	Money Spent Staff & Drug Costs	Money Saved Economic Effectiveness	Effectiveness/ Cost Ratio
Hospital Cost Standard	$1.00 ($1.00)	$1.00 ($1.00)	1.000 (1.000)
Social Learning/Hospital	0.83 (0.67)	2.55 (2.56)	3.072 (3.798)
Milieu/Hospital	0.84 (0.87)	1.99 (2.20)	2.361 (2.522)
Social Learning/Milieu	0.99 (0.77)	1.29 (1.17)	1.302 (1.507)

Figures outside parentheses are for original equated groups; figures in parentheses are for
all treated. Adapted from Table 40.5, Paul and Lentz (1977)

it to be more cost-effective as well. Examination of Table 4 shows that this is
indeed the case. Using conservative data that include only actual direct-cost
dollars spent and saved during the six-year period of investigation, the Social
Learning Program turns out to be well over three times as cost-effective as traditional hospital programs. Rubin (1981) points out that these kinds of data
should assist policy-makers to choose intelligently among types of service. Start-
up costs for effective programs may be initially higher than continuing ineffective ones, but tracking individuals over time shows that the return on investment
for effective programs is often higher in the long run.

Overall, the comprehensive Social Learning Program and integrated aftercare procedures clearly emerged as the treatment of choice for severely disabled
chronically institutionalized mental patients, whether they have severe deficits in
functioning, extremes of psychotic and bizarre behavior, or both. Rates of
change for the most effective procedures evaluated indicate that, installed elsewhere, the program could improve the most severely debilitated to a level of
acceptability for placement in less restrictive community training programs in
26 to 30 weeks. In fact, given appropriate funding and structure, the program
could be conducted in community-based residential facilities (Kohen and Paul,
1976; Lamb, 1980). Two to three years of continuous treatment with the most effective procedures might bring the majority of the most severely disabled to a level
enabling them to function relatively independently and to support themselves.

CONCLUSION

To my knowledge, since the completion of the comparative investigation described here, no studies have been done with designs that allow cause-effect conclusions to be drawn regarding the necessary minimal goals of either psychosocial
or drug interventions during residential treatment. The results of many additional

controlled studies support the principles and procedures incorporated in the intramural social-learning program (for reviews see Barlow and Wolfe, 1981; Curran and Monti, 1982; Hersen and Bellack, 1981; Kazdin, 1982; Liberman, 1982; Marzillier and Birchwood, 1981; Mosher and Gunderson, 1979; Paul, 1978; Paul and Lentz, 1977; Stokes and Baer, 1977). Equally important are studies that have reported ineffective or deleterious effects of some intensive residential psychosocial programs (for reviews see Hemsley, 1978; Hersen and Bellack, 1981; Kazdin, 1982; Liberman, 1982; Marzillier and Birchwood, 1981; Mosher and Gunderson, 1979; Paul and Lentz, 1977; Schooler and Spohn, 1982; Van Putten and May, 1976). In most reports, the assessments of clients, staff, or programs have not been precise or detailed enough to allow firm conclusions regarding the reasons for some of these differences. It seems that the careful structure and pacing of focused, concrete skills training during all of the clients' waking hours carried out in the comprehensive social-learning program may be critical to success, in addition to the application of specific principles and procedures to particular problems. High-demand programs that provide less pacing in concrete problem-solving may overstimulate individuals who are already overaroused as a result of stress, or those who have too few cognitive skills to make use of new information. Such effects could be operating in our milieu therapy program or in less comprehensive operant-based procedures, in skills-training packages that place high demands for cognitive information-processing within time-limited training periods, and in programs that emphasize emotive, insight, and intrapsychic content. In any event, the clear differences in effectiveness of varying psychosocial programs should give pause to those who believe that residential milieus are either unimportant or can be considered a "constant" in the mental health system whose only significant parameter is duration.

Beyond the strong support from the recent literature for the foci and the principles and procedures incorporated in the intramural social-learning program, a remarkable consistency has emerged regarding effective principles and procedures of community-based treatment for the chronically mentally ill. This consistency is in addition to the generalizable commonalities regarding important structural elements in effective operation of mental health systems (Bachrach, 1980; Paul 1978; Lamb, 1981) and discussed in this volume by Elpers, Johnson, Mariotto and Paul, and Talbott. In addition to these structural elements, recent reports of controlled studies of in-community rehabilitation programs, Fairweather Lodges, community training programs, and new approaches to family treatment have yielded impressive data regarding reductions in rehospitalization and relapse rates for the chronically mentally ill (Anthony, 1979; Beels and McFarland, 1982; Dincin and Witheridge, 1982; Goldstein, 1981; Stein and Test, 1980; Zwerling, 1979; and see Anthony and Liberman et al. in this volume).

Especially noteworthy in these recent studies is the general consistency of focus, principles, and procedures concurrent with impressive outcomes. These community-based programs start with a clientele who are less severely disabled than the chronically institutionalized groups who were involved in our comparative investigations. Once the intramural program had improved the clients' functioning to allow their release, the integrated prerelease and aftercare procedures of the social-learning program, which resulted in 97-percent community tenure rates, also seemed to share much of the focus, principles, and procedures of successful programs started in the community for the less disabled (Paul and Lentz, 1977). All emphasize resocialization and instrumental role performance in addition to the reduction, control, or elimination of extreme bizarre behavior. All emphasize concrete education, instruction, skills training, problem-solving, stress management, modeling, reinforcement and contingency management, extra-contact task assignments with performance feedback, generalization training to natural support systems, and graded tasks to successively approximate ultimate goals. All employ therapists or consultants who are identified and knowledgeable, available, predictable, and who are willing to go to the clients in the community rather than relying on office-based appointments during the usual five-day work week. All involve significant others in the clients' life and gradually fade contact over extended periods. Programs that have shown the most promising results for long-term maintenance also systematically shift treatment and consultations from staff-initiated problem identification and solution, to elicited problem-solving, to client-initiated problem-solving. These commonalities in successful community or aftercare programs have appeared from more than 10 clinical research groups in different locales.

To paraphrase some lucid comments by Israel Zwerling (1979), the above citations and information, and that presented in earlier chapters, establish the fact that knowledge regarding system structure and technology now exists to reverse the current gloomy picture for the chronically mentally ill and make effective treatment the rule and not the exception. The political decision to consign the severely disabled and their families to a maze of ineffective and uncoordinated services that drain them emotionally and financially, to continued custodial care in hospitals, or to a rehospitalization rate of 60 to 70 percent and an unemployment rate of 75 percent should be an affront to every mental health professional, taxpayer, or other member of the human race. That decision is no less a decision by virtue of its emergence as an unintended consequence of bureaucratic self-protection, low priorities and underfinancing of improved mental health research and services than if it were a consequence of a deliberate state or national goal. Of course, we do not know all we need to know about schizophrenia or other chronic mental disorders or about effective assessment and treatment procedures in residential settings or in the community. The point is that *we already know all we need to know to make cost-effective treatment a reality* for the greatest number of the chronically mentally ill. It seems about time that we start to do so.

ACKNOWLEDGMENTS

The research reported in this chapter was supported in part by Public Health Service grants MH-15553 and MH-25464 from the National Institute of Mental Health and by grants from the Illinois Department of Mental Health and Developmental Disabilities, the Joyce Foundation, the MacArthur Foundation, and the Owsley Foundation.

REFERENCES

Andreasen, N.D., and Olsen, S. 1982. Negative v. positive schizophrenia. *Arch. Gen. Psychiatry* 39:789-794.

Anthony, W.A. 1979. *Principles of Psychiatric Rehabilitation,* Baltimore: University Park Press.

Anthony, W.A., Buell, G.J., Sharrett, S., and Althoff, M.E. 1972. Efficacy of psychiatric rehabilitation. *Psychol. Bull.* 78:447-456.

Anthony, W.A., and Farkas, M. 1982. A client outcome planning model for assessing psychiatric rehabilitation outcomes. *Schizophr. Bull.* 8:13-28.

Bachrach, L.L. 1980. Overview: Model programs for chronic mental patients. *Am. J. Psychiatry* 137:1023-1031.

Bachrach, L.L. 1981. Continuity of care for chronic mental patients: A conceptual analysis. *Am. J. Psychiatry* 138:1449-1456.

Bachrach, L.L. 1982. Young adult chronic patients: An analytical review of the literature. *Hosp. Community Psychiatry* 33:189-197.

Barlow, D.H., and Wolfe, B.E. 1981. Behavioral approaches to anxiety disorders: A report of the NIMH-SUNY, Albany research conference. *J. Consult. Clin. Psychol.* 49:448-454.

Beels, C.C. 1978. Social networks, the family, and the psychiatric patient: Introduction to the issue. *Schizophr. Bull.* 4:512-521.

Beels, C.C., and McFarland, W.R. 1982. Family treatments of schizophrenia: Background and state of the art. *Hosp. Community Psychiatry* 33:541-550.

Caplan, G. 1981. Mastery of stress: Psychosocial aspects. *Am. J. Psychiatry* 138:413-420.

Carpenter, W.T., and Heinrichs, D.W. 1981. Methodological standards for treatment outcome research in schizophrenia. *Am. J. Psychiatry* 138:465-471.

Curran, J.P., and Monti, P.M. 1982. *Social Skills Training.* New York: Guilford.

Dincin, J., and Witheridge, T.F. 1982. Psychiatric rehabilitation as a deterrent to recidivism. *Hosp. Community Psychiatry* 33:645-650.

Erickson, R.C. 1975. Outcome studies in mental hospitals: A review. *Psychol. Bull.* 82:519-540.

Goldman, H.H., Gattozzi, A.A., and Taube, C.A. 1981. Defining and counting the chronically mentally ill. *Hosp. Community Psychiatry* 32:21-27.

Goldstein, M. (ed.) 1981. *New Developments in Interventions with Families of Schizophrenics.* San Francisco: Jossey-Bass.

Hemsley, D.R. 1978. Limitations of operant procedures in the modification of schizophrenic functioning: The possible relevance of studies of cognitive disturbance. *Behavior Analysis and Modification* 2:165-193.

Hersen, M., and Bellack, A.S. 1981. Treatment of chronic mental patients. In W.E. Craighead, A.E. Kazdin, and M.J. Mahoney (eds.) *Behavior Modification,* 2nd Ed., pp. 357-378. Boston: Houghton-Mifflin.

Herz, M.I., and Melville, C. 1980. Relapse in schizophrenia. *Am. J. Psychiatry* 137:801-805.

HHS (Health and Human Services) Steering Committee, December 1980. *Toward a National Plan for the Chronically Mentally Ill*. Washington, DC: Public Health Service, U.S. Department of Health and Human Services.

Hull, J.T., and Thompson, J.C. 1981. Predicting adaptive functioning among mentally ill persons in community settings. *Am. J. Community Psychol.* 9:247-268.

Kazdin, A.E. 1982. The token economy: A decade later. *J. Appl. Behav. Anal.* 15:431-445.

Keisler, C.A. 1982. Psychology and mental health policy. In M. Hersen, A.E. Kazdin, and A.S. Bellack (eds.), *The Clinical Psychology Handbook*. New York: Pergamon.

Kirshner, L.A. 1982. Length of stay of psychiatric patients: A critical review and discussion. *J. Nerv. Ment. Dis.* 170:27-33.

Kohen, W., and Paul, G.L. 1976. Current trends and recommended changes in extended-care placement of mental patients: The Illinois system as a case in point. *Schizophr. Bull.* 4:575-594.

Lamb, H.R. 1980. Structure: The neglected ingredient of community treatment. *Arch. Gen. Psychiatry* 37:1224-1228.

Lamb, H.R. 1982. *Treating the Long-Term Mentally Ill: Beyond Institutionalization*. San Francisco: Jossey-Bass.

Liberman, R.P. 1982. Assessment of social skills. *Schizophr. Bull.* 8:62-84.

Marsh, A., Glick, M., and Zigler, E. 1981. Premorbid social competence and the revolving door phenomenon in psychiatric hospitalization. *J. Nerv. Ment. Dis.* 169:315-319.

Marzillier, J.S., and Birchwood, M.J. 1981. Behavioral treatment of cognitive disorders. In L. Michelson, M. Hersen, and S.M. Turner (eds.) *Future Perspectives in Behavior Therapy*, pp. 131-159. New York: Plenum.

Mendel, W.M. 1974. Lepers, madmen—who's next? *Schizophr. Bull.* 11:5-8.

Möller, H.J., Zerssen, D.V., Werner-Eilert, K., and Wüschner-Stockheim, M. 1982. Outcome in schizophrenic and similar paranoid psychoses. *Schizophr. Bull.* 8:99-108.

Mosher, L.R., and Gunderson, J.G. 1979. Group, family, milieu and community support systems treatment for schizophrenia. In L. Bellack (ed.), *Disorders of the Schizophrenic Syndrome*, pp. 399-452. New York: Basic Books.

Paul, G.L. 1969a. The chronic mental patient: Current status—future directions. *Psychol. Bull.* 71:81-94.

Paul, G.L. 1969b. Behavior modification research: Design and tactics. In C.M. Franks (ed.), *Behavior Therapy: Appraisal and Status*, pp. 29-62. New York: McGraw-Hill.

Paul, G.L. 1978. The implementation of effective treatment programs for chronic mental patients: Obstacles and recommendations. In J.H. Talbott (ed.), *The Chronic Mental Patient*, pp. 99-127. Washington, DC: American Psychiatric Association.

Paul, G.L. 1980. Comprehensive psychosocial treatment: Beyond traditional psychotherapy. In J.S. Strauss, M. Bowers, T.W. Downey, S. Fleck, S. Jackson, and I. Levine (eds.), *Psychotherapy of Schizophrenia*, pp. 167-179. New York: Plenum.

Paul, G.L. 1981. Social competence and the institutionalized mental patient. In J.D. Wine and M.D. Smye (eds.), *Social Competence*, pp. 232-257. New York: Guilford.

Paul, G.L. in press, a. The impact of public policy and decision-making on the dissemination of science-based practices in mental institutions: Playing poker with everything wild. In R.A. Kasschau, L. Rehm, and L.P. Ullmann (eds.), *Psychological Research, Public Policy and Practice: Towards a Productive Partnership.* New York: Praeger.

Paul, G.L. (ed.) in press, b. *Observational Assessment Instrumentation for Institutional Research and Treatment.* Cambridge, MA: Harvard University Press.

Paul, G.L., and Lentz, R.J. 1977. *Psychosocial Treatment of Chronic Mental Patients.* Cambridge, MA: Harvard University Press.

Power, C.T. 1979. The Time-Sample Behavioral Checklist: Observational assessment of patient functioning. *Journal of Behavioral Assessment* 1:199-210.

Price, R.H. 1981. Risky situations. In D. Magnussen (ed.), *Toward a Psychology of Situations: An Interactional Perspective*, pp. 103-112. Hillsdale, NJ: Erlbaum.

Redfield, J.P. 1979. Clinical Frequencies Recording Systems: Standardizing staff observations by event recordings. *Journal of Behavioral Assessment* 1:211-219.

Rhoades, L.J. 1981. *Treating and Assessing the Chronically Mentally Ill: The Pioneering Research of Gordon L. Paul.* DHHS Publication No. (ADM) 81-1100. Rockville, MD: Science Reports Branch, Division of Scientific and Public Information, National Institute of Mental Health.

Rubin, J. 1981. Cost measurement and cost data in mental health settings. *Hosp. Community Psychiatry* 33:750-754.

Schooler, C., and Spohn, H.E. 1982. Social dysfunction and treatment failure in schizophrenia. *Schizophr. Bull.* 8:85-98.

Stein, L.I., and Test, M.A. 1980. Alternative to mental hospital treatment. *Arch. Gen. Psychiatry* 37:392-397.

Stokes, T.F., and Baer, D.M. 1977. An implicit technology of generalization. *J. Appl. Behav. Anal.* 10:349-367.

Strauss, J.S., and Carpenter, W.T. 1978. The prognosis of schizophrenia: Rationale for a multidimensional concept. *Schizophr. Bull.* 4:56-67.

Strauss, J.S., and Carpenter, W.T. 1979. The prognosis of schizophrenia. In L. Bellack (ed.), *Disorders of the Schizophrenic Syndrome*, pp. 472-491. New York: Basic Books.

Tessler, R.C., Bernstein, A.G., Rosen, B.M., and Goldman, H.H. 1982. The chronically mentally ill in community support systems. *Hosp. Community Psychiatry* 33:208-211.

Tessler, R.C., and Manderscheid, R.W. 1982. Factors affecting adjustment to community living. *Hosp. Community Psychiatry* 33:203-207.

Van Putten, T., and May, P.R.A. 1976. Milieu therapy of the schizophrenias. In L.J. West and D.E. Flinn (eds.), *Treatment of Schizophrenia; Progress and Prospects.* New York: Grune & Stratton.

Vaughn, C., and Leff, J. 1981. Patterns of emotional response in relatives of schizophrenic patients. *Schizophr. Bull.* 7:43-45.

Zwerling, I. 1979. Community psychiatric treatment. In L. Bellack (ed.), *Disorders of the Schizophrenic Syndrome*, pp. 453-469. New York: Basic Books.

15
Schizophrenia: Implications of the Treatment Approach in Predicting Outcome

SAMUEL J. KEITH AND SUSAN MATTHEWS

Of the major health problems of the twentieth century, none combines the disability, the frequency, and the early onset of schizophrenia. If one were to add the number of person years of wasted human potential, no other health problem would even come close to the impact of schizophrenia. The term itself, schizophrenia, calls forth an image of the sometimes bizarre, isolated, empty shells of human beings we all have known. Somewhere in this nightmare collage, perhaps, is a unifying concept that brings meaning to this powerful and highly emotional charged term. For many disorders the diagnosis provides this unifying concept, bringing together conceptual understanding, etiologic discrimination, and treatment implication. Unfortunately, the diagnosis of schizophrenia falls short of this. Much of the problem comes from our having no means of validating the diagnosis of schizophrenia as we do for such entities as diabetes or anemia. Because of this absence of validating criteria, a profound effort has been made to establish the reliability of the diagnosis by selecting symptoms that can be rated reliably. And yet, even the very best reliability has failed to bring validity to the diagnosis. To date, no single, multiple, or cluster of biologic, psychophysiologic, psychologic, or social variables can be found in all schizophrenic patients or only in schizophrenics. The basic heterogeneity of the disorder seems inescapable.

The clinical utility of schizophrenia as a *diagnostic entity* is clearly weakened because of the heterogeneous population it describes. Potentially useful strategies can, however, be derived from recent conceptual descriptions of schizophrenia that may have implications for treatment strategies and may provide us with a rationale for the use of various treatment modalities.

From the time of Kraepelin and Bleuler, diagnosis has assumed an ascendant position in research on schizophrenia. This follows from the basic assumption that, because certain symptoms occur in combinations with a recognizable frequency, there may be common etiologies, treatments, or even prevention strategies to be discovered. Examples from general medicine for which the categorization of symptoms is important in establishing a diagnosis include such infectious diseases as measles and such neurological diseases as amyotropic lateral sclerosis. For symptoms to be of importance in this particular strategy, however, it becomes extremely important to select characteristics that can be rated reliably regardless of their conceptual relationship to the disease. Indeed, until potential diagnostic variability is reduced, we cannot be sure that phenomenologically similar populations are being addressed and, as a consequence, the findings of different investigators cannot be compared.

There are, however, certain limitations to making improved symptom reliability the sole means of creating a classification. If we take an example from general medicine—coughing—and apply the principles of classification to it, perhaps we can illustrate this point. One could reliably classify cough by frequency (number of coughs/minutes), depth of inspiratory effort preceding it, force of expiratory effort associated with it, association with fever, etc. One could even examine potential prognostic factors such as cough followed by a broken rib (excellent short-term prognosis—no one with a broken rib coughs at all, but long-term outcome may lead to pneumonia) or duration of cough ("if cough persists for more than two weeks, consult your physician"). But would any of this lead to a better understanding of the pathophysiology of coughing? We know that the cause of coughing may range from centralized brain tumor, to ear infections, to postnasal drip, to bronchogenic carcinoma; the reliability or frequency of association of the "subsymptoms" that occur in conjunction with the "cough syndrome" does little to improve our understanding. Indeed, we even have effective targeted cough-suppressant treatments that, for some forms of cough, are all that is needed; with other forms, the visible symptoms may go away, but the process continues.

For schizophrenia, the issue can be examined similarly. *DSM-III* describes six specific forms of hallucinations or delusions, deterioration based on level of functioning, duration, occurrence before or after the six forms of hallucinations and, in the deterioration category, eight specific kinds of prodromal or residual symptoms (American Psychiatric Association, 1980). What does this level of detail add to our understanding of schizophrenia and our clinical treatment of it? The answer to the first is in doubt, and we fear that because *DSM-III* offers so little treatment implication to practicing clinicians, the success of this facet of our work also remains in doubt. Yet, it would be unfortunate if we were to discard all descriptive psychiatry based on this argument. There are ways of organizing our current knowledge about the phenomenology of schizophrenia that can provide an interface with our current treatment armamentarium. Several approaches are described in this volume, and we would like to take one and develop it a little further.

Drawing from the work of Hughlings Jackson on the evolution/dissolution theory, Strauss, Carpenter, and Bartko in 1974, well before the current revival of this concept, presented a rather compelling argument (based on precursors and prognosis) for the existence of three groupings of problems associated with schizophrenic symptoms: positive symptoms, negative symptoms, and disorders of personal relationships. By positive symptoms they refer to symptoms of schizophrenia that characterize it by their presence—hallucinations and delusions; by negative symptoms they refer to symptoms that characterize it by their absence—lack of goal-directed behavior, blunting of affect, deteriorative affect, verbal paucity; by disordered personal relationships they refer to patterns of asociality, withdrawal, and lack of close personal ties. Their data supported the following conclusions:

- *Positive Symptoms*
  Develop over short period of time
  Are a reaction to biologic or socioenvironmental causes
  Have minimal prognostic importance
- *Negative Symptoms*
  Develop over extended period of time
  Are conceptualized as either the source of chronicity or the result of it
  Are prognostically important
- *Disordered Personal Relationships*
  Develop over long term
  Are conceptualized as an interactive process of uncertain etiology
  Are prognostically important for predicting functioning in its own area as well as in negative symptomatology and positive symptomatology

TREATMENT

Using this same conceptual framework, we are able to examine the relative contribution of various treatment approaches to schizophrenic patients for impact in each of the three areas. Although advances in psychopharmacologic and psychosocial treatments combined to produce a major revolution in the treatment of schizophrenia in the 1950s, the ensuing two decades have seen a parallel but, until recently, distinctly separate development of knowledge about these two elements of treatment. The well-designed, rigorous clinical trials of neuroleptic drugs have produced an imposing body of data pointing to their efficacy in the control of the positive symptoms of schizophrenia. Almost no one would question that positive symptomatology is profoundly affected by pharmacologic treatments. Further, controlled studies of maintenance chemotherapy demonstrate a decided advantage for patients assigned to receive drugs compared with those assigned to placebo (Davis et al., 1980). The issue of safety vs. relative efficacy must however, be considered. In a review of 56 studies of tardive dsyskinesia (TD) in groups of patients treated with neuroleptics, Kane and Smith (1982) reported an average TD prevalence of 20 percent as compared with a five-percent prevalence of "spontaneous" dyskinesia in 19 samples of untreated individuals.

Psychosocial treatments with their high consumption of time and dollars have proved more difficult to assess and clearly create problems for their advocates. The reasons for this are myriad. At least three, however, deserve noting:

First, our need for the "magical cure." Schizophrenia is a disorder of terrifying magnitude in terms of the disability it causes and the fear that irrational behavior engenders in all of us. It is not unreasonable, therefore, for people to search for the "magic cures" of schizophrenia. Of the many positive things one can say about psychosocial treatments, their resemblance to anyone's concept of "magic cure" is remote.

Second, administrative, political, and fiscal decisions have made short-term hospital treatment a reality of our times. Many psychosocial treatments by their very nature do not lend themselves to brief treatment of patients at the time they experience florid positive symptoms.

Third, although positive symptoms are the least enduring and least prognostic aspect of schizophrenia, they are its most dramatic and characteristic aspect. A treatment that is successful for the positive symptoms becomes, therefore, a treatment standard against which other treatments are measured. Unfortunately, the vast majority of psychosocial treatments address their impact at improving either negative symptoms or social competence and not positive symptoms. When only positive symptoms are examined, the practice of comparing drugs with psychosocial treatments for schizophrenia is not a valid comparison. Would any of us be willing to compare the effects of surgical intervention and physical rehabilitation for a broken hip, the effects of insulin and diet in diabetes, polio vaccine and the "iron lung"? The debate over whether drugs are better or worse than psychosocial treatments for schizophrenic patients is meaningless. Although the efficacy of pharmacologic treatments is well established for the positive symptoms of schizophrenia, it can be argued convincingly that this is only a part and, in fact, only the stage-setting part of the overall long-term treatment plan. In other words, without pharmacologic treatment, other treatments may never get the chance to work.

We should resist the current dangerous trend toward narrowing our diagnostic concept of schizophrenia to only its positive symptoms or face a therapeutic tautology in which the pharmacologic response determines the nature of what is schizophrenia and the positive symptoms determine what treatments are effective.

Psychosocial Treatment

Given the long and rich history of psychosocial treatment, including individual, group, and family therapies for schizophrenic patients, that long precedes the advent of neuroleptics, the scarcity of reported studies evaluating its utility is serious. In searching for explanations for this, we have come up with two thoughts. The first was expressed eloquently by Carpenter and Heinrichs (1980): "Psychotherapy was the most prestigious form of psychiatric treatment, and the need for testing the therapeutic efficacy was not readily appreciated by those who presumed a treatment effect. We looked to the philosopher, the essayist, the metapsychologist, and the indoctrinated clinician for new knowledge. Many leading psychiatrists came from the ranks of those who had a prolonged educational experience which stressed inculcation of beliefs, with neglect of scientific principles of hypothesis testing and theory disproof. Arrogance is no friend of science and we now face the consequences of having failed to establish a data base suitable for testing therapeutic efficacy of social treatments in general, and psychotherapy of schizophrenia in particular" (p. 242).

The second reason is that *maybe* psychotherapy, as we have traditionally defined it, does not work. It becomes essential, however, to distinguish between psychotherapy and psychosocial treatment. By psychotherapy we refer to the traditional format of treating the patient through an approach that anticipates that the patient will be able to take corrective steps outside of therapy based on what he or she has learned inside the therapeutic situation. For many patients with disorders other than schizophrenia and even for some exceptional few with schizophrenia this occurs. For the vast majority of people suffering from schizophrenia, this does not occur. The transfer of information from a brief, intense therapeutic situation into the outside world does not take place or takes place incompletely. The therapeutic experience is either not received, not transferred into an operational system within the schizophrenic person, or it is not encompassing or powerful enough to affect the overwhelming all-encompassing process of schizophrenia. Is it realistic to expect a maximum of a few hours a week of therapeutic contact to offset the effects of a disorder that is constantly present and affecting response to and from an environment? In those few instances in which the traditional psychotherapeutic modalities have an impact, it would seem to be just as plausible to posit factors other than the technique for producing results. Unfortunately, replicating charisma has not been easy. The positive impact of treatment that contains as an integral component an optimistic belief that the patient can be helped has been amply demonstrated. The power of megavitamins, hemodialysis, and many of the other breakthroughs of the past 50 to 60 years will attest to this. And how many of us could deny the phenomenon that occurs when we have a new schizophrenic patient for whom we have high hopes and who improves temporarily? What happens 12 to 18 months later when our clinical enthusiasm has been tempered by the missed goals—the patient's withdrawn affect and the disappointment spread liberally across the faces of the family, friends, and finally to ourselves?

Where then do we turn to provide the restitutive process or preventive interventions for the negative symptoms of schizophrenia? We believe it must come from the psycho*social* approaches (examples of which may be read in this volume). By psychosocial we refer to approaches that integrate the psychological/psychiatric knowledge of schizophrenia with the environment or milieu in which the schizophrenic patient operates. In a disorder that is as pervasive as schizophrenia, to fail to consider the interaction of the disordered process with the environment is to invite treatment failure. Whether one gains total environmental control to reverse the most severe schizophrenic syndrome as Gordon Paul (Chapter 14) has done, or whether it should be done in the community as Stein and Test (1980) have done, or whether one can use a significant component of the person's environment—the family—as Liberman and associates (Chapter 12) have done, is not as crucial as is the basic principle of all of these: considering the impact of the schizophrenic person on his or her environment and, in turn, the environmental impact on the schizophrenic would appear to be a *sine qua non* for treatment.

The power of a milieu or environment to affect a patient's functioning has been demonstrated in ways other than the positive directions described in this volume. Wing (1978) reported on the detrimental effects of a too-forceful, overstimulating rehabilitation program in bringing about relapse. Indeed, the initial treatment failures reported in many studies and the high attrition rates from intensive therapy reported in others may possibly be explained in this manner. Perhaps it is this generalized overstimulating, overinvolved environmental interaction that is being captured by "expressed emotion" (EE), and it explains the success of the current psychoeducational family approaches that attempt to reduce EE.

Some will attempt to explain away the potential direct impact of psychosocial treatments by saying that their influence is only in the area of increasing medication compliance. Although this is probably *one* factor, in instances in which nondrug-responsive symptoms have been assessed as outcome measures—either by using outcome measures that tap negative symptoms or letting drug dosage itself be an outcome measure—the impact of psychosocial treatments becomes more than a profound wish fulfillment on the part of their advocates. Obviously, greater attention needs to be paid to a broader spectrum of outcome measures and more research needs to be conducted to provide replicable interventions. We are past the time when our confidence in and enthusiasm for the power of psychosocial treatments, regardless of their form or the group of schizophrenics to whom they are addressed, can carry the day.

We know that humanitarian goals and the logic of treatment approach are becoming less compelling factors in our increasingly fiscally accountable society. When we examine the impact of psychosocial treatments on factors on which we might expect them to have their greatest effect, negative symptoms and deficits in interpersonal skills, we can find not only a logic for expecting improvement, but considerable evidence to support it. What is also apparent is that the technologies for assessing treatment impact in this area are underdeveloped and that measurement is a complex, frustrating undertaking. Measuring presence or absence of a positive symptom or measuring readmission to a hospital is a far easier and more reliable undertaking than assessing negative symptoms and interpersonal competence. We should not, however, emulate the apocryphal story of the drunk looking for his lost watch near the lamp post only because the light is better there than where he lost it. Schizophrenia is not solved by positive symptom reduction and freedom from hospitalization. The nonproductive lives, so frequently the outcome in this disorder, become far more important even if less dramatic than positive symptoms. Further, we should abandon our bimodal approach to treating schizophrenia: drugs vs. psychosocial treatment. Our acknowledgment that both are useful—perhaps for different aspects, perhaps at different times, perhaps in ways we have not yet considered—will help us take a major step toward a better life for our patients.

REFERENCES

American Psychiatric Association 1980. *DSM III: Diagnostic and Statistical Manual of Mental Disorders (Third Edition)*. Washington, DC.

Carpenter Jr., W.T., and Heinrichs, D.W. 1980. The role of psychodynamic psychiatry in the treatment of schizophrenic patients. In J.S. Strauss, M. Bowers, T.W. Downey, S. Fleck, S. Jackson, and I. Levine (eds.), *The Psychotherapy of Schizophrenia*. New York: Plenum.

Davis, J.M., Schaffer, C.B., Killian, G.A., Kinard, C., and Chan, C. 1980. Important issues in the drug treatment of schizophrenia. *Schizophr. Bull.* 6:70-87.

Jackson, H. 1887. Remarks on evolution and dissolution of the nervous system. *J. Ment. Sci.* 33:25-48.

Kane, J.M., and Smith, J.M. 1982. Tardive dyskinesia: Prevalence and risk factors, 1959 to 1970. *Arch. Gen. Psychiatry* 39:473-481.

Stein, L.I., and Test, M.A. 1980. Alternative to mental hospital treatment. *Arch. Gen. Psychiatry* 37:392-397.

Strauss, J.S., Carpenter, Jr., W.T., and Bartko, J.J. 1974. Part III. Speculations on the processes that underlie schizophrenic symptoms and signs. *Schizophr. Bull.* 11:61-69.

Wing, J.K. (ed.) 1978. *Schizophrenia: Towards a New Synthesis*. New York: Academic Press.

V
Special Populations

16
Chronic Alcoholism:
Broad-Spectrum Clinical Programming

DAVID W. FOY

Current treatment programs for alcoholism reflect a broad-spectrum or multi-modal approach that tacitly recognizes alcoholism as a biopsychosocial phenomenon. Many programs are designed, therefore, to address the physical, psychological, and social concomitants of alcohol abuse. In this respect alcoholism is similar to other chronic mental disorders for which comprehensive treatment is concerned with acute symptom control *and* improvements in psychological and social-role functioning. Ideally, symptomatic treatment and psychosocial rehabilitation are complementary components in an integrated approach to alcoholism (Miller and Foy, 1981).

In terms of reducing abusive drinking, symptomatic treatment, consisting of at least two weeks of inpatient care or five outpatient visits, has consistently produced better outcomes when compared to minimal or no treatment (Emrick, 1975; Polich et al., 1980). These findings hold true regardless of the type of treatment offered. It is now amply clear, however, that simple elimination or reduction of abusive drinking does not ensure that the patient will experience similar improvements in psychological and social adjustment. Most alcoholism treatment outcome studies that include quality-of-life measures as well as drinking indices show few significant pre-post or between-group differences on measures of psychosocial functioning in vocational, social, and psychological areas (Emrick, 1975).

It seems the current "state of the art" in treatment for chronic alcoholics is that effective methods are available for symptomatic relief but more powerful psychosocial rehabilitation methods need to be developed. A general finding from both human and animal studies is that alcohol dependence is heightened by impoverished environmental reinforcers (Falk et al., 1982). Many chronic alcoholics return to their natural environments determined to adjust after treatment without alcohol, a previous significant source of reinforcement. Unless environmental

273

prostheses are used to enrich personal and social sources of available reinforcers, the individual must rely on his/her own skills for selecting and extracting other reinforcers. In many cases, chronic alcoholics do not possess the requisite self-management and social skills to improve their use of nonalcohol reinforcers. In fact, recent findings on relapse factors indicate that anger-producing interpersonal conflicts and peer pressure to resume drinking are particular stressors for which treated alcoholics have ineffective coping skills (Marlatt, 1978).

The focus of this paper will be on broad-spectrum programming that includes symptomatic and psychosocial rehabilitation components. In particular, current social-skills training methods available for use with chronic alcoholics will be highlighted.

BROAD-SPECTRUM PROGRAMMING

Numerous examples of broad-spectrum alcoholism treatment have appeared in the literature in recent years (Miller and Foy, 1981). Despite variations in the combination of treatment components offered, program objectives are remarkably similar. Most programs attempt to:

Provide up-to-date alcohol education to patients and their significant others (Stalonas et al., 1979);

Assess the individual's drinking pattern so that specific situational cues may be identified (Marlatt, 1975);

Decrease the immediate reinforcing properties of alcohol (Miller and Eisler, 1977);

Teach new coping skills (e.g., problem-solving and drink-refusal skills (Miller and Eisler, 1977);

Rearrange the patients' social and vocational environments to maximize self-management without alcohol (Hunt and Azrin, 1973).

Focal areas for intervention include the drinking response per se, the individual's self-management and interpersonal skills, and the physical and interpersonal environments.

The Alcohol Dependence Treatment Program at the Veterans Administration Medical Center in Jackson, Mississippi, for which I served as chief from 1975 to 1980, is an example of a broad-spectrum approach that emphasized psychosocial rehabilitation. Table 1 depicts the program components offered in a 28-day inpatient context. In addition, a schedule of 12 aftercare visits was provided for discharged patients during the first follow-up year.

As shown, the program focused on major self-management and interpersonal skills believed necessary if significant psychosocial improvements were to occur. For example, patients were taught elements of self-management skills such as recognizing past strong situational cues for drinking, problem-solving to identify ways of avoiding difficult situations or dealing with them without drinking, de-

Table 1   Broad-Spectrum Treatment Components

Focal Area	Component	Hours Planned
Drinking Response	Disulfiram (Antabuse) (contract with significant other encouraged)	
Individual	Alcohol education	3
	Group therapy	16
	Individual therapy	6
	Relaxation training	12
	Social-skills training	12
Environment	Marital therapy	(p.r.n.)
	Vocational assistance	4 (+p.r.n.)

fining "craving" for a drink as a temporary phenomenon that is manageable without drinking.

Disulfiram, individual and group therapy, marital therapy, relaxation training, and vocational assistance are familiar components of a multimodal approach to alcoholism. A more recent addition to treatment programming, however, is the application of social-skills training to predictable interpersonal difficulties faced by chronic alcoholic patients. This approach focuses on increasing their adaptive skills in a systematic fashion and seems to hold promise for improving state-of-the-art alcoholism treatment.

SOCIAL-SKILLS TRAINING FOR ALCOHOLICS

Several kinds of social-skills training (general assertiveness, drink refusal, job interviewing, and job interpersonal relations) were conducted to enhance the patients' ability to elicit social reinforcement from their natural environments (Foy et al., 1976, 1979). All training sessions were held in a small-group format in which instructions, goal-setting, modeling, feedback, and social reinforcement were the behavioral techniques used by the trainer. The training vehicle was role-playing, with patients serving as surrogate participants in problem situations derived from their own histories. Target behaviors usually identified for change included both response topography (eye contact, voice volume or intonation, response latency, smiles or other affective expression), and content behaviors (requests for change, compliance, hostile comments, seeking more information).

After each role-played scene, the trainer and patient observers reviewed the patient's performance, giving positive and corrective feedback and instructions for improvement in the next trial. Training trials were repeated for each scene until the performance level was judged acceptable by the patient, trainer, and other patient observers. During each session each patient was expected to role-play in at least one of his own scenes.

Although drink-refusal and job interpersonal skills training methods were developed in individual sessions, all subsequent social-skills training was conducted in small groups. Our comparison study showed no differences in terms of skill acquisition between individual versus group training modalities. A subsequent comparison study (Oei and Jackson, 1980) found similar results for skill maintenance but showed the group format to be better in terms of the speed of skill acquisition. Group training is advantageous from a staff resource and time standpoint as well. Other advantages and disadvantages of the two formats have been described in detail (Liberman et al., 1975; Trower et al., 1978).

To illustrate the social-skills training methods developed specifically for chronic alcoholics, formats for drink refusal, job interviewing and job interpersonal skills training will be presented, each with a sample training scene, problem-solving goals, and response strategies.

Drink-Refusal Skills

First described by Foy et al. (1976), teaching alcoholics to "say no" in difficult situations is now a technique commonly used in many treatment settings. Since social pressure to drink by friends and former drinking partners is a prominent factor in relapse, increasing patients' competence in managing situations in which drinking is pushed is crucial (Marlatt and Gordon, 1979).

Sample training scene. It has been three weeks since you were discharged from inpatient alcoholism treatment. You are downtown on Saturday afternoon taking care of some errands when you meet one of your old drinking buddies whom you haven't seen in four months. Your friend says, "Let's go get a cool one."

Goals set:

1. Refuse the offer for an alcoholic drink
2. Inform friend you have decided not to drink anymore
3. Make friend an ally for the future

Strategies taught:

1. Firm noncompliance (e.g., "No, I'm not drinking.")
2. Request for change (e.g., "Next time we meet it would help me if you didn't ask me to drink.")
3. Change the topic (e.g., "I'm refinishing an old desk as a project. Have you done any woodworking?")
4. Offer an alternative (e.g., "Come with me to the hobby store. We can visit while I finish my shopping.")

Job Interview Skills

Since many patients are unemployed at the time of discharge from treatment, making positive contacts with prospective employers to get a job is an important rehabilitation issue.

Sample training scene. You have journeyman-level skills as a carpenter. You have prepared a résumé, dressed and groomed yourself neatly, and arrived punctually for an interview at a cabinet manufacturing company. The interviewer knew you by reputation as a skilled craftsman whose work was sometimes affected by your drinking. The interviewer says, "Now what about your drinking problem?"

Goals set:

1. Present work history and skills positively

2. Respond openly to questions about problem drinking

Strategies taught:

1. Describe drinking problem in past tense (e.g., "I had some difficulty with alcohol in the past.")

2. Describe positive efforts to overcome drinking problem ("I successfully completed _____ treatment program and am confident of my ability to manage without alcohol now.")

3. Show interest in the job and company (e.g., "Could you tell me about some of the current projects that you are working on?")

Job Interpersonal Skills

Anger-producing interpersonal conflicts have been identified as another important precipitant of alcoholic relapse (Marlatt and Gordon, 1979). In recent studies alcoholics have shown the same social-skill deficits in negative assertion situations as have other hospitalized psychiatric patients (Miller and Eisler, 1977; Monti et al., 1981). Our alcoholic patients frequently reported that on-the-job difficulties with the boss were especially hard for them to handle. Difficulties with peers and, less frequently, with subordinates were also mentioned (Foy et al., 1979).

Sample training scene. You are a carpenter working as a cabinet maker. You and the boss have had several discussions about how to proceed with a difficult corner-joining. The boss tells you how he thinks it can be done but you don't agree. He says, "It's your job, so make it fit."

Goals set:

1. Control urge to attack the boss verbally

2. Keep a problem-oriented focus

Strategies taught:

1. Inhibit immediate angry response (e.g., use wait, absorb, slowly proceeding cognitive instructions to "cool off")

2. Restate the problem (e.g., "I'm still having trouble understanding how to finish the corner.")

3. Suggest an alternative (e.g., "Maybe we can talk about this again in a little while. I'd like to try again then.")

The chronic alcoholic population for whom this social-skills training was provided is described in Table 2.

Table 2   Chronic Alcoholic Population

Descriptive Variable	Mean (N=62)
Age	45.5 yrs
Education	11.5 yrs
Race	
Caucasian	74%
Black	26%
Marital status	
Married	48%
Separated/divorced	52%
Occupational skill level (1-7)	3.3 (semiskilled)
Employment status on admission	
Full-time	29%
Part-time	11%
Unemployed	44%
Other (retired, disabled, student)	16%
Personal income past 12 months	$8,500
Length of problem drinking	10 years
Previous alcohol hospitalization	1.5
D.W.I. arrests	1.5
Minor withdrawal symptoms	90%
Major withdrawal symptoms	36%
Days intoxicated past 12 months	184

Although the veteran alcoholic population for whom these social-skills training methods were developed fits most definitions of "chronic alcoholism," these patients did not have obvious cognitive deficits. In addition, group therapy and individual therapy time beyond the 12 hours of structured social-skills training was required to help the patients actually to use the training in their natural environments. Individual plans to use new skills during the patients' weekend passes and "troubleshooting" actual attempts after their return from passes were critical adjuncts to the role-played training. Booster training also was available during the aftercare phase of the treatment program.

Overall, we estimated that about one third of the 55 programmed hours of treatment focused on social-skills training or implementation. Because the training was included in a broad-spectrum program, the specific contribution of social-skills training to treatment outcome is not known.

Current Status of Social-Skills Training for Alcoholics

It is now a replicated finding that hospitalized chronic alcoholics have demonstrable social-skills deficits in situations that require the expression of anger for interpersonal problem-solving (Miller and Eisler, 1977; Monti et al., 1981).

This is highly congruent with recent research on chronic alcoholics' vulnerability to relapse, which identified anger-producing interpersonal conflicts, along with social pressure to drink, as key relapse precipitants (Marlatt and Gordon, 1979). Thus it seems that many alcoholics need treatment aimed at increasing their social competence in at least these two areas.

The application of social-skills training to alcoholics is a recent clinical development, first case reports having appeared in the mid-1970s. That alcoholics can learn and maintain training effects from social-skills training in the treatment setting has been demonstrated repeatedly. The extent to which such training generalizes to the natural environment is not clear, however (Van Hasselt et al., 1978). Nor is the unique contribution of social-skills training to alcohol treatment outcome understood. Recent preliminary research on the relationship of concurrent adaptive skills to drinking outcome suggests that post-treatment coping competence is positively related to outcome (Jones and Lanyon, 1981).

The current limitations of empirical validation of social-skills training as a viable treatment for alcoholism parallel the status of social-skills training technology in general. Persuasive demonstration of generalization of training outside the treatment setting is still lacking (Foy et al., in press). For the present, social-skills training seems promising as a means of meeting the often extensive social rehabilitation needs of some chronic alcoholic persons.

ACKNOWLEDGMENT

Support for the dissemination of the training procedures described was provided, in part, by Research and Training Center Grant No. G-008006802 from the National Institute of Handicapped Research.

REFERENCES

Emrick, C. D. 1975. A review of psychologically oriented treatment of alcoholism. II. The relative effectiveness of treatment versus no treatment. *J. Stud. Alcohol* 36:88-108.

Falk, J. L., Schuster, C. R., Bigelow, G. E., and Woods, J. H. 1982. Progress and needs in the experimental analysis of drug and alcohol dependence. *Am. Psychol.* 37:1124-1127.

Foy, D. W., Massey, F. H., Duer, J. D., Ross, J. M., and Wooten, L. S. 1979. Social skills training to improve alcoholics' vocational interpersonal competency. *Journal of Counseling Psychology* 26:128-132.

Foy, D. W., Miller, P. M., Eisler, R. M., and O'Toole, D. G. 1976. Social skills training to teach alcoholics to refuse drinks effectively. *J. Stud. Alcohol* 37:1340-1345.

Foy, D. W., Wallace, C. J., and Liberman, R. P. in press. Advances in social skills training for chronic mental patients. In K. D. Craig and R. J. McMahon (eds.), *Advances in Clinical Behavior Therapy*. New York: Brunner/Mazel.

Hunt, G. M., and Azrin, N. H., 1973. A community-reinforcement approach to alcoholism. *Behav. Res. Ther.* 11:91-104.

Jones, S. L., and Lanyon, R. I. 1981. Relationship between adaptive skills and outcome of alcoholism treatment. *J. Stud. Alcohol* 42:521-525.

Liberman, R. P., King, L. W., DeRisi, W. J., and McCann, M. 1975. *Personal Effectiveness: Guiding People to Assert Themselves and Improve Their Social Skills*. Champaign, IL: Research Press.

Marlatt, G. A. 1975. The drinking profile: A questionnaire for the behavioral assessment of alcoholism. In E. J. Marsh and L. G. Terdal (eds.), *Behavior Therapy Assessment: Diagnosis and Evaluation*. New York: Springer.

Marlatt, G. A. 1978. Craving for alcohol, loss of control, and relapse: A cognitive-behavioral analysis. In P. E. Nathan and G. A. Marlatt (eds.), *Experimental and Behavioral Approaches to Alcoholism*. New York: Plenum.

Marlatt, G. A., and Gordon, J. R. 1979. Determinants of relapse: Implications for the maintenance of behavior change. In P. D. Davidson and S. M. Davidson (eds.), *Behavioral Medicine: Changing Health Lifestyles*. New York: Brunner/Mazel.

Miller, P. M., and Eisler, R. M. 1977. Assertive behavior of alcoholics: A descriptive analysis. *Behavior Therapy* 8:146-149.

Miller, P. M., and Foy, D. W. 1981. Substance abuse. In S. M. Turner, K. S. Calhoun, and H. E. Adams (eds.), *Handbook of Clinical Behavior Therapy*. New York: John Wiley and Sons.

Monti, P. M., Corriveau, D. P., and Zwick, W. 1981. Assessment of social skills in alcoholics and the psychiatric patients. *J. Stud. Alcohol* 42:526-529.

Oei, T. P. S., and Jackson, P. 1980. Long-term effects of group and individual social skills training with alcoholics. *Addict. Behav.* 5:129-136.

Polich, J. M., Armor, D. J., and Braiker, H. B. 1980. *The Course of Alcoholism: Four Years After Treatment*. Santa Monica: Rand.

Stalonas, P. M., Keane, T. M., and Foy, D. W. 1979. Alcohol education for in-patient alcoholics: A comparison of live, videotape and written presentation modalities. *Addict. Behav.* 4:223-229.

Trower, P., Bryant, B., and Argyle, M. 1978. *Social Skills and Mental Health*. Pittsburgh: University of Pittsburgh Press.

Van Hasselt, V. B., Hersen, M., and Milliones, J. 1978. Social skills training for alcoholics and drug addicts: A review. *Addict. Behav.* 3:221-233.

17
Chronic Mental Illness in Aged Patients

Charles M. Gaitz

Aging and being old are factors worth considering in a volume on chronic mental illness. I shall focus on these factors rather than attempt a hurried overview of the psychiatry of old age, and I shall comment on aspects that are important to clinicians who care for older people.

DEFINITIONS

Definitions of health and illness, normality, chronicity, and even what we mean by aged, are often vague. The imprecision is especially apparent when our goal is to diagnose the mental state of elderly persons. We have only broad guidelines for defining who is aged. An Olympic swimming champion may be old at 22, a baseball player at 35, a Supreme Court justice at 75. People who grow up in situations of chronic malnutrition and poverty may be elderly at 45. Persons with congenital abnormalities may have a short lifespan and appear aged at 30 or even earlier. Persons who have lived under severe, prolonged stress, such as chronic physical disorders or confinement in a concentration camp, and persons with a long history of alcoholism or other substance abuse may age rapidly and prematurely.

Nevertheless, age categories are useful if we recognize that the parameters of interest determine what groupings are appropriate. In any case, we must understand that "the elderly" are much more heterogeneous than, say, a sample of 10- or 12-year-old children. For some purposes it has been useful to divide the "old" into the "young old" (45 to 65), the "middle old" (65 to 75), and the "old old" (75 and older). One could argue for another arbitrary breakdown, but defining the "aged" in any group requires attention to the group's other characteristics.

Defining normality and mental illness is especially difficult among older persons. That changes occur with aging is well documented, but much remains to be learned about aging processes. Chronologically old people are different from young people, but we are uncertain whether the physiologic and psychologic changes are normal or not. When does forgetfulness move from being a benign sign of aging to being symptomatic of a mental illness? Should one relate limited activity, loss of interest and appetite, and mood disturbances to a demonstrable physical disease or to an affective disorder? How does one interpret depressive symptoms in the face of circumstances or losses that realistically call forth depressive feelings? Distinguishing between grief and abnormal affective states can be a problem at any age, but perhaps the need to do so arises more frequently when the patient is old.

As to chronicity, changes in cognitive function, affect, and thinking usually progress insidiously. Some disorders are, of course, a recurrence, if not a continuation, of an illness manifested earlier in life; others are a response to stresses of late life. Dating the onset of mental illness in late life is often very difficult because acute disorders, for which precipitating stresses can be identified, occur infrequently. Whether the onset of a mental disturbance is slow or fast, however, it is a mistake to assume than an impairment is likely to be irreversible because the patient is old. Though aging may reduce their resources to cope with problems, elderly people are likely to be competent and strong and to have learned how to overcome much adversity during their long lives.

Chronological age, then, should be *one* factor in planning for and treating mentally ill persons, but it should not be a major deterrent to undertaking appropriate diagnostic tests and therapeutic interventions, much like those for younger patients.

ETIOLOGIC AND HISTORIC TRENDS

In addition to genetic and biochemical abnormalities that contribute to mental illness in late life, Blazer (Busse and Blazer, 1977) noted that at least five other factors have been implicated: psychosocial stress, loss of social support, maladaptive personality development, previous history of mental illness, and physical illness. Mental illness in late life is likely to have a multidimensional origin that includes social, psychological, and health factors. Although this approach to understanding mental disorders should not be restricted to those manifested in late life, it emphasizes the importance of the increasing prevalence of physical disorders in older persons and makes us more cognizant of the possibility that physiologic disorders may affect mental status.

As Blazer points out, disease rates in the population increase and decrease over time. The incidence of pellagra psychosis, conversion disorders, and general paresis is lower, the decrease in the latter having special importance to geriatric psychiatry. Clinicians should remember general paresis when making a differential diagnosis of organic mental disorders or other psychotic reactions in an elderly patient. Few studies have actually looked at historical trends of mental illness in the aged, although such studies would be useful because, over decades, changes in diagnostic criteria for certain illnesses make it difficult to compare data. Today, preoccupation with quality of life in addition to survival has led us to be more concerned about depression. Symptoms now considered pathological were accepted previously, and mistakenly, as a normal concomitant of aging.

EPIDEMIOLOGIC RESEARCH

Epidemiologic studies confirm that age affects the prevalence and incidence of mental illnesses but, as the figures tend to be repeated from one paper to another, they take on a credibility they may not deserve. One major chronic mental disorder of late life is senile dementia. The Steering Committee on the Chronically Mentally Ill of the U.S. Department of Health and Human Services (DHHS, 1980) reported in 1980 that five percent of the population aged 65 and older has senile dementia, and that this rate increases to 20 percent at age 80, and to 40 percent by age 90. Another repeated quotation in this and similar reviews is that dementia is the fourth leading cause of death in the United States and that it affects at least one-half of the elderly residents of nursing homes. Unfortunately, efforts to establish prevalence and incidence of senile dementia and other conditions are plagued by the difficulties of establishing diagnoses, obtaining adequate samples, collecting relevant data, and securing the cooperation of subjects. We are left with variations from one study to another and sometimes lack information that would help us understand the differences.

One can readily agree with the government report that both the etiology of mental illness and the causes of chronicity should be studied, but the studies should be multidisciplinary and provide data that integrate the biological, psychosocial, and environmental influences on mental health status.

One does not need the confirmation of epidemiologic studies to know that organic brain syndrome, or late-life dementia, is a devastating disorder and a serious public health problem. The DHHS report states correctly than many older persons are misdiagnosed as suffering from senile dementia when they are, in fact, depressed. Eight to 15 percent of elderly patients who complain about memory deficits or other symptoms of dementia respond favorably to antidepressant drug treatment, the report points out, and another 20 percent of dementing conditions other than Alzheimer disease are treatable and reversible.

These numbers are potentially misleading, if not incorrect. In my opinion, the percentages will vary, depending on where the patients have been examined. Patients referred to a public mental health clinic are likely to have not only dementia but other behavioral disorders, and they are less likely to have reversible dementias than are patients seen in medical facilities. Patients referred to neurologists are more likely to have cerebrovascular disease than those seen by psychiatrists. Patients examined in their homes, or at a senior center, may have little evidence of dementia, and few of them have serious affective or thought disorders.

The scope of the problem, then, is difficult to evaluate if the prime focus is on the residence of persons being studied or if referral sources and examination sites are ignored. Nursing home populations have been studied, but nursing homes are not homogeneous institutions. Some nursing homes do not admit persons who have behavioral problems. Information obtained in such a home could be valid, of course, for that home, but it would not have much relevance to a nursing home whose population includes former state hospital patients.

Diagnosing psychiatric disorders is discouraged, or ignored, in states that determine level of care and payment for services on the basis of physical health factors; introducing psychiatric diagnoses only complicates matters. One need only spend a few minutes talking with residents in a nursing home to discover that many have psychiatric problems, but, for obvious reasons, someone interested in the mental status of nursing home residents cannot rely on diagnoses in the charts or reports to a licensing agency. Estimates are that perhaps 20 percent of nursing home residents have a primary mental disorder and another 30 percent are senile but not psychotic. Those considered "mentally healthy" are also at risk because of the increasing prevalence of senile dementia with advancing age, the susceptibility of the physically ill aged to depression, and the psychological trauma associated with institutional placement. When one realizes that about 1.3 million persons are in nursing homes in the United States, it becomes clear that this population represents a seriously handicapped and underserved group. Yet, under current regulations of payment for care, and in view of the small number of mental health professionals willing to work in nursing-home settings, there is not much hope for change soon.

PROGNOSIS

A flippant pronouncement covers prognosis: elderly patients, like younger ones, get better, get worse, or stay the same. Criteria are based on value judgments, which critically affect expectations, treatment plans, and caregiving. The outcome of an elderly patient's illness depends on an endless list of factors that interact positively and negatively. We often disagree on their importance and impact. Should we infer, for example, that the absence of a specific treatment for senile dementia means we have no treatment? Should treatment effectiveness be measured only by marked improvement in a patient's memory and cognitive function? Respite care relieves caregivers somewhat, but does it affect the patient? Should regulating the dosage of a tranquilizer require the services of a psychiatrist especially knowledgeable about age-related effects of drug metabolism, or should all physicians have this competence? Does relieving external pressures and providing external support represent a medical treatment, eligible for reimbursement by third-party payors, or is it a social service not covered by insurance? And are we really certain that attending to a patient's psychosocial condition affects the primary problems of memory loss and cognitive impairment?

For reasons that are not clear, we have rigid and demanding criteria for judging improvement. In clinical drug trials, for example, we look, of course, for measurable changes in cognitive functions—but the measurement techniques available to us have shortcomings. Behavior rating scales have been justly criticized; other techniques or tests may not have been standardized for old people. Sampling and other methodological problems are more easily identified than solved.

Young patients with schizophrenia may be evaluated as improved on a number of parameters; return to gainful employment and independent living are not the only criteria that count. But for aged patients we are inclined to have expectations that apply more realistically to healthier, younger individuals: we don't use enough age cohort-based data as criteria.

Our shortcomings probably flow from several sources. One is society's intolerance of aging and the tenaciously held belief that aging is associated inevitably with decline and hopelessness. Our etiologic and prognostic concepts are skewed also by the assumption that organic factors cause most mental illnesses of late life. We may set higher standards and expect more concrete evidence of improvement for treatment of organic disorders than we do for treatment of illnesses of uncertain origin. In fairness to psychiatrists and psychiatry, one should note that our colleagues who treat patients for cancer or heart disease acknowledge that many factors affect prognosis. Predicting a precise course for any one patient is as difficult for them as it is for us.

The history of a woman now living in a nursing home illustrates the interaction of multiple factors in a patient's adjustment. For many years this 73-year-old housewife had had various psychophysiologic complaints and was quite dependent on her family. Her dependence increased in late life; she was depressed and afraid of being separated, even briefly, from her still older husband who wanted to work part-time. She responded to outpatient treatment, and for several years before her husband's sudden death her symptoms were less severe. She accompanied her husband to various activities and often stayed alone for a few hours.

When he died suddenly, however, she fell apart and became totally helpless. After considering several possibilities, she agreed to enter a nursing home where, in a few weeks, she blossomed. Compared to other residents, she functioned better intellectually and accepted graciously the role of demonstrating to the outside community that aged persons, including nursing home residents, have energy, vitality, and interests. She is able to do this in a setting where little else is expected of her. She delights in reporting, as often as she can, that she is happy, contented, and productive (to the extent that productivity is expected in a nursing home).

This woman has a chronic mental illness of long standing. Her symptomatology had varied little during most of her adult and late adult life, but it became much less obvious late in life when she received support and admiration in a protected setting, at a time when age probably altered her own expectations and that of others and facilitated the satisfaction of dependency needs.

Illnesses manifested early in life may change with time. Personality traits and symptoms like irritability, seclusiveness, withdrawal, paranoid tendencies, affective disorders, and substance abuse remain the same or become more severe. Some older people, on the other hand, "mellow" with age as they begin to find time for activities they value differently from judgments made earlier in life. Persons driven to overachieve may become more sedate. Being a grandparent may be easier than being a parent. Tension between spouses, or between children and parents, is often reduced in late life, although changes in social roles, especially reversal of the child-parent role, may exacerbate latent conflicts and raise intergenerational tension again. We talk about "midlife crises" as stresses likely to be experienced in middle age; similarly, conflicts and resolutions arise as people experience stresses unique to late life. Some are not able, for example, to accept the changes associated with aging—altered social position, reduced income, loss of external supports, death of supportive relatives and friends, changes in physical appearance. These disturb emotional equilibrium, and mental illness may be the consequence. Many elderly people, however, cope effectively with these late-life crises, none of which should be associated categorically with decline and deterioration. Given even minimal support, old patients may discover hidden resources and surprise us with their resilience.

TREATMENT

Almost all of the modalities used by psychiatrists are effective and applicable in treating aged persons. The chronological age of the patient is not especially important in deciding to undertake individual or group psychotherapy, behavioral modification, biofeedback, or medication. Electroconvulsive therapy is an effective treatment for severe depression, and the patient's age is not a contraindication. Some psychiatrists believe that electroconvulsive therapy actually may be safer than antidepressants that may produce serious side effects. Pharmacotherapy also can be very helpful, but special observation is necessary because the physiological changes associated with aging affect drug metabolism and may cause side effects more frequently. The prescribing physician must be certain that the patient or someone else understands the dosage schedule and will follow instructions. Because they may be receiving treatment for a number of conditions, aged persons tend to take several medications concurrently. Sometimes these are prescribed by different physicians; to avoid adverse drug interactions, each physician must know all medications the patient is taking to minimize the negative effects of drug interactions. This is an especially important responsibility of psychiatrists because aged patients may have behavioral abnormalities that are drug-related.

CASE HISTORY

The following case history illustrates some aspects of treating an elderly person.

A 70-year-old woman, widowed three years ago, complained of memory impairment and feeling "mixed up" when she was first referred to me by her physician. She had undergone a careful diagnostic evaluation in a hospital. The neurologist had noted loss of memory, some tension, elevated blood pressure, and some evidence of mild, irreversible dementia. Radiologic examination had shown duodenal deformity without evidence of peptic ulcer disease, osteoporosis, or diverticulosis of the colon. The electroencephalogram had been normal, and a brain scan had shown features compatible with mild, generalized cerebral atrophy without focal lesions.

The patient's evaluation had been done after she had brought her 93-year-old mother to a specialist in internal medicine because the mother had severe organic brain syndrome and was becoming increasingly difficult to manage. The physician asked both women to be examined. The patient's mother died soon after her hospital stay, and the patient was living alone. Her husband had died after a long illness, having spent his last few months in a nursing home because the patient had been unable to manage two severely ill persons, her husband and mother, at home. There had been two fires in the home, both suspected as being arson.

I interviewed the patient seven times, about a month apart. After the first visit I prescribed Hydergine, 1 mg three times daily, to help her with problems I considered to be associated with primary degenerative dementia.

During each subsequent visit, the patient remembered more and more details about her life. She sometimes brought notes. She was aware of sometimes getting lost and not being able to find things. She had stopped driving, and she was lonely and dependent. Although she had a maid, a woman older than herself, and a close friend interested in her welfare, she showed little interest in her own care and no initiative for outside activities.

Her mother had been very demanding, and the patient still thought that occasionally she heard her mother calling. She spoke of feeling upset and exhausted, sad, and tense, but she slept well and was rarely hungry. She was extremely careful about smoking and not forgetting lighted cigarettes.

I discussed alternative living arrangements, live-in help, and participation in senior center activities with the patient each time. Her friend came to see me as well, and she showed great interest in the patient but was ambivalent about taking direct responsibility. The patient had a daughter with whom she had some conflicts. Because of the patient's depressive symptoms, I added doxepin to the Hydergine prescription, but the patient, complaining of drowsiness, did not take the doxepin reliably.

After several visits, she had not acted on any of the suggestions, but agreed to take her medications regularly and to undergo psychological tests. These confirmed that the patient's depression was a secondary reaction to organic brain syndrome with cognitive impairment and not, primarily, an affective disorder.

About six months later, arrangements had been made for live-in help. The patient was in much better spirits and much more active. Her attendant—in contrast to the former maid whom the friend had described as "the blind leading the blind"—was stimulating and insistent that the patient leave home to shop and participate in social functions. The patient was well dressed and groomed. Although she knew major news stories, she still could not do a serial-three test or remember dates of major events in her life. She knew the year of her birth but could not calculate her age or give it spontaneously.

By now the friend felt more comfortable in talking about the conflicts between the patient and her daughter, and she discussed some problems of guardianship with me. She was reluctant about using the power of attorney, which she already had, because of questions it might arouse in the family. We discussed the patient's mental competence and how to deal with these issues, and we agreed that value judgments had to be made about various expenditures.

COMMENTS

Continuing attention must be paid to changes in status of both the patient and persons in the support system. For dependent, elderly persons who take little initiative and whose capacity to care for themselves is limited, the support of others must be enlisted. The therapist must be aware of the cumulative effects of stress and, in this instance, the strains of caring for and losing two loved ones, and the anxiety of experiencing two fires. Combined with physical disorders, all contributed to the patient's condition at first examination.

Steps in a treatment plan may take several months to accomplish, no matter how logical, rational, and relatively easy they seem. Timing is critical, and issues concerning the welfare and attitude of others often arise. Fluctuation in the patient's condition also emphasizes the value of longitudinal observations and information from others. When others become involved in the treatment plan, one must recognize their needs as well.

These principles apply to treatment of persons of all ages but, in the case of elderly patients, there are some quantitative and qualitative differences. Given an opportunity, older patients also will participate in planning and be more willing to cooperate if a treatment plan is not imposed on them. Clinicians are often pleasantly surprised to discover that working with elderly persons is no more frustrating or fruitless than working with chronically ill persons of any age.

Aged patients tend to respond favorably to minimal intervention and often require less, rather than more, intensive therapy. Much has been said about the extra time required, but for psychiatrists the problem is related more to whether or not they will invest even a small amount of time. The tendency is, of course, to have less time for aged than for young patients and to use therapies that do not require close personal contact. A psychiatrist who treats young patients knows from experience that a significant investment of time will be necessary if treatment is to be effective. When the patient is old, however, attitudes about the aged take over. It takes a conscious effort to understand that an older patient may require more time to come into the examining room, to undress, or to express an idea; but the total investment of time required to treat elderly patients is, on the average, probably less.

Let me remind the skeptics about the time invested in treating young persons with character disorders, neuroses, and psychoses, and ask for comparison to the time invested in treating elderly persons who typically come to a psychiatrist expecting help in overcoming a crisis and little more. Rational goals and reasonable expectations are critical issues. Yet negative, socially determined attitudes about aging and the aged prevail, and therapists incorporate these values. They often accept the stereotype that elderly persons are severely impaired, have multiple problems and a poor prognosis; consequently, they believe, little satisfaction will come from working with them.

In reality, elderly persons are likely to have a combination of assets and impairments. At all ages, adjustment and adaptation are based on compensations and compromises. To some extent, we may be justified in believing that dementia is the disorder of late life least likely to respond to treatment, but we know also that its severity is affected by many factors. A demented person who lives in a situation that provides support, attention, and few demands for performance and achievement may be relatively asymptomatic. Moving the person to another setting, one demanding a great deal of self-care, and isolating the patient from warm, supportive family members, or subjecting the person to a drastic environmental stress like moving from familiar surroundings to a hospital, is often associated with sudden deterioration and an exaggeration of impairment. Subject the mildly demented person to the consequences of a stroke, a heart attack, or a fracture, and the clinical picture may change. At any time, but certainly late in life, a marginally adjusted person will be adversely affected by such sensory losses as impaired vision or hearing. That these losses, more prevalent in old age, affect outcome when elderly persons with chronic mental illness are being treated is no surprise.

We do not give enough attention to remediable conditions, and sensory losses are often in this category. Fractures heal. Even old people recover from strokes and heart attacks, and they survive major surgical procedures. As therapists, we owe it to our patients to plan and provide treatment with minimal attention to our patients' chronological age.

Environmental manipulations are especially effective in helping aged patients. Providing adequate shelter and nutrition and meeting other basic needs, like social opportunities, are especially useful in helping elderly persons. Perhaps they have learned over the years to rely mainly on themselves to resolve internal conflicts, so that satisfaction of their external needs may be more helpful for them than such approaches are for younger patients.

Therapists willing to work with aged persons may have some conflict about their own functions. If they accept the concept that mental illness in late life has a multifactorial etiology, they have taken the first step toward providing comprehensive treatment themselves or being willing to work with persons of other disciplines. Still, the tendency to treat elderly patients in a rather impersonal way dies hard.

Giving elderly patients time to talk and, at least, to share in planning the agenda is another thing to learn. Too many therapists believe that psychotherapy is for young people: "Old people are rigid, set in their ways." How can a psychiatrist help a 70-year-old widow or widower who is struggling with desires for love and affection and even, heaven forbid, a sexual relationship? Who is ready to listen to a 92-year-old man, a little deaf and not seeing as well as before, when he begins to be afraid of being discharged from his nursing home? And what about the frustration of treating patients who have recurrent episodes of depression or schizophrenia?

Help may be on the way. A few psychiatrists are willing to be identified as geropsychiatrists. What a relief it will be to refer these problem patients when they are 60 or 65, and we realize they deserve to be treated by a specialist!

Obviously, my experience leads me to conclude that the barriers we envision in treating old people have usually been erected by ourselves. Treating aged persons may be good for the patients *and* their therapists.

REFERENCES

Busse, E. W., and Blazer, Dan G. (eds.) 1979. *Handbook of Geriatric Psychiatry*. New York: Van Nostrand Reinhold.

U.S. Department of Health and Human Services 1980. *Toward a National Plan for the Chronically Mentally Ill*. Washington, DC: U.S. Public Health Service.

Suggested Reading

Birren, J. E., and Schaie, K. W. (eds.) 1977. *Handbook of the Psychology of Aging*. New York: Van Nostrand Reinhold.

Cyrus-Lutz, C., and Gaitz, C. M. 1972. Psychiatrists' attitudes toward the aged and aging. *Gerontologist* 12(2)Part 1:163-167.

Gaitz, C. M. 1978. Aged patients, their families and physicians. In G. Usdin and C. Hofling (eds.), *Aging: The Process and the People*, pp. 206-239. New York: Brunner/Mazel.

Gaitz, C. M. 1980. Diagnosing mental illness in the elderly. *J. Am. Geriatr. Soc.* 28:176-179.

Gaitz, C. M., and Varner, R. V. 1979. Adjustment disorders of late life: Stress disorders. In E. W. Busse and D. G. Blazer (eds.), *Handbook of Geriatric Psychiatry*, pp. 381-389. New York: Van Nostrans Reinhold.

Talbott, J. A. (ed.) 1978. *The Chronic Mental Patient: Problems, Solutions, and Recommendations for a Public Policy*. Washington, DC: American Psychiatric Association.

Talbott, J. A. (ed.) 1981. *The Chronically Mentally Ill: Treatment, Programs, Systems*. New York: Human Sciences Press.

18
Chronicity in Mental Retardation

HERBERT J. GROSSMAN

Mental retardation is one of the major handicapping conditions in our population. Mental retardation, as the term is commonly used today, affects a heterogeneous population ranging from totally dependent to nearly "normal" people. The definition of mental retardation according to the *Classification in Mental Retardation* (Grossman, 1983) published by the American Association on Mental Deficiency, is as follows:

Mental retardation refers to significantly subaverage general intellectual functioning in or associated with concurrent impairments in adaptive behavior and manifested during the developmental period.

General intellectual functioning is operationally defined as results obtained by assessment with one or more of the individually administered, standardized general intelligence tests developed for that purpose.

Significantly subaverage is defined as an IQ of 70 or below on standardized measures of intelligence. This upper limit is intended only as a guideline and could extend upward through an IQ of 75, especially in school settings, if behavior is impaired and clinically determined to be caused by deficits in reasoning and judgment.

Impairments in adaptive behavior are defined as significant limitations in individuals' effectiveness in meeting the standards of maturation, learning, personal independence, and/or social responsibility that are expected for their age level and cultural group, as determined by clinical assessment and usually standardized scales.

Developmental period is defined as the period of time between conception and the eighteenth birthday. Developmental deficits may be manifested by slow, arrested, or incomplete development resulting from brain damage, degenerative processes in the central nervous system, or regression from previously normal states as a result of psychosocial factors.

Impairment in mental function may be caused by physical trauma or central nervous system deterioration at any age beyond the developmental period. When manifestations occur later, the condition is more properly classified as *dementia*.

Conceptually, the identifiable mentally retarded population may be divided into two distinct, albeit overlapping groups. One group, about 25 percent of the total, is affected by "clinical types" of retardation, which means the individuals in this group generally have some central nervous system defect, IQs usually in the moderate range or below, have associated handicaps or stigmata, which can often be diagnosed at birth or during early childhood. Persons in the second group, which includes the majority of the mentally retarded population of the United States and elsewhere in the world, seem to be neurologically intact, have no readily detectable physical signs or clinical laboratory evidence related to retardation, function in the mildly retarded range of intelligence, and are heavily concentrated in the lower socioeconomic segments of society. Often, they are identified as retarded only during their school years.

Neither group represents a "pure" entity. Children with central nervous system abnormalities can and do function in the mildly retarded range of intelligence, and many retarded but neurologically intact children may become further handicapped by biological deficiencies as the result of poverty. Nevertheless, the association of IQ and physical defects is very high, and differentiating the two groups by primary agents of biological versus social-environmental origin has meaning for prevention, planning, and treatment.

The term, developmental disabilities, has caused some confusion in recent years. The complex of manifestations subsumed as *mental retardation* overlaps considerably with the legislative definition of developmental disabilities as contained in Public Law 94-103 and amended in Public Law 95-602, Title V, of the Developmental Disabilities Assistance and Bill of Rights Act. In this legislation, *developmental disabilities* are defined as severe, chronic disabilities that are "attributable to a mental or physical impairment or combination of mental and physical impairments" and are (a) manifested before age 22, (b) likely to continue indefinitely, and (c) result in substantial limitations in three or more areas of major life activity.

The areas of limitation clearly apply to the more severe and profound forms of mental retardation and to some mildly retarded individuals during certain periods of their lives. For severely retarded people, nearly all of the defined areas of limitation are substantial and applicable: self-care, receptive and expressive language, learning, mobility, self-direction, capacity for independent living, and economic self-sufficiency. For mildly retarded individuals, many of whom achieve self-sufficiency in adulthood, the disability may be confined primarily to impairments of learning and possibly self-direction.

Other conditions defined as developmental disabilities that share some characteristics with mental retardation are cerebral palsy, epilepsy, and autism. Many people affected by these disorders function intellectually at retarded levels and, among the most severely impaired, clusters of mental retardation, cerebral palsy, and epilepsy are often found in the same individual.

Developmental disabilities are therefore distinguishable from the milder forms of mental retardation and less severe conditions of cerebral palsy, epilepsy, and autism by the nature of the functional limitations described. To satisfy the definition, individuals must demonstrate substantial functional limitations that are age-specific. Although "substantial" is not explicity defined, the requirement that these limitations reflect a need for services that are of lifelong or extended duration and are planned and coordinated for the individual clearly delimits the target population. Important also is the fact that the term developmental disabilities is not a clinical definition but one that refers to planning services for people with the substantial handicaps indicated.

The *Classification in Mental Retardation* (Grossman, 1983) indicates that the words mild, moderate, severe, profound should be used to describe levels of retardation. Mild retardation is roughly equivalent to the educational term "educable"; moderate retardation includes those individuals who are likely to fall into the educational category of "trainable"; the severely retarded group includes persons sometimes known as "dependent retarded"; individuals at the profound retardation level are among those sometimes requiring "life support." These are, of course, not absolute or static. A child classified as mildly retarded may function better in a class for "trainable" children than in one for "educable" ones; some children at the severe retardation level may function successfully in a "trainable" group; children may move up or down between categories. The level does not necessarily dictate the service needed, but it may be helpful as one criterion in planning.

The characteristics of persons at each level of mental retardation are of interest. The overall prevalence of mental retardation in the United States is close to one percent of the population. Males predominate at a ratio of about 65 to 35. About three percent of the population score below 70 on the usual IQ test. About two-thirds (particularly those of preschool age or adults) are not clinically retarded because their general adaptation is adequate. About three percent of newborns will be diagnosed as being retarded some time during their lives.

The two broad groups of individuals diagnosed as being mentally retarded have, as indicated, very dissimilar characteristics. In the first group, that of children and adults in whom mental retardation is accompanied by an identifiable, specific abnormality, the degree of mental retardation may be moderate or severe, but some individuals are only mildly impaired. From a diagnostic viewpoint, the condition is often stable throughout life, and the deficits, both in cognition and general adaptation, are clearly observed in most social contacts and outside the home. The difference in intelligence between the parents and the child usually is substantial: The child's condition is readily suspected by family members who begin a search for clinical assistance early. The mortality rates of this group, which are much above average, correlate highly with severity of retardation and lack of ambulation. Profoundly mentally retarded, nonambulatory individuals have a mortality rate about three times higher than do profoundly mentally retarded ambulatory persons. As a consequence, age-specific prevalence rates of mental retardation decline over the life span, adult mentally retarded persons representing the survivors diagnosed during childhood. A biomedical explanation for their retardation can usually be found: About one-third have a problem caused by a known biomedical or other genetic or chromosomal abnormality, one-third have problems in which known factors were implicated but not conclusively, and for about one-third no clearcut etiological factor can be identified. The condition is not social class-dependent and involves about 0.25 to 0.35 percent of all strata of the population.

In the second group, composed of children or adolescents whose mental retardation may be associated with psychosocial disadvantages, the degree of impairment is mild. As indicated, the diagnosis usually is established after the child enters school and the disability is not obvious after the child leaves school. For the most part, investigation of these problems with laboratory methods does not reveal any consistent, concomitant somatic pathology; the mortality rate of this group approximates the average. Overt symptomatology is much more observable in the classroom than at home, which has led to a description of the phenomenon as "six hour" retardation. This type of retardation is highly social class-dependent. In one study, for example, 30 percent of the population held low socioeconomic status but accounted for 43 percent of persons identified as mentally retarded. Among Caucasians, who represented 86 percent of the group, 51 percent were labeled mentally retarded. Mexican Americans made up 8.5 percent, with 36 percent labeled mentally retarded. While the black group in the study accounted for 4.7 percent, 13 percent were identified as mentally retarded.

Etiological factors that relate to mental retardation associated with or caused by psychosocial disadvantage are complex. Three sets of factors are potentially related: genetic influence, the consequences of sequential nonheritable somatic problems, and the sequelae of early life experiences. Each set probably plays a role in the causation of psychosocial retardation.

THE CHANGING ROLE OF SERVICES FOR MENTALLY RETARDED INDIVIDUALS

The last decade has revealed a vast increase of options for the care and management of individuals who have problems of mental retardation (Landesman-Dwyer, 1981). Certainly a major factor has been mandatory public education for the handicapped under Public Law 94-142. In addition, even for individuals more severely impaired, options of placement in other than traditional institutions are increasing. These represent a variety of clusters called family care homes, nursing homes, convalescent hospitals, and others. For individuals who require some care outside of their homes, we have a complex array of problems. The population and functions of community living arrangements and services for the mentally retarded are in a state of flux and surrounded by controversy. The past ten to 15 years have brought a major change in social policy geared to broader opportunities and a commitment to have individuals live in their own homes or in community settings comparable to their own homes to the fullest extent possible. Clichés like deinstitutionalization, normalization, and community living have emerged. There have been major efforts across the nation to depopulate state-run institutions that provide care for the mentally retarded. Some principles are embraced by some individuals and opposed by others. The belief that smaller is better is common. The crudest comparison of very large, traditional institutions with small group homes confirms the obvious, that depersonalizing practices are found more frequently in institutions. Within a given type of residential setting, however, size per se is not related to the quality of care. Sometimes very small family-style homes are evaluated as more restrictive for clients than are larger board and care settings in the same geographic region. Probably more crucial are such factors as social grouping. None of the studies is without flaw.

The courts and states are often involved with decisions concerning the size of facilities that serve no more than three people or six people or 10 people, but the data are insufficient to support these major policy decisions. Inadequate staffing is often given as a reason for inappropriate care or management, yet it is clear that indiscriminately increasing personnel is not the most efficient way to improve the quality of care for the mentally retarded. Staffing patterns vary widely, and, all too often, the human factor is ignored. The economic aspects of providing care for the mentally retarded are a complex subject, studied many times. One assumption is that care in the community is less expensive than that provided in institutions. Few studies, however, compare levels of service for similar groups.

The characteristics of individual retarded persons have also been researched. Relationships between specific personal and social competence and community adjustment are difficult to study because the complex nature of individuals, their environments and life history often precludes making simple predictions about success. The most consistently reported finding is that individuals' behavioral difficulties, primarily antisocial aggressive tendencies, often lead to reinstitutionalization. Lack of environmental support is often as much to blame for the observed failures as are the specific problems. For the most part, individuals in the program designed correctly for them will experience beneficial growth regardless of the degree of their previous impairment.

Types of community residential and other programs and their patterns of daily activity vary greatly in definition, in staffing patterns, and quality of care. Among the crucial factors are the location of facilities and community support. There is a great deal of concern because community facilities like foster homes, group homes, and board and care homes must deal with individuals who have a variety of chronic disorders ranging from mental illness to the disorders of aging to mental retardation. Community opposition often arises from fears that property values will be lowered and neighborhoods disrupted. Those living close to facilities are sometimes less hospitable than those who live farther away.

Nonetheless, there has been great progress on this issue. Urban settings often provide more specialized services and opportunities for activities, including recreation, than do rural communities. There is no evidence, on the other hand, that rural environments necessarily are segregated or isolated or that they limit the involvement of mentally retarded persons in their communities. Obviously an array of community support and training options is needed.

Another important factor is the movement of individuals from one setting to another. It has long been known that moving is stressful for everyone. It may lead to physical illness and depression in "normal" persons, and more so for disabled persons and the elderly. Older people are particularly vulnerable to these stresses, and the mentally retarded have patterns of difficulty identical to those of the elderly. Some moves may be beneficial, but far more important, of course, is the fact that moves must be planned individually and that attention must be given to enabling the person to maintain peer support and friendships established in residential settings. Keeping the family involved is crucial, and to a great extent this has not been given proper attention. Sometimes continued family involvement with mentally retarded adults may be detrimental. This does not mean that family involvement should be discouraged, but that appropriate planning and sensitivity to these factors should be kept in mind.

REFERENCES

Grossman, H. J. (ed.) 1983. *Classification in Mental Retardation*. Washington, DC: American Association in Mental Deficiency.

Landesman-Dwyer, S. 1981. Living in the community. *Am. J. Ment. Defic.* 86: 223-234.

VI
Economic-Political Issues
and the Future
of the Chronically Mentally Ill

19
Economic-Political Issues and the Impact of Chronic Mental Illness

BERTRAMS S. BROWN

In the United States, the number of institutionalized mental patients rose for a century until it reached 557,000 in 1957, when the situation turned around and the number declined to 150,000 patients in institutions. Everyone is familiar with these figures. We know about the use of psychotropic drugs that started at about that time, before the community mental health center movement. If things had continued as they had for a century, we would now have 1.3 million patients in mental institutions. Where are those people right now? About one third of them are walking the streets of the country, a third are in nursing homes, and a third were in nursing homes or state hospitals. That is the story of more than one million people for the last 20 years.

Let's look at another country. Nobody knows how many people were in the mental hospitals of Japan after World War II but the number was something like 80,000. As of 1980, it was 350,000. It's easy to think about Japan because it has half our population, about 110 million people compared to our 220 million. How does a country half the size of ours have fourfold per capita institutionalization? In a class I taught at the University of Texas, we tried to analyze this dramatic phenomenon, especially in view of the fact that the two countries are similar in gross national product, per capita income, and all those other factors, and my purpose here is to ask these questions.

The answers are complex. They have to do with culture, with the use of inpatient versus outpatient care, with shame and family relationships, but they also have to do with the fact that 90 percent of the hospitals in Japan are private, owned by physicians, while ten percent are state- and government-owned. Any doctor worth his salt acquires a hospital with a few hundred beds. With national health insurance in place, the government covers the cost, which is why my liberal friends never understand why I am not quite in favor of national health insurance, much as they would like me to be. If you have unlimited hospital coverage, this is what happens. I have been a consultant to the Japanese govern-ment for several years, and we have been trying to figure out what to do about a crisis that is bankrupting their treasury. If we had a million or two million people in our state institutions, think about what would be going on here, and you have the feeling for what's going on in Japan.

The case example is interesting, but it is only a way of illustrating that econ-omics, politics, and culture decide whether the patients are in the state hospital or the nursing home or on the street. Those are the driving dynamics, more so than, or not totally excluding, pharmacology and psychotherapy. Mine is the econ-omic and political perspective of the psychiatrist who has been through a four-year training tour in policy analysis. After directing the National Institute of Mental Health, I spent two years at the Woodrow Wilson International Center where I worked on such issues as the relationship of national policies of different countries to health care. I spent a year at the Rand Corporation in Santa Monica, working on refugee and immigration policy, the relationship of illegal aliens and Mexican Americans and the relationship of oil commerce with Mexico to whether or not we extend health care and other benefits when Mexicans cross our border. More recently I have held the Robert Lee Sutherland Chair in Mental Health and Social Policy at the University of Texas.

I shall turn the telescope around to ask, What does the case study of the chronically mentally ill teach us about the political and economic dynamics of our country? It is a reverse twist. The purpose is not to expand understanding of political science and historical analysis, but to turn the telescope around so that we may ask more knowledgeably what we can do about the political and econ-omic dynamics of our country that will help us to do a better job for the chroni-cally mentally ill, wherever we may be working. If I could redo the title that I have of being a political psychiatrist, I would like to be known as a political-economic psychiatrist.

The economics of treatment of the chronically mentally ill are a clear lens on the never-ending debate about which level of government is responsible for meeting the needs of the citizenry, especially when problems are complex; which level of government is responsible for coordinating and integrating resources. First one has to look at how those resources, which are dollars and people, are allocated at the federal, state, and local levels. The process is a political and economic one. We constantly move between an Adam Smith free market, free trade, social Darwinism point of view and the other, that of a centrally led econ-omy, the social welfare, socialist, or communist perspective.

Oversimplified, the more control the political structure has over the total of available resources, the better the complex problems of the chronically mentally ill will fare, as in Scandinavia and the Soviet Union. Our political pluralism has as its price the inability to create government structures that can deal effectively with problems like those of the chronically mentally ill. From this perspective, one can trace the direct impact of the recent changes in our federal, local, and state relationships subsequent to the election of President Reagan. The Budget and Reconciliation Act, passed by the Congress during the Reagan administration's first year, was the most far-reaching legislation since Roosevelt's New Deal laws in the 1930s. It abolished most categorical programs. It reduced the total contribution of the federal government to human services and established new mechanisms, like the block grant.

A second perspective on the case of the chronically mentally ill is how it helps us to understand the political, economic, and professional dynamics of the human services sector, the nondefense sector of our country. The economics of care for the chronically mentally ill illuminate the relationship between the broad field called human services and the more focused field of definable psychiatric illness. Of our gross national product, 9.4 percent is spent on health, 12 percent on education, 10 percent on income transfers and social security. If you add up everything called human services, the total is about a third of the gross national product, one trillion dollars. You have to start thinking in the trillions.

The chronic mental illness component of this is small but complicated, and I would like to describe a vertical flow of this domain. The one-trillion figure includes education, health, welfare. Health costs are about $300 billion now, mental health $30 billion, defined psychiatrist illness, such as schizophrenia, $3 billion, and chronic mental illness $300 million. I oversimplified the numbers. But as we move down the continuum of increasing focus, we pass through the human-services equivalent of a sound barrier, a sort of U-curve. At one end of the U-curve, it is hard to coordinate the billions and trillions that made up the old Department of Health, Education, and Welfare. And that is why we are constantly changing. HEW is now HHS, the Department of Health and Human Services, with the Department of Education separate. The domain keeps splitting, although the department's old name is fixed in stone on the front steps of the building. The names never lasted more than 15 years.

On the other hand, for specific problems like those of the chronically mentally ill, we need all those services—housing, education, vocation. They are very difficult to coordinate, so that the problem is small in dollars but hard to manage, similar to the trillion-dollar problems on the other side of that curve.

Our perspective permits us to think about the meaning of the recent (1982) Congressional election. One major issue was to move responsibility for health care for the poor, Medicaid, from the states to the federal government, and to move all welfare costs back to the states. That momentum was stalemated by the 1982 election, so that the states remain in charge of health care for the indigent. In that sense, the problems of the chronically mentally ill remain deep in the heart of Texas for solution rather than having been brought up to Washington.

The issue of the balance of powers is fundamental to our political and economic structures. How responsible is that federal, state, and local level—with, say, Austin as the capital, El Paso as a local community, and Washington? Our constitutional structure is based on the psychological wisdom of our founding fathers who understood the importance, not of basic trust, but of basic mistrust. They knew that power corrupts and absolute power corrupts absolutely, and they established a tripartite domain—executive, legislative, and judicial—the famous separation of powers, so that no one institution, no one individual, including the president, would have too much power. They were shrewd fellows back then, and their intentions are well understood.

Less well known is that federal, state, and local separation has played an equally important role in the development of the United States. To make this point more concrete: the acme of Dorothea Dix's efforts in the 1830s and 40s to establish the state institutions was her landmark achievement of having the Congress pass a land grant act to give money for building and supporting state hospitals. In 1853 President Franklin Pierce vetoed the legislation. In those days, the mentally ill were the chronically mentally ill. And President Pierce's language is incredible for 1853: "If the federal government takes on responsibility for this unfortunate group, the insane, where will it stop? It may go to unwise and unconstitutional extremes if the federal government be concerned with the sick and the poor, clearly the domain of the states."

Sharp and clear a century ago, the argument remains unchanged. Who is to be responsible for the sick and the poor—the state or the federal government? From this perspective, the issue of Medicaid, the financial responsibility for the medically needy, the sick, the poor, is alive and unresolved and expensive. The balance of power between federal, state, and local domains, and the issue of coordination are interesting, broad concepts, but let us focus on responsibility for the chronically mentally ill as it moves between these different domains.

A major policy feature of the now defunct Community Mental Health Systems Act was its focus on the underserved, particularly the chronically mentally ill. This was the main point of the President's Commission on Mental Health, Rosalynn Carter's effort. The Community Mental Health Systems Act, the climax of 20 years of community health legislation, disappeared entirely with the Budget Reconciliation Act. That's how profound the change was a year and a half ago. Where did that policy emphasis go? It could have disappeared because the community mental health responsibility moved to the states along with the new mechanism of block grants. Now the states can decide their own priorities: they can spend more for prevention, or for the aged, or for children, or for the chronically mentally ill. In implementing policies and procedures for the block grant, we have the mixture of economic resource allocation and a clear new site of setting priorities.

What's happened? Several states, Florida, for example, have clearly decided to set a priority for the chronically mentally ill. But how does this state-set policy for the chronically mentally ill play in Peoria? Or in Houston? Or in Jacksonville? Not so well! It's not that anybody will admit to being against taking decent care of the chronically mentally ill, but the hard-earned prerogative of priority-setting has been taken away from the city and community and their boards. The essence of local community participation and priority-setting is threatened. This is the basic meaning of block grants. In absolute economic size the block grant is small: a few million dollars or tens of millions for human services in relationship to the total state spending for health, education, and welfare, but in policy and priority and power it is large. The block-grant chain is a big one. In essence, it permits the state-level authority to strengthen itself vis à vis its local communities. Austin can tell Austin's community health center what to do through the block grant mechanism. This is the big shift.

The tension, as it is actually building in many states, centers clearly on exactly this patient population, the chronically mentally ill. States are setting priorities to urge or force local clinics, centers, and providers to care for the chronically ill, to give such services as aftercare, to cooperate with the state hospitals. This runs counter to many of the acute, life-problem, social-problem, prevention, and education emphases of the community. In part, the state emphasis on the chronically and seriously mentally ill is the result of the continuing momentum of deinstitutionalization. The state is saying to the local folks, You'd better take care of these patients we are sending back to you.

This also relates to the state's historical responsibility to the mentally ill patient population. The dynamics of the federal-state tension I described earlier are mirrored at the state level by state-local tensions, especially in state-city relationships. This is a particularly cogent issue for the chronically mentally ill. It is unclear how many of the "street people" are chronically mentally ill, probably the majority. And how many have personality disorders, alcoholism, and other forms of mental disturbance? The pressing issue is which level of government shall protect, feed, and house these people, and the burden is on the city-county governments.

The lack of either willingness or resources to deal with this problem of most cities across our country highlights the moral and economic role of the nongovernmental structures of our society, particularly the voluntary organizations like the Salvation Army and the churches. In Austin recently, two church groups opened or sponsored soup kitchens for transients and other impoverished people. The crisis is such that the street-people issue is forcing a reconsideration of the role of the churches, the volunteer sector. It's not surprising when you remember that only a century ago it was the churches and voluntary sector that provided all services to the poor, before the state institutions and the community sector came into being.

Looking at the problems of the chronically mentally ill shows us the dilemma of human-service coordination and integration. One specific issue that illustrates this is housing. Is community housing for the mentally ill a mental health responsibility? Is it a responsibility of the city, the county, the state, or the federal government? Mental health people are not trained to deal with housing; all they know is large-scale congregate housing, known as state hospitals. Why only a few hundred halfway houses have been developed across the country is not clear. We are familiar with problems of zoning and the use of single-room hotels. We can get on our platforms and shout about the need for housing the chronically mentally ill, but who is responsible for getting that housing? An equally interesting case can be made for vocation and education: Who is responsible for educating the mentally ill, for their vocational training, their job placement?

What does all this lead to? The two most important documents on public policy concerning the chronically mentally ill are the statement by the American Psychiatric Association and the book edited by John Talbott, *The Chronic Mental Patient* (see also Talbott, this volume). The book is the best compendium of studies of these issues. The message is, "We need a single point of authority and coordination. It's a mess. There's no place you can go to for these many needs." The economic and political issues are the major ones that need understanding. What is clear also is that, while the mental health field is at the tail end of a 20-year period of deinstitutionalization, other fields such as the criminal justice system are just beginning to institutionalize and are running into interesting and difficult problems—issues of whom to confine and how institutionalization takes place.

Our focus is on the chronic schizophrenic, the young adult mentally ill person, the brain-damaged patient, the organically impaired, the person with a character disorder. How many are there? What's the size and scope of the problem? Goldman, Gattozzi, and Taube's recent paper (Defining and counting the mentally ill, *Hospital and Community Psychiatry* 32:21-27, 1981; see also Goldman, this volume) reviews the issue in detail. Using a definition by the President's Commission on Mental Health and taking into account diagnosis, disability, and duration of illness, institutional and community settings in which the chronically mentally ill are found, and using prevalence data from a variety of sources, they arrived at a national estimate of 1.7 to 2.4 million chronically mentally ill, with 900,000 in institutions. The President's Commission decided that the chronically mentally ill are those who would be in state institutions if state mental health systems had continued to grow and custodial kinds of care were available to the seriously and chronically mentally ill. The commissioners arrived at their operational definitions and numbers very pragmatically. John Talbott (see Chapter 1, this volume) estimates two to four million. Leona Bachrach estimates one to two million, based on the population of state institutions. Taking all these estimates, averaging them and using an intuitive factor, I would say the number is three million chronically mentally ill. When I was director of the National Institute of Mental Health, I could have announced that figure, and it would have become the official number. But the number is somewhere between one and three million chronically mentally ill persons.

The economics are interesting. It costs $10,000 for a person to live in the community. I picked the figure 10 because it's easy—you can decide if you can live on $5,000 or $15,000, but $10,000 per person is reasonable. Ten thousand times three million: suddenly we are dealing with who is going to pay for $30 billion worth of community living. Or 900,000 institutions. The cheapest place now costs $100 a day, a good place $300 a day, so it's at least $3,000 a month. Calculating how much it costs to keep one million people in different kinds of institutions, you suddenly realize that you are dealing with $25 billion of institutional costs. Even at $50 a day, we are talking about $10 billion to care for a million chronically mentally ill people. The arithmetic is very powerful when you start to multiply by numbers we are all familiar with. Is it cheaper or more expensive to care for the chronically mentally ill in the hospital or in the community? These are people who do not get better, and they are out in the community needing drugs and social work follow-up. And is it cheaper? There is no real saving in the community. It may be better for dignity, self-worth, or some institutional dynamics, but it is not clear that caring for most of the chronically mentally ill in the community is cheaper.

The heart of the matter—the reason for the poor care of the chronically mentally ill—is not clinical but economic and political, the political being a subsystem of the definition of economic. The most sensible and clearest point of view is expressed by Talbott who, after noting chronically discoordinated care for the chronically mentally ill, states: "There is no single system of care. Instead, there is a nonsystem which cries out for a single point of responsibility and authority for the chronic mental patient." Why doesn't this happen? It doesn't because there is no obvious way it can happen given the nature of our dispersed political authority in our current working or nonworking democracy. It doesn't happen in the criminal justice system or in the educational system. In practice, coordination of services becomes the overwhelming responsibility of the consumer, the patient, and his or her family. And yet you cannot be a consumer when you are chronically mentally ill. You cannot coordinate your own care, when the nature of your illness is chronic schizophrenia, alcoholism, or brain disease.

Things are awful. But, to quote Winston Churchill: "This democracy is awful, until you consider the alternatives." I spent a lot of time in the Soviet Union, where there's a clear point of responsibility and authority for the care of the mentally ill. And in a serious sense, one way to deal with the economic and political question is to ask whether we want a communist, totalitarian, or socialist regime so that we can deal with this problem.

In China they have made a policy: The chronically mentally ill are the responsibility of the family. One problem in China is that they now have a public policy of allowing only one child per family. Within 20 years they will run out of excess relatives to care for the chronically mentally ill in the home. The serious policy planners anticipate this as a real-life public health problem. In Scandinavia and Great Britain, closer to our own democracy, where they do have a more "socialist" or "social welfare" scheme and a tighter point of authority, the issue becomes what part of the resources are to be allocated to that single point of authority. In those countries, the problem is that not enough is allocated. So when you resolve the authority issue, you see there are two sides to the coin. A single point of authority and adequate resources are needed to do the job well.

Now we, as mental health professionals, psychiatrists, and psychologists, have a fundamental dilemma in trying to meet the needs of the chronically mentally ill. In my own profession, psychiatry, we must attend directly to complex, controversial, big-league economic and political issues. We are doubly handicapped in that psychiatry, as it remedicalizes, seems either to depoliticize itself in the broad sense or to become a more self-centered political interest group in a narrow sense. There are a few psychiatrists who, like me, believe that the social and political realm is critical to good mental health care and that we must not become narrow, medical-model doctors who do not deal with the other professions nor with political and economic issues.

As to economic issues concerning the chronically mentally ill, the problem is one of Yin and Yang, two sides of the same coin. We must define, not only the needs of the chronically mentally ill, but the kind of government structure we need to implement those programs. That elusive single point of authority cannot be self-declared but must come about from our political and economic processes.

I shall conclude with one mind-boggling story about the chronically mentally ill and their relationship to government. In 1980-81, because of tension between Cuba and the United States, a wave of 125,000 Cubans landed in Florida from large ships and fishing boats. Early in this episode, I had heard that patients I had seen in the national mental hospital in Havana only three years before had been taken out of their hospital wards, put on boats and dumped, literally, on our shores. I quickly tried to see what I could do about this, where I could place the chronically mentally ill people who arrived here. I had a sensible thought: Puerto Rico—warm, Spanish-speaking. I ran into a federal-state problem; there was an election going on there and President Carter was not popular. The governors of Puerto Rico and Florida were running for election; neither wanted the federal government to dump the problem on their shores. The Cuban refugees who were chronically mentally ill ended up behind bars and barbed wire at St. Elizabeths Hospital in Washington. Nobody wanted them. It is a terrible problem that has not been resolved, and it is a major example of how governments use the chronically mentally ill in fighting ideological battles. The issue of how to deal with the chronically mentally ill is a clinical and a political issue.

20
The Future of the Chronically Mentally Ill

GARY E. MILLER

Predicting the future is always a risky business. Our historical lack of success in adequately serving the chronically mentally ill, coupled with the fact that we are in an era of political and financial uncertainty, makes it especially difficult to speculate about the fate of the approximately two million Americans (Goldman et al., 1981) who suffer from chronic mental illness.

My suggestions as to what the future may hold for this population derive of necessity from observations of how well the chronically mentally ill are faring today as a result of our past efforts, and of emerging trends and new developments that are currently evident.

At first glance there is reason to be discouraged, for many of the signs suggest that, despite all of our recent talking and writing about the chronically mentally ill, most of the people who are the subject of these communications continue to experience the lack of care and poor living conditions discussed in essays addressing the seamy side of the phenomenon known as deinstitutionalization (Lamb, 1979a; Lamb and Goertzel, 1971; Task Panel Report, 1978). Gaps in residential, vocational, and treatment services are everywhere evident. The infamous lack of coordination among the many federal, state, and local agencies potentially serving the chronically mentally ill continues as though the 1977 General Accounting Office (GAO) report on this subject (Returning the Mentally Disabled to the Community, 1977) had not been written. There is no evidence that the stigma of mental illness has abated. Major breakthroughs in treatment technology have not surfaced yet. There are no large sums of new dollars waiting to be spent on the chronically mentally ill. And the products of the national mandate to serve this population of the years 1977-1980—the GAO report on deinstitutionalization (1977), the report of the President's Commission on Mental Health (1978), the Mental Health Systems Act (1980), and the draft document titled *Toward a National Plan for the Chronically Mentally Ill* (1980)—have all either fallen on deaf ears, by the wayside, or through the cracks between a Democratic and Republican administration.

All of that having been said, I hold a moderately optimistic view of what the future may hold for the chronically mentally ill. I begin by assuming that the future of the chronic patient will be determined by how well we understand the patient's needs, how well we understand the lessons of the past, and how well we put our knowledge to work in shaping the delivery system of the future. Accordingly, I have organized this essay into four subject areas—what the chronically mentally ill need, why we have failed in the past, portents of the future that justify a guarded optimism, and a consideration of some additional more problematic variables that could make the fate of the chronic patient go either way.

WHAT THE CHRONICALLY MENTALLY ILL NEED

We are not ignorant of what chronic patients need nor of the programs that can meet these needs. Many experimental community treatment programs succeeded in greatly reducing the hospital use by the chronically mentally ill (Polak and Kirby, 1976; Test and Stein, 1977, 1978a and b; Bené-Kociemba et al., 1979; Stein and Test, 1981), although some backup inpatient capacity seems generally to be necessary (Bachrach, 1981). A recent evaluation of the Texas Community Support Program, for example, demonstrated a 19-percent one-year recidivism rate for patients treated in the program as compared to 86 percent for control subjects (Norwood and Mason, 1982). Although aggregate recidivism rates are an important measure of the effectiveness of community programs (Anthony et al., 1978; Miller, 1981; Craig and Kline, 1982), they do not, of course, tell the whole story. Satisfaction of consumers with services received, employment figures, clinical evaluations, evaluations by relatives or neutral parties, and several kinds of functional assessment scales also have been used to measure the outcome of programs serving the chronically mentally ill.

Recent overviews of models of community treatment of this population (Test and Stein, 1978a; Braun et al., 1981; Bachrach, 1982a) point to limitations in experimental design, methodology, and cross-study comparability of evaluations of these programs. If community support programs for chronic patients were a pill, the Food and Drug Administration probably would require a good deal of additional research to verify its effectiveness before the pill could be marketed. We need measures that are more sensitive to the interplay of various subjective and objective factors, reflecting not only the patient's behavior and performance, but also the patient's quality of life (Lehman et al., 1982).

Critical reviewers of currently available evaluation research on model programs agree that certain types of community programs cannot only reduce dramatically the admissions of chronic patients to hospitals but also improve their social performance and productivity. Even the guarded and skeptical review by Braun and associates (1981) concludes that "a qualified affirmative response to the question of feasibility of deinstitutionalization can be given with regard to programs of community care that are alternatives to hospital admission and to programs for short-term care or day-care offered as substitutes for conventional hospitalization."

Leona Bachrach (1981) took the additional step of identifying eight operating principles she found to be common to programs that seem successful in helping the chronically mentally ill. Although she cautions against attempting to replicate the program models *per se*, Bachrach suggests that the principles may be transplantable. Thus, in spite of the limitations of current research and evaluation studies of programs serving the chronically mentally ill, we can draw some general conclusions about what these patients need.

Chronic mental patients need, first of all, psychiatric treatment, mainly carefully monitored and skillfully regulated administration of neuroleptic medications that have been demonstrated to reduce the frequency of relapses and rehospitalization in schizophrenia (Anthony et al., 1978; Craig and Kline, 1982; Hansell, 1981; Hogarty and Ulrich, 1977; Strauss and Carpenter, 1977). Some observers have suggested, in fact, that careful attention to patients' needs for neuroleptic medications may have been the principal determinant of the success of certain model community support programs (Braun et al., 1981; Klein, 1980).

Low-dosage maintenance neuroleptic medication, combined with temporary administration of high dosages during acute psychotic episodes, is believed generally to be effective for most schizophrenic patients (Hansell, 1981), although not all patients seem to need or benefit from medication (Buckley, 1982). Neuroleptic medications may be administered intermittently to selected patients to reduce the incidence of dyskinesias, dysphorias, and other undesirable side effects, provided each patient's condition is monitored carefully (Herz et al., 1982). Patients, families, and clinicians, alert to the early nonpsychotic signs of relapse described by Herz and Melville (1980), can prevent reemergence of psychotic breaks by timely increases in the dosage of neuroleptic medications.

Tardive dyskinesia is still an unsolved problem that plagues the drug treatment of chronic mental illness. Our best strategy is to monitor patients carefully for early signs of dyskinesia and hope that new and promising avenues of research will lead to effective ways of controlling the problem (Bergen and Rexroth, 1980).

Schizophrenia is not the only major disorder of the chronically mentally ill. Some depressed patients may respond to tricyclic or other antidepressants; those with bipolar or other cyclical affective or schizoaffective disorders may be good candidates for maintenance with lithium carbonate (Carroll, 1979).

In addition to medication management, a variety of other program elements have been identified by Bachrach (1981), Test and Stein (1978a) and Turner and Shifron (1979) as important to the satisfactory adjustment of chronic mental patients in the community. These include individualized residential living environments, basic health care, adequate finances, transportation, training in skills necessary for community living, programs directed toward improvement of vocational and employment skills, and a group of other people, that is, a "social network" (Greenblatt et al., 1982) capable of meeting the patient's emotional needs in good times and bad.

The chronic mental patient also needs a case manager, an individual or a team who can be the patient's contact to the formal and informal service system indefinitely—for the patient's disability or risk of disability is of indefinite duration (Hansell, 1978). The case manager's task is to orchestrate the programs, services, and resources each individual needs, changing the mix as the patient's needs change. As the focus of continuity, coordination, and accountability for the needs of the individual patient, the case manager is a vital element of the service system (Anthony et al., 1978; Granet and Talbott, 1978; Lourie, 1978; Sullivan, 1981; Curry, 1981; Gerhard et al., 1981; Miller, G. E., 1982).

The special difficulties presented by the so-called "new" young adult chronic population (Caton, 1981; Bachrach, 1982b; Pepper et al., 1982) will, more than ever, require the services of a case manager. These young people who, according to Bert Pepper and colleagues (1982), are the "bane and despair" of the working lives of caregivers, do not use existing services appropriately, and they could benefit from the personal attention and flexible programming a case management system can provide. John Talbott (1981) referred to case management systems as the "human glue" necessary to bind together the disparate program elements chronic patients need. For the young chronically ill person to be served adequately, copious quantities of this human glue will be necessary.

One thing the chronic mental patient does not need is to live with relatives or other people with whom he or she has a stressful relationship. Intrafamilial stress is a recognized cause of relapse and rehospitalization of chronic mental patients (Craig and Kline, 1982; Vaughn and Leff, 1976; Falloon et al., 1982) even when they are maintained on an otherwise adequate level of long-acting neuroleptic medication (Hogarty et al., 1973). For such patients, placement with nonrelatives may be an appropriate solution. Another option that has been shown to reduce significantly the frequency of relapses is direct therapeutic intervention with the patient's family (Falloon et al., 1982; Boyd et al., 1981).

An important question, the answer to which has both programmatic and economic implications, is whether we should teach community survival skills in the community itself or in the hospital. The demonstrated feasibility of *in situ* community training in social and other adaptive skills of severely disabled, often overtly psychotic, patients, and the difficulty such patients have in transferring skills acquired in hospital environments to those in which they will reside leads to the conclusion that the community is the proper locus for such training and that it is unwise and uneconomical to attempt extensive social-skills training in mental hospitals (Test and Stein, 1978a; Wallace et al., 1980).

So, in a general way, we know what the chronically mentally ill—or at least many chronically mentally ill persons—need. Our knowledge is far from comprehensive but it is sufficient for us to do a good deal more than is now being done.

Stated another way, knowing the needs of the chronically mentally ill is not sufficient to accomplish the task of meeting them. There have been times in the past when the mental health field has seemed to possess not only the knowledge, but the commitment and the resources to optimize the care and rehabilitation of the chronic patient. It will be useful, therefore, to review our past failures before looking to the future.

WHY HAVE WE FAILED IN THE PAST?

Chronic mental illness and the many accompanying problems did not suddenly appear on the scene in the early 1970s. Those years, of course, marked the beginning of an era characterized by media exposés of the egregious living conditions of ex-state hospital patients (Lamb and Goertzel, 1971; Lamb, 1979b) and by a series of official publications and gatherings (*Returning the Mentally Disabled to the Community*, 1977; *Report to the President*, 1978; Mental Health Systems Act, 1980; *Toward a National Plan for the Chronically Mentally Ill*, 1980; *The Chronic Mental Patient*, 1978a and b) dealing with the problem. The continuing backlash to deinstitutionalization (Talbott, 1978) is, however, but the most recent phase in the chronic mental patient's odyssey of despair, deprivation, and discrimination.

The sorry living conditions in our nation's state hospitals, reported as early as 1948 by Albert Deutsch in *The Shame of the States*, was the real driving force behind the community mental health movement and deinstitutionalization. A growing awareness during the 1950s and 1960s of the potentially deleterious effect of an institutional environment on the mentally ill (Stanton and Schwartz, 1954; Goffman, 1964), coupled with an appreciation of the effectiveness of the new drugs, created the impetus for federal action. A Joint Commission on Mental Illness and Health was appointed in 1955 and reported to the Congress in 1961. The report, *Action for Mental Health*, recommended a moratorium on construction of large state hospitals, establishment of a large network of community clinics which, together with general hospital psychiatric units, would provide continuing treatment and rehabilitation to the chronically mentally ill, moving those who could be removed from the hospitals and diverting new admissions. The existing state hospitals were intended to shrink in size and carry on specialized functions not feasible in local settings. Indeed, these recommendations are similar to those of John Talbott in his 1978 book on the state hospital, *The Death of the Asylum*.

The federal legislation that initiated the era of community mental health centers (CMHC), Public Law 88-164 (Community Mental Health Centers Construction Act, 1963), while presumably intended to address the needs of the chronically mentally ill in and out of state hospitals, somehow missed the target. Somewhere along the way, the new community centers became side-tracked; although they provided needed and worthwhile services in hundreds of American communities, the needs of the original target population were not adequately addressed (Lamb and Goertzel, 1971; Gardener, 1977; Hogarty, 1971; Kirk and Therrien, 1975; Langsley, 1980).

This failure of the community mental health movement to become integrated fully into the concurrent deinstitutionalization movement by concentrating its efforts on the high-risk population has been attributed to a number of factors. Zusman and Lamb (1977) contended that the failure was not of community mental health *per se*, "but rather a failure to focus on the basic mission of community mental health." Instead of using then-existing models of successful community treatment and rehabilitation of the chronically ill, like that of Pasamanick and his colleagues (1967), Zusman and Lamb argued that "community mental health has tended to focus on treating the 'healthy but unhappy.' "

J. Frank James (1980) recently attributed at least some of the problems to the original federal concept of five basic services for community centers which, in his view, "demonstrated a naiveté seen only in those who are far distant from clinical realities."

Elaine Cumming made a similar observation in 1968 when the CMHC movement was in an early stage of development. With respect to the five-basic-services model, Cumming asked, "Was this new method of delivery designed for the disorders of the chronically ill, in the first place, or was it designed to suit the needs of the people who deliver the care?" Anticipating recent criticism of the alleged failure of community centers to serve the truly mentally ill (Miller, 1981; Langsley, 1980; Zusman and Lamb, 1977; Sharfstein, 1978), Cumming asked "whether the new mental health centers will . . . modify their treatment to suit the patient or, as in the past, succumb to the temptation of selecting the amenable patients to suit the preferred treatment, thereby competing with various other regulative agents, doctors, clergymen and social workers, all of whom also want the same amenable patient."

The reduction of psychiatric leadership and participation in community mental health centers (Zusman and Lamb, 1977; Fink and Weinstein, 1979; Fink, 1975; Ribner, 1980; Winslow, 1979; Stern and Hoover, 1980; Berlin et al., 1981), about which I shall say more later, is clearly another factor since good medical care and medication supervision are essential needs of the chronically mentally ill.

Closely linked to the reduction of psychiatrists' participation in the centers is the philosophical model on which they operate. Steven Sharfstein (1978), noting the relative decline from 1970 to 1975 in the proportion of psychiatric and nursing full-time staff members relative to that of psychologists and social workers, suggested that these shifts in the composition of center personnel support the notion "that the CMHC program is mutating from a clinical-medical program toward a social program." This issue will be mentioned later as a "problematic variable" with the potential of having a significant impact on the future of the chronically mentally ill.

Cumming (1968) suggested that imprecise use of such terms as "community" and "comprehensive" may have led to practices that resulted in a gradual shift of emphasis from the care of the severely disabled to other populations and other activities.

According to Lamb and Zusman (1979), unproved theories of the causation of major mental illnesses have diverted staff time and energy from treating the chronically mentally ill to activities presumably directed toward primary prevention of their disorders. "Prevention's appeal must be resisted by mental health professionals," these authors contend, "lest it become a glamorous rationalization for avoiding treatment of difficult mentally ill persons, such as chronic psychotic, alcoholic, and addicted patients."

Another factor that may have played a role in the current plight of the chronically mentally ill is the string of books by Thomas Szasz which appeared regularly throughout the years the community mental health movement was developing. These writings and those of like-minded authors became widely read, not only by lawyers and members of the general public but also by mental health professionals. For those who were seduced by Szasz's powerful style and deceptive chains of pseudologic, there would be little appeal in serving severely disabled persons because such persons were viewed as needing, above all, freedom from caregivers and, indeed, were not mentally ill, but only so labeled by professionals laboring under the myth of mental illness (Szasz, 1961).

In sum, we don't really know how a movement intended to provide active community treatment for chronically mentally ill people in lieu of hospital care wound up as it has with thousands of patients receiving inadequate care, living in substandard community environments or repeatedly swinging through the revolving doors of state institutions. Doubtless some or all the factors I have discussed played a role. Perhaps our best strategy is to assume the operation of Murphy's Law: If something can go wrong, it will. It may be that our staying on course with respect to the chronically mentally ill will be a function of our vigilance and single-mindedness as well as our unblinking assessment of our performance in the light of the goals we set for ourselves.

I indicated at the beginning of this essay that I am moderately optimistic about the future of the chronically mentally ill. I should like to review now several recent developments which suggest to me that we may be on the verge of success in our effort to improve the lot of these individuals.

PORTENTS OF THE FUTURE

The Role of State Government

The recent dissolution of the mental health services function of the National Institute of Mental Health (NIMH) and the phasing of CMHC project grants into state-administered block grants have resulted in an enhanced role of state mental health agencies as well as local governments in shaping the delivery of services by community mental health centers. As a result we already are seeing greater diversity in service delivery models at the local level. Rather than adhering to a fixed model such as that of five or twelve basic services, the centers are being conceptualized and organized in accord with state and local priorities and preferences as well as available funds.

The end point of this evolution is impossible to discern. There is, however, a strong indication that states are vitally interested in programs for the chronically mentally ill.

This development is the result in large measure of a federal effort begun in 1977. To the credit of NIMH, the relatively low-budget Community Support Program (CSP) (Turner and Shifron, 1979; Turner and TenHoor, 1978), directed the attention of state mental health agencies and community mental health centers to the needs of the chronically mentally ill. This led to many of the model programs on which our future efforts will be based. Although the states certainly had not ignored this population—the traditional responsibility of state government—federal leadership from the CSP program reinforced and, to some extent, legitimized the efforts of the states.

In Texas and several other states, state legislatures have amended their mental health statutes in recent years to place increasing emphasis on services to the chronically and severely disabled. Texas Senate Bill 791, enacted in 1981, requires, for example, that "the first priority for the use of grants-in-aid to be expended for mental health services [by community mental health-mental retardation centers] shall be for services directed to those individuals who are at significant risk of placement in a state facility." The act has teeth: "The department shall develop standards to enforce this policy and may withhold grants-in-aid from any center not found to be in compliance with these standards."

In New Hampshire, the state in which I previously served as state mental health director, the legislature enacted similar legislation in its 1981 session. The amendment to the state community mental health services act reads in part: "Priority emphasis shall be placed on treatment and rehabilitative services for severely mentally disabled persons who are former patients of New Hampshire [State] Hospital and other such psychiatric institutions, and other such severely disabled persons at risk of being so institutionalized. Such priority emphasis shall mean that no funds shall be allocated or expended for any other purpose unless minimum program standards for the severely mentally disabled have been fulfilled" (New Hampshire Code, 1981).

These legislative enactments and other such mechanisms identified by the Strategic Planning Office of the Texas Department of Mental Health and Mental Retardation in a recent survey of other states suggest that state governments, at the level of their legislatures, their governors, and their commissioners of mental health, will continue to place special emphasis on the chronically mentally ill.

A Higher Status for the Chronic Mental Patient

The alleged preference of community program staffs for less severely disabled clients who are more attractive, articulate, better off financially, and possibly better candidates for psychotherapy has been cited by many authors (Lamb and Goertzel, 1971; Miller, 1981; Gardener, 1977; Hogarty, 1971; Kirk and Therrien, 1975; Langsley, 1980; Zusman and Lamb, 1977; Cumming, 1968) as one cause of the drift away from the chronically mentally ill. Although the circumstances certainly vary among community centers, Goldman and colleagues (1980) have observed that, at least with respect to new admissions of patients to the centers, less emphasis is being placed on persons with serious mental disorders.

However we read these reports and these data, their very existence, together with the nationwide attention focused on the chronically mentally ill since about 1977, cannot help but have a beneficial effect on the perceived status of chronic patients and of those who are interested in helping them. While I am not suggesting that chronic mental patients will become the "in" clientele for all mental health service providers, I believe that the high visibility being given these patients, together with other positive signs, indicates that they will be treated better in the future than in the past.

More Realistic Expectations

It seems to me that we are moving from an era of ideology to one of pragmatism. Some of the more extreme views of the 1960s and early 1970s are expressed less frequently today. Community center personnel now rarely claim that they are preventing new cases of mental illness (Lamb and Zusman, 1979). Our "discovery" of the never-hospitalized young chronic patient (Pepper et al., 1982; Lamb and Goertzel, 1972) belies earlier contentions that institutions were the cause of all chronicity (Stanton and Schwartz, 1954; Goffman, 1964). Far from being antithetical to good care as has been alleged in the past, psychiatric inpatient beds are considered by most observers to be an essential element of any realistic delivery system and are required as a backup even for model programs dedicated to avoiding hospitalization at almost any cost (Bachrach, 1981; Kaiser and Townsend, 1981).

We also are more realistic about the prognosis or potential of chronic patients. Observations and studies suggest that the chronically mentally ill are a heterogeneous population that includes subgroups of individuals who do not benefit from even the most intensive rehabilitation effort and may need to remain indefinitely in a highly structured residential program (Strauss and Carpenter, 1977; Auerbach and Pattison, 1976; Lamb, 1981; Morgan and Gray, 1982; Engelhardt et al., 1982; Stephens and Astrup, 1963; Tsuang and Winokur, 1974). Indeed, the post-deinstitutionalization residual chronic hospital population may be made up largely of members of this group (Dowart, 1980).

Even our optimism about the powerful therapeutic effects of neuroleptic drugs is tempered by our knowledge that some schizophrenic patients fail to respond to them (Hansell, 1981). Clinicians have been forced also to accept the unacceptable in the no-win case of the patient whose disorder is controlled successfully by a neuroleptic medication but who develops the signs of tardive dyskinesia (Berger and Rexroth, 1980).

I conclude this rather gloomy section by asserting my belief that optimism, perhaps even idealism, is an important attribute of those working with the chronically mentally ill, and that it is justified by the results obtained in programs that have been studied (Test and Stein, 1978a; Bachrach, 1981). Nevertheless, our recognition that we cannot be successful with every patient to the same degree will give us a more solid grounding in reality as we face the future.

Self-Help

There has been consistent growth over the years in the number of organized groups of consumers who come together to share problems and concerns and to advance their personal and collective causes (Tracey and Gussow, 1976).

The self-help groups include those of chronic mental patients who are capable of benefiting one another through friendship, mutual support, and instruction in social skills (Borck and Aber, 1981). Such groups can be a major ingredient of natural helping networks required for their members' successful adjustment (Greenblatt et al., 1982).

Family members of chronically mentally ill patients also have joined forces and are becoming increasingly vocal advocates of the needs of this patient group (Hatfield, 1981). The newly established Alliance for Mental Recovery is an example of this trend in Texas.

Texas's FAIR (Family and Individual Reliance) program sponsored by the Mental Health Association is a unique mutual-assistance organization that involves patients and their families.

The self-help movement may prove to be a vital force in shaping service delivery to the chronically mentally ill for the remainder of the 1980s and beyond. Durman (1976), commenting on the growth of self-help groups of all kinds, suggests that this growth represents a "mandate for refocusing planning efforts of the next decade from the agency to the helping network; from services which ignore existing 'natural' resources to efforts which encourage and foster the ability of ordinary people, working together, to resolve many of life's difficulties without professional intervention." In Hatfield's view, these groups

> have put a new impetus into the hope for citizens' involvement that was expressed nearly two decades ago in the Community Mental Health Centers Construction Act of 1963. Because consumers are so intimately involved in seeking and selecting services, not to mention paying the bills

and living with the consequences, they will bring a sense of urgency to the whole enterprise not heretofore experienced (1981, p. 6).

The emergence of self-help groups of the chronically mentally ill and their families is a positive development that bodes well for the future of these patients.

Patient Rights

Mentally ill people have constitutional, statutory, and human rights: that message has been driven home since the early 1970s by means of nationwide legal advocacy, a series of lawsuits in the federal courts, and changes in state statutes. Despite the continuing debate over the meaning of such terms as "least restrictive alternative" (Miller, R. D., 1982; Bachrach, 1980) and the right of committed hospital patients to refuse medication (Brooks, 1980; Stone, 1981), I believe that mental health workers in state hospitals and community centers essentially have incorporated the values of the patient rights movement into their attitudes and their practices. Consequently, chronically mentally ill individuals are more likely now than in past years to be treated with respect and as individuals capable of making decisions on their own behalf.

Accountability

In recent years we have seen an increasing emphasis on accountability in mental health programs. It is not surprising that in this era of tightened purse strings, legislators, governors, and the public are requiring that programs spending tax dollars demonstrate that they are effective in helping patients and that the taxpayers are receiving a fair return on their investment. Examples of the "accountability movement" include the designation of priority populations for mental health services by state legislatures, federal initiatives concerned with possibly limiting funding of services to those that have demonstrated effectiveness (Health Services Research, 1978), performance contracting used in the community mental health systems of Texas and other states, and emphasis on outcome measures to determine the performance of programs or entire regional or statewide systems of programs (Wolfe and Schulberg, 1982).

In spite of the myriad technical problems attendant to such efforts (Bachrach, 1982a; Majchrzak and Tash, 1982; Bachrach and Lamb, 1982), state mental health agencies like the Texas Department of Mental Health and Mental Retardation are embarking on the development of comprehensive accountability systems. I regard the accountability movement as another good omen. It may help keep us on track in the future.

These portents suggest that a degree of optimism is justified. There are some other more problematic variables, however, that, depending on their interaction with the more promising developments, could lead to a range of possible futures for the chronically mentally ill, some of them not happy. These variables are money, the role of psychiatry, and leadership.

PROBLEMATIC VARIABLES

Finances

Notwithstanding our good intentions, our commitment to the chronically mentally ill and all of the accountability devices we can construct, absent the money to pay for the care, treatment, and subsistence of chronic patients, our efforts will not take us far in solving their problems. The 1980s clearly will not be a decade of fiscal abundance. It is evident also that the chronically mentally ill are not viewed as the first priority for expenditures of tax dollars, even for the expenditure of human services dollars.

The recently stepped-up eligibility review of recipients of Supplemental Security Income (SSI) and Social Security Disability Income (SSDI), which had the effect of terminating basic financial support to many chronically mentally ill patients, is an example of how vulnerable this population is to cuts in entitlements and other forms of public assistance (Talbott, 1982). The fate of these financial supplements, essential to the survival of thousands of chronic patients in the community, is, at this writing, uncertain.

Although inappropriate nursing home placement is viewed as a part of the de-institutionalization problem (*Returning the Mentally Disabled to the Community*, 1977), such placement is appropriate for many patients. Whether appropriate or not, however, large numbers of patients in nursing homes may be forced to return to state hospitals or the street if the current federal effort to classify private nursing homes as Institutions for Mental Disease (IMD) is successful. Based on unofficial internal agency guidelines for making such determinations, the Health Care Finance Administration of the Department of Health and Human Services has proceeded to declare nursing homes in a number of states ineligible for reimbursement under Title XIX (Medicaid) on the grounds that they are IMDs. Despite a recent setback to this federal campaign by a United States District Court in Minnesota, the future of the community nursing home as an alternative to the state hospital is uncertain (U.S. District Court, 1982).

The future of basic funding of medical services to ambulatory and hospitalized chronically mentally ill patients under Medicaid and Title XVIII (Medicare) is also far from certain (Prevost, 1982).

Funding from state and local governments for mental health services is in question, especially since mental health agencies will face tough competition for scarce funds from other agencies, many of which will be attempting to replace lost federal funds with new state and local dollars.

Technically, the chronically mentally ill now are eligible for low-cost rental housing units under Section 202 of the housing program of the Department of Housing and Urban Development (HUD) (*Mental Health Reports*, 1982). The previous demonstration program for this population and the history of the Section 202 program for the mentally retarded make it clear, however, that from two to five years of time, extensive legal fees, and incredible patience in dealing with a formidable bureaucracy are required for these residential programs to come into existence. Those who have had previous experience in attempting to secure funds for the mentally disabled under the HUD Section 202 program may conclude that it is not worth the trouble.

The Role of Psychiatry

An additional variable, whose future effect is uncertain, is the role psychiatrists will play in public mental health systems, especially community mental health programs from which most of the services to the chronically mentally ill logically should emanate.

Despite the fact that psychiatrists are needed for proper care of the severely and chronically mentally ill in the community (Berlin et al., 1981), their leadership, their numbers, and their active participation in community programs have declined significantly (Winslow, 1979). This may be partly the result of the national shortage of psychiatrists (*ADAMHA News*, 1980), especially in rural areas (Tucker et al., 1981).

Yet a number of commentators have identified abandonment of the medical or clinical treatment model in favor of the social model, and even outright discrimination against psychiatrists by social workers and psychologists as reasons for the psychiatric exodus (Zusman and Lamb, 1977; Fink and Weinstein, 1979; Fink, 1975; Ribner, 1980). The reported tendency of nonmedical community center directors who are now in the majority (Winslow, 1979) to hire their professional brethren in preference to those of other disciplines (Perls et al., 1980) may be a part of the problem.

It is not surprising that psychiatrists are inclined to leave the employ of community centers when they find that they are assigned the care of patients deemed most undesirable by other staff members (Stern and Hoover, 1980), or viewed as a "necessary evil" (Peterson, 1981) and relegated to signing prescriptions and medical records (Winslow, 1979), or deemed to be cost-ineffective because their salaries are higher than those of their nonmedical colleagues (Fink and Weinstein, 1979). Zusman and Lamb (1977) encapsulated the dilemma of the psychiatrist attempting to cope with such working conditions:

> A . . . source of frustration has been the challenge to psychiatry from other disciplines and a feeling that in the area of community mental health the psychiatrist runs a risk of losing his status, his power, and even his high income. It is no wonder then that having ventured forth and tested the water and having found it cold and uninviting, many of us have retreated to more scientific and academic pursuits (p. 889).

The issue of the role of psychiatrists in community mental health centers will be a critical variable in determining the future of the chronically mentally ill. The decline in additions of patients with schizophrenia to the caseload of CMHCs compared to those of patients with less serious disorders (Goldman,

1980) cannot be unrelated to the declining participation of psychiatrists in the centers. I am somewhat encouraged by the new "remedicalization" of psychiatry which may yield better role delineation among professionals working in the centers and perhaps greater respect for the training and potential contribution of the psychiatrist to clinical management of the chronically mentally ill. In the final analysis, however, I must agree with Ribner (1980) who concludes that the future of psychiatrists in CMHCs is "unclear at best and grim at worst."

Before leaving the role of the psychiatrist, it is important to note that state hospitals also have serious problems in attracting and retaining qualified psychiatrists (Knesper, 1978; Talbott, 1979). Although the issues are somewhat different from those in the CMHCs, the problem of the hospitals in recruiting psychiatrists also will affect the future of the chronically mentally ill who are the principal users of state hospital services.

Leadership

An analysis of the factors that may or may not bode well for the future of the chronic mental patient can easily overlook one of the most important determinants—the people who will lead the nation's state mental health agencies, community mental health centers, and state hospitals. The theme of absent or misdirected leadership underlies descriptions of our past failures to address properly the needs of the chronically mentally ill (Gardener, 1977; Hogarty, 1971; Langsley, 1980).

All our good intentions and rhetoric about what we must do to serve these patients will come to naught unless those of the editorial "we" who have the power and influence to shape the future exercise that power and influence on behalf of these patients and the programs they need. The importance of leadership was set forth succinctly by Morgan and Connery (1973) in their analysis of the administration of public mental health programs. According to these authors,

> the degree to which mental health administrators understand and are able to manipulate the governmental/political environment within which they must operate will largely determine both the nature and quality of the programs they manage (p. 241).

Mental health administrators lead an exciting but highly stressful professional life. Commenting in his 1978 book, *Psychopolitics*, on his six years' experience as commissioner of the Massachusetts Department of Mental Health, Milton Greenblatt recalls the

> many constraints, rules, regulations and complications of a sticky system, the personal and professional vulnerability at all times; the vast potential for criticism from patients, families, staff, legislators and citizen groups; the extraordinary demands made on mental and physical energy [and] the relatively brief tenure and the lack of security (p. 9).

On the positive side, Greenblatt observes that the commissioner's task is

> exciting and even exhilarating at times—at least until the veneer of glory
> fades into a smog of day-to-day trials. There are often marvelous oppor-
> tunities to do good on a grand scale—for patients and families and for the
> political organization one serves, which, if it is functioning effectively,
> may someday succeed in raising the individual above the tangles of bureau-
> cracy (pp. 9-10).

This description of the challenges and opportunities as well as the pressures
and frustrations of the state commissioner is applicable to mental health administrators at many levels: in state mental health central offices, community mental health centers, and state mental hospitals (Talbott, 1978; Arce, 1980).

The issue of tenure of mental health leaders is particularly important because a high turnover in top administrators invariably leads to frequent disrup-
tions in policy and program direction which, in turn, cannot help but affect
patients at the level of direct service delivery. We are not encouraged by the most
recent study of the tenure of state mental health directors. Susan Manduke,
deputy executive director of the National Association of State Mental Health
Program Directors, reports (in a personal communication) that the average director holds the job for less than two years.

Our goal of achieving a better life for the chronically mentally ill will depend
not only on adequate funding but on the ability of persons in key positions to
deal effectively with the politics and human resources of the nation's vast public
mental health apparatus. It is impossible to know whether or not such person-
alities will occupy leadership positions in future years and whether, even if they
do, they will stay around long enough to do the job. Therefore, the role of leadership must remain a problematic and uncertain variable in predicting the fate of
the chronically mentally ill.

SUMMARY

There are some fairly good reasons for optimism with respect to the future of
the chronically mentally ill. There are other highly problematic variables that
could result either in repetition of the failures of the past or in a new era of concern and care for the chronically mentally ill. Among these variables, that of
leadership is perhaps the most important.

In a real sense the future of the chronically mentally ill will be up to us—
those of us who inspire colleagues, as teachers and researchers, and those who
serve patients in administrative or clinical roles. Our action or inaction, our
strategies and tactics, our judgment, courage, and persistence will, in the end,
determine just how well the future will treat the chronically mentally ill.

REFERENCES

Action for Mental Health: Report of the Joint Commission on Mental Illness and Health 1961. New York: Basic Books.

ADAMHA News 1980. Psychiatry shortage: "Substitution" only partial answer, says NIMH. August 22, 1980.

Anthony, W.A., Cohen, M.R., and Vitalo, R. 1978. The measurement of rehabilitation outcome. *Schizophr. Bull.* 4:365-383.

Arce, A.A. 1980. Mission impossible: Effects of bureaucratic rigidity. In J.A. Talbott (ed.), *State Mental Hospitals*, pp. 47-59. New York: Human Sciences Press.

Auerbach, E.D., and Pattison, E.M. 1976. Outcome of social rehabilitation: Whom does it help? *Social Psychiatry* 11:33-40.

Bachrach, L.L. 1980. Is the least restrictive environment always the best? Sociological and semantic implications. *Hosp. Community Psychiatry* 31:97-102.

Bachrach, L.L. 1981. Discussion: The role of model programs in the care of chronic mental patients: In J.A. Talbott (ed.), *The Chronic Mentally Ill*, pp. 300-314. New York: Human Sciences Press.

Bachrach, L.L. 1982a. Assessment of outcomes in community support systems: Results, problems and limitation. *Schizophr. Bull.* 8:39-61.

Bachrach, L.L. 1982b. Program planning for young adult chronic patients. In B. Pepper and H. Ryglewicz (eds.), *The Young Adult Chronic Patient, New Directions in Mental Health Services*, no. 14, pp. 99-109. San Francisco: Jossey-Bass.

Bachrach, L.L., and Lamb, H.R. 1982. Conceptual issues in the evaluation of the deinstitutionalization movement. In G.J. Stahler and W.R. Tash (eds.), *Innovative Approaches to Mental Health Evaluation*, pp. 139-161. New York: Academic Press.

Bené-Kociemba, A., Cotton, P.G., and Frank, A. 1979. Predictors of community tenure of discharged state hospital patients. *Am. J. Psychiatry* 136:1556-1561.

Berger, P.A., and Rexroth, K. 1980. Tardive dyskinesia. *Schizophr. Bull.* 6:102-116.

Berlin, R.M., Kales, J.D., Humphrey, F.J., and Kales, A. 1981. The patient care crisis in community mental health centers: A need for more psychiatric involvement. *Am. J. Psychiatry* 138:450-454.

Borck, L.E., and Aber, R.A. 1981. The enhancing of social support for mental health patients through the development of self-help groups. *Community Support Service Journal* 2:11-15.

Boyd, J.L., McGill, C.W., and Falloon, I.R.H. 1981. Family participation in the community rehabilitation of schizophrenics. *Hosp. Community Psychiatry* 32:629-632.

Braun, P., Kochansky, G., Shapiro, R., Greenberg, S., Gudeman, J.E., Johnson, J., and Shole, M.F. 1981. Overview: Deinstitutionalization of psychotic patients, a critical review of outcome studies. *Am. J. Psychiatry* 138:736-749.

Brooks, A.D. 1980. The constitutional right to refuse antipsychotic medication. *Bulletin of the American Academy of Psychiatry and the Law* 8:179-221.

Buckley, P. 1982. Identifying schizophrenic patients who should not receive medication. *Schizophr. Bull.* 8:429-432.

Carroll, B.J. 1979. Prediction of treatment outcome with lithium. *Arch. Gen. Psychiatry* 36:870-878.

Caton, C.L.M. 1981. The new chronic patient and the system of community care. *Hosp. Community Psychiatry* 33:475-478.

The Chronic Mental Patient in the Community 1978a. New York: Group for the Advancement of Psychiatry.

The Chronic Mental Patient: Problems, Solutions, and Recommendations for a Public Policy 1978b. Washington, DC: American Psychiatric Association.

Community Mental Health Centers Construction Act of 1963, Public Law 88-164, 42 U.S.C.A. 6001 *et. seq.*

Craig, T.G., and Kline, N.S. 1982. Factors associated with recidivism: implications for a community support system. *Community Support Service Journal* 2:1-4.

Cumming, E. 1968. Community psychiatry in a divided labor. In *Social Psychiatry*, pp. 100-113. New York: Grune & Stratton.

Curry, J.J. 1981. A study in case management. *Community Support Service Journal* 2:15-17.

Deutsch, A. 1948. *The Shame of the States*. New York: Harcourt Brace Jovanovich.

Dowart, R.A. 1980. Deinstitutionalization: Who is left behind? *Hosp. Community Psychiatry* 31:336-338.

Durman, E.C. 1976. The role of self-help in service provision. *Applied Behavioral Science* 12:433-443.

Engelhardt, D.M., Rosen, B., and Feldman, J. 1982. A 15-year followup of 646 schizophrenic outpatients. *Schizophr. Bull.* 8:493-503.

Falloon, I.R.H., Boyd, J.L., McGill, C.W., Razen, J., Moss, H.B., and Gilderman, A.M. 1982. Family management in the prevention of exacerbations of schizophrenia. *N. Engl. J. Med.* 306:1437-1440.

Fink, P.J. 1975. Problems of providing community psychiatry training to residents. *Hosp. Community Psychiatry* 26:292-295.

Fink, P.J., and Weinstein, S.P. 1979. Whatever happened to psychiatry? The deprofessionalization of community mental health centers. *Am. J. Psychiatry* 136:406-409.

Gardener, E.A. 1977. Community mental health center movement: Learning from failure. In W.E. Barton and C.J. Sanborn (eds.), *An Assessment of the Community Mental Health Movement*, pp. 103-115. Lexington, MA: Lexington Books.

Gerhard, R.J., Dorgan, R.E., and Miles, D.G. 1981. *The Balanced Service System: A Model of Personal and Social Integration*. Clinton, OK: Response Systems Associates.

Goffman, E. 1964. *Asylums: Essays on the Social Situation of Mental Patients and Other Inmates*. Garden City, NY: Anchor Books.

Goldman, H.H., Gattozzi, A.A., and Taube, C.A. 1981. Defining and counting the chronically mentally ill. *Hosp. Community Psychiatry* 32:21-27.

Goldman, H.H., Regier, D.A., Taube, C.A., Redick, R.W., and Bass, R.D. 1980. Community mental health centers and the treatment of severe mental disorder. *Am. J. Psychiatry* 137:83-86.

Granet, R.B., and Talbott, J.A. 1978. The continuity agent: Creating a new role to bridge the gaps in the mental health system. *Hosp. Community Psychiatry* 29:132-133.

Greenblatt, M. 1978. *Psychopolitics*. New York: Grune & Stratton.

Greenblatt, M., Becerra, R.M., and Serafetinides, E.A. 1982. Social networks and mental health: An overview. *Am. J. Psychiatry* 139:977-984.

Hansell, N. 1981. Medication. In J.A. Talbott (ed.), *The Chronic Mentally Ill*, pp. 29-46. New York: Human Sciences Press.

Hansell, N. 1978. Services for schizophrenics: A lifelong approach to treatment. *Hosp. Community Psychiatry* 29:105-109.

Hatfield, A.D. 1981. The organized consumer movement: A new force in service delivery. *Community Support Service Journal* 2:3-7.

Health Services Research, Health Statistics, and Health Care Technology Act of 1978, Public Law No. 95-623, 42 U.S.C.A. 242 *et seq.*

Herz, M.I., and Melville, C. 1980. Relapse in schizophrenia. *Am. J. Psychiatry* 137: 801-805.

Herz, M.I., Szymanski, H.V., and Simon, J.C. 1982. Intermittent medication for stable schizophrenic outpatients: An alternative to maintenance medication. *Am. J. Psychiatry* 139:918-922.

Hogarty, G.E. 1971. The plight of schizophrenics in modern treatment programs. *Hosp. Community Psychiatry* 22:197-203.

Hogarty, G.E., Goldbert, S.C., and the Collaborative Study Group, Baltimore 1973. Drug and sociotherapy in the aftercare of schizophrenic patients. *Arch. Gen. Psychiatry* 28:54-64.

Hogarty, G.E., and Ulrich, R.F. 1977. Temporal effects of drug and placebo in delaying relapse in schizophrenic outpatients. *Arch. Gen. Psychiatry* 34:297-301.

James, J.F. 1980. State hospitals should be replaced. In J.A. Talbott (ed.), *State Mental Hospitals,* pp. 117-146. New York: Human Sciences Press.

Kaiser, J., and Townsend, E.J. 1981. A community support system's use of state hospitalization: Is it still necessary? *Hosp. Community Psychiatry* 32:625-628.

Kirk, S.A., and Therrien, M.E. 1975. Community mental health myths and the fate of former hospitalized patients. *Psychiatry* 38:209-217.

Klein, D.F. 1980. Psychosocial treatment of schizophrenia, or Psychosocial help for people with schizophrenia. *Schizophr. Bull.* 6:122-130.

Knesper, D. 1978. Psychiatric manpower for state mental hospitals: A continuing dilemma. *Arch. Gen. Psychiatry* 35:19-24.

Lamb, H.R. 1979a. The new asylums in the community. *Arch. Gen. Psychiatry* 36:129-134.

Lamb, H.R. 1979b. Roots of neglect of the long term mentally ill. *Psychiatry* 42: 201-207.

Lamb, H.R. 1981. What did we really expect from deinstitutionalization? *Hosp. Community Psychiatry* 32:105-109.

Lamb, H.R., and Goertzel, V. 1971. Discharged mental patients—are they really in the community? *Arch. Gen. Psychiatry* 24:24-34.

Lamb, H.R., and Goertzel, V. 1977. The long-term patients in the era of community treatment. *Arch. Gen. Psychiatry* 34:679-682.

Lamb, H.R., and Zusman, J. 1979. Primary prevention in perspective. *Am. J. Psychiatry* 136:12-17.

Langsley, D.G. 1980. The community mental health center: Does it treat the patients? *Hosp. Community Psychiatry* 31:815-819.

Lehman, A.F., Ward, N.C., and Linn, L.S. 1982. Chronic mental patients: The quality of life issue. *Am. J. Psychiatry* 139:1271-1276.

Lourie, N.V. 1978. Case management. In J.A. Talbott (ed.), *The Chronic Mental Patient: Problems, Solutions and Recommendations for Public Policy,* pp. 159-164. Washington, DC: American Psychiatric Association.

Majchrzak, A., and Tash, W.R. 1982. Performance monitoring: Response to the 1980 mental health systems act. In G.J. Stahler and W.R. Tash (eds.), *Innovative Approaches to Mental Health Evaluation,* pp. 329-343. New York: Academic Press.

Mental Health Reports (newsletter) August 1982. Arlington, VA.

Mental Health Systems Act, Public Law 96-398, 1980. *Congressional Record— House,* September 22, pp. H9541-H9588.

Miller, G. E. 1981. Barriers to serving the chronically mentally ill. *Psychiatric Quarterly* 53:118-131.

Miller, G.E. 1982. Case management: The essential service. In C.J. Sanborn (ed.), *Case Management in Mental Health Services,* pp. 3-15. New York: Haworth Press.

Miller, R.D. 1982. The least restrictive alternative: Hidden meanings and agenda. *Community Ment. Health J.* 18:46-55.

Morgan, J.A., and Connery, R.H. 1973. The governmental system. In S. Feldman (ed.), *The Administration of Mental Health Services,* pp. 241-288. Springfield, IL: Thomas.

Morgan, R., and Gray, S. 1982. Prognosis in chronic disability. *Br. J. Psychiatry* 141:178-180.

New Hampshire Code, 1981. Chapter 126-B, Section 7, Subsection II, New Hampshire Revised Statutes Annotated.

Norwood, L., and Mason, M. 1982. Evaluation of community support programs. Texas Department of Mental Health and Mental Retardation.

Pasamanick, B., Scarpitti, F., and Dinitz, S. 1967. *Schizophrenics in the Community: An Experimental Study of the Prevention of Hospitalization.* New York: Appleton-Century-Crofts.

Pepper, B., Ryglewicz, H., and Kirschner, M.C. 1982. The uninstitutionalized generation: A new breed of psychiatric patient. In B. Pepper and H. Ryglewicz (eds.), *The Young Adult Chronic Patient, New Directions in Mental Health Services,* no. 14, pp. 3-14. San Francisco: Jossey-Bass.

Perls, S.R., Winslow, W.W., and Pathak, D.R. 1980. Staffing patterns in community mental health centers. *Hosp. Community Psychiatry* 31:119-121.

Peterson, L.G. 1981. On being a necessary evil at a mental health center. *Hosp. Community Psychiatry* 32:644.

Polak, P.R., and Kirby, M.W. 1976. A model to replace psychiatric beds. *J. Nerv. Ment. Dis.* 162:13-22.

Prevost, J.A. 1982. The mental health system at risk in the 1980's. *Community Support Service Journal* 2:1-4.

Psychiatric News 1981. Program aims at reducing chronic patient recidivism. Sept. 4, p. 30.

Report of the task panel on deinstitutionalization, rehabilitation and long-term care 1978. *Task Panel Reports Submitted to the President's Commission on Mental Health,* vol. 2, appendix, pp. 356-372. Washington, DC: U.S. Government Printing Office.

Report to the President from the President's Commission on Mental Health, vol. 1, 1978. Washington, DC: U.S. Government Printing Office.

Returning the Mentally Disabled to the Community: Government Needs to Do More 1977. Washington, DC: General Accounting Office.

Ribner, D.S. 1980. Psychiatrists and community mental health: Current issues and trends. *Hosp. Community Psychiatry* 31:338-341.

Senate Bill 791, 1981. Acts, Texas 67th Legislature, R.S.

Sharfstein, S.S. 1978. Will community mental health survive in the 1980s? *Am. J. Psychiatry* 135:1362-1365.

Stanton, A.H., and Schwartz, M.S. 1954. *The Mental Hospital.* New York: Basic Books.

Stein, L.I., and Test, M.A. 1981. A state hospital-initiated community program. In J.A. Talbott (ed.), *The Chronic Mentally Ill,* pp. 160-174. New York: Human Sciences Press.

Stephens, J.H., and Astrup, C. 1963. Prognosis in "process" and "non-process" schizophrenia. *Am. J. Psychiatry* 119:943-953.

Stern, M. S., and Hoover, J. O. 1980. The clinical work of the psychiatrist in a community mental health center. *Hosp. Community Psychiatry* 31:263-265.

Stone, A. A. 1981. The right to refuse treatment: Why psychiatrists should and can make it work. *Arch. Gen. Psychiatry* 38:358-362.

Strauss, J. S., and Carpenter, W. T. Jr. 1977. Prediction of outcome in schizophrenia. *Arch. Gen. Psychiatry* 34:159-163.

Sullivan, J. P. 1981. Case management. In J. A. Talbott (ed.), *The Chronic Mentally Ill*, pp. 119-130. New York: Human Sciences Press.

Szasz, T. S. 1961. *The Myth of Mental Illness: Foundations of a Theory of Personal Conduct.* New York: Harper & Row.

Talbott, J. A. 1978. *The Death of the Asylum: A Critical Study of State Hospital Management, Services, and Care.* New York: Grune & Stratton.

Talbott, J. A. 1979. Why psychiatrists leave the public sector. *Hosp. Community Psychiatry* 30:778-782.

Talbott, J. A. 1981. Successful treatment of the chronic mentally ill. In J. A. Talbott (ed). *The Chronic Mentally Ill*, pp. 15-26. New York: Human Sciences Press.

Talbott, J. A. 1982. Statement of the American Psychiatric Association and other organizations on the Social Security Disability Insurance Program. Testimony before the Senate Committee on Finance, August 18.

Test, M. A., and Stein, L. I. 1977. A community approach to the chronically disabled patient. *Social Policy* May/June, pp. 8-16.

Test, M. A., and Stein, L. I. 1978a. Community treatment of the chronic patient: Research overview. *Schizophr. Bull.* 4:350-364.

Test, M. A., and Stein, L. I. 1978b. Training in community living: Research design and results. In L. I. Stein and M. A. Test (eds.), *Alternatives to Mental Hospital Treatment*, pp. 57-74. New York: Plenum.

Toward a National Plan for the Chronically Mentally Ill 1980. Department of Health and Human Services. Washington, DC: U.S. Government Printing Office.

Tracey, G. S., and Gussow, Z. 1976. Self-help health groups: A grass roots response to a need for services. *Applied Behavioral Science* 12:381-396.

Tsuang, M. T., and Winokur, G. 1974. Criteria for subtyping schizophrenia. *Arch. Gen. Psychiatry* 31:43-47.

Tucker, G. J., Turner, J., and Chapman, R. 1981. Problems in attracting and retaining psychiatrists in rural areas. *Hosp. Community Psychiatry* 32:118-120.

Turner, J. E. C., and Shifron, I. 1979. Community support systems: How comprehensive? *New Directions for Mental Health Services* 2:1-23.

Turner, J. C., and TenHoor, W. J. 1978. The NIMH community support program: Pilot approach to a needed social reform. *Schizophr. Bull.* 4:319-344.

U.S. District Court rules for State of Minnesota against HHS (HCFA) in 'IMD' case: Orders Schweiker to repay Medicaid $$$$ withheld. *Legal Issues*, Aug. 29, 1982. Washington, DC: National Association of State Mental Health Program Directors.

Vaughn, C. E., and Leff, J. P. 1976. The influence of family and social factors on the course of psychiatric illness: A comparison of schizophrenic and depressed neurotic patients. *Br. J. Psychiatry* 129:125-137.

Wallace, C. J., Nelson, C. J., Liberman, R. P., Aitchison, R. A., Lukoff, D., Elder, J. P., and Ferris, C. 1980. A review and critique of social skills training with schizophrenic patients. *Schizophr. Bull.* 6:42-63.

Winslow, W. W. 1979. The changing role of psychiatrists in community mental health. *Am. J. Psychiatry* 136:24-27.

Wolfe, J. C., and Schulberg, H. C. 1982. The design and evaluation of future mental health systems. In G. J. Stahler and W. R. Tash (eds.), *Innovative Approaches to Mental Health Evaluation*, pp. 3-21. New York: Academic Press.

Zusman, J., and Lamb, H. R. 1977. In defense of community mental health. *Am. J. Psychiatry* 134:887-890.

Index

329